Pesticides in Urban Environments

ACS SYMPOSIUM SERIES **522**

Pesticides in Urban Environments

Fate and Significance

Kenneth D. Racke, EDITOR
DowElanco

Anne R. Leslie, EDITOR
U.S. Environmental Protection Agency

Developed from a symposium sponsored
by the Division of Agrochemicals
at the 203rd National Meeting
of the American Chemical Society,
San Francisco, California,
April 5–10, 1992

American Chemical Society, Washington, DC 1993

Library of Congress Cataloging-in-Publication Data

Pesticides in urban environments: fate and significance / [edited by] Kenneth D. Racke, Anne R. Leslie.

    p.   cm.—(ACS symposium series, ISSN 0097–6156; 522)

"Developed from a symposium sponsored by the Division of Agrochemicals at the 203rd National Meeting of the American Chemical Society, San Francisco, California, April 5–10, 1992."

Includes bibliographical references and index.

ISBN 0–8412–2627–X

1. Pesticides—Toxicology—Congresses. 2. Pesticides—Environmental aspects—Congresses. 3. Urban ecology—Congresses.

    I. Racke, Kenneth D., 1959–   . II. Leslie, Anne R., 1931–   . III. American Chemical Society. Division of Agrochemicals. IV. American Chemical Society. Meeting (203rd: 1992: San Francisco, Calif.) V. Series.

RA1270.P4P49   1993
363.17′92′01732—dc20
                                   92–42060
                                      CIP

The paper used in this publication meets the minimum requirements of American National Standard for Information Sciences—Permanence of Paper for Printed Library Materials, ANSI Z39.48–1984. ∞

PRINTED IN THE UNITED STATES OF AMERICA

Foreword

THE ACS SYMPOSIUM SERIES was first published in 1974 to provide a mechanism for publishing symposia quickly in book form. The purpose of this series is to publish comprehensive books developed from symposia, which are usually "snapshots in time" of the current research being done on a topic, plus some review material on the topic. For this reason, it is necessary that the papers be published as quickly as possible.

Before a symposium-based book is put under contract, the proposed table of contents is reviewed for appropriateness to the topic and for comprehensiveness of the collection. Some papers are excluded at this point, and others are added to round out the scope of the volume. In addition, a draft of each paper is peer-reviewed prior to final acceptance or rejection. This anonymous review process is supervised by the organizer(s) of the symposium, who become the editor(s) of the book. The authors then revise their papers according to the recommendations of both the reviewers and the editors, prepare camera-ready copy, and submit the final papers to the editors, who check that all necessary revisions have been made.

As a rule, only original research papers and original review papers are included in the volumes. Verbatim reproductions of previously published papers are not accepted.

M. Joan Comstock
Series Editor

Contents

MOBILITY OF PESTICIDES IN URBAN ENVIRONMENTS

INDEXES

x

Preface

WHEN PESTICIDE USE and the concomitant considerations of efficacy and environmental safety come to mind, our first thoughts tend to gravitate toward agriculture. Images of the farmer or crop duster diligently battling the ravages of boll weevils, rootworms, and giant foxtail with a modern arsenal of chemical weapons are easily envisioned. However, the importance of pesticide use in urban environments is being increasingly recognized. We need look no further than our front lawns, home gardens, or kitchens for pesticide interest and issues to be raised.

Currently, a great deal of interest and research activity is focused on pesticide use in the urban environment. The urban environment includes homes, yards, gardens, public parks, golf courses, and restaurants. Some common products for the urban market are turf pesticides, termiticides, home and garden pesticides, indoor pesticides, and rodenticides. Topics of contemporary concern regarding the use of these products revolve around their fate in the environment and their potential effects on humans and environmental quality. This book represents the first compilation of research information addressed to these concerns. Chapters have been contributed by researchers and scholars drawn from industry, academia, and government agencies.

This book is divided into five sections, each of which focuses on one facet of urban pesticide use. The first section provides background information on the use patterns and practices characteristic of the urban pesticide market and includes perspectives on the key issues facing the arena. The second section centers around the topic of persistence and degradation of pesticides in urban environments. The topic of mobility (leaching, runoff, and volatility) is the focus of the third section of the book. The final two sections address the topics of biological exposure and risk assessment, the fourth and fifth sections dealing with humans and nontarget animals, respectively.

We thank those who have contributed their technical expertise to this volume, including authors and reviewers. We also express our thanks to the Division of Agrochemicals, sponsor of the symposium on which this book is based, and the ACS Books Department staff for their efforts in presenting this volume. The assistance of Debbie Allen in formatting the chapters into final shape was much appreciated. Finally, special thanks are offered to Jim Gibson and DowElanco, whose financial support made both the arrangement of the symposium and publication of this book possible.

KENNETH D. RACKE
DowElanco
Indianapolis, IN 46268

ANNE R. LESLIE
U.S. Environmental Protection Agency
Washington, DC 20460

October 23, 1992

PESTS AND PESTICIDES IN URBAN ENVIRONMENTS

Chapter 1

Urban Pest Control Scenarios and Chemicals

K. D. Racke

Environmental Chemistry Laboratory, DowElanco, 9410 North Zionsville Road, Indianapolis, IN 46268

The urban environment represents an important arena of pesticide use. The scope of the urban environment encompasses a variety of non-agricultural settings in which human activities or properties are threatened by insect, weed, microbial, or vertebrate pests. Examples of such areas are homes, yards, gardens, public parks and recreation areas, and industrial properties. Pesticides are employed by both homeowners and pest control professionals to protect investments, maintain aesthetics, reduce nuisances, and minimize disease threats. Some typical examples of urban pest control scenarios would be turf pest control, structural pest control, ornamental plant pest control, garden pest control, and indoor and outdoor nuisance pest control. A wide array of insecticides, repellents, herbicides, fungicides, disinfectants, and rodenticides are used in urban pest management programs. The fate of pesticides in the urban environment is of interest due to considerations of human and environmental safety. This chapter provides a general overview of pesticides in the urban environment, and serves as an introduction to the environmental research on pesticide degradation, transport, and nontarget organism exposure summarized in this book.

It is increasingly recognized that urban environments represent important arenas for consideration of pesticide fate and exposure. Thus, significant research efforts have recently been directed toward understanding the behavior of pesticides following urban use. Due to the high level of scrutiny these urban pesticide uses entail, there is a critical need for information on pesticides in urban environments to be generated, summarized, and communicated to government regulators, pesticide manufacturers and formulators, pest product retailers, pest control professionals, and perhaps most importantly, consumers and homeowners.

The Urban Environment. The focus of this volume is on the fate and significance of pesticides in urban environments, but just what constitutes an urban environment?

0097–6156/93/0522–0002$06.00/0

First, use of the term is meant to distinguish this arena of pesticide use from agricultural pest control. The employment of pesticides in urban environments, then, would constitute non-agricultural pesticide use. Second, in reflection of the diversity of scenarios encountered, the urban environment may be considered as any non-agricultural setting in which human activities or properties are threatened by insect, weed, microbial, vertebrate, or other pests. Examples of urban environments which are the primary focus of this volume include homes, yards, gardens, public parks, golf courses, and public and commercial buildings. There are several important non-agricultural pesticide uses that have not been extensively dealt with in this book, and these include forestry pest control, rights-of-way pest control, and aquatic pest control.

Pests in the Urban Environment. A wide variety of pests are present and active in the urban environment. An exhaustive treatment is not possible here, but general categories of urban pests and a few examples will be highlighted (Table I).

As opposed to the agricultural arena, in which weeds are the primary pests, in the urban environment insects represent the most important pests for which control measures are instituted. Indoor nuisance insects and arachnids such as cockroaches, ants, fleas, spiders, houseflies, and carpet beetles provide examples of commonly encountered intruders. Outdoors, nuisance arthropod pests such as mosquitoes, ticks, ants, spiders, and stinging Hymenoptera (wasps, bees, hornets) are of concern. In addition to the obvious nuisances posed by these pests, certain ones may serve as vectors of serious human diseases (e.g., encephalitis, Lyme disease). In the turf arena, both surface-feeding (e.g., chinch bug, sod webworm) and burrowing (e.g., beetle grub, mole cricket) insects may cause damage to home, park, and commercial lawns as well as golf courses. The depredations of such pests as hornworms, flea beetles, codling moths, and aphids are familiar to most home gardeners and horticulturalists. Finally, there are several structural insect pests such as subterranean termites, carpenter ants, and wood-boring beetles that often merit control measures. The activities of these wood-destroying pests can literally "bring down the house".

Weeds are plants that tend to grow well in the disturbed ecosystems characteristic of many urban areas. Although they may be encountered in a variety of settings, weeds found in turfgrass are the ones most often the target of chemical control. Virtually everyone with a home lawn has witnessed the amazing ability of such weeds as dandelions and crabgrasses to compete with cultured grasses (e.g., Kentucky bluegrass, St. Augustinegrass) for sunlight and space. There are also situations in which nuisance weeds growing in proximity to human activities must be controlled for health or safety considerations. These would include such noxious plants as poison ivy, ragweed, and thistles.

There are various fungal and microbial pests in the urban environment that are the objects of chemical control measures. These would include plant pathogens causing such turf, ornamental plant, houseplant, and vegetable plant diseases as anthracnose, fusarium blight, powdery mildew, verticillium wilt, and Dutch elm disease. Various molds and mildews can also damage building timber and siding, wallpaper, carpeting, and other interior furnishings under the right conditions.

Vertebrate pests at times may cause considerable damage and disturbance in the urban environment. Chief among these are commensal rodents such as rats and mice. These creatures may be pests of stored food products or building structures, and in addition, may serve as reservoirs for such diseases as bubonic plague and Lyme disease. There are a variety of other animals that at times may become nuisance pests in urban settings, including bats, moles, pigeons, and skunks. In some cases chemical control measures may be used, whereas in others the use of repellents or traps may be employed.

Table I. Urban Pest Categories and Examples

Urban Pest Category	Typical Pests
Indoor Nuisance	Cockroach, ant, flea, spider, housefly, carpet beetle Mold, mildew Mouse, bat
Outdoor Nuisance	Mosquito, tick, ant, spider, bee, wasp Poison ivy, ragweed, thistle Rat, pigeon
Turf and Ornamental Plants	Beetle grub, webworm, mole cricket, aphid, chinch bug, plant bug Crabgrass, dandelion, plantain, thistle Anthracnose, fusarium blight, powdery mildew Mole, chipmunk
Home Garden	Aphid, hornworm, codling moth, flea beetle Slug, snail Fusarium wilt, verticillium wilt
Structural	Subterranean termite, carpenter ant, wood-boring beetle

PESTICIDE USE IN URBAN ENVIRONMENTS

Pest Management Rationale and Strategy. In the urban environment, there are several considerations that spur the implementation of pest management practices, a single component of which may be chemical control. The primary objective of these pest management systems is to improve the quality of life in urban areas. There are

definite economic concerns associated with the activities of pests. Damage to home
and building structures, lawns and landscaping, and produce are major reasons for
intervention. There are several other considerations associated with urban
environments that are also important. Elimination of nuisance pests (e.g.,
mosquitoes, cockroaches, fleas, rats) is certainly an important consideration. Urban
aesthetics is also a desirable commodity to preserve and enhance, and pests with
activities impacting this area often stimulate pest management practices. Finally,
disease threats present in urban environments (e.g., tick transmission of Lyme
disease) merit pest control measures that may include pesticide use. Due to the
predominance of insect pests in all these categories of urban pest control, insecticides
are much more important in relation to overall pesticide use in urban environments
than they are in agricultural environments. Chapter 3 by Whitmore et al. discusses
results of the National Home and Garden Pesticide Use Survey and provides more
details on the rationale and key target pests for pesticide use in urban areas.

Pesticides in urban environments are applied by both homeowners and pest
control professionals. Characteristics of the consumer and professional markets for
pesticides are discussed in detail in Chapter 2 by Hodge; each represents
approximately $1.1 billion of annual pesticide sales. Many consumers and
homeowners utilize over-the-counter pesticide products. According to Whitmore et
al. (Chapter 3) and Bunting (1992, personal communication), approximately 70 and
62% of consumers have applied a pesticide or insecticide product within the last
year, respectively. In addition, professional pest control services are often relied
upon. Whitmore et al. (Chapter 2) estimates that approximately 15% of
homeowners with private lawns had pesticides applied professionally, and 20% of all
households had commercial applications for indoor pests. Professional pest control
applications are also commonly employed for public and commercial properties
(e.g., restaurants, factories and office buildings, parks, golf courses).

Urban Pest Control Scenarios. Pesticide use patterns in urban areas can be
grouped into several loose categories. These will be briefly discussed, and although
a comprehensive treatment is not possible here, the examples highlighted should
provide an introductory overview of the variety of pest control scenarios which exist
in the urban environment (see also Table I).

Indoor Nuisance Pest Control. Nuisance insects and arthropods indoors are
subject to various control measures. Broadcast floor sprays may be made for pests
such as fleas. Spot and surface treatments as well as crack-and-crevice applications
of insecticide sprays are often directed at such common indoor pests as cockroaches
and ants. In some cases insecticidal baits are employed for these same invaders.
Total release aerosol bombs, which provide immediate control, or slow-release pest
strips, which provide continuous control, may be employed in some circumstances.

Outdoor Nuisance Pest Control. Control of outdoor nuisance pests is often
directed at insect and arachnid pests. High-volume, low concentration perimeter
sprays of insecticides may be made to exterior building surfaces. Insecticidal sprays
may also be applied to the soil surface surrounding structures or directly to pest

activity areas (e.g., wasp nests, ant mounds). Area-wide control measure such as ground or aerial fogging with insecticides may at times be employed for very mobile pests such as mosquitoes or blackflies. Nuisance vegetation growing in undesirable locations may be controlled by selective or nonselective herbicide sprays. For rat and mouse pest control, rodenticidal baits are most often employed.

Turf and Ornamental Pest Control. The depredations of insect, weed, fungal, and vertebrate pests in turfgrass and ornamental plants often result in implementation of pest control measures. Both foliar sprays and granular applications of insecticides may be applied during the growing season for control of surface feeding as well as thatch- and soil- dwelling insect pests. Selective preemergent and postemergent herbicide sprays may be employed for grass and broadleaf weeds. In many cases, these insecticides and herbicides are carried on fertilizer granules, especially for use by homeowners. Fungicide sprays or dusts may also be applied to diseased turfgrass areas. For ornamental plants, shrubs, and trees, foliar sprays are most commonly applied to combat insect pests.

Home Garden Pest Control. Chemical control measures in the home garden are most often directed at the ravages of arthropod and other invertebrate pests. Insecticide sprays, granules, and dusts may all be employed for vegetable pest control. Fungicide dusts are also employed to some extent on crops such as tomatoes and potatoes. Fruitbearing trees and vines in the home garden or orchard are often subject to foliar insecticide sprays.

Structural Pest Control. Distinctive pesticide use patterns are associated with attempts to control structural pests such as termites and fungi. A preventative approach is at times used, which involves the treatment of lumber with fungicides or insecticides prior to construction. A more common control practice is the creation of insecticidal soil barriers to termite invasion. For buildings under construction, application of insecticide formulations may be made to the soil underneath the slab or foundation. Existing structures commonly have insecticides injected through the building foundation or deposited in trenches surrounding the foundation to prevent termite invasion. Exposed wood surfaces may be subject to insecticide drenches for control of wood-boring beetle pests. In extreme cases an entire structure may be tented and fumigated to provide control of an insect infestation.

Urban Pest Control Chemicals. A diversity of chemical pesticides are utilized in urban pest management systems. Insecticide products are most commonly employed, but substantial use of herbicides, fungicides, rodenticides, and other classes also find use. A significant number of the products used in urban environments have been around for many years. Examples of such older products would be carbaryl, chlorpyrifos, diazinon, 2,4-D, and malathion. Some of these same chemicals find substantial use in agricultural pest control. In a few cases, specific pesticide products may be developed primarily or exclusively for urban use, such as isazophos, isofenphos, or oryzalin. Table II provides a listing of examples of commonly encountered urban pesticide chemicals. In many instances products destined for over-the-counter sale to consumers have been formulated and packaged in small volumes, as ready-to-use dilutions, or in safety containers (e.g., childproof lids) for ease of use and minimization of human exposure.

Table II. Examples of Common Urban Pest Control Chemicals

Product Class	Common Urban Pesticide	
Insecticide	Acephate	Ethoprophos
	Bendiocarb	Isazophos
	Carbaryl	Isofenphos
	Chlorpyrifos	Malathion
	Cypermethrin	Propoxur
	Diazinon	Pyrethrins
	Dimethoate	Rotenone
	Ethion	Trichlorfon
Repellant	Diethyl toluamide	Para-
	Naphthalene	dichlorobenzene
Nematicide	Ethoprophos	Fenamiphos
Fumigant	Sulfuryl fluoride	
Herbicide	Arsenates	Glyphosate
	Bensulide	MCPA/MCPP
	Choroxuron	Oryzalin
	2,4-D/2,4-DP	Oxadiazon
	DCPA	Pendimethalin
	Dicamba	Simazine
	Diuron	Triclopyr
Fungicide	Benomyl	Fenarimol
	Captan	Thiophenate
	Chlorothalonil	Triadimefon
Disinfectant	Cresol	Phenol
Rodenticide	Brodifacoum	Bromethalin
	Bromadiolone	
Molluscicide	Metaldehyde	Methiocarb

Environmental Considerations and Issues. The use of pesticides in urban environments is accompanied by consideration of human and environmental safety. The issues surrounding urban pesticide use are often difficult and controversial due to the high profile of these use patterns and close proximity to humans. Chapters 4 and 5 in this volume provide regulatory and professional pest control perspectives on the key issues and concerns associated with urban pesticide use. Following this introductory section of chapters, the remaining chapters of this book deal with research related to the fate and significance of pesticides in urban environments. Consideration of the fate of pesticides involves examination of both transformation and transport processes. These processes interact to determine the magnitude and duration of exposure of humans and nontarget organisms.

Persistence. The persistence of urban pesticides in soil, on turfgrass and plant foliage, in water, and in air is of prime interest. Persistence not only determines to a great extent the efficacy of the products involved, but also whether significant quantities of pesticide will be available for transport processes or for nontarget organism exposure. The chapters in the second section of this book, "Dissipation of Pesticides in Urban Environments", are organized around the topic of persistence. Chapters 6 and 7 deal specifically with the persistence and degradation of termiticidal soil applications of insecticides. Chapter 8 details a comparison of the similarities and differences between pesticide dissipation in urban and agricultural environments. Pesticide dissipation from foliar (i.e., turfgrass) surfaces is the topic of chapters 9 and 10. Finally, the dissipation of pesticides in aquatic environments and waste disposal systems are covered in chapters 11 and 12.

Transport. The transport of pesticides within the soil and in the atmosphere is also an important consideration. Issues of potential concern from urban pesticide use include groundwater contamination due to leaching, and surface water contamination resulting from erosion and runoff. In addition, volatilization or drift of pesticides in the atmosphere may result in nontarget organism exposure. Chapter 13 deals with the subsurface mobility of pesticides applied for termiticidal control efforts. The subject of pesticide leaching through soil following turf application is covered by chapters 14 and 15, whereas chapter 16 presents a comparison of pesticide and nutrient leaching in urban and agricultural areas. The primary focus of chapters 17, 18, and 19 is the surface runoff of pesticides from turfgrass areas, with both field research and modeling assessments included. Mobility in air following volatilization from treated urban surfaces and drift from agricultural areas into the urban environment is covered by chapters 20 and 21, respectively.

Human Exposure. Assessment of human exposure to pesticides in urban environments is of prime consideration from a safety perspective. This is the topic of the chapters in the section of this book titled "Urban Pesticides and Humans". Chapters 22 and 23 cover the potential exposure of both pesticide applicators and bystanders from outdoor pest management programs, primarily involving applications to turfgrass and ornamental plants. Chapters 24 and 25 in turn deal with exposure of applicators and bystanders during and following application of indoor pesticides and structural pesticides (i.e., termiticides). Chapter 26 focuses on exposure of humans to biocides used in indoor paints.

   Nontarget Animal Exposure. Exposure of pesticides to animals, whether domestic pets or urban wildlife, is also of concern. Chapters 27 and 28 deal with the potential effects of turfgrass pesticides on nontarget vertebrate (e.g., birds) and invertebrate (e.g., earthworms) wildlife, respectively. Adverse effects of pesticides on domestic pets is discussed in chapter 29. Finally, the nontarget evaluation of urban rodenticide uses provides the focus of chapter 30.

CONCLUSIONS

This book presents a summary of what is known about the fate and significance of pesticides in urban environments. The research information herein reflects the current state of knowledge on the topic. It is likely that interest, concern, and controversy regarding pesticides in the urban arena will continue. However, a substantial knowledge base regarding urban pesticides has been assembled, and it continues to be added to and refined through many ongoing studies. This insight provides an excellent tool with which to promote wise stewardship in the implementation of urban pest management systems.

RECEIVED November 2, 1992

Chapter 2

Pesticide Trends in the Professional and Consumer Markets

J. E. Hodge

Kline & Company, Inc., 165 Passaic Avenue, Fairfield, NJ 07004

Professional and consumer end users are major purchasers and applicators of a wide variety of pesticides in the U.S. This presentation provides an overview of the special characteristics of and current trends within each of these markets, including size, structure, customer behavior and attitudes, regulatory influences, and future growth. Leading suppliers in each market are also identified.

Kline & Company estimates that the professional and consumer markets for pesticides in the U.S. each represented about $1.1 billion in sales at the manufacturers' level in 1991. The agricultural market, in contrast, was about $4.9 billion in sales.

MARKET DEFINITIONS

The professional and consumer markets for pesticides are defined by the following factors:

- The intended customers or end users
- Channels of distribution
- Certification and other regulatory requirements
- Product categories in each market
- Product characteristics

The consumer market is essentially comprised of a single end user group whose members, though large in number and diverse in behavior, typically buy pesticides which require no special certification or training, purchase through normal retail outlets, and do so for private use. The professional market, in contrast, commonly involves products that do require licensing, multiple channels of distribution, use for public or commercial purposes, and distinct clusters of different types of end users. These include:

0097–6156/93/0522–0010$06.00/0

Turf management

- Lawn care operators (LCOs)
- Golf courses
- Landscapers
- Educational facilities
- Parks
- Cemeteries
- Turf farms

Industrial and rights-of-way vegetation control

- Industrial facilities
- Electric utilities
- Roadways
- Railroads
- Pipelines

Public health and other publicly funded programs

- Mosquito abatement districts
- Rodent control areas
- Fire ant control programs
- Rangeland
- Aquatic areas

Non-agricultural crops

- Commercial forestry
- Horticulture/nurseries

Pest control operators (PCOs)

There is some one-way overlap between the professional and consumer markets in that some professional end users, especially smaller ones, occasionally purchase consumer products. Although this behavior represents only a tiny fraction of pesticide usage in the professional market, it has become more noticeable in the last two years as more end users have moved away from professional products because of applicator certification/licensing costs, reduced product usage, or concerns about product safety.

PRODUCT CATEGORIES

There are several noticeable differences between the professional and consumer markets in the types of pesticides sold and the relative importance of different product categories. Combination pesticide-fertilizer products, primarily for use on turf, are a significant product category in terms of both dollar sales and physical volume in the consumer market but are rarely seen in the professional market. Moth control and pet (flea and tick) insecticides are also sizeable product categories in the consumer market that have no counterpart in the professional market. Aquatic pesticides, including aquatic herbicides, algicides, and piscicides, avicides, and plant growth regulators (PGRs), are all primarily sold in for professional use only, although PBI/Gordon now offers consumer formulations of two of its professional PGRs. Insecticides of various kinds account for roughly three-quarters of pesticide sales in the consumer market but substantially less than that in the professional market. The size of other product categories also varies between these two markets, as shown in Figure 1.

MARKET CHARACTERISTICS

The consumer market is driven primarily by external factors, including the weather, demographic changes in population size, location, age, and income, regulatory activity, and changes in public attitudes. It is characterized by the following:

- Mature product categories
- A blurred market structure
- Two sets of customers, retailers and end users
- Intense competition
- Thin profit margins
- Marked seasonality for most product categories
- Emphasis on nonproprietary active ingredients

External factors, including weather conditions, regulatory activity, public attitudes, and national and regional economic vitality, are influential in the professional market. It is driven, however, by internal factors, including treatment site characteristics, application requirements, end user budgets, product characteristics and performance, and application-related costs for labor, equipment, and insurance. The professional market is characterized by the following:

- Mature product categories
- A fairly well-defined market structure
- Multiple sets of primary customers
- Distributors/dealers as secondary customers
- Variable levels of competition between product categories
- Declining profit margins
- Seasonality for most product categories, spread over a broader period than in the consumer market
- Emphasis on proprietary active ingredients

CONSUMER MARKET

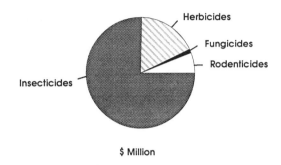

$ Million

TOTAL MARKET: $1.1 Billion

PROFESSIONAL MARKET

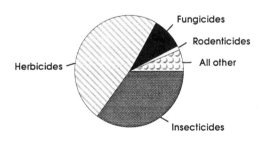

$ Million

TOTAL MARKET: $1.1 Billion

Figure 1. Relative Distribution of Pesticide Sales by Product Category and Market 1991

MARKET STRUCTURE

Companies selling pesticides in the consumer market include:

- Basic manufacturers, such as American Cyanamid, Monsanto, and Roussel Bio
- Formulators and reformulators, such as Scotts, S.C. Johnson, and Chevron
- Marketers with no manufacturing involvement, such as K mart, WalMart, and Bengal

There is considerable overlap between these categories in the consumer market because of the prevalence of subcontracting arrangements, private label manufacturing, and marketing agreements and other joint efforts. There are also some examples of vertical integration by suppliers to the retail level, most notably Agway and Vigoro.

Companies selling pesticides in the professional market include:

- Basic manufacturers, such as DowElanco, DuPont, Monsanto, and ICI
- Formulators and reformulators, such as Scotts, Lesco, and UAP

There is little overlap between these categories in the professional market, and there is little direct integration in the distribution system. There are direct connections or relationships involving product development and testing, however, between leading suppliers and some major end users, such as Chemlawn, Orkin, and others.

CUSTOMERS

Suppliers in the consumer market have three sets of customers, end users, retailers, and distributors. End users constitute a very large, diffuse, poorly defined population. They purchase pesticides intermittently and are characterized by highly variable levels of product knowledge, brand loyalty, and product consumption. Retailers and distributors, in contrast, constitute well-defined subsets within which consolidation is occurring. Chains, especially mass merchandisers, are becoming increasingly important in the consumer market, leading to reduced access by some suppliers to end users and reduced access by end users to product expertise. Retailers and distributors differ from each other as well as from consumers in what they require of suppliers, making the process of selling pesticides more complex. Distributors are important in product placement in retail accounts but do not directly influence end user product selection.

Suppliers in the professional market also serve two different types of customers, end users and distributors/dealers. End users in the professional market, however, can be grouped into very defined market segments, although end user populations in some segments can be very hard to identify, locate, and/or reach. End users in the professional market are characterized by variable levels of product knowledge and consumption, willingness to try new products, based in part on weak brand/product loyalty, and different requirements from segment to segment. They typically rely on agricultural universities, extension agents, and professional associations for information on pesticides, as well as on manufacturers and distributors. As in the consumer market, distributors/dealers constitute well-defined subsets within which consolidation is occurring. A number of leading distributors serve both the professional and consumer markets. Distributors are very important in the professional market not only for their role in product placement but as sources of information on pesticides. They are often directly influential in end user product selection.

COMPETITION

The consumer market exhibits low rates of growth and a significant degree of market concentration in most product categories and large numbers of existing suppliers. Product categories typically feature one dominant supplier, a small group of regional suppliers, and many very small competitors. Consolidation is occurring through both outright acquisition and supplier departure from certain categories, most notably household insecticides. Suppliers are primarily U.S.-owned companies. New competitors entering the consumer market include some basic manufacturers, agricultural suppliers, and some foreign companies. Major competitive strategies include:

- Manufacturing efficiencies
- Broad distribution
- Expansion through acquisition
- Niche marketing
- Changes in product characteristics
- Advertising and promotion

In the professional market, growth is limited to a few end user segments, and sales are in fact declining noticeably in some segments. The market is highly concentrated, although supplier dominance varies by product category and end user segment, with market share tied to the development and success of proprietary products. Major suppliers are typically very large companies, for many of which their presence in the professional market represents spillover or incremental business from the agriculture market. There is also a very high incidence of foreign ownership of suppliers to the professional market. Leading suppliers with foreign parents include:

- Ciba-Geigy
- Hoechst-Roussel
- ICIw   ISK
- Miles (formerly Mobay)
- NorAm
- Rhone-Poulenc
- Roussel Biow Sandoz
- Valent

Regulatory activity and public attitudes concerning pesticide usage in recent years have been much more hostile in the professional market than in the consumer market. Major competitive strategies include:

- Development of new proprietary products
- Label expansion
- Product variations (formulations and packaging)
- Licensing agreements and other shared efforts
- Expansion through acquisition
- Niche marketing
- Label/registration defense

REGULATORY CONSIDERATIONS

Regulatory activity in the last few years has become a paramount consideration in both the professional and consumer markets. Most suppliers are concerned not simply because of the additional or changed requirements with which they must deal but because many believe that their pesticide businesses face an increasingly uncertain future. Fungicides have been a high priority for EPA review, followed by insecticides and toxic inerts. The costs of registration of new actives and reregistration of existing actives have skyrocketed, and the timeframe required to develop test data has lengthened. State and local regulations are now widely regarded as even more of a problem than federal regulations. State registration fees have increased substantially, and differing regulatory requirements are making national sales and distribution increasingly difficult. Other agencies, in particular OSHA and the Department of Transportation, and regulations, including those dealing with waste disposal, container recycling, and site cleanup, are also having an impact on these markets.

LEADING SUPPLIERS

Leading suppliers of pesticides (including combination fertilizer-pesticide products) in the consumer market, as measured by dollar sales at the manufacturers' level, include:

- Chevron
- Clorox
- Eastman Kodak
- Hartz
- S.C. Johnson
- Monsanto
- Reckitt & Colman
- Scotts
- United Industries

Leading suppliers on the same basis in the professional market include:

- American Cyanamid
- Ciba-Geigy
- DowElanco
- DuPont
- ICI
- Miles (formerly Mobay)

- Monsanto
- Rhone-Poulenc
- Sandoz
- Scotts

CONCLUSION

Suppliers of both professional and consumer pesticides find themselves facing an increasingly inhospitable world. Real growth has slowed due to the maturity of most product categories, and expansion now comes most readily through acquisition or at the expense of a competitor. Changing public attitudes are fostering, or in some cases forcing, reductions in pesticide use, and the costs associated with product development, commercialization, and maintenance in the market have skyrocketed. The fragmentation of the U.S. regulatory system is also damaging suppliers' ability to function efficiently.

The consumer and professional markets for pesticides, each accounting for more than $1 billion a year in manufacturer level sales in this country, are nonetheless large and valuable businesses. Despite the problems noted above, both markets also present individual suppliers with opportunities for expansion. Over the long term, the pesticide industry is likely to follow the pattern evolving in the pharmaceutical industry, relying on joint ventures, mergers, partnerships, and licensing agreements to achieve and maintain the critical mass needed to remain viable. This will ultimately result in a smaller number of bigger major suppliers (as, for example, with the DowElanco joint venture) and a related group of technology-driven smaller firms with links to leading suppliers. The heightened level of research on biopesticides, pesticide-resistant plants, and other alternative methods of pest control will also broaden suppliers' focus considerably and may offer benefits in areas outside of the pesticide industry. In the meantime, consumption of pesticides in the consumer and professional markets is expected to remain substantial.

RECEIVED October 23, 1992

Chapter 3

National Home and Garden Pesticide Use Survey

R. W. Whitmore[1], J. E. Kelly[1], P. L. Reading[1], E. Brandt[2], and T. Harris[2]

[1]Research Triangle Institute, Research Triangle Park, NC 27709
[2]Biological and Economic Analysis Division, U.S. Environmental Protection Agency, 401 M Street, SW, Washington, DC 20460

The National Home and Garden Pesticide Use Survey represents an attempt to compile data on the reasons why home pesticides are used, the extent of their use, and the methods used to apply, store, and dispose of them. The survey was conducted under contract to EPA by Research Triangle Institute. Data were collected by trained interviewers that visited each home personally. Data are available on specific pest problems, whether they are considered major or not, and whether the pests are managed in some way with pesticides. Other data are included on storage and disposal, use of child resistant packaging, and use of commercial pest control services.

In March 1988, the EPA contracted Research Triangle Institute (RTI) to design the National Home and Garden Pesticide Use Survey (NHGPUS). After designing the survey and obtaining approval from the Office of Management and Budget (OMB), field data collection was conducted during August and September 1990. The study was designed as a national, probability-based sample of households with interviews conducted in person at the sample residences. Prior to the current survey, the last national survey of household pesticide use was conducted by the U.S. Environmental Protection Agency (EPA) in 1976-77.

The Agency's Office of Pesticide Programs (OPP) performs risk/benefit analyses for home and garden pesticide registrations that will be better informed using the survey data. Survey data on frequency of use and safety precautions will be used in risk assessments. Data on pests and sites treated and on consumer satisfaction will be used in benefit analyses. Information regarding child resistant packaging (CRP), disposal methods, and commercial pesticide treatments will help guide Agency policy in these areas.

0097–6156/93/0522–0018$06.00/0
© 1993 American Chemical Society

STUDY OBJECTIVES AND TARGET POPULATION

The NHGPUS is a one-time, cross-sectional survey of the use of pesticides in and around homes in the United States. The dwellings in the target population are the housing units1 in the 48 coterminous States and the District of Columbia that are occupied as primary residences, excluding institutions, group quarters, military reservations, and Indian Reservations. A housing unit, as defined by the U.S. Bureau of the Census, is a room or groups of rooms occupied or intended for occupancy as a separate living quarters in which the occupants (1) live and eat separately from any other persons in the building and (2) have direct access from the outside of the building or through a common hall. Questions regarding pesticide use in and around the home would not be well-defined for people living in institutions or group quarters. Indian reservations and military reservations are excluded from the NHGPUS primarily because pesticide applications in these places are likely to be atypical of the remainder of the U.S. household population. The States of Alaska and Hawaii were excluded for the same reason and to control the costs of field data collection.

The following types of data were collected by the NHGPUS regarding use of pesticides by the households in the target population (Pesticides that were used solely for crops or livestock grown for sale were excluded from consideration):

1. which pesticides were used;
2. what they were used for;
3. how often they were used;
4. how they were applied, including safety precautions;
5. how unused portions were stored and/or disposed of;
6. how product containers were disposed of;
7. how child resistant packaging was used;
8. how effective the pesticides were judged to be; and
9. which pests were major problems (either treated or untreated).

Most data were collected for the 12-month reference period ending on the date of the interview. However, the data for specific pesticides were limited to those in storage at the residences at the time of the interview. Because pesticides tend to be used more in the summer than during the winter, data collection was performed late in the summer (August and September 1990) to temper the effects of these limitations.

The NHGPUS was not designed to collect quantitative usage data (i.e., estimates of aggregate quantities of pesticides actually used for a specific purpose over a period of time). However, the frequency of application data collected in the NHGPUS are helpful for preparing quantitative usage estimates because quantitative usage can be derived from frequency, extent, and rate of application. Moreover, the Agency has access to quantitative data from commercial subscriptions and from production reports submitted to EPA under the reporting requirements of Section 7 of the Federal Insecticide, Fungicide, and Rodenticide Act (FIFRA).

Summary Description of the Sampling Design. The sampling design for the NHGPUS can be summarily described as a stratified, three-stage probability sampling design. The areas selected at the first two stages of sampling were selected with probabilities proportional to estimates of the number of housing units currently in these areas. This strategy achieved approximately equal overall probabilities of selection with approximately equal interviewer assignments with each sample country.

Fifty-eight sample counties located in 29 different States were selected at the first stage of sampling. The locations of the 58 sample counties are shaded on a map of the United States in Figure 1. Approximately five subcounty areas defined by Census blocks and enumeration districts were selected at the second stage of sampling within each sample county for a total of 298 sampled subcounty areas, called sample segments. A list of current housing units was then prepared for each segment, from which the third-stage sample of housing units was selected.

A sample of 2,674 housing units was selected, of which 2,447 housing units were eligible for the NHGPUS (i.e., occupied primary residences). Of these 2,447 eligible households, 2,078 participated in the survey for a response rate of 84.9 percent (2,078/2,447). Because of the high response rate, the potential for nonresponse bias affecting the survey statistics is low.

The NHGPUS was designed to provide defensible national inferences, not regional inferences. Regional inferences would require a much larger sample. A sample of approximately 30 or more counties per region would be necessary. Because the NHGPUS is based on a sample of 60 counties, no more than limited inferences for two regions that each contain approximately 30 counties are supported. Limited regional analyses were performed by combining the Northeast and North Central Census Regions and comparing them to the combined South and West Regions.

RESULTS

Population Characteristics. The estimated breakdown of the NHGPUS target population by selected household characteristics is presented in Table I. The statistics presented in Table I are relative frequencies of occurrence for urban versus rural households,5 single-versus multi-family households, (based on interviewer observation, potential pesticide application sites, such as lawns, swimming pools, fruit trees, vegetable gardens, and roses.

Storage of Pesticide Products. One task of the NHGPUS data collection was to construct an inventory of all the pesticide products in storage at each sample residence, excluding plant growth regulators, pool chemicals, anti-fouling paints, and products used exclusively for agricultural production. The types of pesticide products inventoried include disinfectants, fungicides, insecticides, molluscicides, rodenticides, herbicides, and repellents. The total number of pesticide products identified and inventoried in storage at the 2,078 participating residences was 7,945. The estimated total number of pesticide products in storage at residences in the target population at the time of the NHGPUS survey (August and September 1990) is approximately 324,538,000 with a standard error of 22,213,000. Thus, a 95 percent confidence interval estimate of the number of pesticide products in storage at residences in the target population at that time is 280,102,000 to

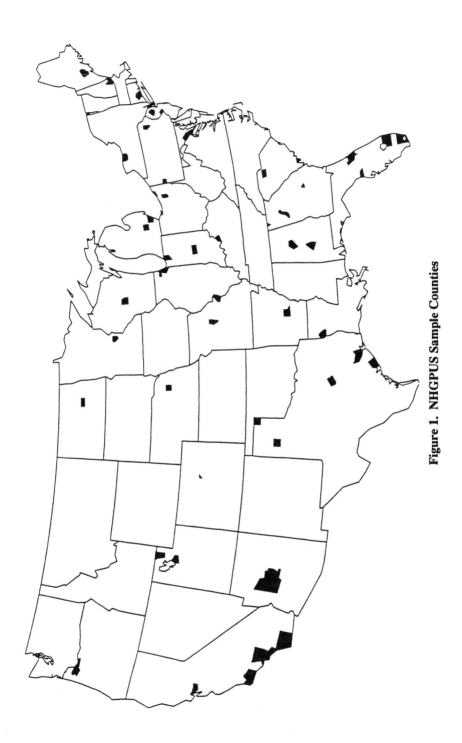

Figure 1. NHGPUS Sample Counties

Table I. Selected Characteristics of Households in the Target Population

Population Characteristic	Estimated Thousands of Households	Estimated Percentage of All Households
All Households	84,573	100.00
Urbanization[a]		
Urban	70,468	83.32
Rural	14,105	16.68
Type of Dwelling		
Single-Family	63,335	74.89
Multi-Family	21,237	25.11
Have private lawn		
Yes	66,828	79.02
No	17,744	20.98
Have private swimming pool		
Yes	5,978	7.07
No	78,595	92.93
Have hot tub		
Yes	2,500	2.96
No	82,073	97.04
Grew edible fruit/nut trees or grape vines[b]		
Yes	18,421	21.78
No	66,151	78.22
Grew tomatoes, vegetables, berries, or melons in past year[b]		
Yes	23,180	27.41
No	61,392	72.59
Grew roses in the past year[b]		
Yes	27,150	32.10
No	57,423	67.90

[a]Based on interviewer observation.
[b]Excluding any grown for sale.

368,954,000. Likewise, a 95 percent confidence interval estimate of the mean number of products that were in storage at residences in the target population is 3.34 to 4.34, or 3.84 + 0.50.

The estimated distribution of the number of products in storage at residences in the target population at the time of the survey (August and September 1990) is shown in Table II for single-family and multi-family residences . The estimated percentage of residences that had at least one pesticide product in storage is 90 percent for single-family residences, which is significantly greater than the estimated 70 percent for multi-family residences. About 85 percent of all households had at least one pesticide product in storage at the time of the survey. Most households (about 63 percent) had one to five products in storage. About 22 percent had more than five products in storage.

The estimated number of products in storage at the time of the survey is presented for each type of pesticide product in Table III by when the product was last used. About 5 to 10 percent of each type of pesticide product (disinfectants through repellents) that was found in storage had not been used yet. With the exception of disinfectants, about 15 to 30 percent of the pesticide product of each type had last been used over a year ago. Only about 5 percent of the disinfectants in storage had last been used over a year ago.

Table IV presents the estimated distribution of the number of pesticide products in storage at the time of the survey by size of container and length of time in storage. The length of time in storage was found to decrease with increasing size of container. This pattern of storage was observed consistently for all types of pesticide product containers except bait boxes, which are seldom found in large containers.

Most pesticide products have labels that ask the users to keep the products out of the reach of children. Products found in storage at sample residences were classified as being stored "securely" if they were:

1.   stored in a locked or childproof room or cabinet, or
2.   stored more than 4 feet off the floor (i.e., out-of-reach for small children).

Otherwise, when the products were:

1.   stored no more than 4 feet off the floor, and
2.   not stored in a locked or childproof room or cabinet,

they were classified as being stored "insecurely." Tables V and VI present estimates of the conditional percentages of households that had each type of pesticide stored "insecurely," given that the household had at least one product of the given type in storage. Table V presents the results for households with children under 5 years of age (a cut-off for regulations regarding CRP), and Table IV presents the results for all other households.

Table VI shows that approximately 75 percent of households that had no children under 5 years of age and had pesticides in storage had at least one stored "insecurely." The corresponding estimate from Table V for households with children under 5 years of age is about 47 percent, which is significantly less. For each type of pesticide, except rodenticides, the estimated percentage of households with the pesticide in storage that had at least one stored "insecurely" is less for households with children under 5 years of age. For rodenticides, there is no significant difference because of the small numbers of rodenticide products in storage. Therefore, the overall impression is that households with

Table II.   Household Distribution of the Number of Products in Storage by Type of Dwelling

Number of Products	Single-Family		Multi-Family		Total	
	Estimated Thousands of HH	Estimated Percentage of HH	Estimated Thousands of HH	Estimated Percentage of HH	Estimated Thousands of HH	Estimated Percentage of HH
TOTAL	63,335	100.00	21,237	100.00	84,574	100.00
0	6,364	10.05	6,454	30.38	12,818	15.16
1-5	39,613	62.55	13,765	64.80	53,378	63.12
6-10	11,148	17.60	700	3.29	11,848	14.01
>10	6,207	9.80	323	1.52	6,530	7.72

Abbreviations: HH = Households

Table III. Number of Products in Storage by Type of Pesticide and When Last Used[a]

Type of Pesticide[b]	Not Yet Used		Used in Past Year		Used Over 1 Year Ago		Total
	Estimated Thousands	Estimated Percentage	Estimated Thousands	Estimated Percentage	Estimated Thousands	Estimated Percentage	Estimated Thousands[c]
ALL TYPES OF PESTICIDES	23,153	7.13	227,767	70.18	73,619	22.68	324,538
Disinfectant	3,515	4.55	69,898	90.40	3,907	5.05	76,888
Fungicide	3,144	4.60	54,024	79.00	11,216	16.40	68,190
Insecticide	14,301	8.09	114,556	64.82	47,864	27.08	176,454
Molluscicide	250	4.42	3,995	70.69	1,407	24.89	5,551
Rodenticide	328	7.01	3,499	74.73	855	18.25	4,829
Herbicide	3,255	9.90	19,447	59.12	10,191	30.98	32,984
Repellent	1,838	5.78	21,357	67.19	8,592	27.03	32,260

[a] For pesticide products (excluding those used exclusively for agricultural production, plant growth regulators, pool chemicals, and anti-fouling paints) in storage at residences in the target population at the time of the survey (Aug–Sept 1990).

[b] An individual pesticide product can be of more than one type (e.g., insecticide and fungicide). Therefore, the estimates for the individual types of pesticides sum to more than the total for all types of pesticides.

[c] The estimated totals are not identical to the sum of the columns. The totals were estimated separately and are more reliable than the sum of the columns.

Table IV.   Percentage of Products in Storage by Size of Container and Time in Storage[a]

Size of Container[b]	Months in Storage			
	<6	6-12	13-24	>24
All Sizes of Containers	42.58	19.74	14.95	22.74
≤ 4 Ounces	40.65	18.82	12.62	27.90
4 < Ounces < 8	32.95	20.25	15.04	31.77
8 < Ounces < 16	37.93	20.72	16.92	24.44
16 < Ounces < 32	47.61	19.14	15.18	18.07
32 < Ounces < 128	58.19	16.75	9.73	15.32
> 128 Ounces	55.66	20.05	12.47	11.82

[a] For pesticide products (excluding those used exclusively for agricultural production, plant growth regulators, pool chemicals, and anti-fouling paints) in storage at residences in the target population at the time of the survey (Aug-Sept 1990).

[b] The number of ounces can be considered either ounces by weight (avoirdupois ounces) or ounces by volume (fluid ounces) assuming an equivalency rate of 8 pounds per gallon.

Table V. Number of Households with at least One Pesticide Product Stored Insecurely by Type of Pesticide for Households with Children under 5 Years of Age[a]

Type of Pesticide[b]	At Least One Stored Insecurely		None Stored Insecurely	
	Estimated Thousands	Estimated Percentage[c]	Estimated Thousands	Estimated Percentage[c]
All types of Pesticides	6,078	46.88	6,887	53.12
Disinfectant	3,481	41.61	4,885	58.39
Fungicide	2,831	38.12	4,594	61.88
Insecticide	3,749	36.04	6,655	63.96
Molluscicide	43[d]	6.45[d]	617	93.55
Rodenticide	319[d]	40.65	466	59.35
Herbicide	617	21.18	2,295	78.82
Repellent	1,261	24.30	3,928	75.70

[a] For pesticide products (excluding those used exclusively for agricultural production, plant growth regulators, pool chemicals, and anti-fouling paints) in storage at residences in the target population at the time of the survey (Aug–Sept 1990).

[b] An individual pesticide product can be of more than one type (e.g., insecticide and fungicide). Therefore, the estimates for the individual types of pesticides sum to more than the total for all types of pesticides.

[c] Conditional percentage, given that at least one product of the designated type was in storage.

[d] Estimate has poor precision because of the small number of observations in this cell.

Table VI.   Number of Households with at least One Pesticide Product Stored Insecurely by Type of Pesticide for Households with No Children Under 5 Years of Age[a]

Type of Pesticide[b]	At Least One Stored Insecurely		None Stored Insecurely	
	Estimated Thousands	Estimated Percentage[c]	Estimated Thousands	Estimated Percentage
All types of Pesticides	43,909	74.69	14,881	25.31
Disinfectant	26,149	77.35	7,658	22.65
Fungicide	21,461	67.55	10,310	32.45
Insecticide	28,934	61.57	18,062	38.43
Molluscicide	1,427	34.89	2,663	65.11
Rodenticide	791	21.20	2,942	78.80
Herbicide	5,006	34.77	9,390	65.23
Repellent	8,462	48.10	9,130	51.90

[a] For pesticide products (excluding those used exclusively for agricultural production, plant growth regulators, pool chemicals, and anti-fouling paints) in storage at residences in the target population at the time of the survey (Aug-Sept 1990).

[b] An individual pesticide product can be of more than one type (e.g., insecticide and fungicide). Therefore, the estimates for the individual types of pesticides sum to more than the total for all types of pesticides.

[c] Conditional percentage, given that at least one product of the designated type was in storage.

small children are less likely to have pesticide products stored within their reach. Of course, children can be exposed to pesticides at homes other than their own (e.g., at homes of friends or relatives).

Difficulty Opening Containers. The NHGPUS questionnaire asked if any of the users of pesticide products had difficulty opening the container. If so, the ages of the users who had difficulty opening the package were determined. Table VII shows that approximately 10.5 percent of pesticide product users reported difficulty opening CRP pesticide containers, which was significantly greater than the estimated 1.5 percent for non-CRP pesticide containers.

The data suggest that the percentage of users aged 75 or older who have difficulty opening CRP pesticide containers (18 percent) is greater than the percentage for other age groups, but this difference is not statistically significant. The data also suggest that the percentage of users aged 75 or older (5 percent) who have difficulty opening non-CRP pesticide containers is greater than the percentage for other age groups, but again this difference is not statistically significant.

Disposal of Pesticides. Households participating in the NHGPUS were asked about their disposal, if any, of insecticides, herbicides, fungicides, or empty containers thereof during the past year. Table VIII shows that approximately 62 percent of households (about 52 million) disposed of at least one empty ready-to-use container of insecticide, fungicide, or herbicide in the past year, and that approximately 23 percent (about 19 million) disposed of an empty concentrate container. Much smaller percentages of households (under 10 percent) disposed of leftover insecticides, fungicides, or herbicides (concentrate, diluted, or ready-to-use).

Among the households that disposed of leftover concentrates of insecticide, fungicide, or herbicide in the past year, approximately 13 percent took the leftover chemicals to special collection sites and 67 percent disposed of the concentrates in their regular household trash. For disposing of empty containers (either for concentrated or ready-to-use products), only about 2 to 3 percent of households took them to a special collection site. However, because many more households disposed of empty containers than disposed of leftover pesticides, the overall percentage of households that took empty pesticide containers to special collection sites, about 1 percent, was greater than the percentage of households that took leftover pesticides, less than 0.5 percent, to those sites.

In response to a separate, but related question, the survey also determined that about 6 percent of all households in the survey population had pesticides in storage at the time of the survey (August and September 1990) that they had not disposed of because they did not know how to do so safely. Many households have products in storage for registrations that have been cancelled by the Agency. For example, approximately one million households (1.4 percent) still have products containing chlordane; about 150,000 (0.2 percent) have products containing DDT; around 70,000 (0.1 percent) have heptachlor; and about 85,000 (0.1 percent) have silvex.

Severity of Pest Problems. Each household that participated in the NHGPUS was asked to identify: (a) all types of pests that had been treated by a household member in the past

Table VII. Child Resistant Packaging by Age of Household User[a]

Age Group	Percentage Users that have Difficulty Opening		
	CRP	Non-CRP	Total
All Ages	10.48	1.68	3.34
18-44	11.04	1.32	3.03
45-59	8.74	1.63	3.28
60-74	8.95	2.44	3.92
75 or Older	18.02	4.97	7.01

[a]For pesticide products (excluding these used exclusively for agricultural production, plant growth regulators, pool chemicals, and anti-fouling paints) in storage at residences in the target population at the time of the survey (Aug-Sept 1990) that were used in the past year.

Table VIII. Percentage of Households Using Specified Disposal Methods in the Past Year for Insecticides, Herbicides, or Fungicides

Type of Item Disposed	Households Disposing of Pesticides		Regular Trash[a]	Special Home Collection[a]	Special Collection Site[a]	Other Disposal Methods[a]
	Estimated Thousands	Estimated Percentage				
Concentrated Pesticide	1,458	1.72	66.53	2.69 [b]	12.96	20.51
Diluted from Concentrate	3,194	3.78	28.83	-[c]	2.47[b]	68.69
Ready-to-Use Product	6,414	7.58	86.36	1.29 [b]	6.16	6.88
Empty Concentrate Container	19,240	22.75	91.90	2.95	2.91	3.58
Empty Ready-to-Use Container	52,368	61.92	95.15	1.46	2.36	2.33

[a]Conditional percentages, given disposal.

[b]Estimate has poor precision because of the small number of observations in this cell.

[c]None observed in the survey.

year; and (b) all types of pests that had been a major problem (in the respondent's opinion) in the past year, whether or not the pest had been treated. Table IX presents the estimated percentage of households that had a major problem with each pest in the past year and the estimated percentage of households that treated each type of pest. In addition, the four sites of application that were reported most frequently (for household treatment) are presented for each pest.

The two types of pests most frequently reported to be a major problem are household nuisance pests, ants, and cockroaches. The next two pests most frequently reported to be a major problem are pests that directly attack people and pets, namely mosquitoes and fleas. The estimated percentage of households that had a major problem with fire ants in the past year, about 6 percent, is quite high considering that fire ants only inhabit certain regions of the U.S. Pests that inhibit the growth of ornamental plants, gardens, and lawns (plant-sucking and -chewing insects plus related pests and weeds) were less frequently reported to be a major problem.

The pest category treated by the highest percentage of households, nearly 50 percent, is "mildew, mold, bacteria, or virus," even though this pest was not often reported to be a major problem.7 The top five insect pests in terms of the estimated percentage of households treating the pest in the past year are: ants; mosquitoes; cockroaches; fleas; and flies, gnats, or midges. The sites most frequently treated for these pests were kitchen, person, or pet. For other pests, other outside areas, including lawns and ornamental plants, were often reported as the sites treated.

Consumer Satisfaction. For each pesticide product in storage that had been used in the past year, the NHGPUS questionnaire determined if the household users were satisfied with its effectiveness. For each pest, Table X presents the number of pesticide products for which the household was not satisfied with the effectiveness of the product as a percentage of all products used to treat the pest. The percentage of products with which the household was not satisfied was significantly greater than the overall average of 8 percent for two pests:

1.   mammals other than mice, rats, or bats (36 percent), and
2.   fleas (14.5 percent).

The "other mammals" category includes squirrels, moles, skunks, prairie dogs, woodchucks, and rabbits, plus cats and dogs for repellent products. Other pests for which elevated levels of dissatisfaction with the pesticide products were recorded include:

1.   mice or rats (14.5 percent),
2.   broadleaf weeds (13 percent),
3.   grass-like weeds (11.5 percent),
4.   ticks or chiggers (11 percent), and
5.   soil-dwelling insects or nematodes (11 percent).

Household dissatisfaction with pesticide products could be the result of poor product efficacy or a number of other factors, including improper applications, not treating as frequently or extensively as recommended, or poor sanitation.

Table IX. Households Reporting Major Pest Problems or Problems Treated by a Household Member

Pest Problem	Households Reporting Major Problem		Households Reporting Treated Problem		Most Frequently Treated Sites[a] (in order of treatment frequency)
	Estimated Thousands	Estimated Percentage	Estimated Thousands	Estimated Percentage	
MICROORGANISMS					
Mildew, Mold, Bacteria, Virus	2,486	2.94	40,361	47.72	Bathroom; Kitchen; Living area; Fabric
Plant Diseases	1,826	2.16	8,356	9.88	Roses; Ornamentals[e]; Lawn; Garden[f]
INSECTS AND RELATED PESTS					
Ants	10,830	12.81	30,443	36.00	Kitchen; OOA[c]; Bathroom; OIA[d]
Mosquitoes	6,884	8.14	24,056	28.44	Person; OOA[c]; Living area; Kitchen
Cockroaches	8,320	9.84	20,687	24.46	Kitchen; Bathroom; Living area; OIA[d]
Fleas	6,482	7.66	20,107	23.77	Cat, dog or kennel; Living area; Kitchen; Bathroom
Flies, Gnats, Midges	4,961	5.87	17,448	20.63	Person; Kitchen; OOA[c]; Living area
Bees, Hornets, Wasps	4,995	5.91	15,611	18.46	OOA[c]; OIA[d]; Detached structures; Living area
Spiders, Crickets, Pillbugs, Milli/Centipedes	5,105	6.04	13,177	15.58	OOA[c]; OIA[d]; Kitchen; Living area
Plant-Chewing Insects	3,468	4.10	11,858	14.02	Ornamentals[e]; Garden[f]; Roses; Lawn
Plant-Sucking Insects and Mites	2,994	3.54	11,730	13.87	Ornamentals[e]; Roses; Garden[f]; Lawn

Continued on next page

Table IX.　Households Reporting Major Pest Problems or Problems Treated by a Household Member (*Continued*)

Pest Problem	Households Reporting Major Problem		Households Reporting Treated Problem		Most Frequently Treated Sites[a] (in order of treatment frequency)
	Estimated Thousands	Estimated Percentage	Estimated Thousands	Estimated Percentage	
Ticks, Chiggers	1,659	1.96	9,542	11.28	Cat, dog or kennel; Person; Lawn; OOA[b]
Fire Ants	4,966	5.87	7,907	9.35	Lawn; OOA[c]; Kitchen; OIA[d]
Mice, Rats	2,571	3.04	7,388	8.74	Kitchen; OIA[d]; Bathroom; Living area
Slugs, Snails	2,076	2.45	5,100	6.03	Ornamentals[e]; Lawn; OOA[c]; Garden[f]
PLANTS					
Broadleaf Weeds	3,692	4.37	12,345	14.60	Lawn; OOA[c]; Ornamentals[e]; Garden[f]
Grass-Like Weeds	3,158	3.73	11,707	13.84	Lawn; OOA[c]; Ornamentals[e]; Roses

[a] "Treated" or "not treated" refers to treatment by a household member; thus, pests treated only by a pest control service are reported as "not treated" in this table.

[b] Excluding fire ants, carpenter ants, and termites.

[c] Other Outside Area (such as walls, driveway, patio, deck, fences, or roof, including air treated by fogging).

[d] Other Inside Area (such as attached garage, attic, basement, crawlspace, attached utility room or workshop, etc.).

[e] Roses are the only ornamental identified separately.

[f] Food crops such as tomatoes and vegetables (excluding fruit or nut trees and grapes).

Table X. Number of Pesticide Products for Which Households Were Not Satisfied with Their Performance by Type of Pest Treated[a]

Pest Treated	Estimated Thousands of Products Not Satisfactory	Estimated Percentage of Products Not Satisfactory
All Pests	25,033	8.17
Plant Diseases	593	8.99
Cockroaches	1,550	7.96
Fire Ants	579	8.67
Other Ants	2,425	8.21
Bees, Hornets, Wasps	913	7.77
Mosquitoes	1,586	7.41
Flies, Gnats, Midges	1,603	9.13
Fleas	3,453	14.51
Ticks, Chiggers	1,289	11.09
Spiders, Crickets, Pillbugs, Millipedes, Centipedes	986	8.27
Soil-Dwelling Insects, Nematodes	395	10.73
Plant-Chewing Insects	1,032	7.59
Plant-Sucking Insects and Mites	1,082	7.70
Grass-Like Weeds	1,213	11.52
Broadleaf Weeds	1,654	13.21
Mice, Rats	384 [b]	14.62[b]
Other Mammals[c]	426	35.59

[a] For pesticide products (excluding those used exclusively for agricultural production, plant growth regulators, pool chemicals, and anti-fouling paints) in storage at residences in the target population at the time of the survey (Aug-Sept 1990) that were used in the past year. Moreover, this analysis assumes that the product satisfaction reported in response to Question 32 is applicable to all the pests reported in response to Question 28a.

[b] Estimate has poor precision because of the small number of observations in this cell.

[c] Such as squirrels, moles, skunks, prairie dogs, woodchucks, and rabbits, plus cats and dogs for repellent products.

Table XI. Number of Households That Used Pest Control Services and Received Written Precautions in the Past Year

TYPE OF SERVICE Utilization Written Precautions	Estimated Thousands of Households	Estimated Percentage of Households
COMMERCIAL LAWN-CARE COMPANY[a]		
Utilized	8,003	12.07
Informed of Chemicals Used[c]	3,626	49.51
Informed of Safety Precautions[c]	3,746	50.42
TREATMENT FOR FLEAS, ROACHES, ANTS[b]		
Utilized	16,557	19.58
Informed of Chemicals Used[c]	3,637	23.46
Informed of Safety Precautions[c]	3,216	20.67

[a] The inference population for lawn care services is the population of all households with a private lawn.

[b] The inference population for treatment of fleas, roaches, or ants is the population of all private households.

[c] Conditional percentages, given that the service was used.

Use of Pest Control Services. Each household that participated in the NHGPUS was asked about their use of a commercial lawn care company or a pest control service for treatment of fleas, roaches, or ants in the home. About 15 percent of the 66.8 million households that have a private lawn (about 10 million households) had pesticides applied in the past year by someone other than a member of the household, usually by a commercial lawn care company. Also, about 20 percent of all households (about 16 million) had their homes commercially treated for indoor pests, such as cockroaches, ants, or fleas.

Estimates of the percentages of the households utilizing these services that received written notification of the chemicals used and safety precautions to be taken are presented in Table XI. The estimates indicate that the proportion of households receiving written notification is higher for commercial lawn-care companies than for pest control companies.

RECEIVED November 2, 1992

Chapter 4

Federal and State Issues Related to Pesticide Use

T. E. Adamczyk

U.S. Environmental Protection Agency, 401 M Street, SW, Washington, DC 20460

In addressing federal and state issues related to pesticide use,this paper will concentrate on lawns or, more precisely, ornamental turf. Although there are many pesticide applications made in urban environments, both indoor and outdoor, the program of this symposium is weighted towards lawn use.

FEDERAL INSECTICIDE, FUNGICIDE, AND RODENTICIDE ACT

To register lawn pesticides, or any pesticide for that matter, the Environmental Protection Agency is required by law to consider the risks and benefits of the proposed chemical use pattern(s). Some critics argue that maintenance of ornamental turf is an exercise in aesthetics only; that lawns serve no essential purpose beyond the economic aspects of supporting a huge industry that sells products and services for that segment of the market. These critics further charge that, since benefits are small, any risk associated with turf pest control is unacceptable. Of course, many people dispute that view by citing numerous benefits, other than economic, of having a lush lawn. These include retardation of noxious weeds, supplying oxygen to the atmosphere, absorption of pollutants and noise, minimization of soil erosion, and cooling of the immediate area. Whatever your viewpoint, I believe it is safe to say that lawns will continue to be important to a large segment of the population and products, including pesticides, will be needed for their care.

Before a pesticide is registered data must be submitted or referenced which informs EPA of the physical and chemical properties of the product, toxicity to non-target organisms as well as mammalian effects, the persistence and fate of the active ingredient(s), leaching and runoff, and other data as needed. Efficacy data and target site phytotoxicity data are not required to be submitted; many people knowledgeable in the pesticide field don't realize that fact. Before 1979, EPA did require complete batteries of efficacy testing to be conducted and submitted but that is no longer the case except for products that control pests of human health significance. It deserves to be pointed out that, especially with lawn chemicals, EPA has had few reports of products that do not perform their intended function. On the whole, lawn pesticide manufacturers have done a commendable job of marketing pesticides that deliver the level of pest control claimed, when applied according to label directions.

ADVERTISING

One area that has received congressional and news media criticism is advertising. FIFRA regulates advertising claims that may be made by pesticide registrants by. It is unlawful to make advertising claims that exceed those made in connection with registration. Since safety claims or any false or misleading statements are not permitted on labels, those claims cannot legally be used in advertising by pesticide manufacturers or distributors. The EPA has no such authority, however, over pest control operators, lawn care services, custom applicators or others who use pesticides in performing a service for customers. There have been cases, related in congressional hearings, where lawn service companies have allegedly made false or misleading claims about pesticide safety in an effort to assure potential customers concerned about hazards to their families or pets. Because these cases reflect unfavorably on the industry as a whole, the Professional Lawn Care Applicators Association (PLCAA) has asked EPA to work with them on formulating advertising guidelines for use by their members. In addition, EPA is working with the Federal Trade Commission, which has overall jurisdiction in advertising, to establish uniform and consistent enforcement efforts in the area of pesticide advertising by users and applicators.

PUBLIC, PRESS AND CONGRESSIONAL CONCERNS

Because the lawn care industry has grown so rapidly over the last decade, it is inevitable that it is receiving increased public attention and concern. People wonder if such widespread pesticide use is necessary and whether the products are safe. Concerned citizens are worried about pesticides used on their own or their neighbors lawns. Their primary concern is with the safety of the chemicals; the basic question they always ask concerns safety. No pesticide and few other common household chemicals are totally free of hazard. While pesticides have varying degrees of toxicity, they all have some degree of hazard. EPA, in registering pesticides, makes the determination that when used as directed, those pesticides will not cause unreasonable effects to man or the environment. But that finding does not translate to hazard-free. There are also persons who claim to be severely affected by any exposure to any pesticide and demand that applications be stopped or severely reduced. Ironically, the same concerns are seldom expressed about homeowners treating their own lawns, even though they are likely using the same pesticides at the same rates as the professional applicators. It seems to be largely a matter of visibility and the professionals are far more conspicuous.

Although PLCAA recommends, and some state laws require, a homeowner or customer to be notified of the pesticide being used on their premises and any precautions to be taken, a recent survey indicated that a large percentage of customers claim they did not receive such notifications. As a result concerns expressed in Senate hearings and in numerous news media articles and programs, the lawn care industry has taken steps to improve their service and image; customer notification, accurate advertising, pesticide application on a "as needed" program rather than by the calendar, better worker training, increased emphasis on diagnosis and prevention of pest problems, are all being strongly recommended and increasingly employed.

STATE AND FEDERAL REGULATIONS

With increasing numbers of persons claiming to be sensitive to any pesticide, some states have instituted registries of chemical- sensitive individuals. With a doctor's written verification, a person's name and address is added to a list which is periodically distributed to professional applicators throughout the state. Individuals are supposed to be notified in advance before pesticide applications are made in their vicinity. Most comments I have received by persons residing in states with such registries have been very critical of the design, implementation, and enforcement of the program. Since most such programs rely on the voluntary response of the applicators, rather than mandating notification, individuals on the lists claim they often do not receive notification. Connecticut is the only state at this time that requires homeowners as well as professional applicators to post and notify. Enforcement of those regulations is difficult because of resource restraints.

At the local level, there is an ongoing dispute in some areas of the country by county and municipal governments that have imposed pesticide regulations for their jurisdictions. State attorney generals have usually over-ruled such regulations as being reserved for the state. In a recent case, however, the Supreme Court upheld the right of a local jurisdiction to impose its own pesticide laws. While that case was narrow and did not address the broader issue of federal or state pre-emption, it does cause concern for pesticide manufacturers and applicators. Because of the fear of "Balkanization" (i.e. dealing with a host of differing pesticide regulations) there is sentiment among pesticide producers and users for federal pre-emption. That authority would require changes in FIFRA, which now only prohibits states from imposing labeling requirements different from those required by the Act. Since any change in the law must be made through congressional action, it is impossible to predict if, when, or how this issue will be resolved.

LAWN CARE FOCUS GROUP

Since lawn pesticide issues continue to receive attention and concern, the EPA convened, in February of this year, a Lawn Care Focus Group composed of pesticide manufacturers and formulators, user groups, state and university researchers, environmental and consumer groups and congressional staffers. Under the direction of Vic Kimm, EPA, the group discussed a large array of problems and possible solutions in regulation of lawn pesticides. As you can imagine, a long list of concerns emerged. Four major areas evolved; labeling, chemically-sensitive registries at the federal level, communication and consumer education, and advertising guidelines. EPA intends to consult with state officials in order to get a sense of the feasibility of making a registry work; resources needed, program design, other problems. It is too early to say if a federal registry is workable.

In the labeling area, criticism was voiced about "clutter". Too many labels try to be all things to all people. Some participants suggested labels aimed at only one consumer group or broad use site (e.g. lawns) rather than trying to list food crops, ornamentals, rights-of-way, industrial sites and many other sites on a single label. Consumers say that labels often contain technical or scientific terms not easily understood by the average user. Suggestions were made that all liquid pesticides marketed to homeowners should be packaged ready-to-use rather than requiring mixing on-site with water. A color-coding idea was also presented; that low toxicity products bear green labels, for example, while more toxic products bear yellow or red. While some of the above ideas have merit, there are many factors to be considered before adopting them. The ready-to-use mixes, for example, could be costlier since it is expensive to ship water. Also, there would be a far greater number of containers to dispose of for a given amount of pesticide applied. The color-coding sounds attractive until one realizes that hazard encompasses a wide area. A product that is low in acute mammalian toxicity may be extremely toxic to birds or fish. A product that is not persistent may be prone to leach into groundwater. Because few pesticides can be grouped into one convenient hazard niche, it would be difficult to institute an accurate color scheme. Additionally, there is the concern that a consumer would, if he or she purchased a "green" product, be prone to disregard or ignore the labeling in the mistaken belief that the product was harmless.

All suggestions and ideas are being carefully considered. Additional Lawn Care Focus Group meetings are planned in order to concentrate on details. Any major labeling changes will be published for comment before being adopted. Since most lawn pesticide user organizations are represented in the Focus Groups, a wide range of input and concerns will be considered.

COMMUNICATION

Another area of concern involves communication. Communicating with the general consumer and with special interest groups can certainly be improved. EPA is presently receiving comments on a consumer lawn care bulletin that is intended to provide a balanced presentation of the benefits and hazards of lawn pesticides.

Responses from those who have reviewed the draft have generally been favorable. It is not surprising that the environmental and consumer groups feel that more emphasis should be placed on hazard, while pesticide producers favor more emphasis on benefits. But considering the diversity of viewpoints among the Focus Group participants, reaction to the bulletin has been good.

Finally, there are the news reports on pesticide incidents and issues, some accurate and some less so. All we can do, public and private sector groups alike, is to try to get out factual information and discuss frankly what is known and what is unknown about a pesticide and it's effects on man and the environment.

Unfortunately, there is an avid market for bad news and we can expect to hear loud reaction to cases of mis-use or accidents. It does little good to complain that the positive aspects of pesticide uses are largely ignored and risks, real or perceived, are emphasized. Such is the nature of news. But everyone, regardless of professional affiliation, must do their best to use, and advise others to use, pesticides in a responsible manner. Read the label and remember to add a maximum amount of common sense.

RECEIVED November 16, 1992

Chapter 5

Professional Pest Control Industry Perspective on Public Concerns and Regulatory Issues

T. J. Delaney

Professional Lawn Care Association of America, 1000 Johnson Ferry Road, Northeast, Suite C–135, Marietta, GA 30068

The professional pest control industry feels that the public's concerns about urban/suburban pesticide use must be taken seriously. The industry is addressing these concerns by using the well-established concept of risk communication--an approach that consists of giving the public open and complete information about pesticide applications. As part of the industry's risk communication program, it is promoting its support of reasonable and responsible legislation, including a requirement for notifying the public when pesticides are applied. It is also pursuing regulations requiring additional education for all pesticide applicators. The industry believes this approach will lessen the public's fear of pesticides, and make them feel more comfortable about urban/suburban pesticide use.

Today's heightened environmental movement has galvanized into an anti-pesticide movement. And the anti-pesticide groups are focusing on what they see as the weakest, most visible pesticide user--the urban/suburban user. Citing aesthetics as the only benefit of outdoor pesticide applications, these groups try to make the urban/suburban customer feel guilty for having a green lawn, or for hiring any kind of pesticide applicator. They frighten these people with hype about high risks, such as the cancer-scare tactic. They launch the kind of public relations campaigns that are almost always picked up by the media because of their controversial, sensational news value. Headlines, articles, and even cartoons have been used to single out the urban/suburban pesticide users and portray them in a negative light. The Dan Rather "CBS Nightly News" segment that aired during the 1991 U.S. Senate lawn care hearings is a prime example of this type of negative media coverage.

This negative publicity--fueled by local pesticide ordinances, federal and state bills, Government Accounting Office (GAO) reports, and congressional hearings--creates a negative perception of pesticides in the public's mind. The urban/suburban pesticide user industry is trying to respond to this negative perception with a two-pronged approach: 1) by using the well-established concept of risk communication; and 2) by pursuing regulations, including requiring additional education for all pesticide applicators.

0097–6156/93/0522–0041$06.00/0

RISK COMMUNICATION

To counteract the media's portrayal of us as an uncaring, unregulated industry, we promote our support of reasonable and responsible legislation. We believe the issue we are addressing is the public's desire to know more about the pesticide application process. What, when, and why is a pesticide being applied? The public would like to know these things and would like to feel that they have some control over the process.

Famous risk communicators Peter Sandman, Director of the Environmental Communications Research Program at Rutgers University, and Vincent Covello, Director of Columbia University's Center for Risk Communications, agree that posting and notification of pesticide applications fits into the proven principles of risk communication.

Scientists don't understand why the public's *perception* of the risks of pesticides is much higher than the actual risks. They believe that if they tell the public there is no scientific evidence of unacceptable risks from pesticides, the public will stop worrying and the perceived risk will disappear. But their approach is wrong.

The pesticide user industry is trying to alleviate the public's fears by letting them feel that they have control over the pesticide application process--by notifying them when pesticides are applied. This approach lets individuals decide for themselves whether they want to expose themselves to a pesticide. It helps gain the public's trust and gives credibility to our industry.

Consider the public's perception of risk:

1. Voluntary risks are accepted more readily than those that are imposed.

2. Risks that individuals feel they have some control over are better accepted than risks that individuals feel they have no control over.

3. Risks that seem fair are more acceptable than those that seem unfair.

4. Natural risks seem more acceptable than artificial risks.

5. Risks that are known are more acceptable than those that are not known.

Based on these points of perceived risk, the pesticide user industry believes that the following, when reasonable and consistent, is the best approach for communicating risk:

1. Post a sign to allow individuals to decide for themselves whether they want to expose themselves to the pesticide.

2. Have an open notification registry so that people can decide for themselves whether they want to be pre-notified or not.

3. Give people information about what product is being applied, how much, and for what reason. Also provide them with the opportunity to request copies of product labels.

4. Explain that these products are the same ones that homeowners or "do-it-your-selfers" can buy; and if they apply these products, they should be posting too.

5. Be responsive to a customer's request for additional information about a product.

6. Provide customers with an open-ended service agreement that spells out the terms of the pest control program. This puts the customers in control--they can cancel the service agreement at any time.

7. Offer the customer alternative programs, such as an organic, natural, or pesticide-free program.

EDUCATION OF PESTICIDE APPLICATORS

The urban/suburban pesticide user industry believes that proper training of pesticide applicators is one of the most important factors in providing responsible pest control services to the public. The pest control industry also believes that the Federal Insecticide, Fungicide and Rodenticide Act (FIFRA) should have requirements for licensing applicators of general use pesticides, and required training for technicians making applications.

In addition, the pesticide user industry is concerned that even with these additional requirements, many of the non-commercial users of pesticides--the homeowner "do-it-your-selfers"--often apply these products without sufficient information or instruction. We feel that the pesticide user industry and the state extension agencies should consider adopting voluntary training programs aimed at these pesticide users.

These provisions are part of an approach that should help address the public's concerns about pesticides. Also, the Professional Lawn Care Association of America (PLCAA) has developed a document containing commonly asked questions and answers about lawn care. PLCAA consulted closely with the Environmental Protection Agency and the Federal Trade Commission on this document, which it feels will help in the risk communication process by supplying more information to the public. "What You Should Know About Lawn Care Products and Services" covers such topics as pesticide safety, regulation of lawn care products and services, posting and notification, and the pesticide registration process. It also discusses the terms natural organic, natural based, and organic based.

The pesticide user industry feels that with increased education for all users of pesticides, and a commitment to a proper communications program by the entire industry including manufacturers, suppliers, users, *and scientists*, we will be on the road to solving the problem of a negative perception of urban/suburban pesticide use.

RECEIVED December 18, 1992

DISSIPATION OF PESTICIDES IN URBAN ENVIRONMENTS

Chapter 6

Field Evaluation of the Persistence and Efficacy of Pesticides Used for Termite Control

B. M. Kard and C. A. McDaniel

Forestry Sciences Laboratory, Forest Service, U.S. Department of Agriculture, P.O. Box 2008, GMF, Gulfport, MS 39505

Separate quantities of soil were each treated with one of seven currently registered termiticides and placed in trenches along the inside and outside of reduced-scale concrete foundation walls. Each termiticide was applied at its lowest label rate. Composite soil samples were collected after 1, 30, 60, 120, 180, 270, and 365 days. For each termiticide, mean ppm recovered $\pm$ SD of eight composite samples after 1 day was: Dursban TC (1.0% AI rate), 924 $\pm$ 192; Pryfon 6 (0.75%), 782 $\pm$ 48; Demon TC (0.25%), 430 $\pm$ 108; Prevail FT (0.30%), 353 $\pm$ 57; Dragnet FT (0.50%), 471 $\pm$ 127; Torpedo (0.50%), 590 $\pm$ 213; Tribute (0.50%), 681 $\pm$ 255; water controls (0.0%), 0.0 $\pm$ 0.0. Using a standard soil sampling protocol developed for this study, initial recoveries of active ingredients were within a 95% or better confidence interval of theoretical ppm. Termiticide residue analyses are provided for the first year of this investigation, which will continue for a minimum period of five years. Differences in degradation of active ingredients between inside and outside concrete foundation walls are provided for the first 12 months. Additionally, evaluations of long-term field tests of currently marketed termiticides are provided. Organophosphate and pyrethroid termiticides provided several years of termite control depending on rates applied to the soil and test site location.

Subterranean termites annually cause hundreds of millions of dollars in damage to wooden structures in the United States (1-3). Chemical treatments to soil are used protect wooden structures from termite attack, and eight termiticides representing five active ingredients are currently registered by the Environmental Protection Agency (EPA) for use under and around buildings. Chlorinated hydrocarbon, organophosphate (OP), and pyrethroid (PR) termiticides have been used, often providing 10 to 20 or more years of control (4-5). Currently OP and PR termiticides are marketed in the United States. However, little work has been published concerning a standard soil sampling protocol or expected concentrations of termiticide residues in soils after by-the-label termiticide treatments.

TERMITICIDE RESEARCH

Soil sampling techniques and methods of chemical residue analysis of soils vary from state to state and from laboratory to laboratory. There are a great number of different soil types and conditions across the United States; therefore, the ppm of termiticides in soil reported from different areas of the United States varies. This makes it difficult for pest control operators, researchers, state regulators, and other interested parties to know what to expect from a proper termiticide treatment to soil. If consistent and reliable sampling and analysis are to be achieved, standardized soil sampling and laboratory analysis methods should be accepted and implemented nationwide.

A soil sampling method developed by the Association of Structural Pest Control Regulatory Officials (ASPCRO) and representatives from each termiticide manufacturer is detailed herein. Also, the nationally accepted APHIS QA/QC laboratory analysis methods for determining amounts of termiticide residues in soil samples are cited in Appendix A and will be used in this study. These methods are accepted and recommended by ASPCRO.

Additionally, ASPCRO is conducting field studies in several states in order to establish a protocol and guidelines for the collection and interpretation of residue data for soils treated with termiticides. These studies will provide additional information concerning expected residues in soil after termiticide treatments.

Termiticide Persistence and Soil Sampling. Members of ASPCRO, the National Pest Control Association, state regulators, university and government termite researchers, and manufacturers of termiticides recognize the need to establish a standardized soil sampling method for collecting soil treated with a termiticide. A standardized method is needed to ensure consistency in soil samples arriving at residue analysis laboratories as well as provide confidence that quantities of termiticides have been recovered with a known degree of reliability.

In response to these needs, ASPCRO formed a "committee on termiticide sampling and concentrations in soils" (Committee). The Committee met in January 1990, and established the interim guideline that if a termiticide treatment to soil is to be considered adequate, 50 to 150 parts per million (ppm) of termiticide must be present. This interim ppm range may be modified as determined by future research using the field soil sampling and laboratory soil analysis protocols followed in this study. The Committee also decided to develop a standard soil sampling protocol for use in the current research. This protocol was developed by extracting portions of several proposals submitted by Committee members and manufacturer's representatives. The intent of the Committee is that a reliable protocol will be adopted and used in future field sampling around structures to determine levels of termiticides expected in soils following by-the-label termiticide treatments. The Committee again met in March 1990, at the Forest Service Wood Products Insects Research Laboratory in Gulfport, Mississippi. A specific soil sampling protocol was developed for field tests with currently marketed termiticides. The basic design of the termiticide soil residue study was also developed. In August, 1990, this study was placed on the Harrison Experimental Forest, ca. 20 miles north of Gulfport, Mississippi, and consisted of termiticide treatments to soil which was then placed in trenches around the inside and outside of reduced-scale concrete building foundations.

Termiticide Efficacy. In nationwide field tests, evaluations of termiticide treatments to soil are continued for as long as the termiticides remain effective barriers against subterranean termites. Chlorpyrifos (Dursban TC; Equity), cypermethrin (Demon TC, Prevail FT), fenvalerate (Tribute), isofenphos (Pryfon 6), and permethrin (Dragnet FT; Torpedo) field tests were initiated from 1967 through 1980 *(6)*. These tests provided the information necessary to register currently marketed soil termiticides in the United States. Test sites are located in Arizona, Florida, Mississippi, and South Carolina, representing varying climatic conditions and different soil types. Several *Reticulitermes* species are found in Florida, Mississippi, and South Carolina. In Arizona, the desert subterranean termite, *Heterotermes aureus* (Snyder), causes extensive damage to wooden structures and products. Mention of a company or trade name does not imply endorsement by the USDA.

Objectives. The objectives of the studies described herein are to:

(1) Establish and verify a standard soil sampling protocol for use by regulatory officials, pest control operators, researchers, and other interested individuals.

(2) Determine the concentrations (ppm) of the currently marketed termiticides in soil 1 day and 30 days after a proper by-the-label termiticide application to soil in trenches along the inside and outside of a building foundation wall.

(3) Determine degradation rates of all currently marketed termiticides in the Rumford sandy loam soil in the test site.

(4) Determine the concentration of termiticide in the soil at which subterranean termites penetrate the soil to attack bait wood.

(5) Evaluate "years-of-effectiveness" of currently registered and marketed termiticides in long-term field tests through 1991, using ground-board and concrete slab test methods.

MATERIALS AND METHODS

Precast Concrete Blocks. Plywood forms were constructed and used to produce 30 reduced-scale, steel-reinforced poured concrete blocks to simulate vertical walls of a crawl space building foundation (Figure 1). The blocks measure 30.0-inches (76.2-cm) square outside by 14.0-inches (35.6-cm) high with 2.0-inch (5.1-cm)-thick walls, and are reinforced with nine gage, 6-inch (15-cm)-square steel wire mesh (1- by 10-feet; 0.3- by 3-m).

Concrete-Block Wall Trenching Test. This test simulates application of a termiticide emulsion or solution under ideal conditions in trenches along the outside and inside of a building foundation wall that had been back-filled with soil thoroughly mixed with termiticide. To establish a field test site, a level, rectangular block of land, 45- by 150-feet (14- by 46-m), was cleared of leaves and duff and divided into thirty square plots, each 15.0-feet (4.6-m) on a side. A 42-inch (107-cm)-square (outside perimeter) by 14-inch (36-cm)-wide by 8-inch (20-cm)-deep trench was excavated in the center of each plot. One precast concrete block was centered in each trench (block sides parallel to the plot lines), establishing a 3 by 10 grid of blocks. Following placement of a concrete block in each plot, 2-inches (5-cm) of soil was placed in the bottom of each trench and compacted, resulting in a 6-inch-square trench cross-section on the inside and outside of each concrete block (Figure 1).

The remaining soil previously excavated from each trench was sifted through a 0.25-inch (0.64-cm)-square mesh screen to remove rocks, pebbles, leaves, and debris, and retained for treatment with termiticides. One cubic foot (0.0283-m³) of the sifted soil was placed in a clean drum of a motorized concrete mixer. Using a 3-gallon hand-pressurized sprayer, a known concentration and volume of termiticide (label rates) was sprayed over the soil as the drum rotated, and allowed to mix for 15 minutes. The treated soil was placed back into the outer trench, evenly distributed, and tamped down to the level of the original soil surface. Outer trenches required 3 cubic feet of soil for each concrete block. This procedure was repeated for the trenches inside blocks using 1.7 cubic feet (0.048-m³) of soil treated with termiticide at the same rate as the outer trench soil.

For these treatments, the lowest label rate for each of the seven registered termiticides was randomly assigned to four concrete blocks within the 30-block grid (Table I). Trenches outside and inside the blocks in the two control plots were back-filled with soil treated with water at the same volume as termiticide treatments. The water used in all treatments was non-chlorinated with a pH of 7.0.

After filling trenches with soil treated with termiticides or water, two 2- by 4- by 4-inch (5- by 5- by 10-cm) pine sapwood blocks were placed on top of the treated soil both outside and inside of the four block walls (16 pine blocks per plot). During each posttreatment sampling of soil, blocks were checked for termite attack. Decayed blocks were replaced. Concrete blocks were capped with a square (1.0- by 32.0- by 32.0-inch; 2.5- by 81.3- by 81.3-cm) plywood cover that was sealed against moisture. This provided a 1.0-inch (2.5-cm) overhang on all block sides. Tops of covers were painted glossy white to reflect heat. The underside of each cover had four 1.0- by 2.0- by 25.5-inch (2.5- by 5.1- by 64.8-cm)-long fir strips attached in a 25.5-inch (64.8-cm)-square configuration arranged parallel to the sides of the cover and fitting inside the block, keeping the cover centered on the block. A brick was placed on top of each cover at its center to hold it in place. Covers that became decayed or damaged during the test were replaced. To provide ventilation holes, a 1.5-inch (3.8-cm)-inside diameter by 2.0-inch (5.1-cm)-long PVC pipe was horizontally inserted ca. 2-inches (5-cm) below the top and centered on each side of all concrete blocks during their fabrication (Figure 1).

Ten 300-gram samples of sifted, non-treated soil from trenches were dried at 221°F (105°C) for 24 hours, cooled in a desiccator for 24 hours, and weighed. Dry soil

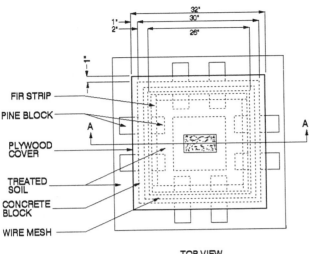

TOP VIEW

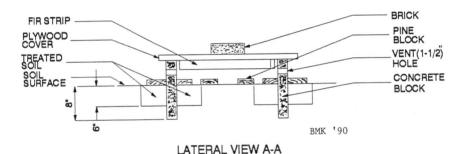

BMK '90

LATERAL VIEW A-A

Figure 1. Concrete block test unit.

Table I. Termiticides and Rates Used in the Concrete Block Wall Trenching Test[a]

Trade Name	Active Ingredient	Formulation AI Concentration %
Dursban TC	Chlorpyrifos	1.0
Pryfon 6	Isofenphos	0.75
Demon TC	Cypermethrin	0.25
Prevail FT	Cypermethrin	0.30
Tribute	Fenvalerate	0.50
Dragnet FT	Permethrin	0.50
Torpedo	Permethrin	0.50

[a] All termiticides were applied at 4.0 gallons (15.14-l) per 10.0 linear feet (3.05-m) of trench per foot (0.305-m) of trench depth

volumes were then measured to determine mean weight per cubic foot for use when calculating termiticide ppm in soil.

The inside of the concrete mixer barrel was cleaned before and after mixing each termiticide with soil. The barrel was thoroughly rinsed with water, scrubbed out with non-bleach detergent and again rinsed with water. Following this second rinse, the barrel was rinsed with 200-ml of a hexane and isopropyl alcohol mixture (3:1), followed by a third water rinse. The hexane and alcohol rinsate and the third water rinsate were collected in a waste container and removed from the test site. The two water treatments (controls) were placed in plots first.

Termiticide Residues and a Standard Soil Sampling Protocol. Each manufacturer provided an analysis of its termiticide concentrate for use in the study. Samples of each concentrate were also analyzed by the National Monitoring and Residue Analysis Laboratory (NMRAL) in Gulfport, MS. Each concentrate was diluted to its lowest label rate for use in this investigation. A sample of each dilution was also analyzed by the NMRAL. Immediately after mixing each termiticide with soil in the concrete mixer, a ca. 200-gram sample of treated soil was removed for chemical analysis. Trenches were then filled with treated soil.

Soil samples were collected from the trenches in each plot at the following times: 1, 30, 60, 120, 180, 240, 300, and 365 days after treatment. Additional samples will be collected annually for 5 years in order to determine long-term degradation curves. All samples, other than the first ones collected 24 hours after treatment, were collected within a ±5-day range of the specified sampling day.

To collect soil samples, a 1.0-inch (2.5-cm) inside diameter by 8-inch (20-cm) stainless steel soil probe was used. Leaves and duff were removed from a small area (ca. 2-in²; 14-cm²) of filled trench, 2-inches (5-cm) from the four inside and outside walls of each concrete block. One 4.5-inch (11.3-cm) vertical core of treated soil was collected from the trench along each outer wall and the top 0.5-inch (1.3-cm) of treated soil removed. These four cores were placed in an aluminum-foil (uncoated)-lined plastic soil sampling bag, and mixed with a clean glass stirring rod for 2 minutes to provide one homogeneous composite sample. One 4-inch vertical core from the trench along each inner wall was similarly combined and mixed to provide a single composite sample. This resulted in sixty composite samples being collected on each posttreatment sampling date. The locations where soil cores were removed were plugged with a 1-inch (2.5-cm) outside diameter by 5-inch (13-cm)-long PVC cylinder to ensure the same location would not be resampled and prevent soil from collapsing into the holes.

Each sample bag was labeled with indelible ink directly on the outside and with a tag wired to its top. Labels designated the sample number, date collected, and the test site location. Sample bags were placed into an ice chest containing sealed, frozen, refreezable "blue ice" to maintain soil at 70°F (21°C) or less, and delivered to the NMRAL within 2 hours for analysis. Samples were maintained a -10°C while awaiting analysis.

Test Site Description. The Harrison Experimental Forest is located in Harrison County, on the central gulf coast of Mississippi. Soil type is Rumford sandy loam with the following characteristics: pH-5.1; clay-4.9%; silt-25.2%; sand-69.9%. Average yearly rainfall is 67 inches (170 cm). The site supports widespread, numerous populations of the native subterranean termites *Reticulitermes flavipes* (Kollar), *R. virginicus* (Banks), and *R. hageni* (Banks).

Laboratory Analyses of Soils Treated with Termiticides. Appendix A cites the laboratory protocols used to analyze for each termiticide.

Data Analyses. Residue analyses of soils treated with termiticides will be used to develop multi-year "time-rate-of-decay" curves for each termiticide. Rates of degradation between outside and inside foundation walls are compared. Means and standard deviations of termiticide ppm recovered will be used to indicate the precision of the sampling procedure and to indicate expected concentrations in soil over time following the thorough termiticide treatments to soil. Residues will be determined over a 5-year minimum period. The ability of *Reticulitermes* spp. to penetrate soil treated with each termiticide to attack pine blocks was evaluated as the concentrations of termiticide changed in the soil during the first year. These evaluations will be continued for at least 5 years.

Termiticide Efficacy. Field evaluations were conducted at test sites in Arizona, Florida, Mississippi, and South Carolina. At each test site, an experimental area was established that contained 10 blocks (each 10.7- by 10.7-m), with each block subdivided into 49 plots (each 1.5- by 1.5-m). Each termiticide treatment was replicated once in each block (one treatment in a plot) in a randomized complete-block design. Non-treated plots in each block were reserved for future tests.

Termiticides were evaluated in both ground-board and concrete slab tests *(1,7)*. Aqueous solutions or emulsions of termiticides were applied to the soil at several active ingredient concentrations, usually ranging from 0.00% (water only controls) to 1.0% [AI] by weight. These dilutions were applied at a volume of 1.0 pt/ft^2 (5.1 liters/m^2) of soil surface area. Each block contained one concrete slab and one ground-board treatment of each concentration.

The concrete slab method simulates conditions which exist under a poured concrete slab house foundation. The steps involved in establishing test plots were as follows: leaves and debris were removed to expose soil in a square area 24 inches (61 cm) on a side. A square wooden frame [21 inches (53 cm) on a side] constructed of 1- by 1-inch (2.5- by 2.5-cm) spruce strips was placed in the center of the cleared area, and a trench ca. 2-inches (5-cm) deep and 2-inches (5-cm) wide was dug around the inside of and adjacent to the frame. A square metal frame 17 inches (43 cm) on a side by 4-inches (10-cm) high was then centered within the wooden frame and the termiticide applied evenly to the soil surface within the metal frame. The metal frame was then removed and a vapor barrier [6-mil thick, square polyethylene sheet, 21 inches (53 cm) on a side] placed over the treated area [sheet extended ca. 1 inch (2.5 cm) into the trench on all sides]. A cylindrical plastic tube [4-inches (10-cm) diameter- by 4-inches (10-cm) high] was then placed upright on the vapor barrier in the center of the treated area, and concrete was poured over the vapor barrier until it reached the top of the wooden frame. The concrete was finished with a trowel, resulting in a smooth-surfaced slab. The wooden frame was left in place. When the concrete hardened, the vapor barrier at the bottom of the tube was cut out to expose treated soil. A pine sapwood block [2-by 3- by 4-inches (5.1- by 7.6- by 10.3-cm)] was placed inside the tube and in direct contact with the treated soil. The tube was capped to reduce loss of moisture and to preclude rain and sunlight from affecting the termiticide.

The ground-board method is similar to the concrete slab method except that no concrete slab or vapor barrier is used. A 6- by 6- by 1-inch (15- by 15-by 2.5-cm) pine sapwood board was placed in direct contact with the soil in the center of the treated area and weighted down with a brick. Thus, the treated area remained exposed to weathering.

Treated plots were evaluated annually for a minimum of five years. Evaluations were continued if the termiticide remained an effective barrier against subterranean termites past this period. Blocks and boards that became severely decayed were replaced during posttreatment evaluations. In all treatments, the response variable was "yes" (wood attacked and treated soil penetrated by termites) or "no" (wood not attacked and treated soil not penetrated by termites) as evidenced by the condition of the treated soil and the block, stake, or board in contact with the soil. When termites had penetrated treated soil and attacked the wood in 50% or more of the replicates of a particular treatment, that treatment was no longer evaluated.

RESULTS

Termiticide Residues and a Standard Soil Sampling Protocol. Initial samples of soil that were separately treated with one of each registered termiticide were removed from their respective trenches after 24 hours. For each termiticide, applied at its least concentrated label rate, soil sample average ppm recovered $\pm$ the standard deviation of eight composite samples were as follows: Dursban TC (1.0% AI rate), 924 $\pm$ 192; Pryfon 6 (0.75%), 782 $\pm$ 48; Demon TC (0.25%), 430 $\pm$ 108; Prevail FT (0.30%), 353 $\pm$ 57; Dragnet FT (0.50%), 471 $\pm$ 127; Torpedo (0.50%), 591 $\pm$ 213; Tribute (0.50%), 681 $\pm$ 181; water control (0.0%), 0.0 $\pm$ 0.0 (Table II). The ppm recoveries were achieved under near ideal conditions in a carefully controlled experiment with as homogeneous a mixture of termiticide and soil as possible. All recoveries were within a 95% or higher confidence interval for theoretical ppm, validating the soil sampling protocol.

The additional cores of soil treated with each termiticide that were removed at regular intervals during the first year of the test, were analyzed for termiticide residues and the $\pm$ 95% confidence limits calculated *(8)*. Termiticide residues recovered from inside and outside concrete block walls, and combined and theoretical ppm are provided in Table II.

The changes in ppm recoveries for each termiticide at each sample interval did not always show a gradual degradation of AI. Since variability is to be expected with each composite sample recovered, increases as well as decreases in ppm are considered normal, especially during the first sampling year. As more ppm data are collected over several years, normal degradation curves showing steady decreases of AI are expected. Field data beyond one year are needed to establish realistic curves.

A similar perspective is needed when evaluating attack by termites to wooden blocks placed on top of the treated soil in both the outside and inside trenches. For all

Table II. Termiticide Residues in Soils Treated at Lowest Label Rates

Termiticide		Day 1	Day 30	Day 60	Day 120	Day 180	Day 240	Day 300	Day 360[a]
		PPM (±95% CL)							
DURSBAN	Inside[b]	858 (127)	699 (272)	601 (237)	967 (344)	956 (437)	808 (150)	469 (130)	777 (224)
	Outside[b]	990 (304)	636 (223)	654 (397)	793 (288)	822 (100)	1214 (204)	586 (118)	791 (121)
	Combined[c]	924 (147)	668 (149)	627 (193)	880 (199)	889 (194)	1011 (196)	527 (87)	784 (106)
	Theoretical[d]	846							
PRYFON 6	Inside[b]	787 (42)	514 (54)	511 (146)	898 (100)	409 (150)	265 (112)	444 (135)	221 (163)
	Outside[b]	778 (76)	507 (124)	396 (208)	689 (238)	563 (615)	163 (53)	491 (144)	229 (219)
	Combined[c]	782 (36)	511 (56)	454 (116)	794 (137)	486 (271)	214 (67)	467 (84)	225 (114)
	Theoretical[d]	636							
DEMON TC	Inside[b]	453 (193)	188 (85)	156 (47)	357 (127)	214 (88)	239 (99)	177 (27)	147 (46)
	Outside[b]	407 (27)	200 (17)	157 (33)	326 (82)	260 (47)	232 (121)	190 (81)	110 (49)
	Combined[c]	430 (83)	194 (36)	156 (24)	342 (64)	237 (46)	235 (65)	184 (36)	128 (32)
	Theoretical[d]	247							
PREVAIL	Inside[b]	353 (26)	254 (73)	223 (33)	409 (166)	294 (73)	318 (91)	296 (67)	158 (14)
	Outside[b]	352 (101)	269 (68)	256 (68)	429 (67)	272 (33)	279 (111)	281 (31)	157 (29)
	Combined[c]	353 (43)	262 (42)	239 (34)	419 (75)	283 (34)	298 (62)	288 (31)	158 (13)
	Theoretical[d]	292							

TRIBUTE	Inside[b]	692	(196)	457	(101)	424	(70)	639	(87)	349	(71)	578	(241)	751	(70)	869	(106)
	Outside[b]	641	(419)	442	(189)	448	(134)	631	(58)	562	(185)	501	(212)	726	(148)	867	(152)
	Combined[c]	681	(195)	449	(89)	436	(64)	635	(44)	455	(120)	540	(137)	739	(69)	868	(77)
	Theoretical[d]	484															
DRAGNET	Inside[b]	471	(54)	605	(278)	419	(76)	281	(43)	434	(233)	537	(52)	400	(52)	519	(23)
	Outside[b]	465	(226)	661	(200)	389	(54)	341	(76)	307	(163)	543	(187)	446	(99)	493	(13)
	Combined[c]	471	(97)	633	(144)	404	(40)	311	(44)	371	(129)	540	(81)	423	(50)	506	(15)
	Theoretical[d]	427															
TORPEDO	Inside[b]	685	(188)	616	(112)	342	(29)	316	(108)	263	(123)	279	(224)	419	(76)	454	(33)
	Outside[b]	497	(290)	710	(253)	388	(130)	285	(81)	157	(30)	442	(69)	280	(93)	402	(38)
	Combined[c]	591	(163)	663	(121)	365	(58)	300	(58)	210	(68)	360	(118)	399	(52)	428	(30)
	Theoretical[d]	506															

SOURCE: Adapted from ref. 12.
[a] because of inclement weather samples were taken on day 365.
[b] analyses from 4 replicate samples of pooled soil cores.
[c] values from 8 replicate samples in [a].
[d] ppm calculated from amount of termiticide applied, using a measured dry soil density of 71.71 lbs/ft^3, and assuming homogenous distribution

termiticides tested, during the first year there was no attack to wooden blocks on top of the treated soil in the inside block wall trenches. However, for outside trenches, a few wooden blocks on top of soil treated with five of the seven termiticides sustained attack. When investigating the treated soil directly under the attacked blocks, it was noted that termites were tunnelling only through approximately the upper inch of soil to reach the blocks. This soil is directly exposed to weathering, and significant rainfall occurs in the test site. Thus, termiticides in the top inch of soil may have degraded more rapidly than termiticides at greater depths. Termite attack to wooden blocks must be evaluated over a few years to gain reliable data on long-term differences between termiticides.

Termiticide Efficacy. Table III provides years-of-effectiveness of currently registered termiticides in long-term field tests as of 1991, using both the ground-board and concrete slab test methods. To clarify Table III, the following examples are provided. In Mississippi, a 1.0% concentration of chlorpyrifos placed under concrete slabs in 1971 provided 100% control of subterranean termites for 11 years; control then declined to 90% during the 12th year, where it remained for the next 4 years before declining further to 70%. It remained at 70% for 1 year before falling below 50% effectiveness.

In Arizona, 0.5% cypermethrin under concrete slabs remained 100% effective against subterranean termites for 4 years; effectiveness then declined to 90% during the 5th year, where it remained for 1 year before declining to 70%. It remained at 70% for 1 year before declining to 50%, where it remained for at least 1* year. The asterisk after a 1 indicates that evaluation of this treatment was ended after 1 year at 50%; thus the total number of years that 0.5% cypermethrin remained at 50% control was not recorded. Other asterisks found in the table indicate the same situation. The arrow between 90% and 70% effectiveness represents a greater than 10% loss in termite control during the 6th test year. A dash represents termite control percentages not yet observed.

In Florida, 1.0% permethrin (Dragnet FT) under concrete slabs has remained 100% effective in preventing penetration of subterranean termites through treated soil for more than 13 years of testing. However, the same treatment at the South Carolina site was 100% effective for 10 years; effectiveness then declined to 90% during the 11th year, where it remained for 1 year before declining to 80%, where it has remained for more than 2 years.

Because termiticides were placed in field tests in different years, a termiticide reported as 100% effective for a certain number of years is not necessarily less successful than one listed as 100% effective for a longer period. The termiticides simply have not been evaluated for an equal period.

DISCUSSION

Soil sampling and termiticide residue analyses will continue for a minimum period of 5 years, and termiticide "time-rate-of-decay" curves will be determined for the sandy loam soil type in the experimental site. Rates of degradation between outside and inside foundation walls will be evaluated for at least 5 years. These data will be reported in future publications.

Additionally, the ability of subterranean termites to penetrate soil treated with each termiticide and attack pine blocks on top of the treated soil will be evaluated as the study continues. Since changes in ppm of termiticides in the soil will be determined over time simultaneously with the evaluation of termite penetration through the treated soil, it may be possible to establish a range of termiticide concentrations in the soil through which the termites are able to penetrate. This would allow a pest control operator, researcher, or other interested party to use degradation tables to estimate a point in time when a termiticide retreatment is needed to prevent a termite infestation.

It should be noted that the termiticide residue portion of this study analyzed only the parent active ingredient of each termiticide in soil. Amounts of degradation products such as oxon metabolite of isofenphos, or TCP from chlorpyrifos were not determined *(9-11)*. Some degradation products are known to be insecticidal and may partially account for prolonged effectiveness of a termiticide barrier in concrete slab tests although the primary insecticide is degrading relatively rapidly compared to another termiticide. Further studies concerning degradation products are being conducted by other researchers.

Generally, termiticides placed under concrete slabs were 100% effective for 5 or more years when applied at the highest label rates but were less effective when applied at the lowest label rates. Termiticides protected under concrete slabs remained effective against subterranean termites longer than when placed in the exposed conditions of ground-board tests.

Organophosphates placed under concrete slabs were not effective as long in Arizona as in the other test sites. Relatively high soil surface temperatures and low soil moisture conditions in this arid climate may affect degradation rates. In contrast, except for cypermethrin, pyrethroids generally have remained effective for longer periods in Arizona than in the other sites. This indicates that climatic conditions may have a significant affect on termiticide longevity. Thus, to achieve termite control for the years indicated by research results, termiticides must be applied as a continuous barrier in the soil at the rates required by their labels.

In other field studies related to those described herein, the ASPCRO Committee is currently completing a 1- to 2-year multi-state study in order to establish a protocol and guidelines for the collection and interpretation of actual field data, relative to termiticide residues in soils which have been treated according to product label use dilution rates and application directions. Studies in Arizona, Georgia, Indiana, and Oklahoma using all currently marketed termiticides (except Equity) are scheduled for completion in 1993.

In the participating states, each product was placed around the exterior of at least three houses. Slab foundations and structures with basements also were included in the study. Local pest control operators (PCOs) performed the treatments according to standard practices, with state pesticide regulatory agency staff members present as quality control observers. Equipment and treatment methods were consistent across all PCOs. Three composite soil core samples were collected on each of several sampling dates. These samples were collected immediately prior to termiticide application, within 24 to 48 hours after initial application, and after 30, 120, and 365 days (± 5

Table III. Number of Years that Termiticides have been Effective Against Subterranean Termites in Concrete Slab (CS) and Ground-Board (GB) Field Tests (1991)

Termiticide and percent [AI]**	Test Method	Arizona						Florida						Mississippi						South Carolina					
		100	90	80	70	60	50	100	90	80	70	60	50	100	90	80	70	60	50	100	90	80	70	60	50
		\multicolumn{24} Years at each Percent																							
Chlorpyrifos (1971)[x]																									
0.5	CS	4	2	↑	↑	2	↑	7	↑	1	1	1	↑	3	↑	4	↑	↑	1	7	1	1	↑	↑	1
1.0	CS	6	↑	2	↑	↑	↑	9	4	4	1	↑	1	11	4	↑	1	↑	↑	12	↑	↑	2	↑	1
1.0	GB	2	2	↑	1	↑	1	7	↑	↑	↑	↑	↑	4	↑	2	↑	1	↑	8	1	↑	↑	↑	1
1.0	CS[xx]	-	-	-	-	-	-	-	-	-	-	-	-	21	3+	-	-	-	-	-	-	-	-	-	-
Isofenphos (1974)[x§]																									
0.5	CS	5	1	↑	↑	↑	↑	7	1	1	1	1	↑	5	↑	↑	↑	2	↑	-	-	-	-	-	-
1.0	CS	7	4	1	1	1	↑	14	2	1+	-	-	-	12	1	1	1	↑	↑	-	-	-	-	-	-
1.0	GB	3	↑	↑	1	1	1*	4	↑	↑	↑	↑	1	1	1	1	1	↑	↑	2	↑	1	↑	↑	↑
Cypermethrin (1982)[x]																									
0.25	CS	4	↑	1	↑	↑	1*	9+	-	-	-	-	-	3	2	1	↑	↑	1	4	↑	↑	↑	↑	1*
0.5	CS	4	1	↑	1	↑	1*	5	4+	-	-	-	-	7	2+	-	-	-	-	9+	-	-	-	-	-
1.0	CS	8	1+	-	-	-	-	8	1+	-	-	-	-	6	3+	-	-	-	-	9+	-	-	-	-	-
1.0	GB	5	1	↑	↑	↑	↑	5	↑	2	↑	1	1*	5	↑	1	↑	1	↑	5	1	↑	1	2+	-

Location and Percent Control

Fenvalerate (1978)[x]																						
0.5	CS	12	1+	-	-	3	4	1	5+	-	-	7	↑	2	↑	1	1*	4	4	4	1+	-	-
1.0	CS	12	↑	↑	1+	-	-	6	7+	-	-	10	1	↑	2+	-	-	6	7+	-	-	-
1.0	GB	7	1	1	1*	4	1	3	↑	1	↑	4	↑	↑	↑	1	6	1	↑	↑	1	↑
Permethrin																						
Dragnet® (1978)[x]																						
0.5	CS	13+	-	-	-	4	↑	2	7+	-	-	5	1	↑	↑	1	5	3	1	↑	↑	1*
1.0	CS	13+	-	-	-	13+	-	-	-	5	3	2	1	↑	1*	10	1	2+	-	-
1.0	GB	9	2	↑	2+	6	↑	3	↑	↑	↑	2	1	↑	↑	1	3	↑	↑	↑	1	↑
Torpedo® (1980)[x]																						
0.5	CS	11+	-	-	-	6	3	2+	-	-	4	1	↑	↑	1	1	3	3	↑	1	↑
1.0	CS	11+	-	-	-	11+	-	-	-	3	4	1	2	↑	6	1	2	1	1+	-
1.0	GB	8	1	↑	↑	5	1	1	1	↑	1	2	↑	↑	1	1	↑	↑	↑	↑	↑

* Evaluations stopped after 1 year at 50%.

** AI = the active ingredient concentration in the termiticide dilution applied to the soil.

[x] Year test initiated.

[xx] Initial 1967 test in Mississippi only.

§ CS tests not installed in South Carolina.

NOTE: An arrow indicates a greater than 10 percent loss in termite control since the preceeding evaluation.
Dashes represent termite control percentages not yet observed.
A "+" after the number indicates that control did not decline below the indicated percent as of the most recent evaluation.

days). Composite samples are delivered to participating state soil analysis laboratories as well as the appropriate termiticide manufacturer for residue analyses. Samples initially analyzed were the 24- to 48-hour samples; the 365-day samples also will be analyzed. Other samples will be retained for future reference and analysis as needed. Thus, seventy-two composite samples per termiticide will be analyzed during the study.

Analytical results of this study will be consolidated in a centralized database maintained by the Clemson University Department of Fertilizer and Pesticide Control. Once all data collection and consolidation is complete, the information will be made available.

Some benefits of the termiticide residue and soil sampling protocol and termiticide efficacy studies described herein, and the related ASPCRO multi-state study, will be an improved understanding of expected termiticide residue levels following a "by-the-label" treatment, as well as expected years-of-effectiveness of termiticide barriers in the soil. This knowledge will be useful to homeowners, PCOs, termiticide manufacturers, and regulators.

ACKNOWLEDGMENTS

Thanks to J. B. Terry and B. S. Dunn for collecting soil cores, consolidating and calculating data, and preparing Table II. Thanks also to R. E. Daniel, E. J. Mallette, N.M. Rich, and C. A. Stringer for planning and technical help and to T. A. Roland for computer assistance.

LITERATURE CITED

1.   Beal, R. H. *Pest Control* **1980a**, *48*, 11, 46, 48, 50, 52, 54.
2.   Beal, R. H. *Sociobiology* **1980b**, *5(2)*, 163-170.
3.   Beal, R. K.; Mauldin, J. K.; Jones, S. C. *Home and Garden Bull. No. 64*; Forest Service-USDA: Washington DC, **1989**. 36 p.
4.   Kard, B. M.; Mauldin, J. K.; Jones, S. C. *Sociobiology* **1989**, *15(3)*, 285-297.
5.   Kard, B. M. *Pest Management* **1991**, *10(5)*, 30-31.
6.   Kard, B. M. *Pest Control* (in press) **1992**.
7.   Smith, V. K.; Beal, R. H.; Johnston, H. R. *Pest Control* **1972**, *40(6)*, 28, 42-44.
8.   Steel, R. G. D.; Torrie, J. H. Principals and Procedures of Statistics (*2d ed.*); McGraw-Hill: New York, NY, **1980**.
9.   Chapman, R. A.; Harris, C. R. *J. Environ. Sci. Health* **1985**, *B17*, 355.
10. Felsot, A. *J. Environ. Sci. Health* **1984**, *B19*, 13.
11. Racke, K. D.; Robbins, S. T. *American Chemical Society Symposium Series No. 459*, **1991**, 93-107.
12. Kard, B. M.; McDaniel, C. A. In *56th Annual Purdue Pest Control Conference*; Purdue University Press: Lafayette, IN, **1992**, 94-96.

APPENDIX A

Protocols for Residue Analysis of Specific Insecticides. The protocols in this appendix have been developed by a manufacturer or are under copyright. They can be obtained from the manufacturer or found in the cited publication.

A. Manufacturer's Protocols:

A.1.   Wetters, J. H. *Determination of Residues of Chlorpyrifos (0,0-diethyl-0-(3,5,6-trichloro-2-pyridyl) phosphorothioate) in Soils by Gas Chromatography*. Dow Chemical U.S.A., Agricultural Products Dept., Midland, MI. ACR 77.7, **1977**.

A.2.   Shaw, H. R., II. *Gas Chromatographic Method for Residual of Oftanol and Oftanol Oxygen Analog in Soils*. Chemagro Agric. Div. of Mobay Chemical Corp. Research and Development Dept. Report No. 53690, Doc. No. AS79-506, **1977**.

B. Published Protocols:

A.3.   Sapiets, A.; Swaine, H.; Tandy, M. J. *Analytical Methods for Pesticides and Plant Growth Regulators, Cypermethrin,* Vol. XIII. Chap. 2, Academic Press, Inc. **1984**.

A.4.   Shell Development Company. *Analytical Methods for Pesticides and Plant Growth Regulators, Pydrin: Insecticide*, Vol. XIII. Chap. 7, Academic Press, Inc. **1984**.

A.5.   Swaine, H.; Tandy, M. J. *Analytical Methods for Pesticides and Plant Growth Regulators, Permethrin,* Vol. XIII. Chap 6, Academic Press, Inc. **1984**.

RECEIVED October 23, 1992

Chapter 7

Effect of Concentration, Temperature, and Soil Moisture on the Degradation of Chlorpyrifos in an Urban Iowa Soil

J. H. Cink and J. R. Coats

Department of Entomology, Iowa State University, Ames, IA 50011

The effect of concentration, temperature, and soil moisture on chlorpyrifos degradation were investigated in an urban Iowa soil. Soil samples were brought into the laboratory for treatment. Formulated Dursban TC at 10, 500 or 1,000 ppm was applied with water to establish soil moisture tensions of 0.03, 0.30 or 3.00 bar. Treatments were then placed in incubation chambers maintained at 20° and 27°C. Temperature did not affect the degradation of chlorpyrifos or mineralization of its primary metabolite, 3,5,6-trichloro-2-pyridinol (TCP). Soil moisture greatly affected mineralization. The highest percent of mineralization occurred in soil maintained near field capacity (0.30 bar) while the lowest percentage occurred in soil maintained under the driest condition (3.0 bar). Concentration had the greatest effect on the degradation of chlorpyrifos to TCP. At higher concentrations of chlorpyrifos applied, the amount of chlorpyrifos remaining was greater. The highest concentration of chlorpyrifos applied (1,000 ppm) had the highest amount of chlorpyrifos remaining and the lowest relative percentage of TCP formed.

Since the removal of chlordane and other chlorinated cyclodiene termiticides from the market, the organophosphorus insecticide chlorpyrifos (Dursban TC) has become the most widely used termiticide. Estimates, based on annual chlordane use, place the annual application of chlorpyrifos for termite control at approximately 1.7 million pounds of active ingredient (1). Chlorpyrifos is widely used in rural and urban settings for preventative soil barriers around and under buildings and in direct applications to posts, poles, and other wood products for protection from damage caused by termites. The primary damaging termite species in the United States include the eastern subterranean termite and the Formosan subterranean termite.

0097–6156/93/0522–0062$06.00/0

Chlorpyrifos (as Lorsban) has been used for many years in agriculture for the control of various field crop insect pests. In Iowa alone, over one million acres of corn soils are treated with chlorpyrifos annually *(2)*. Although several studies have focused on the persistence and degradation of chlorpyrifos in soils *(3-9)*, these studies have examined rates comparable to those used for the control of pests in field crops and have not addressed the higher rates used in termite control. Degradation kinetics of soil-applied pesticides can be highly concentration-dependent in some cases. Herbicides applied to soil at high concentrations (e.g., 10,000 ppm) were degraded extremely slowly compared to a normal field application rate *(10)*. Chlorpyrifos degradation involves both chemical and microbial processes *(11)*. Studies have shown that, although chlorpyrifos is not mobile in soil *(12)*, its primary degradation product, 3,5,6-trichloro-2-pyridinol (TCP), is potentially more mobile in a wide range of soil types *(13)*. TCP has also been shown to be more toxic to one microorganism than chlorpyrifos *(14)*. The degradation rates for TCP are variable depending on the specific soils *(15, 16)*. The purpose of this study was to determine how moisture, temperature, and application rate can influence the degradation of chlorpyrifos in soil. Although these factors have been investigated for application rates suitable for agriculture, they have not been examined at the rates used for termite control, which are two orders of magnitude higher. It is important that we understand how this chemical will react in the environment so that adequate termite control can be obtained without adverse effects to human health or the environment.

METHODS AND MATERIALS

Chemicals. Radiolabeled [2,6-ring-^{14}C]chlorpyrifos (25.5 µCi/mmol) *(16)* and non-labeled Dursban TC were obtained from DowElanco for use in this study. The [^{14}C]chlorpyrifos was dissolved in acetone to yield a treating solution. The radiopurity of this material was tested by thin-layer chromatography (TLC) immediately prior to study initiation and found to be >99%. Addition of Dursban TC-formulated material to the treating solution was based on normal labeled concentrations of the active ingredient. Treating solutions were prepared by combining [^{14}C]chlorpyrifos, non-labeled Dursban TC and water in sufficient amounts to yield 0.5 µCi per 50 g dry soil; chlorpyrifos concentrations were 10, 500 or 1,000 µg/g. Soil moisture tensions were established within treatment jars at 0.03, 0.30 or 3.00 bar. All other chemicals and solvents used were reagent grade.

Soil. The soil used for this study was surficial (0-15 cm), taken from the north and south sides of an established urban building. Soil samples were combined, mixed thoroughly, then sieved to remove debris and large particles. The prepared soil was then stored at 4°C prior to use to minimize effects on microbial activity. Properties of the soil are listed in Table I. All soil data are expressed on a dry weight basis.

Table I. Characteristics of the Iowa soil used for laboratory degradation studies

Soil type	pH	OC[a]%	Texture Sand%	Silt%	Clay%	P[b]	K[b]	CEC[c]
Loam	7.8	3	52	34	14	56	2.2	16.5

[a]OC - organic carbon content
[b]P and K reported in ppm.
[c]CEC - cation exchange capacity (meq/100g)

Soil Treatment and Incubation. For determination of chlorpyrifos degradation rates, 50 g (dry weight) portions of soil were weighed out into individual 8-oz French square bottles. Treating solution was then uniformly applied so that samples received 0.5 μCi at 10, 500 or 1,000 μg/g chlorpyrifos and appropriate water to establish soil moisture tensions at either 0.03, 0.30 or 3.00 bar. Once the soil was treated, a 20-ml glass scintillation vial containing 10 ml of 0.1 N NaOH was placed inside to serve as a CO_2 trap. Treatments were divided between two incubators maintained at 20° and 27°C. During the experimental period, filtered HPLC-grade water was added to each sample as needed, to maintain the desired soil moisture tension. Each treatment was replicated six times.

Extraction and Analysis. NaOH traps were removed at regular intervals during the 12-wk incubation period and sampled for evolved $^{14}CO_2$. At time 0 and 12 wk after incubation, samples were removed and extracted three times by shaking with 100 ml of acetone/phosphoric acid (99:1). Extracts from the 0-wk samples were used to quantify (confirm) the amount of [^{14}C]chlorpyrifos initially applied. Unextractable, soil-bound ^{14}C residues in the 12-wk incubation samples were recovered by combustion of aliquots of soil to $^{14}CO_2$ in a Packard Bell model 300 oxidizer. Radiocarbon in NaOH traps, soil extracts, and soil combustions were analyzed by liquid scintillation counting (LSC).

Qualitative identification of ^{14}C residues in the 12-wk soil extracts was determined by thin-layer chromatography. Soil extracts were concentrated and spotted with nonradioactive standards of chlorpyrifos and TCP on 250 μm thick silica gel plates and developed with hexane/acetone/acetic acid (20:4:1) *(11)*. Developed plates were air-dried and then placed under 254 nm UV light to determine positions of nonradioactive standards. The chromatogram was then cut into sections, which were placed in 7-ml scintillation vials with 5 ml cocktail and counted to determine quantities of chlorpyrifos and TCP.

Statistical Analysis. Each treatment combination was replicated six times. Data on the evolution of $^{14}CO_2$ was plotted using all six replications, with error bars expressing ± one standard mean error (Figure 1-3). Data for soil extracts and soil combustions are based on two replications randomly selected from the original six. Analysis of variance and L.S.D. for pair-wise contrasts were used to evaluate treatment effects.

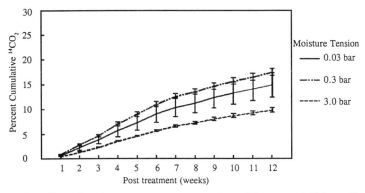

Figure 1. Effect of moisture on the degradation of Dursban TC in an Iowa soil when applied at 10 ppm and incubated at 27°C.

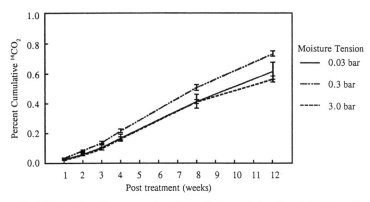

Figure 2. Effect of moisture on the degradation of Dursban TC in an Iowa soil when applied at 500 ppm and incubated at 27°C.

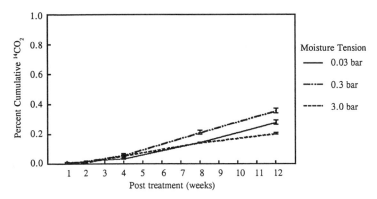

Figure 3. Effect of moisture on the degradation of Dursban TC in an Iowa soil when applied at 1,000 ppm and incubated at 27°C.

RESULTS

Effect of Concentration, Temperature, and Moisture on the Mineralization of Chlorpyrifos. The rate of mineralization, measured by $^{14}CO_2$ evolution, was not significantly affected by temperature (Figure 1-3). Therefore, data for individual treatments were combined across temperatures before statistical analysis. The result of this combination revealed that concentration, moisture, and the interaction between these two factors all were significant. All data are presented as percent of ^{14}C applied.

The interaction between chlorpyrifos concentration and soil moisture tension revealed that samples treated with 10 ppm chlorpyrifos evolved the greatest percent of $^{14}CO_2$ at each moisture tension (Table II). Samples maintained at 0.30 bar evolved a significantly higher percentage of $^{14}CO_2$ than samples maintained at either 0.03 or 3.0 bar tension. Samples maintained at 3.0 bar evolved significantly less $^{14}CO_2$ than samples maintained at either 0.03 or 0.3 bar moisture tension (Table II).

Samples treated with either 500 or 1,000 ppm chlorpyrifos evolved a significantly lower percent $^{14}CO_2$ at all moisture tensions compared to samples treated at 10 ppm. However, no significant differences in mineralization were found between or within 500 or 1,000 ppm treatments.

Table II.   Effect of chlorpyrifos concentration and soil moisture tension on the degradation of Dursban TC in an urban Iowa loam soil (averaged for 2 temperatures)

	Chlorpyrifos Concentration in Soil (ppm)								
	10			500			1,000		
	Soil Moisture (bar tension)								
	0.03	0.30	3.00	0.03	0.30	3.00	0.03	0.30	3.00
	% of ^{14}C recovered after 12 weeks								
Chlorpyrifos	4.6	3.8	6.7	17.0	37.0	25.0	59.0	58.0	53.0
TCP	66.0	63.0	72.0	80.0	59.0	72.0	40.0	40.0	45.0
CO_2	14.0	17.0	9.8	0.55	0.67	0.55	0.24	0.30	0.18

Effect of Chlorpyrifos Concentration on its Degradation. Preliminary analysis of the data from the soil extracts indicated temperature did not affect the degradation of chlorpyrifos or its metabolite (TCP). Data were then combined across all incubation temperatures and reanalyzed. This analysis showed that there were no significant interactions between the concentration of chlorpyrifos applied and soil moisture tension ($P < 0.19$). The same trend also appeared with TCP ($P < 0.18$). There was a significant effect, however, due to concentration of chlorpyrifos applied on both the percent of chlorpyrifos remaining and the percent of TCP present ($P < 0.001$).

Based on the percent of ^{14}C applied, soil treated with 10 ppm chlorpyrifos had the lowest percentage of chlorpyrifos remaining, with only 5% at the end of the 12-wk incubation. This was significantly less than either the 26% remaining for samples treated with 500 ppm chlorpyrifos or the 57% remaining in the samples treated with 1,000 ppm. The percent TCP present was significantly greater in samples treated with 10 or 500 ppm with 67% and 70%, respectfully. The percent of TCP detected was significantly lower (42%) in samples treated with 1,000 ppm.

The degradation pattern of 10 ppm chlorpyrifos is comparable to those in the literature for agricultural application rates *(8, 15, 16)*. For the higher rates (500 and 1,000 ppm), the rates of degradation were much slower and concentration dependent.

Effect of Soil Moisture Tension on the Degradation of Chlorpyrifos. Although soil moisture tension did not affect chlorpyrifos degradation at the same level of significance as the concentration effect ($P < 0.05$), a trend seemed apparent ($P < 0.078$). The percent of TCP formed, however, was significantly affected by soil moisture tension ($P < 0.05$). Based on the percent of ^{14}C applied, samples maintained at near field capacity (0.30 bar) had 33% of the chlorpyrifos remaining at the end of the 12-wk incubation period. Samples maintained at the wettest moisture level (0.03 bar) had only 26% of the applied concentration remaining, compared to 28% remaining in soil samples maintained at the driest moisture level (3.0 bar).

In contrast, the percent of TCP present was the least (54%) for samples maintained at 0.30 bar. Soil samples maintained at 0.03 and 3.0 bar had a significantly higher percentage of TCP, with no significant differences detected between either of these moisture tensions.

Effect of Chlorpyrifos Concentration, Temperature, and Moisture on Bound Soil Residues. Based on statistical analysis, temperature did not significantly affect soil bound residues ($P < 0.17$). However, a significant interaction was detected between the concentration of chlorpyrifos applied, incubation temperature, and soil moisture tension maintained ($P < 0.015$). The percent of ^{14}C applied remaining in unextractable or bound residues was highest (5.8-10%) in soil samples treated with 10 ppm chlorpyrifos. Over 10% of the ^{14}C applied was bound in samples incubated at 20°C and maintained at the highest moisture level (0.03 bar). The amount of bound ^{14}C was lower, less than 2%, in the soil samples treated with 500 or 1,000 ppm (Table III).

DISCUSSION

In this experiment, temperature did not significantly affect the degradation of chlorpyrifos. However, the concentration of chlorpyrifos applied and the soil moisture did play important roles in modifying the rates of chlorpyrifos degradation and mineralization. At the lowest concentration of 10 ppm, the amount of chlorpyrifos remaining at the end of 12 wk was only 0.5 ppm. However, the concentration of its TCP metabolite was 6.7 ppm. TCP has been found to be toxic to one microorganism *(14)*, and may reduce mineralization in soil *(17)*; however, the amount of TCP formed in the 10 ppm treatment did not appear to adversely affect the soil microorganisms' capability to degrade or mineralize chlorpyrifos.

Table III. Effect of concentration, moisture and temperature on the percent of bound residues in an Iowa soil

	Temperature					
	20°C			27°C		
	Soil moisture (bar tension)					
	0.03	0.30	3.00	0.03	0.30	3.00
	% of ^{14}C recovered after 12 weeks					
10 ppm	10.0	8.1	6.8	7.4	10.0	5.8
500 ppm	1.5	1.6	1.7	1.2	1.4	1.6
1,000 ppm	1.0	1.3	1.3	1.0	1.2	1.4

The greatest influence on degradation at the lowest concentration was the soil moisture tension. Soil samples maintained at near field capacity (0.3 bar) provided optimal conditions for mineralization at 10 ppm. At the higher soil moisture, near saturated conditions (0.03 bar), the rate of mineralization was lower. A significantly lower rate was seen when the soil was maintained at its driest level (3.0 bar). The main effect of applying higher concentrations (500 or 1,000 ppm) of chlorpyrifos was to greatly reduce the percent of mineralization. However, the same moisture effect trend appears as in the soil treated at the lower concentration; mineralization of chlorpyrifos was higher in the samples maintained at 0.3 bar, with reduction in mineralization as the soil becomes saturated, and greater reduction when the soil was driest.

The percent hydrolysis of chlorpyrifos to its metabolite (TCP) was influenced the most by the concentration of chlorpyrifos applied. Soil moisture did not appear to significantly influence this process. We speculate that as the concentration of chlorpyrifos increases, the mechanisms by which it is hydrolyzed (chemical and microbial) are slowed or reach saturation. The concentration effect is also quite apparent for the mineralization of TCP. At the higher concentrations of chlorpyrifos, the concentration of TCP formed was also higher. The mineralization of ^{14}C-TCP to ^{14}CO$_2$ can be significantly reduced due to the toxicity of the TCP to soil microorganisms *(14)*. Although the relative percentage of TCP is lower in the soil treated with 1,000 ppm, the actual concentration of TCP is greater, resulting in greater toxicity to soil microorganisms and extended residual activity of the insecticide.

The persistence of chlorpyrifos is greatly influenced by the concentration applied to the soil. At higher concentrations the rates at which chlorpyrifos is degraded to TCP and the TCP is subsequently mineralized are dramatically lower. Soil moisture also influences degradation. This effect is mainly seen in the percent of mineralization of TCP. Conditions for the degradation of chlorpyrifos appear to be optimal when the soil is near field capacity (0.3 bar); however, at a higher soil moisture the persistence of chlorpyrifos was greater. Persistence is greatest when the soil is dry. Understanding how the degradation of chlorpyrifos is affected by concentration, temperature, and soil moisture may help us predict how long this chemical can provide adequate protection against termite infestation. Furthermore, this data provides valuable information based on climate and soil conditions which may allow a pesticide applicator to adjust the application rate of chlorpyrifos, for either the initial or repeat application, that will avoid over-application and possible environmental insult.

ACKNOWLEDGMENT

We thank Mr. Michael Wallendorf for his assistance with statistical analysis of the data. Partial funding for this project was provided by DowElanco, Indianapolis, IN. This chapter is Journal Paper No. J-14966 of the Iowa Agriculture and Home Economics Experiment Station, Ames, Iowa; Project No. 2306.

LITERATURE CITED

1. Federal Register. *Chlordane and Heptachlor Termiticides; Cancellation Order.* Vol. 52, No. 212. 42145-42149.
2. Wintersteen, W.; Hartzler, R. *Iowa Coop. Ext. Serv. Pamph.* **1987**, Pm-1288.
3. Davis, A. C.; Kuhr, R. J. *J. Econ. Entomol.* **1976**, *69*, 665-666.
4. Tashiro, H.; Kuhr, R. J. *J. Econ. Entomol.* **1978**, *71*, 904-907.
5. Miles, J. R. W.; Tu, C. M.; Harris, C. R. *Bull. Environ. Contam. Toxicol.* **1979**, *22*, 312-318.
6. Getzin, L. W. *J. Econ. Entomol.* **1981**, *74*, 707-713.
7. Chapman, R. A.; Chapman, P. C. *J. Environ. Sci. Health.* **1986**, *B21*, 447-456.
8. Racke, K. D.; Coats, J. R. *J. Agric. Food Chem.* **1988**, *36*, 193-199.
9. Racke, K. D.; Laskowski, D. A.; Schultz, M. R. *J. Agric. Food Chem.* **1990**, *38*, 1430-1436.
10. Dzantor, E. K.; Felsot, A. S. *Environ. Toxicol. Chem.* **1991**, *10*, 649-655.
11. Getzin, L. W. *J. Econ. Entomol.* **1981**, *74*, 158-162.
12. Wauchope, R. D.; Young, J. R.; Chalfant, R. B.; Marti, L. R.; Sumner, H. R. *J. Econ. Entomol.* **1978**, *71*, 904-907.
13. Somasundaram, L; Coats, J. R.; Racke, K. D. *Environ. Toxicol. Chem.* **1991**, *10*, 185-194.
14. Somasundaram, L; Coats, J. R.; Racke, K. D.; Stahr, H. M. *Bull. Environ. Contam. Toxicol.* **1990**, *44*, 254-259.
15. Racke, K. D.; Coats, J. R.; Titus, K. R. *J. Environ. Sci. Health.* **1988**, *B23*, 527-539.
16. Racke, K. D.; Laskowski, D. A.; Schultz, M. R. *J. Agric. Food Chem.* **1990**, *38*, 1430-1436.
17. Somasundaram, L.: Coats, J. R.; Racke, K. D. *J. Environ. Sci. Health.* **1989**, *B24*, 457-478.

RECEIVED November 2, 1992

Chapter 8

Comparative Fate of Chlorpyrifos Insecticide in Urban and Agricultural Environments

K. D. Racke, R. N. Lubinski, D. D. Fontaine, J. R. Miller, P. J. McCall, and G. R. Oliver

Environmental Chemistry Laboratory, DowElanco, 9410 North Zionsville Road, Indianapolis, IN 46268

The fate and degradation of pesticides in both agricultural and urban environments are of interest. Chlorpyrifos insecticide is employed for both agricultural and urban pest control scenarios, and was used as a model compound to compare the environmental fate processes operating in the two environments. Agricultural use patterns examined included application to corn (soil-incorporated and foliar/soil spray) and citrus (foliar/soil spray). Urban use patterns selected for study included application to turfgrass via foliar/soil spray and soil trench treatment for termite control. Chlorpyrifos dissipated rapidly from the surface of cornfield soil, citrus grove soil, turfgrass, and fallow urban soil with observed half-lives of between 1 and 17 days. Chlorpyrifos applied as a pre-plant, soil-incorporated application displayed slightly greater persistence, with observed dissipation half-lives of 33-56 days. Application of chlorpyrifos as a termiticidal soil barrier resulted in initial residues of several hundred ppm in the soil and increased persistence versus other use patterns; nearly 70% of the initially applied chlorpyrifos remained in soil after 18 months. Subsequent laboratory investigations revealed chlorpyrifos degradation half-lives of between 116 and 1576 days in 5 soils treated at termiticidal application rates (1000 ppm). Results demonstrated that an increase in application rate from typical agricultural use (10 ppm) to that for urban termiticide application (1000 ppm) resulted in a dramatically decreased rate of dissipation. It appears that chlorpyrifos soil application for termite control achieves long residual control due to both the high application rate and retardation in degradation at the resultant elevated concentrations. Results of these studies illustrate the importance of examining pesticide environmental fate under the different conditions characteristic of both agricultural and urban environments.

Pesticides are used for various pest control scenarios in a wide variety of agricultural environments. Many studies have addressed the fate of pesticides in such agricultural

0097–6156/93/0522–0070$06.00/0

commodities as corn, cotton, soybeans, and citrus. The behavior of pesticides under these and other agricultural conditions has been fairly well characterized, and environmental fate models have been developed to allow prediction of pesticide dissipation and mobility. Urban environments represent important use arenas for pesticides as well. Common urban pest control scenarios include turfgrass pest control (home lawns, golf courses), shrub and ornamental plant pest control, termite control, and home garden pest control. The fate of pesticides under these conditions has also received attention, but the behavior of these materials in urban environments has not been as thoroughly characterized. Because of the high profile of urban pest control efforts and potential for direct exposure of humankind, more attention should and is being directed toward elucidating the environmental behavior of pesticides in urban environments. Additionally, it will be increasingly important to understand the similarities and differences in the behavior of pesticides for the various agricultural and urban scenarios in which pesticides are used.

INTRODUCTION

Pesticides in Urban and Agricultural Environments. There are many similarities but also a few important differences between the rationale for use of pesticides in agricultural and urban environments. In agricultural situations, potential economic losses caused by pest depredations drive the implementation of pest management systems which incorporate pesticide use as a key component. The goal is to provide maximum economic benefit to the agriculturalist by maximizing the quantity and quality of commodity produced. Thus, when economics justify the cost of pest control measures, the use of pesticides plays a key role in realizing the economic gain obtained through avoidance of pest damage. In agricultural pest control scenarios most pesticide use involves herbicide application to control various weeds that compete with crop plants for nutrients, moisture, and sunlight. Insecticides are also important chemicals in agricultural production, with fungicides of somewhat lesser significance. In urban situations, although economic concerns are also important factors in encouraging pest control measures, they are of a different nature. The major economic driving force in the urban pest control arena is the desire to protect investments such as lawns, horticultural landscaping, and home and building structures. There are several other considerations associated with urban environments that are also important. Elimination of nuisance pests (e.g., mosquitoes, cockroaches, fleas, rats) is certainly an important consideration. Urban aesthetics is also a desirable commodity to preserve and enhance, and pests with activities impacting this area often stimulate pest management practices. Finally, disease transmission threats present in urban environments (e.g., tick transmission of Lyme disease) merit pest control measures that may include pesticide use. Due to the predominance of insect pests in all these categories of urban pest control, insecticides are much more important in relation to overall pesticide use in urban environments than they are in agricultural environments.

Pesticide use patterns are fairly similar between agricultural and urban environments. In both situations foliar pesticide sprays are important application modes for combatting weed pests and foliar-feeding insect pests. In agricultural environments these sprays may be made with ground (e.g., groundbooms, airblast sprayers) or aerial application equipment. In urban environments by contrast, spray applications are usually limited to ground application equipment with much application occurring via hand-held sprayers. In both agricultural and urban environments direct soil treatments with liquid or granular formulations of insecticides and herbicides are common. In agricultural situations (e.g., row-crop agriculture), however, soil-incorporated applications of insecticides and herbicides are much more common than under most urban conditions. A distinctive pesticide use pattern is also represented by termite control practices in urban environments. Under these conditions, insecticidal soil barriers to termite invasion are created by termiticides injected through building foundations or deposited in trenches surrounding the structure. One common outcome of pesticide application in both urban and agricultural environments is that soil serves as the major sink of initial and/or ultimate pesticide deposition. Thus, in both environments fate of pesticides in soil will be an important focus of experimental activity.

A number of common pesticide products are employed in both agricultural and urban pest control practices. This is not surprising since many similar types of pests are the targets of control efforts. Insecticides such as acephate, carbaryl, chlorpyrifos, diazinon, dimethoate, and malathion all find use for both agricultural and horticultural pests. For weed control in both scenarios, common herbicides such as 2,4-D, dicamba, glyphosate, and pendimethalin are utilized. There is a larger suite of pesticides available for agricultural use than for urban use. Widely used agricultural pesticides such as alachlor, aldicarb, metribuzin, paraquat, parathion, and terbufos may not commonly be used in urban environments due to poor product fit into the urban market, higher-than-average mammalian toxicity, or environmental concerns. Less commonly, a handful of pesticides may almost exclusively be used in urban environments. These include products such as isazophos, isofenphos, and oryzalin, and their heavy specialization for urban environments is most likely due to good product matches for specific urban pest control scenarios and/or poor matches for significant agricultural pest control scenarios. Of major significance for comparison of pesticide behavior in urban and agricultural environments are the pesticides which are commonly employed in both. Thus, direct comparisons made for a specific chemical under several agricultural and urban conditions may provide insight into the similarities and differences in environmental fate processes operating in the two spheres.

Chlorpyrifos Insecticide. Chlorpyrifos (O,O-diethyl O-(3,5,6-trichloro-2-pyridyl) phosphorothioate) is an insecticide that has broad application for control of various insect pests in both agricultural and urban settings. It is widely applied both foliarly and to the soil in row crops, orchard crops, turf, landscaping, and around structures for termite control. Agricultural products include both an emulsifiable concentrate (Lorsban* 4E) (*Trademark of DowElanco) and a granular formulation (Lorsban 15G). Urban, specialty products include emulsifiable concentrate (EC) formulations for turf pests (Dursban* Turf Insecticide) (*Trademark of DowElanco), various outdoor insect pests (Dursban 4E), and termites (Dursban TC). Thus, chlorpyrifos presents a unique opportunity for the comparison of environmental fate processes operating in agricultural and urban environments.

The chemical properties and environmental fate of chlorpyrifos have been recently reviewed (*1*), but a few notable points are worth emphasis. Chlorpyrifos is an organophosphorus insecticide characterized by a low water solubility (<2 ppm), moderate vapor pressure (2×10^{-5} mm Hg @ 25°C), and high tendency for sorption to soil and sediments (average soil $K_{oc} = 8498$). Chlorpyrifos is a degradable compound, and both abiotic and biotic transformation processes effect its dissipation from environmental compartments. In all cases, the major pathway of transformation involves cleavage of the phosphate ester bond to form 3,5,6-trichloro-2-pyridinol (TCP), an insecticidally inactive metabolite. In general, chlorpyrifos displays rapid dissipation from foliar surfaces (typical half-lives of from 1-7 days) and moderate to rapid dissipation in soil (typical half-lives of from 7-35 days).

Purpose of Current Studies. The purpose of the current set of studies was to compare the environmental fate of chlorpyrifos applied under urban and agricultural conditions. Urban use patterns selected for study included application to turfgrass via foliar spray and soil treatment for termite control. Agricultural use patterns examined included application to corn (soil-incorporated and foliar spray) and citrus (foliar spray). The goal was to determine how similar the kinetics of dissipation would be under the various scenarios investigated, with the major focus of the studies falling on fate in soil.

METHODS AND MATERIALS

Field Dissipation Studies. Field dissipation studies were conducted by using formulated chlorpyrifos products applied under typical use conditions. For each experimental design the analytical procedures used were similar and will not be elaborated on at great length. On the day of chlorpyrifos application and at various times afterwards, samples of soil or plant materials were collected from the field, extracted with organic solvents, and analyzed by Gas-Liquid Chromatography (GLC) for chlorpyrifos residues. Specific details of the field sites, application practices, and sampling patterns will be discussed for each agricultural and urban scenario.

Corn: Soil-Incorporated. Soil-incorporated applications of chlorpyrifos are used to control one of the major pests of corn, the corn rootworm. Corn sites chosen for the study were plots (0.01-0.09 ha) located in Illinois, Michigan, and California. The soil present at the Illinois site was a Catlin silt loam soil (pH 5.7, 1.8% organic carbon). The Michigan soil was a Londo sandy loam soil (pH 7.7, 0.9% organic carbon) and the California soil a Yolo loam (pH 7.8, 0.5% organic carbon). The field at the California site was furrow irrigated (23 cm/3 months), whereas only natural rainfall occurred at the other two sites. An EC formulation of chlorpyrifos (Lorsban 4E) was applied at 3.36 kg/ha a.i. as a broadcast, preplant application during May. The surface-applied chlorpyrifos was immediately incorporated to a depth of 5-10 cm. At each site, soil samples in 15.24 cm depth increments (2.54 cm diameter) to 45.72 cm were taken on the day of application and at later intervals. On each sampling date, 24 sample cores were taken from each site, and these were combined into 3-4 composite samples for residue analysis.

Corn: Soil/Foliar Spray. Foliar sprays of chlorpyrifos in corn are used to control various lepidopterous pests such as cutworms and corn borers. A field site planted to corn in Illinois (1.33 ha) was used for the study. Several soils were present at the study site, and these included Ada loamy fine sand (pH 5.7, 0.8% organic carbon), Hoopeston fine sandy loam (pH 6.5, 1.3% organic carbon), and Gilford fine sandy loam (pH 7.0, 1.3% organic carbon). Two foliar applications of an emulsifiable concentrate of chlorpyrifos (Lorsban 4E) at 1.68 kg/ha a.i. were made to the corn, the first during May when the corn was at the 2-4 leaf stage, and the second during June when the corn was at the 60-90 cm height stage. On the days of chlorpyrifos application and at later intervals 9 soil samples of 2.54 cm depth (10.16 cm diameter) were collected for chlorpyrifos residue determination. In addition, samples of corn foliage (500 g) were randomly collected on the days of application and subsequently for determination of foliar chlorpyrifos residues.

Citrus: Soil/Foliar Spray. Chlorpyrifos sprays are applied to the foliage of citrus trees for control of various lepidopterous pests (e.g., cutworms, leafrollers), and also pests such as aphids, thrips, mealy bugs, and rust mites. A Valencia orange grove in Florida was selected for the citrus dissipation study. The total site was 2 ha in area, and both St. Lucie and Lakewood sands and fine sands were present (pH 6.4-7.0, 0.16-0.37% organic carbon). The site was sprinkler irrigated as is common in Florida citrus production (48.5 cm/10 months). Three separate foliar applications of an emulsifiable concentrate of chlorpyrifos (Lorsban 4E) at 1.12 kg/ha a.i. were made, with the first two during November, and the third during December. For sampling purposes, 3 test plots of 9 trees each were delineated within the grove, and triplicate soil samples to 2.54 cm depths (10.16 cm diameter) were collected from each test plot for chlorpyrifos analyses. Some soil samples down to 76-107 cm depth were collected on some sampling dates.

Turf: Soil/Foliar Spray. Chlorpyrifos is applied to turfgrass to control surface-feeding and soil-dwelling insect pests such as chinchbugs, mole crickets, sod webworms, and white grubs. Turfgrass dissipation studies were conducted at sites in both Indiana and Florida. At both sites, triplicate plots (0.01 ha) of turfgrass and fallow soil were included in the experimental design. A Crosby clay loam soil (pH 6.2-6.3, 1.30-1.65% organic carbon) was present at the Indiana site, portions of which were sodded with Kentucky bluegrass mixtures. The Florida site was underlain by a Millhopper sand (pH 6.3-6.4, 0.57-0.70% organic carbon), and the turf plots there were sodded with a St. Augustinegrass variety. At both sites, an emulsifiable concentrate of chlorpyrifos (Dursban Turf Insecticide) was spray applied to both the turf and fallow soil plots in June at a rate of 4.48 kg/ha a.i. On the day of application and subsequent dates, 5 cores (5-15 cm diameter) were collected, to a depth of 10-15 cm, from each triplicate turf and fallow soil plot. Composite samples from each replicate were then analyzed for chlorpyrifos residues. Throughout the growing season either sprinkler or overhead boom irrigation was applied regularly to turf and fallow soil plots alike.

Termite Control: Soil Trench. Chlorpyrifos is applied underneath and surrounding buildings and structures for termite pest control. The goal of termiticidal soil treatment is to create an impenetrable insecticidal barrier in the soil to prevent termite invasion and damage. The site selected for the field dissipation study was a structure in Georgia. This field test was established in cooperation with U.E. Brady of the University of Georgia. A 15.24 cm wide (10.16 cm depth) trench was dug in the sandy loam soil surrounding the building foundation, and a 1% dilution of a chlorpyrifos emulsifiable concentrate formulation (Dursban TC) was applied to the trench at 5 L/linear meter. At various times after application soil cores down to 15.24 cm depth (1.9 cm diameter) were removed from the trench and analyzed for chlorpyrifos remaining.

Laboratory Degradation Studies. Investigations were also conducted to examine the degradation of chlorpyrifos in soils under laboratory conditions. These studies represented an attempt to understand some of the differences in chlorpyrifos behavior that had been observed in soil following field application to soil under agricultural and urban conditions. For laboratory studies, technical [14]C-(2,6-pyridyl)-chlorpyrifos was utilized, and it was applied to soils (50 g) contained in soil biometer flasks (2). These flasks permit carbon dioxide resulting from mineralization to be collected, and are attached to an oxygen manifold to permit replenishment of oxygen and maintenance of aerobic conditions. Samples were incubated for up to 18 months in this fashion. During this period, soil flasks were regularly sampled for evolved carbon dioxide and soils taken for extraction and subsequent analysis of chlorpyrifos, extractable metabolites, and soil-bound (unextractable) residues (3). Relative concentrations of chlorpyrifos and metabolites in soil extracts were quantified via high-performance liquid chromatography with radiomonitor detection.

Degradation Kinetics at Termiticidal Rates. Several soils were selected for study of chlorpyrifos degradation at termiticidal application rates. For the study, soils from areas in which termiticides are commonly used were selected. Two Florida sand soils were chosen, with one having a pH of 6.4 and organic carbon content of 0.66% (designated FL1) and the other having a pH of 7.5 and organic carbon content of 1.92% (designated FL2). In addition, two sandy loam soils were examined, including a Hawaiian soil (pH 5.7, 5.7% organic carbon) and an Arizona soil (pH 8.3, 0.88% organic carbon). Finally, a clay loam soil from Texas (pH 8.0, 1.20% organic carbon) was employed. To approximate the concentration resulting from trench application of chlorpyrifos (i.e., Dursban TC) a nominal initial concentration of 1000 ppm chlorpyrifos was used. Soils treated with ^{14}C-chlorpyrifos at 1000 ppm were adjusted to 75% of 0.3 bar soil moisture tension (SMT) and incubated at 25°C for the duration of the experiment.

Effect of Application Rate on Degradation Kinetics and Pathway. To further examine the effect of concentration on the rate of chlorpyrifos degradation in soil, samples of a sand soil from Florida (FL1: pH 6.4, organic carbon 0.66%) were treated with several concentrations of ^{14}C-chlorpyrifos. A 10 ppm application was chosen to represent soil concentrations commonly reached during agricultural use, whereas a 1000 ppm application was selected to typify concentrations expected from urban, termiticidal use of chlorpyrifos. An intermediate concentration of 100 ppm was also examined. Samples of soil treated with ^{14}C-chlorpyrifos were adjusted to a soil moisture of 75% 0.3 bar SMT and incubated at 25°C. The common metabolites of chlorpyrifos in soil, 3,5,6-trichloro-2-pyridinol (TCP), 3,5,6-trichloro-2-methoxypyridine (TMP), soil-bound (unextractable) residues, and carbon dioxide were all analyzed in samples incubated for up to 18 months.

RESULTS AND DISCUSSION

Field Dissipation Studies. Results of field dissipation studies for each scenario will be discussed individually. Data on chlorpyrifos dissipation in the various studies is presented in Table I and Figures 1-6. Half-lives were calculated assuming first order kinetics.

Table I.   Comparative Dissipation of Chlorpyrifos in Agricultural and Urban
          Environments Under Field Conditions

Crop/Use Pattern	Location	Application Rate (a.i.) kg/ha	Application Pattern	Dissipation Half-Life (Days)
Corn	Illinois	3.36	Soil-Incorporated	56
Corn	Michigan	3.36	Soil-Incorporated	33
Corn	California	3.36	Soil-Incorporated	46
Corn	Illinois	1.68	Soil Surface	13.5-17.2
Citrus	Florida	1.12	Soil Surface	1.3-4.4
Turfgrass	Indiana	4.48	Soil Surface	8.6
Fallow Soil	Indiana	4.48	Soil Surface	9.5
Turfgrass	Florida	4.48	Soil Surface	5.7
Fallow Soil	Florida	4.48	Soil Surface	7.6
Termiticide	Georgia	392	Soil Trench	>1095

Corn: Soil-Incorporated. At the three locations, application of chlorpyrifos as a preplant, soil-incorporation (3.36 kg/ha a.i.) resulted in initial soil surface (0-15.24 cm) residues of 0.72-1.4 ppm. Chlorpyrifos dissipation half-lives at the Illinois, Michigan, and California sites were determined to be 56, 33, and 46 days, respectively (Figure 1). After 1 year, residues at all sites had declined below detectable levels (0.05 ppm). Regarding vertical mobility, no residues of chlorpyrifos were detected at depths greater than 30.5 cm at any site. The half-lives observed for these soil-incorporated applications of chlorpyrifos correspond well with previous investigations on chlorpyrifos persistence in soil. Chapman and Harris (4) reported chlorpyrifos dissipation half-lives of 2 and 8 weeks in treated sand and muck soils, respectively. Getzin (5) reported soil-incorporated half-lives of 22-58 days for chlorpyrifos. For effective control of such major corn soil pests as larval corn rootworms, several weeks of persistence at insecticidally significant levels are required (6). The long history of effective control provided by chlorpyrifos indicates that the persistence pattern of chlorpyrifos is well matched to the control scenario presented by corn soil pests (7).

Corn: Soil/Foliar Spray. Application of chlorpyrifos as a foliar/soil surface spray to a cornfield in Illinois resulted in initial residues of 118-145 ppm on corn foliage. Chlorpyrifos residues on corn foliage dissipated rapidly, with observed half-lives of approximately 1.5 days for the two applications. This is similar to dissipation patterns reported for chlorpyrifos on other foliar surfaces. Comparatively similar half-lives on foliage of corn (1 day), soybean (3.95 days), tomato (<1-5.8 days), cotton (<1-4.0 days), citrus (<1-2.4 days), and bluegrass (7 days) have been reported (8-11). The major mechanism of chlorpyrifos dissipation from foliar surfaces is volatility, and the rapid rate of decline in chlorpyrifos residues on a variety of foliage is presumably due to this factor (*12*).

The average initial concentration of chlorpyrifos residues in the soil surface layer (0-2.54 cm) following the first and second applications was 4.1 and 6.2 ppm, respectively. In comparison with the previous studies (i.e., soil-incorporated application), chlorpyrifos applied to the soil surface dissipated more rapidly. Dissipation half-lives of 13.5 and 17.2 days were observed for the May and June applications, respectively (Figure 2). Near the end of the growing season (August) less than 1 ppm chlorpyrifos remained in soil. The relatively rapid dissipation of chlorpyrifos from the soil surface has been previously reported. Similar applications of formulated chlorpyrifos (EC) to the soil surface have yielded dissipation half-lives of 4 days in Georgia (*8*), 6 days in Washington (*5*), and 30 days in Italy (*13*). The more rapid dissipation of chlorpyrifos on the soil surface is most likely due to several factors including volatility and photodegradation, occurrence of higher temperatures, and rapid hydrolysis on air-dry soil particles (*1*).

Citrus: Soil/Foliar Spray. Similarly short chlorpyrifos dissipation half-lives were noted for 3 successive applications of chlorpyrifos on the surface of citrus soils in Florida (Figure 3). Initial residue levels in the upper 2.54 cm of soil underneath and between plant canopies were 0.4-0.8 and 0.2-2.3 ppm, respectively, and average soil dissipation half-lives of 1.3-4.4 days were observed. Residues of chlorpyrifos were confined to the upper 15.24 cm of soil for the duration of the study. The high temperatures and alternating moist (irrigation) and dry conditions present on the citrus soil surface may have contributed to the very rapid chlorpyrifos dissipation observed.

Turf: Soil/Foliar Spray. For the urban investigations, chlorpyrifos dissipation on both turf and bare soil plots at two locations was examined. Initial residues of between 1.5 and 2.5 ppm were present in the upper 10-15 cm of soil/thatch/grass (turf plots) or soil (fallow soil plots) at both the Indiana (Kentucky bluegrass) and Florida (St. Augustinegrass) sites. At the Indiana site (Figure 4), half-lives of 8.6 and 9.5 days were noted for turf and fallow soil plots, respectively, whereas slightly shorter half-lives of 5.7 (turf) and 7.6 days (fallow soil) were noted at the Florida site (Figure 5). These dissipation rates are similar to those observed by previous turf researchers, who have reported half-lives of 7 days (*11*) and 7-14 days (*14*).

What is striking is the similarity between the dissipation rates for chlorpyrifos applied to either the turf or fallow soil surface. This coincidence may appear deceivingly simple, but the similarity in dissipation rates between turf and soil may be the result of entirely different mechanisms. Due to the dense foliar surface of the turfgrass plots, nearly all of the application is intercepted by the foliage. This has been documented by Sears and Chapman (*14*), who reported that 97% of a chlorpyrifos (EC) application to annual bluegrass was intercepted by the grass/thatch layer, whereas only 3% was initially present in the soil root zone (0-1 cm depth). With the majority of turfgrass residues present on the turf foliage, volatility would be expected to be the major route of dissipation, as from other foliar surfaces (e.g., corn). However, dissipation from the soil surfaces was most likely due to a combination of soil-catalyzed hydrolysis, photodegradation, and volatility.

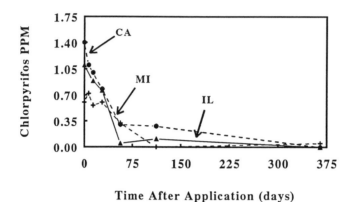

Figure 1. Field Dissipation of Soil-Incorporated Chlorpyrifos in Cornfields at 3 Locations (3.36 kg/ha).

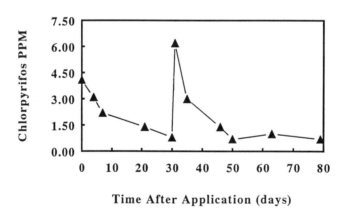

Figure 2. Field Dissipation of Soil Surface Applied Chlorpyrifos in an Illinois Cornfield (1.68 kg/ha).

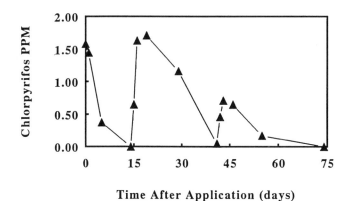

Figure 3. Field Dissipation of Soil Surface Applied Chlorpyrifos in a Florida Citrus Grove (1.12 kg/ha).

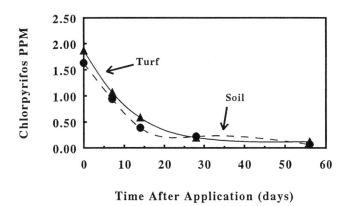

Figure 4. Field Dissipation of Chlorpyrifos Applied to the Surface of Turfgrass or Fallow Soil in Indiana (4.48 kg/ha).

What is significant from an agricultural/urban fate comparison vantage is the very similar dissipation pattern of chlorpyrifos noted for turf and urban soil surfaces and that observed for corn and citrus soil surfaces.

Termite Control: Soil Trench. Application of chlorpyrifos for termite control to a soil trench surrounding a building structure resulted in much higher initial residue levels than were observed under any of the other urban or agricultural scenarios examined. The average initial residue in the soil (0-15.24 cm) was 357 ppm, but individual analyses ranged as high as 703 ppm for the soil surface layer (0-5.08 cm). Sampling and residue analyses conducted over a 3 year period indicated only modest decline in residue levels during that period; after 36 months an average of 245 ppm chlorpyrifos remained (Figure 6). This would indicate a dissipation half-life of >1095 days, which is far longer than under the other scenarios examined. The termiticidal use of chlorpyrifos underneath structures and in trenches alongside building foundations, for which high per unit application rates are used, represents a unique situation for consideration of its environmental fate. Field efficacy studies at a number of sites have revealed that soil applications of chlorpyrifos may provide control of termites for as long as 10-20+ years, indicating a long persistence at insecticidal levels (*15,16*). Thus, the extended persistence of chlorpyrifos is not surprising in light of the residual termiticidal efficacy that has been observed and which is expected of termiticides in the marketplace.

Field Dissipation Study Conclusions. In summary, the dissipation pattern for chlorpyrifos on the soil surface was similar for urban and agricultural conditions. Investigations of chlorpyrifos behavior on the surface of cornfield soil, citrus soil, fallow urban soil, and turfgrass revealed that soil behavior will be largely similar for this compound in the two environments. In agricultural settings in which chlorpyrifos is incorporated into the soil profile, somewhat longer dissipation half-lives are observed. However, the one use pattern which appears to present a variant picture of chlorpyrifos soil fate is that associated with urban termiticidal control practices. This difference, represented by the apparently extended soil dissipation half-life observed (>1095 days), indicated that further investigation of chlorpyrifos soil fate under termiticidal use conditions was merited.

Laboratory Degradation Studies. Studies on the degradation of chlorpyrifos in soil were initiated in the laboratory in an attempt to explain the increased persistence noted in the termiticidal trench field dissipation study. Results of the various experiments will be discussed individually, and data has been summarized in Table II and Figures 7 and 8.

Degradation Kinetics at Termiticidal Rates. Application of chlorpyrifos at termiticidal rate (1000 ppm) to 5 different soils incubated under laboratory conditions resulted in degradation half-lives measured in months rather than days (Table II). Observed half-lives ranged from 116-335 days in 4 of the soils to as high as 1576 days in one Florida soil (FL1). These observed chlorpyrifos half-lives are substantially longer than those observed in previous laboratory soil degradation studies. Typical

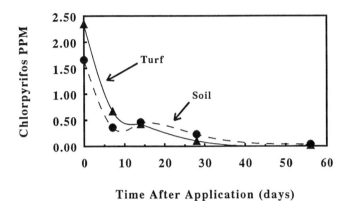

Figure 5. Field Dissipation of Chlorpyrifos Applied to the Surface of Turfgrass or Fallow Soil in Florida (4.48 kg/ha).

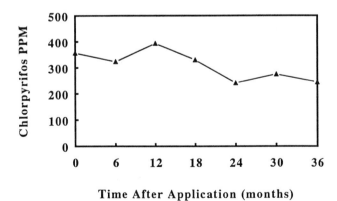

Figure 6. Field Dissipation of Chlorpyrifos Applied to a Soil Trench for Termite Control in Georgia (392 kg/ha).

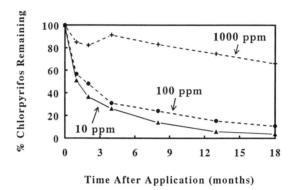

Figure 7. Effect of Initial Chlorpyrifos Concentration on its Degradation in a
Florida Sand Soil Under Laboratory Conditions.

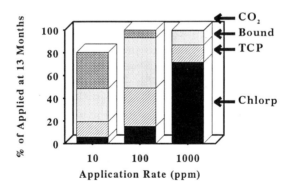

Figure 8. Effect of Initial Chlorpyrifos Concentration on its Dissipation and
Formation of Metabolites in a Florida Sand Soil Under Laboratory
Conditions. Chlorp = chlorpyrifos; TCP = 3,5,6-trichloro-2- pyridinol;
Bound = unextractable soil residues.

Table II. Degradation of Chlorpyrifos in Soil Under Laboratory Conditions at Termiticidal Application Rate

Soil Collection Site	Texture	pH	Organic Carbon %	Half-Life (Days)
Florida (1)	Sand	6.4	0.66	1576
Hawaii	Sandy Loam	5.7	5.70	335
Arizona	Sandy Loam	8.3	0.88	230
Florida (2)	Sand	7.5	1.92	214
Texas	Clay Loam	8.0	1.20	116

chlorpyrifos soil degradation half-lives of from 11 to 141 days have been reported, with most falling in the range of 25-35 days (*1,3*). Based on observations of 95+% mortality of termites in soil containing 0.4 ppm chlorpyrifos (*17*), the predicted length of termiticidal control based on these laboratory results would be from many months to more than 20 years. This corresponds well with field observations of >80% control of termites by chlorpyrifos after 8, 17, 15, and 12 years at sites in Arizona, Florida, Mississippi, and South Carolina, respectively (*16*). The variability in the soil degradation rates of chlorpyrifos observed in the present study also indicates its persistence will be dependent on soil type. This variability represents differences due to soil variables alone (e.g., microbial populations, pH), and does not take into account environmental variables such as moisture and temperature.

Effect of Application Rate on Degradation Kinetics and Pathway. A direct comparison of chlorpyrifos degradation at agricultural (10 ppm) and termiticidal (1000 ppm) application rates in a Florida sand soil (FL1) revealed an interesting phenomenon (Figure 7). Chlorpyrifos dissipated in an apparent first-order fashion at the agricultural rate (10 ppm), with less than 40% of the applied chlorpyrifos remaining after 2 months of incubation. When applied at the termiticidal application rate (1000 ppm), chlorpyrifos exhibited much greater persistence, with nearly 80% of the application remaining after some 18 months. The degradation rate at 1000 ppm application rate was somewhat linear in nature, and did not fit first-order kinetic assumptions very well. These results clearly demonstrated that an increase in application rate from typical agricultural use (10 ppm) to that for urban termiticide application (1000 ppm) resulted in a dramatically decreased rate of dissipation. The 100 ppm application demonstrated a slightly increased persistence versus the 10 ppm rate. Observations of decreasing pesticide degradation in soil with increasing concentration are not new (18-22), but the underlying mechanisms have not been conclusively elucidated. Hance and McKone suggested that decreased degradation rates observed at higher application concentrations might result from a limitation in the number of available reaction sites in soil (19). An alternative theory focused on the potential for toxic effects on soil microbial activity or inhibition of soil enzymes at high pesticide application rates (23). In the case of chlorpyrifos, it appears that not only does use of a high initial application rate enhance residual control (i.e., many ppm remaining even after a number of half-lives), but also that degradation processes are retarded at the termiticidal application rate, thus contributing further to the length of termiticidal efficacy.

The pathway of degradation of chlorpyrifos in soil typically involves hydrolytic cleavage of the phosphate ester to form 3,5,6-trichloro-2-pyridinol (TCP). This cleavage occurs via both abiotic reactions in soil and microbial activities. The TCP metabolite is itself further transformed and ultimately mineralized to carbon dioxide by the soil microbial community. The relative recovery of chlorpyrifos and its metabolic products in soil after 13 months is illustrated in Figure 8 for the Florida sand soil (FL1) treated with 10, 100, or 1000 ppm. For the 10 ppm application rate, very little chlorpyrifos remained, and nearly equal quantities of carbon dioxide and soil-bound residues were produced. For the soil treated at 100 ppm some differences are evident. Over 30% of the initially applied chlorpyrifos was transformed and present as TCP in this soil, but very little subsequent mineralization occurred. Greater formation of soil-bound residues occurred at the 100 ppm versus the 10 ppm treatment. For the 1000 ppm treatment, very little mineralization was evident as well, but due to the fact that most chlorpyrifos remained unaltered, the significance of this finding is unclear. The major difference in the metabolic pathway between chlorpyrifos degradation at agricultural versus termiticidal rates involved further degradation of the TCP metabolite. Decreased degradation of TCP in soil containing elevated levels of this metabolite has been previously reported. For example, Racke et al. reported that for one soil that mineralized 80% of an applied TCP dose of 5 ppm only 4% of an applied dose of 50 ppm was likewise mineralized (24). Further work demonstrated that TCP does have some anti-bacterial activity, and an EC_{50} for the bacteria tested was approximately 19 ppm (25).

CONCLUSIONS

In both agricultural and urban environments, the fate and degradation of pesticides are of interest. Comparison of the fate of chlorpyrifos insecticide in agricultural and urban environments suggests that fate processes will be largely similar under most conditions. Due to the high application rates characteristic of the urban termiticidal use pattern, however, the rate of degradation in soil was significantly slower than under all other conditions examined. These results highlight the importance of examining pesticide environmental fate under the different use patterns employed for both agricultural and urban pest control scenarios.

LITERATURE CITED

1. Racke, K.D. *Rev. Environ. Contam. Toxicol.* **1992**, *131*, in press.
2. Laskowski, D.A.; Swann, R.L.; McCall, P.J.; Bidlack, H.D. *Residue Rev.* **1983**, *85*, 139-147.
3. Racke, K.D.; Laskowski, D.A.; Schultz, M.R. *J. Agric. Food Chem.* **1990**, *38*, 1430-1436.
4. Chapman, R.A.; Harris, C.R. *J. Environ. Sci. Health* **1980**, *B15*, 39-46.
5. Getzin, L.W. *J. Econ. Entomol.* **1985**, *78*, 412-418.
6. Felsot, A.S.; Steffey, K.L.; Levine, E.; Wilson, J.G. *J. Econ. Entomol.* **1985**, *78*, 45-52.
7. Foster, D.; Bailey, W. *Summary of Insecticide Uses in Iowa for 1985 Corn Production.* Iowa State University Cooperative Extension Service Bulletin IC-404, 1984.
8. Wauchope, R.D.; Young, J.R.; Chalfant, R.B.; Marti, L.R.; Sumner, H.R. *Pestic. Sci.* **1991**, *32*, 235-243.
9. Abdel-All, A.; Khamis, A.E.; Edrisha, M.S.; Antonious, G.F. *Alexandria Sci. Exch.* **1990**, *11*, 1-17.
10. Veierov, D.; Fenigstein, A.; Melamed-Madjar, V.; Klein, M. *J. Econ. Entomol.* **1988**, *81*, 621-627.
11. Kuhr, R.J.; Tashiro, H. *Bull. Environ. Contam. Toxicol.* **1978**, *20*, 652-656.
12. McCall, P.J.; Swann, R.L.; Bauriedel, W.R. **1985** DowElanco unpublished report.
13. Leoni, V.; Hollick, C.B.; D'Alessandro de Luca, E.; Collison, R.J.; Merolli, S. *Agrochimica* **1981**, *25*, 414-426.
14. Sears, M.K.; Chapman, R.A. *J. Econ. Entomol.* **1979**, *72*, 272-274.
15. Mauldin, J.; Jones, S.; Beal, R. *Pest Contr.* **1987**, *55*, 46-59.
16. Kard, B.M. In: *Fate and Significance of Pesticides in Urban Environments;* Racke, K.D., Leslie, A.R., Eds.; Symposium Series, American Chemical Society, Washington (in press).
17. Su, N.-Y.; Scheffrahn, R.H. *J. Econ. Entomol.* **1990**, *83*, 1918-1924.
18. Armstrong, D.E.; Chesters, G.; Harris, R.F. *Soil Sci. Soc. Am. Proc.* **1967**, *31*, 61-66.
19. Hance, R.J.; McKone, C.E. *Pestic. Sci.* **1971**, *3*, 31-34.
20. Walker, A. *Pestic. Sci.* **1976**, *7*, 41-49.
21. Ou, L.-T.; Rothwell, D.F.; Wheeler, W.B.; Davidson, J.M. *J. Environ. Qual.* **1978**, *7*, 241-246.
22. Racke, K.D.; Lichtenstein, E.P. *J. Environ. Sci. Health* **1987**, *B22*, 1-14.
23. Hurle, K. *Acta Phytomedica* **1981**.
24. Racke, K.D.; Coats, J.R.; Titus, K.R. *J. Environ. Sci. Health* **1988**, *B23*, 527-539.
25. Somasundaram, L.; Coats, J.R.; Racke, K.D.; Stahr, H.M. *Bull. Environ. Contam. Toxicol.* **1990**, *44*, 254-259.

RECEIVED November 2, 1992

Chapter 9

Dissipation of Turfgrass Foliar Dislodgeable Residues of Chlorpyrifos, DCPA, Diazinon, Isofenphos, and Pendimethalin

K. A. Hurto and M. G. Prinster

ChemLawn Services Corporation, 135 Winter Road, Delaware, OH 43015

Field studies were conducted to determine the influence of posttreatment irrigation on dislodgeable pesticide residues following applications to a Kentucky bluegrass turf. Turfgrass clippings were harvested 0,1,2,3,7, and 14 days after treatment (DAT) and analyzed for pesticide residue. Irrigation (1.3 cm) was applied 2 hours after treatment (HAT), after which water was withheld until after the 7 DAT harvest. Total pesticide residue retained on clippings harvested 1 HAT averaged 21.3% of the applied rate. Irrigation 2 HAT reduced concentrations of F-, DG-, and WP- formulated pesticides 45%, but did not significantly reduce concentration of EC-formulated pesticide residues retained on foliage. Dislodgeable residues averaged 5.6% of the applied rate 0 DAT, and dissipated exponentially over time to 1% at 7 DAT, and to 0.3% by 14 DAT. Dissipation rates varied among pesticide treatments but not between irrigation treatments. Results suggest a very low percentage of lawn-applied pesticides are dislodgeable, and that levels decrease rapidly with time. Secondly, irrigation can further reduce levels depending upon pesticide formulation applied.

Incidence of pesticide use on residential lawn turfgrass has increased as homeowner awareness of weed and insect problems has grown, largely as a result of the rapid expansion of the lawncare industry in the United States and southern Canada. Pesticides used to treat lawns are formulated either as a dry granule product on an inert carrier such as clay, vermiculite, corncob, or fertilizer granules and applied with a mechanical spreader; or are formulated as concentrates that are applied as a very dilute mixture with water or in fertilizer solutions. Recent attention by the public to lawncare application of pesticides has raised a concern over the exposure risk to humans and pets from these applications.

Thompson et al. *(1)* reported on the persistence and dislodgeable residues of 2,4-D following its application to Kentucky bluegrass in Guelph, Ontario. Sprayable liquid formulations had higher dislodgeable residues of 2,4-D on foliage immediately after application compared with granule formulated product. They reported very rapid

0097–6156/93/0522–0086$06.00/0

dissipation of dislodgeable residues within days of application. At 3 days after treatment (DAT), less than 1% of 2,4-D applied at 1 kg ha^{-1} was dislodged by vigorous wiping of foliage with moistened cheesecloth regardless of formulation. Irrigation or rainfall after application and mowing 3 DAT significantly reduced dislodgeable residue levels compared to unmowed areas.

Bowhey et al. *(2)* reported dislodgeable residues of 2,4-D the day of application increased proportionately as use rate applied increased from 1 to 4 kg ha^{-1}, but by 7 DAT less than 1% of the target rate applied was recovered regardless of concentration applied, and decreased to less than 0.2% by 10 DAT. Dislodgeable residues immediately after application were greater for liquid formulations than for granule formulations of 2,4-D; but at 1 DAT residues dislodged from granular applications were not lower than residues dislodged from the liquid application. Premix formulations of 2,4-D + mecoprop + dicamba did not alter level of 2,4-D dislodged compared to 2,4-D applied alone, either as a liquid or as a granule formulation.

Dissipation of dislodgeable residues of chlorpyrifos applied to a Kentucky bluegrass in Sacramento, CA in very dilute concentrations using a formulated concentrate of 3% chlorpyrifos + 2.6% dichlorvos applied at 74.5 l ha^{-1} in 4883 l ha^{-1} of water were measured using a detergent-stripping procedure *(3)*. Dislodgeable levels of chlorpyrifos immediately after application were well below the estimated safe level of 0.5 µg cm$^{-2.}$ Irrigation immediately following application significantly increased dissipation rate of residues on foliage.

Sears et al. *(4)* reported on dislodgeable residues of three insecticides applied to turfgrass in Guelph, Ontario. In a laboratory study dislodgeable residues of diazinon removed immediately after application by mechanical wiping with moistened cheesecloth constituted about 10% of the applied rate, yet declined to less than 0.3% within a day. These values were over 6 times higher than that dislodged immediately following application in a field experiment. Residues of isophenfos, diazinon, and chlorpyrifos dislodged 1 DAT in field experiments were less than 1% of the target rate applied. Comparison between granule and liquid diazinon formulations applied to turf indicated significantly higher levels (20X) for liquid diazinon the day of application (5.67 mg m^{-2}), but by 1 DAT residue dislodged was equal for both formulations (0.42 mg m^{-2}).

In the studies on dislodgeable foliar residues of liquid formulated pesticides described above, procedures used to apply pesticides were different from that used by commercial lawncare operators. Commercial lawncare applications of pesticides are usually applied as very dilute concentrations in mixtures with fertilizer solutions at 1627 l ha^{-1} spray volume, using a coarse spray droplet emitting nozzle. One system widely used in commercial lawncare emits droplets that have a MMD of 2128 æm with less than 1% of the spray droplet volume smaller than 250 æm in diameter *(5)*.

This study reports on the influence of irrigation on dissipation of foliar dislodgeable residue levels of two herbicides and three insecticides applied to lawn turf at recommended rates as tank mixtures with fertilizer solutions using application equipment and techniques employed by lawncare operators.

MATERIALS AND METHODS

Turf Site. Treatments were applied to a 4-yr-old stand of 'Baron:Merion:Glade' Kentucky bluegrass (*Poa pratensis* L) growing on a Blount silt loam soil (32% sand, 36% silt, 32% clay) in Delaware, Ohio that was mowed weekly at 7.6 cm, irrigated as needed to avoid visual drought stress, and was fertilized four times per growing season to supply 195 kg N ha^{-1} from a complete fertilizer source. The turf quality and density is typical of a well-maintained residential lawn area. Three days before treatments were applied, the site was mowed and irrigated. Thereafter, irrigation and mowing were withheld until 7 DAT when plots were irrigated and mowed at 7.6 cm.

Treatment Procedure. A CO_2-propelled small plot sprayer equipped with a Lesco/ChemLawn spray gun and 4GPM nozzle (Lesco, Inc., Rocky River, OH) calibrated to deliver 63 ml s^{-1} flow rate was used to apply commercial formulations of pendimethalin (Pre-M 60DG, Lesco, Inc., Rocky River, OH), DCPA (Dacthal 75WP, ISK Biotech Corp., Mentor, OH), chlorpyrifos (Dursban 4EC, DowElanco, Indianapolis, IN), diazinon (Diazinon AG-500, Prentiss Drug and Chemical Co., Inc., Floral Park, NY), and isophenfos (Oftanol 2F, Miles, Inc., Kansas City, MO) at recommended rates (Table I) to the turf site in three separate studies. Each pesticide treatment was prepared as a tank mixture with a fertilizer solution containing 22 g N kg^{-1} spray solution from a 17-0.87-4.2 (N-P-K) analysis fertilizer derived from urea, ammonium polyphosphate and potassium chloride and applied at 1627 l ha^{-1} spray volume. Treatments were applied between 0900 to 1000 h to 3.8 by 6.1 m plots replicated four times.

An applicator certified in the use of the Lesco/ChemLawn spray gun applied the treatments in a manner consistent with normal use practices. The gun is held at waist height and angled down toward the turf. To treat the area the gun is swept parallel to the ground with a left-to-right-to-left arm swing motion as the applicator moves forward across the turf. The effective spray swath width is 4 m. On the initial pass the applicator positions himself 2 m in from the edge of the plot and walks forward at 0.7 m s^{-1}. At the end of the plot he turns and repositions himself 2 m down from his original foot path and overlaps the spray swath back to his initial footpath. In the trim areas of the plot the applicator directs the spray swath back towards his previous footpath, trimming the area up to the plot edge with a half-arm swing pattern as he doubles his walking speed forward across the plot. Hence, the spray is uniformly applied across the treatment area using a 50 percent overlap spray pattern. Exactly 3.8 l of spray mixture per plot is applied.

Meteorological Data. Wind speed, air temperature, relative humidity, and soil temperature at 8 cm were recorded at time of application. Rainfall occurrence and irrigation applied were recorded for the duration of the study (Table I).

Irrigation Schedule. Two of the four replicated treatment plots were irrigated after total residue samples were harvested using a hand-held shower nozzle to uniformly distribute 284 l water per plot which is equivalent to 13 mm irrigation. Thereafter, irrigation was withheld from all plots until 4 DAT or longer as noted in Table I; at which time the entire study was irrigated to moisten the surface 3-cm of soil. In the event of a rainfall occurrence, rain-out shelters were placed on non- irrigated plots.

Table I. Application schedule, meterological conditions, and irrigation schedule for dislodgeable residue studies conducted in Delaware, OH

	Study I	Study II	Study III
Date Applied:	17-May-88	6-June-88	23-June-88
Treatment rate	pendimethalin 60DG	DCPA 75WP 11.8 kg ha^{-1}	chlorpyrifos 4EC 1.1 kg ha^{-1}
Treatement rate		Isophenfos 2F 2.2 kg ha^{-1}	diazinon 4EC 6.2 kg ha^{-1}
Air Temp: 0 MAT min/max R.H. wind speed	 11 C 8/17 C 85% <1.3 m s^{-1}	 27 C 17/32 C 44% <1.3 m s^{-1}	 22 C 9/27 C 23% <1.3 m s^{-1}
Soil Temp @ 8cm min/max	9/13 C	17/27 C	18/28C
Rainfall	18-May (2 mm)* 23-May (9 mm)*	8-June (8 mm)* 16-June (7 mm)	
Irrigated	25-May (13 mm)	14-June (13 mm)	1-July (13 mm) 2-July (13 mm) 3-July (13 mm) 4-July (13 mm) 5-July (13 mm) 6-July (13 mm)

*Rain-out shelters positioned on non-irrigated plots for this precipitation event.

Determination of Foliar Surface Area. Dislodgeable foliar residue is measured in weight of pesticide residue per foliar surface area. Turfgrass foliar surface area was determined from leaf blade lamina dissected from tillers collected in 10.8 cm diameter turf cores removed from the treatment plots for each study date. Grass blades were harvested from each plug by manually clipping blades two inches above the thatch surface and immediately determining fresh weight of the clippings. These clippings were then positioned on a 10 cm by 10 cm template and weighed to determine weight of grass blades per 200 sq. cm. of foliar surface area (both sides of leaves). The remaining clippings were weighed again. The total weight of clippings measured the second time divided by initial weighing determines % moisture loss during handling and was used to calculate corrected foliar surface area per gram fresh weight values as follows:

$$\frac{(LFwtSArea)t_1 + (LFwtTFR)\,t_1}{(LFwtTF)t_0} \quad \times \quad \frac{200\ cm^2}{(LFwtSArea)t_1} \quad = cm^2\ gram\ LFwt^{-1}$$

where: $(LFwtTF)t_0$ =   fresh weight of grass foliage measured initially

       $(LFwtSArea)t_1$ =   fresh weight of grass foliage placed in 10 by 10 cm template

       $(LFwtTFR)t_1$ =   fresh weight of remaining grass foliage not placed in 10 by 10 cm template

     Mean value of all turf samples measured for foliar surface area (both sides of leaf blade) per gram freshweight was 139.6 ± 36.7 cm^2 g^{-1} (n = 34). In study I the foliar surface area value used to calculate dislodgeable pesticide residue was 153.8 ± 53.8 cm^2 g^{-1} (n = 10); for study II the value was 130.2 ± 17.4 cm^2 g^{-1} (n = 16); and for study III the value was 138.9 ± 10.9 cm^2 g^{-1} (n = 8).

     Turfgrass foliar clippings collected at each harvest interval were weighed to determine clipping yield per meter^2 land area. Yields fluctuated reflecting differences in intervals between initial mowing and harvest dates, plant water content, etc. The average clipping yield for all harvest dates and treatments was 227 gm^{-2} land area.

Foliar Sampling Procedure. Grass clippings to be analyzed for pesticide residues were collected from treatment plots using a rotary mower set at 5 cm cutting height and equipped with a bagger attachment to collect clippings. Before the initial residue harvest, a 45 cm-wide strip was mowed from each side of the treatment plot and clippings discarded. The center 3.3 by 5.2 m area of the plot remaining was sampled at 1 and 2 HAT and 1, 2, 3, 7 or 8, and 14 DAT. At each sampling interval, the previously mowed areas of each plot were mowed again at 5 cm and the clippings discarded. For each harvest, a 0.3 m by 5.2 m area of the plot was mowed. The clippings collected were weighed and a 50 gm subsample of foliage removed and reserved for residue analysis.

The subsample was wrapped in aluminum foil, enclosed in a sealable plastic bag, and refrigerated until the next morning when pesticide residues contained on the foliage were extracted.

Residue Extraction and Analysis. An independent contract laboratory (A&L Great Lakes Agricultural Laboratories, Inc., Fort Wayne, IN) performed the detergent extraction and analysis of pesticide residues on the foliage at 2 HAT, 1, 2, 3, 7 or 8, and 14 DAT. Additionally, total residue analysis was performed for all treatments on foliage harvested at 1 HAT and for samples harvested from all but pendimethalin treatments on 1 and 2 DAT. Dislodgeable pesticide residues were estimated using a detergent stripping procedure initially described by Gunther et al. *(6)* and modified later by Iwata et al. *(7)*. The day following clipping collection, 2 grams of leaf clippings were detergent extracted from each replicate. Extracts from each harvest date, including blank standards, were refrigerated until all extracts were partitioned, cleaned up, and analyzed for pesticide residues.

RESULTS

Pesticide concentration retained in the upper canopy of lawn turf immediately after treatment varied among treatments (Tables II and III). When adjustments are made to compare residue concentration at nominal application rate equivalent to 1.1 kg ha^{-1}, concentration of total residue 1 HAT were similar for pendimethalin, chlorpyrifos, and diazinon (0.60 ± 0.07 µg cm^{-2}) while levels were almost twice as high for DCPA and isophenfos (1.18 ± 0.09 µg cm^{-2}).

Total residue on foliage dissipated rapidly within 2 days for all pesticide treatments. Irrigation reduced total residue of pesticides evaluated. DCPA levels decreased 65.7 and 24.6%, respectively, 2 DAT for irrigated and non-irrigated treatments, while average insecticide concentration decreased 61.7 ± 5.1 and $52.2 \pm 9.5\%$, respectively.

Total residue concentration as a percent of the targeted application rate retained in the upper canopy 1 HAT averaged $21.3 \pm 8.8\%$ for all pesticides and ranged from a low of 9.0 to a high of 42.8% (Tables IV and V). Foliar concentration of residues were more similar among formulation systems than within pesticide groups (eg insecticide vs herbicide). The petrochemical solvent-based formulations (4EC) of chlorpyrifos and diazinon retained on foliage was $15.1 \pm 3.1\%$ of nominal application rates while dry or aqueous-based formulations (60DG, 2F, 75WP) of pendimethalin, isophenfos, and DCPA retained were $27.6 \pm 5.8\%$ of the targeted application rate.

Dislodgeable residues as a percent of targeted application rate ranged from a low of 0.6% for chlorpyrifos to a high of 10.7% for isophenfos 2 HAT (Table II and III). Irrigation after treatments had dried on the foliage did not have a significant affect on reducing concentration of diazinon or chlorpyrifos dislodged from foliage at any sampling date after application. Among dry or aqueous formulated pesticides studied, there were significant differences in concentration of pesticides dislodged between irrigated and non-irrigated plots. Levels of pendimethalin and DCPA dislodged from irrigated plots were significantly lower compared to non-irrigated plots at all sampling dates through 7 DAT, while differences in isophenfos levels dislodged were significant through 3 DAT. Beyond the aforementioned sampling dates there were no significant differences in residues dislodged from irrigated and non- irrigated plots.

Table II.   Effects of irrigation on concentration of herbicide residues of
            pendimethalin 60DG and DCPA 75WP found on grass clippings
            harvested over time from a Kentucky bluegrass lawn turf. **Mean values
            ± standard deviation are expressed as µg pesticide residue cm^{-2} of fresh
            foliage surface area**

Sampling	Pendimethalin 60 DG		DCPA 75WP	
Interval	Irrigated	Nonirrigated	Irrigated	Nonirrigated
	total residue in foliage, µg cm^{-2}			
1 HAT	1.20 ± 0.06	1.33 ± 0.01 (p > .085)	12.60 ± 1.36	12.50 ± 0.77 (ns)
1 DAT	-	-	5.03 ± 0.43	10.39 ± 0.80 (p > .013)
2 DAT	-	-	4.32 ± 0.16	9.42 ± 0.17 (p > .001)
	detergent-stripped residue on foliage, µg cm^{-2}			
2 HAT	0.20 ± 0.06	0.40 ± 0.01 (p > .044)	1.66 ± 0.07	3.30 ± 0.17 (p > .005)
1 DAT	1.13 ± 0.03	0.28 ± 0.02 (p > .025)	1.16 ± 0.09	2.60 ± 0.26 (p > .017)
2 DAT	0.07 ± 0.01	0.24 ± 0.03 (p > .016)	1.04 ± 0.03	2.58 ± 0.12 (p > .003)
3 DAT	0.04 ± 0.00	0.12 ± 0.01 (p > .020)	0.80 ± 0.04	12.02 ± 0.44 (p > .059)
7 DAT	0.01 ± 0.00	0.03 ± 0.00 (p > .006)	0.73 ± 0.03	1.89 ± 0.28 (p > .027)
14 DAT	0.00 ± 0.00	1.01 ± 0.00 (p > .204)	0.27 ± 0.02	0.43 ± 0.03 (p > .019)

Table III. Effects of irrigation on concentration of insecticide residues of chlorpyrifos 4EC, diazinon 4EC, and isophenfos 2F found on grass clippings harvested over time from a Kentucky bluegrass lawn turf. Mean values ± standard deviation are expressed as µg pesticide residue cm⁻² of fresh foliage surface area

Sampling Interval	Chlorpyrifos 4EC		Diazinon 4EC		Isophenfos 2F	
	Irrigated	Nonirrigated	Irrigated	Nonirrigated	Irrigated	Nonirrigated
	total residue in foliage, µg cm⁻²					
1 HAT	0.68 ± 0.02	0.53 ± 0.01	3.37 ± 0.25	2.86 ± 0.24	2.15 ± 0.10	2.49 ± 0.06
	($p > .007$)		($p > .175$)		($p > .055$)	
1 DAT	0.41 ± 0.01	0.36 ± 0.00	1.64 ± 0.25	1.97 ± 0.11	0.79 ± 0.04	1.48 ± 0.09
	($p > .037$)		($p > .225$)		($p > .008$)	
2 DAT	0.30 ± 0.03	0.31 ± 0.06	1.23 ± 0.25	1.16 ± 0.17	0.74 ± 0.00	1.10 ± 0.11
	(ns)		(ns)		($p > .046$)	
	detergent-stripped residue on foliage, µg cm⁻²					
2 HAT	0.03 ± 0.00	0.03 ± 0.00	1.60 ± 0.14	1.35 ± 0.20	0.50 ± 0.10	0.91 ± 0.07
	($p > .231$)		($p > .276$)		($p > .037$)	
1 DAT	0.03 ± 0.00	0.02 ± 0.00	0.78 ± 0.17	0.83 ± 0.02	0.42 ± 0.05	0.73 ± 0.10
	($p > .087$)		(ns)		($p > .057$)	
2 DAT	0.02 ± 0.00	0.02 ± 0.00	0.55 ± 0.15	0.50 ± 0.10	0.22 ± 0.00	0.44 ± 0.05
	($p > .292$)		(ns)		($p > .026$)	
3 DAT	0.02 ± 0.00	0.01 ± 0.00	0.52 ± 0.05	0.50 ± 0.05	0.19 ± 0.02	0.29 ± 0.02
	($p > .127$)		(ns)		($p > .032$)	
7 DAT	0.01 ± 0.00	0.01 ± 0.00	0.13 ± 0.04	0.10 ± 0.03	0.11 ± 0.00	0.19 ± 0.05
	($p > .105$)		(ns)		($p > .160$)	
14 DAT	0.00 ± 0.00	0.00 ± 0.00	0.03 ± 0.01	0.02 ± 0.00	0.03 ± 0.01	0.04 ± 0.01
	(ns)		(ns)		(ns)	

Table IV.   Effects of irrigation on concentration of herbicide residues of
pendimethalin 60DG and DCPA 75WP found in clippings harvested
over time from a Kentucky bluegrass lawn turf. Mean values ±
standard deviation are expressed as a percent of nominal application
rates

Sampling Interval	Pendimethalin 60 DG		DCPA 75WP	
	Irrigated	Nonirrigated	Irrigated	Nonirrigated
	total residue as % of nominal applied rate			
1 HAT	27.41 ± 1.30	30.44 ± 0.32	21.95 ± 1.66	27.39 ± 4.10
		(p > .085)		(p > .223)
1 DAT	-	-	7.88 ± 0.18	20.30 ± 2.31
				(p > .017)
2 DAT	-	-	7.08 ± 0.11	22.15 ± 0.74
				(p = .001)
	detergent-stripped residue on foliage, $\mu g\ cm^{-2}$			
2 HAT	4.53 ± 1.41	9.21 ± 0.34	3.41 ± 0.51	6.40 ± 1.39
		(p > .045)		(p > .103)
1 DAT	2.89 ± 0.73	6.52 ± 0.40	1.83 ± 0.34	3.21 ± 3.00
		(p > .045)		(p > .010)
2 DAT	1.66 ± 0.16	5.59 ± 0.73	1.70 ± 0.03	6.07 ± 0.04
		(p > .017)		(p > .000)
3 DAT	0.94 ± 0.09	2.64 ± 0.34	1.55 ± 0.26	4.58 ± 1.09
		(p > .020)		(p > .070)
7 DAT	0.35 ± 0.09	0.75 ± 0.09	1.05 ± 0.13	3.27 ± 0.16
		(p > .005)		(p > .004)
14 DAT	0.03 ± 0.00	0.09 ± 0.05	0.50 ± 0.04	1.04 ± 0.25
		(p > .256)		(p > .097)

Table V.   Effects of irrigation on concentration of herbicide residues of chlorpyrifos 4EC, diazinon 4EC, and isophenfos 2F found in clippings harvested over time from a Kentucky bluegrass lawn turf. Mean values ± standard deviation are expressed as a percent of nominal application rates

Sampling Interval	Chlorpyrifos 4EC		Diazinon 4EC		Isophenfos 2F	
	Irrigated	Nonirrigated	Irrigated	Nonirrigated	Irrigated	Nonirrigated
	total residue in foliage, $\mu g\ cm^{-2}$					
1 HAT	17.65 ± 1.76	14.20 ± 2.93	16.78 ± 0.00	11.94 ± 4.20	24.56 ± 3.26	33.97 ± 12.55
	(p > .291)		(p > .244)		(p > .413)	
1 DAT	7.45 ± 1.05	7.07 ± 1.27	5.54 ± 1.64	6.60 ± 2.49	6.85 ± 0.45	17.38 ± 7.17
	(ns)		(ns)		(p > .173)	
2 DAT	6.15 ± 0.43	6.65 ± 2.43	4.45 ± 1.32	3.67 ± 1.42	7.90 ± 0.69	13.49 ± 4.9
	(ns)		(ns)		(p > .254)	
	detergent-stripped residue as % nominal applied rate					
2 HAT	0.96 ± 0.01	0.62 ± 0.22	7.98 ± 0.91	5.56 ± 2.50	6.61 ± 0.76	10.65 ± 4.1
	(p > .156)		(ns)		(p > .304)	
1 DAT	0.46 ± 0.07	0.40 ± 0.11	2.66 ± 0.94	2.79 ± 1.12	3.63 ± 0.53	8.62 ± 4.15
	(ns)		(ns)		(p > .232)	
2 DAT	0.39 ± 0.03	0.36 ± 0.11	2.00 ± 0.77	1.61 ± 0.71	2.40 ± 0.17	5.36 ± 2.04
	(ns)		(ns)		(p > .177)	
3 DAT	0.33 ± 0.02	0.22 ± 0.03	1.83 ± 0.23	1.68 ± 0.37	1.99 ± 0.22	3.67 ± 0.77
	(p > .052)		(ns)		(p > .097)	
7 DAT	0.23 ± 0.02	0.20 ± 0.06	0.64 ± 0.16	0.58 ± 0.33	1.04 ± 0.25	1.74 ± 0.93
	(ns)		(ns)		(p > .410)	
14 DAT	0.12 ± 0.04	0.08 ± 0.00	0.16 ± 0.06	0.10 ± 0.01	0.47 ± 0.162	0.48 ± 0.13
	(p > .296)		(p > .355)		(ns)	

Dislodgeable residues dissipated exponentially (1nl, P > .05) for all treatments (Figures 1-5). Dissipation rate varied among pesticides, but were not significantly different between irrigation treatment for any pesticide treatment. A linear regression for dissipation of dislodgeable residues from foliage was calculated using the following equation:

$$Y = 10^{a+bX}$$

where Y = concentration of residue ($\mu g\ cm^{-2}$) at each sampling date (X). Individual regression equations and correlation coefficients are presented in Figure legends.

DISCUSSION

Previous reports concluded that there was a rapid decrease in dislodgeable residues after application of pesticides applied to lawn turfs (1, 2, 3, 4). The results of our studies were similar for rates of dissipation, but varied in response to post- treatment irrigation practices. We did not observe significant reductions in foliar residues of diazinon and chlorpyrifos as reported by Goh et al. (3) and Sears et al. (4) following irrigation. These differences cannot be attributed to spray volume as the former study was applied at 7.3X our spray volume (1627 l ha^{-1}) and the latter was applied at 12.3% of our spray volume. In one study (3) irrigation rates were similar to ours (13 mm), while in Sears et al. (4) 18 mm of rainfall occurred after application. It is possible that our tank mixtures with fertilizer solutions and/or the spray droplet spectral characteristics of the Lesco/ChemLawn 4 GPM nozzle are influencing spray deposit retention differently for these pesticides compared to dilutions in water only (8). Irrigation significantly reduced isophenfos residue levels and agrees with unpublished reports by Miles Inc. (D.C. Eberhart, personal communication). Our results suggest irrigation influence on pesticides will vary more with formulation than with active ingredient and warrants further investigation to compare dislodgeable residue levels among formulations of the same pesticide. However, what we consider to be ideal irrigation practices for immediate watering-in of pesticides following application only reduced dislodgeable residues on foliage, by at best, to 50% of values measured for non-irrigated turfs.

Comparison of total residue on foliage immediately following application among treatments suggests there may be compounding factors that influence retention of pesticides on foliage. Low application rates of isophenfos, chlorpyrifos, and pendimethalin yielded similar retention rates when adjustments were made to normalize values at 1.1 kg ha^{-1}, while rates were almost double for DCPA and diazinon applied at higher nominal application rates. It is worth noting that foliar residues retained do not appear to be influenced as much by formulation as they may be by pesticide use rate applied.

From our studies, it would appear that dislodgeable pesticide levels on foliage dissipate naturally at a rapid rate dropping to less than 10% of target applied rate within 1 day of application and to less than 5% and 2%, respectively at 3 and 7 DAT, and to below 1% by 14 DAT, if not watered in immediately. Where concern exists over pesticide residues on turf foliage, irrigation can reduce levels of some pesticides (eg dry or aqueous-based formulations) yet not others (EC formulations). Because pesticides applied

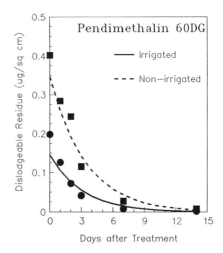

Figure 1. Predicted dissipation rate of foliar dislodgeable residues for pendimethalin in post-application irrigated (circles) and non-irrigated (squares) lawn turf. Irrigated dissipation rate $Y = 10^{-0.85-0.14X}$ ($r^2 = -0.953$) while non-irrigated dissipation rate $Y = 10^{-0.46-0.13X}$ ($r^2 = -0.945$).

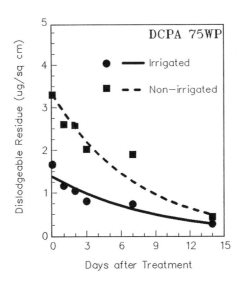

Figure 2. Predicted dissipation rate of foliar dislodgeable residues for DCPA in post-application irrigated (circles) and non-irrigated (squares) lawn turf. Irrigated dissipation rate $Y = 10^{-0.14-0.05X}$ ($r^2 = -0.939$) while non-irrigated dissipation rate $Y = 10^{-0.52-0.06X}$ ($r^2 = -0.914$).

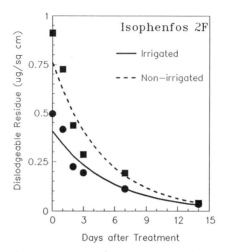

Figure 3. Predicted dissipation rate of foliar dislodgeable residues for isophenfos in post-application irrigated (circles) and non-irrigated (squares) lawn turf. Irrigated dissipation rate $Y = 10^{-0.39-0.08X}$ ($r^2 = -.953$) while non-irrigated dissipation rate $Y = 10^{-0.12-0.09X}$ ($r^2 = -.958$).

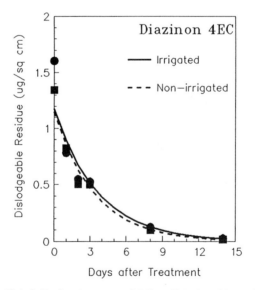

Figure 4. Predicted dissipation rate of foliar dislodgeable residues for diazinon in post-application irrigated (circles) and non-irrigated (squares) lawn turf. Irrigated dissipation rate $Y = 10^{-0.07-0.12X}$ ($r^2 = -.964$) while non-irrigated dissipation rate $Y = 10^{-0.06-0.13X}$ ($r^2 = -.988$).

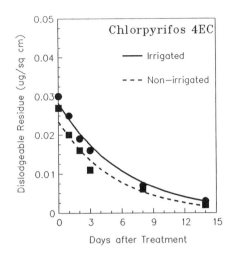

Figure 5. Predicted dissipation rate of foliar dislodgeable residues for chlorpyrifos in post-application irrigated (circles) and non-irrigated (squares) lawn turf. Irrigated dissipation rate $Y = 10^{-1.53-0.07X}$ ($r^2 = -.990$) while non-irrigated dissipation rate $Y = 10^{-1.63-0.08X}$ ($r^2 = -.978$).

commercially are often tank mixed with fertilizers and occasionally two or more pesticides are applied simultaneously, further studies are needed to understand interactions between pesticide formulations in tank mixture applications.

LITERATURE CITED

1. Thompson, D.G., Stephenson, G.R., and Sears, M.R. *Pestic. Sci. 15*, 353-360, **1984.**
2. Bowhey, C., McLeod, M.T., Stephenson, G.R. *Proc. British Crop Protection Conf. - Weeds*, **1987,** 8.A-10:799-805.
3. Goh, K.S., et.al. *Bull. Environ. Contam. Toxicol.* **1986,** *37*, 27-32.
4. Sears, M.K., et.al. *Pestic. Sci.*, **1982,** *20*, 233-231.
5. Hurto, K.A. *Proc. Northeastern Weed Sci. Soc.* **1987,** *42*, 164-165.
6. Gunther, et.al. *Bull. Environ. Contam. Toxicol.* **1973,** *9*, 243-249.
7. Iwata, et.al. *Bull. Environ. Contam. Toxicol.* **1977,** *18*, 649-655.
8. Hull, H.M., Davis, D.G., Stolzenberg, G.E. *In Adjuvants For Herbicides*; Hodgson, R.H., Ed.; Weed Sci. Soc. Amer., Champaign, IL., **1982,** pp 26-67.

RECEIVED October 30, 1992

Chapter 10

Comparison of Foliar Dissipation and Turf Dislodgeable Residue Sampling Techniques

J. E. Cowell, S. A. Adams, J. L. Kunstman, and M. G. Mueth

The Agricultural Group of Monsanto Company, St. Louis, MO 63198

Several studies have been performed to evaluate foliar dissipation of turf applied chemicals and techniques for estimation of dislodgeable residues of these compounds. The experimental design and conduct of these studies are described herein. A number of parameters that have an effect upon foliar dissipation and reentry exposure have also been examined. Mass balance, turf intercept, turf density, and climatic conditions of foliar applications of two example compounds were investigated. Studies evaluating the difference in surface residues versus total (including endogenous) residues for a particular herbicide were performed. Data showing the effect of formulation type upon residue dislodgeability were compiled and several experiments comparing dislodgeable residue techniques and different types of dislodgeable sampling media were conducted. The goal of these experiments was to identify a procedure for realistic estimation of reentry exposure.

In the development of a new turf maintenance chemical, there are numerous human and environmental safety factors which need to be studied and evaluated prior to the actual commercialization decision. Hazard evaluations are made from results of toxicological studies. Exposure assessments usually based on field studies are then needed to complete the estimate of risk to the subject.

This area of study which traverses human and environmental safety from the standpoint of exposure is identified as "Reentry Protection" by the Environmental Protection Agency in Subdivision K of the Pesticide Assessment Guidelines (1). This Subdivision gives guidance in the conduct of studies which measure foliar dissipation and dislodgeable residues of pesticides. Numerous studies have been undertaken to evaluate exposure to humans entering and working in areas recently treated with pesticides (2-7). These studies can be directed at the actual work practices and in many cases do assess the specific exposure. However, in the case of pesticide applications to turf or lawns, the reentry activities of humans or animals cannot be exactly defined, and thus pesticide

0097–6156/93/0522–0100$06.00/0

exposure assessment may be difficult. Traditional means of assessing this type of exposure have been based on a foliar wash to measure removable pesticide residues. This approach is limited to measurement with respect to time of the amount of pesticide residues adhering to particulate matter that could be transferred from the foliage. Other researchers have evaluated the amount of turf maintenance chemical that can physically be removed or dislodged from the treated foliage *(8)*. This latter approach takes into account the fact that there may be additional factors preventing complete foliage contact or residue removal. This paper presents the findings of our studies directed toward comparison of techniques and the assessment of this reentry exposure scenario for turf maintenance chemicals.

FOLIAR DISSIPATION

Traditionally in exposure measurement one encounters much variation. Although one plot of turf may look identical to another plot, there exist subtle differences which can affect measurements. In order to include as much of this variation in the measurements, experimental design should encompass sites representative of the climatic conditions expected in the intended use areas and representative sampling of the treated plots.

Our method to address this representative sampling was to divide a relatively large plot of turf at each location into quadrants and columns producing 64 sampling plots which measured 4 feet by 9 feet as shown in Figure 1. Prior to each study, sets of four sampling plots were defined by computer selection to include one sample plot from each quadrant of the test plot with at least one sample plot from each column. This sampling technique attempts to account for differences in turf density, pesticide application variation, and environmental factors which affect chemical distribution within each treated plot. Sets of four sampling plots were used to collect four replicates of each sampling type per time interval from the treated test plot to allow statistical examination of the data. Each sampling plot was used only once in the study.

Foliar dissipation of a turf maintenance chemical can be viewed from two perspectives: "surface residue" which is available unbound chemical and "total residue" which includes foliage absorbed chemical. A study to compare these two types of foliar residues was conducted with dithiopyr (Structure shown in Figure 2), a newly registered herbicide (Tradename: Dimension™) for control of crabgrass and other weed species in turf.

Turf clippings were collected from four sampling plots at each sampling interval with a rotary lawn mower equipped with a grass catcher. Each turf sample was well mixed and subsamples analyzed by two different procedures. Samples of the fresh foliage were washed with a relatively mild 20% acetonitrile in water solution in order to determine the "surface residues". This solvent-wash system was compared to the traditional soap and water wash and found to be quantitatively equivalent but without the chromatographic interferences observed with the traditional approach. To determine "total residues", another subsample was extracted with a solution of 2.2% acetonitrile: 8.9% water: 88.9% isooctane. Table I shows comparative data of surface residues versus total residues at three climatologically stratified sites. The application of dithiopyr was made at a rate of 1.0 lb/A at each site and left to dry for one hour before the "0" sample was collected.

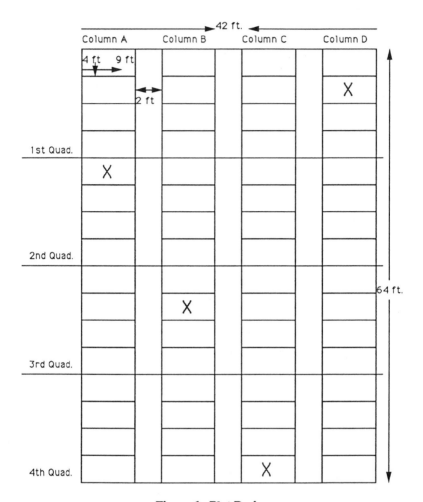

Figure 1. Plot Design

Figure 2. Structure of Dithiopyr

Table I. Comparison of Foliar Surface Wash and Total Extraction

Days After Treatment	Foliage	Dithiopyr Residues in mg/m^2		
		Atlanta	Columbus	Cleveland
0	Surface	1.84	6.59	2.37
	Total	8.81	27.9	14.6
1	Surface	1.32	4.78	1.83
	Total	4.25	19.0	10.6
3	Surface	0.953	5.54	1.86
	Total	4.44	14.8	12.0
7	Surface	0.610	2.84	1.01
	Total	2.98	13.8	4.17
14	Surface	0.302	2.46	0.327
	Total	1.14	6.86	1.83
30	Surface	0.091	0.487	0.052
	Total	0.232	2.49	0.398
60	Surface	0.0086	0.0302	0.0023
	Total	0.0266	0.322	0.0138

Surface residues averaged 23% $\pm$ 8% (s.d.) of the total residues throughout the course of the study. Both surface and total foliar residues were found to decline to about 40% of initial levels within 7 days of the application. Dissipation was found to vary as a function of weather conditions with more rapid dissipation occurring in warm, dry conditions (i.e. Atlanta) and slower dissipation occurring in cool, wet conditions (i.e. Columbus).

As shown in Figure 3, total residues even from identical rate applications varied in magnitude from site to site. The same type of application equipment was used at all three sites and the same amount of chemical was mixed and applied.

Mass balance has been achieved (average > 92 %) in other studies with dithiopyr by placing polyurethane foam sheets on the soil surface as spray interception plates in the application area *(9)*. Thus the residue magnitude differences at each site are believed to be due to differences in turf density and chemical intercept. At these three sites, each of which had a different variety of fescue or bluegrass, we also measured turf surface area and turf density. Turf density was determined by cutting several one square foot sections of turf at the soil surface and weighing the collected grass. Leaf surface areas were determined for turf samples from several subplots at each site by measuring the leaf-lamina single surface areas of a weighed turf subsample with a LI-3000 Portable Leaf Area Meter similarly to the procedure of Goh *et al (10)*. Surface areas per gram of fresh weight were determined from the sampling plots. These leaf surface area and turf density measurements have been calculated and are shown in Table II. Residue measurements also seem to be more consistent with greater surface area as exhibited by the mean Coefficient of Variation calculated at each site.

Table II. Leaf Surface Area and Turf Density

Location	Surface Area (cm²/g)	Turf Density (g/ft²)	Residue V.C. (%)
Atlanta	104.7	126.6	54
Columbus	129.7	334.5	35
Cleveland	129.5	103.4	35

If the leaf surface area and turf density measurements from Table II are applied to the total extraction data from Table I, the results as graphically displayed in Figure 4 demonstrate in stark contrast to Figure 3, that the magnitude of residue on or in foliage is fairly consistent from site to site.

Higher values at 1, 7 and 14 days from the Columbus site are believed to be due to the cooler, wet weather and the fact that dithiopyr, being somewhat hydrophobic, would partition under wet conditions into the waxy cuticle of the grass blades and therefore dissipate at a slower rate.

In another study, applications of dithiopyr from three different types of formulations were made to turfgrass at a rate of 2.0 lb/A at a plot at Troy, Missouri. Dithiopyr was applied as an emulsifiable concentrate (EC), a micro-encapsulated (ME) and a clay granule (GR) formulation. Figure 5 shows total foliar residues of dithiopyr for each formulation type over 60 days following application. Notice that the EC and ME dissipate similarly while the GR formulation does not leave much foliar residue and does not dissipate as fast.

DISLODGEABLE RESIDUES

Thompson, Stephenson and Sears in a 1984 article in *Pesticide Science* described their use of cotton cheese-cloth worn on researchers' shoes to physically dislodge herbicide residue by scuffling vigorously back and forth over 1 square meter subplots *(8)*. This technique was used in a study at a site in St. Charles, Missouri to investigate the dislodgeable residue of amidochlor, a turf plant growth regulator,(Structure shown in Figure 6) and to compare the residues to those obtained by a polyurethane foam (PUF) covered paint roller technique.

Results (Table III) revealed that only about 0.4% of amidochlor from a 4.0 lb/A application could be dislodged by the cotton gauze technique or the PUF covered paint roller. The paint roller technique residue was slightly lower, although not significantly, and some researchers have suggested that additional roller weight might have improved this comparison.

Because the comparison of two different techniques was made with two different sampling media, there was some uncertainty in comparing results. In another study, the two sampling media, cotton gauze and PUF, were used to dislodge dithiopyr with the scuffling technique. Results shown in Table IV indicate that PUF is significantly better at

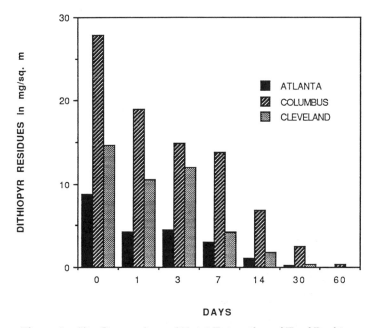

Figure 3. Site Comparison of Total Extraction of Turf Residues

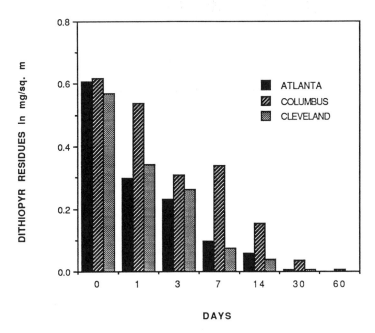

Figure 4. Comparison of Total Extraction Residues by Surface Area and Turf Density

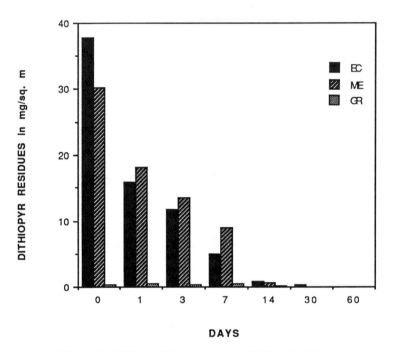

Figure 5. Effect of Formulation on Foliar Residues

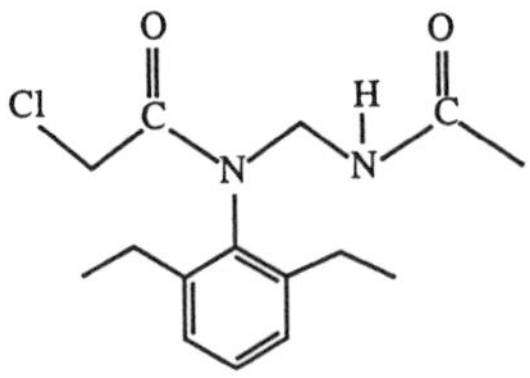

Figure 6. Structure of Amidochlor

trapping and retaining dithiopyr than cotton gauze. Field fortification, transport and storage stability tests have demonstrated that PUF recovers >99% of dithiopyr that is trapped while similar studies with cotton gauze retained an average of only 77% of the applied dithiopyr *(11)*.

Table III. Comparison of Dislodgeable Residue Sampling Media and Techniques

Days After Treatment	Amidochlor Residues in mg/m^2 from 4lb/A Trmt.	
	Shoe Pads - Cotton Gauze	Paint Roller - Polyurethane Foam
0	2.21	1.74 (± 0.71)
1	0.19 (± 0.09)	0.14 (± 0.026)
3	0.017 (± 0.004)	0.005 (± 0.003)
7	0.008 (± 0.005)	Not Sampled
14	0.003 (± 0.004)	Not Sampled
21	0.001 (± 0.002)	Not Sampled

Table IV. Comparison of Dislodgeable Residue Sampling Media

Days After Treatment	Dithiopyr Residues in mg/m^2 Cotton Gauze	From 2 lb/A EC Treatment Polyurethane Foam
0	1.62	3.14
1	0.283	0.636
3	0.148	0.298
7	0.0437	0.117
14	0.00353	0.00954
30	0.00160	0.00410
60	<0.00061	<0.00061

The effect of different weight or pressure on the dislodgeable media was studied with specially designed platform shoes and PUF media in the removal of dithiopyr from turf. Table V displays the four replicate samplings for a couple of sampling days performed by different individuals and their respective body weights.

There does not appear to be a correlation of residue with body weight in the resulting samplings. However, this does not imply that there is not some minimal threshold weight.

Experiments evaluating the dislodgeability of the three different formulations of dithiopyr described previously were performed with the PUF-lined platform shoes.

Figure 7 displays the data which again indicates that the granular formulation was not easily dislodged while the microencapsulated formulation was the easiest to dislodge. It is believed that dithiopyr, when applied as an emulsifiable concentrate formulation, more easily penetrates the grass foliage than does the microencapsulated dithiopyr. It is important to note that the total foliar residue from the two formulations (Figure 5) were approximately the same.

Table V. Effect of Body Weight on Foam Pad Dislodgeable Residues

Days After Treatment		Plot No.	Body Weight	Dithiopyr Residues in ug/pads
CLE	0	13	160 lb	12,028
	0	49	160 lb	8,972
	0	26	140 lb	9,362
	0	39	190 lb	6,818
ATL	3	33	159 lb	356
	3	64	150 lb	574
	3	7	180 lb	534
	3	22	160 lb	519

A comparison was made of the surface foliar residue after application of dithiopyr as an emulsifiable concentrate formulation presented earlier in Table I with the amount of dithiopyr that can be physically removed from turf with the PUF scuffling technique presented in Table IV. The foliar wash and dislodgeable wipe data were fit to the non-linear first order model described by Gustafson and Holden *(12)*. Surface foliar residues were shown to dissipate rapidly with an average DT_{50} of 6.3 days as shown in Table VI. Dislodgeable residues, as measured by collection on PUF pads, were found to dissipate more rapidly (i.e. DT_{50} of 0.9 day).

Table VI. Dithiopyr Residue Dissipation Time

Location	Foliar Wash		PUF Wipe	
	DT_{50}	DT_{90}	DT_{50}	DT_{90}
Atlanta	6.0	22	0.9	3.1
Columbus	7.9	26	0.8	2.6
Cleveland	5.0	17	1.1	3.6
Average	6.3	22	0.9	3.1

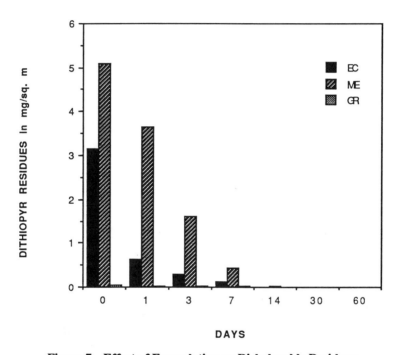

Figure 7. Effect of Formulation on Dislodgeable Residues

Only 10% of the amount present on the day of application still remaining after 3 days and only 1% remaining after 7 days were dislodgeable. Table VII compares the actual dithiopyr residue values of each technique.

Table VII. Comparison of Foliar Surface Wash and Dislodgeable Residues

Days After Treatment	Foliage	Dithiopyr Residues in mg/m^2		
		Atlanta	Columbus	Cleveland
0	Surface	1.84	6.59	2.37
	Wipe	1.42	6.02	2.78
1	Surface	1.32	4.78	1.83
	Wipe	0.646	5.83	0.708
3	Surface	0.953	5.54	1.86
	Wipe	0.162	0.597	0.0404
7	Surface	0.610	2.84	1.01
	Wipe	0.0071	0.0182	0.0326
14	Surface	0.302	2.46	0.327
	Wipe	0.0033	0.0174	0.0060
30	Surface	0.091	0.487	0.052
	Wipe	0.0020	0.0017	0.0016
60	Surface	0.0086	0.0302	0.0023
	Wipe	0.0008	0.0008	0.0012

In the estimation of dermal exposure from contact with treated surfaces, a commonly used concept is the transfer coefficient. This coefficient is defined as the ratio of the amount of pesticide adhering to exposed skin of a person reentering the treated area in this case, to the measured amount on the treated foliage surface. In our study, the amount adhering to the exposed skin could be said to be equivalent to the amount dislodged by the foam pads (Table VII) while the amount on the treated surface was equivalent to the surface foliar residue (Table VII). Transfer coefficients have been calculated in Table VIII for all the sampling intervals from 0 to 30 days after application at each location. Samplings conducted 1 hour after application show equivalent results whether estimated from grass clippings or foam pads and yield a transfer coefficient of approximately 1. Transfer coefficients decline to about 0.1 after day 3 and to about 0.01 after day 7. It is believed that the probable explanation for this fact is that surface residues become less available for dislodgement over time due to the binding of the dithiopyr with the waxy cuticle of the grass blades. At the Columbus site, there was considerable precipitation between the 0 day sampling and the day 1 sampling. Although the long-term effect of precipitation seems to be the partitioning of dithiopyr into the grass, the short term effect of a rainfall after application is to retain the availability for dithiopyr to dislodge with PUF due to its almost hydrophobic nature.

Table VIII. Transfer Coefficients

Days After Treatment	Atlanta	Columbus	Cleveland
0	0.979	0.914	1.00
1	0.490	1.00	0.387
3	0.170	0.108	0.022
7	0.012	0.006	0.032
14	0.011	0.007	0.018
30	0.022	0.003	0.031

CONCLUSIONS

Several parameters for determining foliar dissipation of turf maintenance chemicals have been investigated in these studies. The surface residue, although only about 25% of the total residue, is the most relevant when considering reentry exposure. Magnitude of foliar residues is dependent on turf density and mass balance is difficult to determine by grass analysis due to fractional turf intercept. Formulation of the active ingredient can have a significant effect upon foliar residues.

Several techniques for determining dislodgeable residues of turf maintenance chemicals have been investigated. Dislodgeable residues, obtained by thoroughly wiping a treated turf plot with polyurethane foam pads, are a good estimator of reentry exposure to herbicides. Polyurethane foam is preferred for many turf maintenance chemicals because of its chemical affinity for organic chemicals and its residue transport storage stability. The scuffling technique does produce quantitative transfer coefficients after applications and, although differing from foliar residues with time, probably provides a better estimate of unbound available dislodgeable residues. The use of dislodgeable residue data should provide an estimate of the maximum exposure because of the vigorous bi-directional wipe and the chemical affinity of the media. In a practical reentry situation, only a small part of the foliage in the treated plot is expected to be contacted, and skin and clothing materials are expected to have less affinity for the turf maintenance chemicals than the PUF sampling media. In the case of clothing materials, cotton gauze has been shown in this study to be inferior to the PUF for dislodgeable residue sampling. Skin, which has an abundance of water stored in the dermis for periods of water deprivation (13), would also be less likely to retain a somewhat hydrophobic chemical than the waxy cuticle of grass blades. Therefore, this technique should give a worst case estimate of the potential for exposure to a turf maintenance chemical upon reentry of a treated plot.

LITERATURE CITED

1. *U.S. Environmental Protection Agency*, **1984**, Pesticide Assessment Guidelines, Subdivision K, EPA 540/9-84-001, Washington, DC
2. Gunther, F.A., W.E. Westlake, J.H. Barkley, W. Winterlin, and L.Langbehn, **1973**, *Bull. Environ. Contam. Toxicol. 9*:243-249.
3. Iwata, Y., J.B. Knaak, R.C. Spear, and R.J. Foster, **1977**, *Bull. Environ.Contam. Toxicol. 18*:649-655.
4. Winterlin, W.L., W.W. Kilgore, C.R. Mourer, and S.R. Schoen, **1984**, *J. Agric. Food Chem. 32*:664-672.
5. Stamper, J.H., H.N. Nigg, and R.M. Queen, **1986**, *Bull. Environ. Contam. Toxicol. 36*:693-700.
6. Knaak, J.B., P. Schlocker, C.R. Ackerman, and J.N. Seiber, **1980**, *Bull.Environ. Contam. Toxicol. 24*:796-804.
7. Zweig, G., R. Gao, J.M. Witt, W.J. Popendorf, and K.T. Bogen, **1985**, In *Dermal Exposure Related to Pesticide Use*, R.C. Honeycutt, G. Zweig and N.N. Ragsdale (Eds), ACS Symposium Series No. 273, *9*:123-138.
8. Thompson, D.G., G.R. Stephenson, and M.K. Sears, 1984, *Pestic. Sci. 15*:353-360.
9. Manning, M.J. and J.E. Cowell, **1992**, "Terrestrial Dissipation of Dithiopyr" (Study in -progress).
10. Goh, K.S., S. Edmiston, K.T. Maddy, D.D. Meinders, and S. Margetich, **1986**, *Bull. Environ. Contam. Toxicol. 37*:27-32.
11. Cowell, J.E., C.M. Lottman, and M.J. Manning, **1991**, *Arch. Environ.Contam. Toxicol. 21*:195-201.
12. Gustafson, D.I., and L.R. Holden, **1990**, *Environ. Sci. Technol. 24*(7):1032-1038.
13. Rongone, E.L. (1983) In *Dermatotoxicology* F.N. Marzulli and H.I.Maibach (Eds), Hemisphere Publishing Corporation, Washington, DC *1*:1-70.

RECEIVED October 30, 1992

Chapter 11

Biologically Based Sorbents and Their Potential Use in Pesticide Waste Disposal During Composting

D. E. Mullins[1], R. W. Young[2], D. F. Berry[3], J.-D. Gu[3], and G. H. Hetzel[4]

Departments of [1]Entomology, [2]Biochemistry and Nutrition, [3]Crop and Soil Environmental Sciences, and [4]Agricultural Engineering, Virginia Polytechnic Institute and State University, Blacksburg, VA 24061

Pesticide usage and inappropriate disposal of pesticide wastes have been identified as a source of soil as well as surface and groundwater contamination. Currently, there are few options available to small-scale pesticide applicators and homeowners to safely and effectively dispose of pesticide waste. To help alleviate this situation, we are developing a pesticide wastewater clean-up procedure employing biologically-based materials. These materials serve as a sorbent for effective removal of pesticides from aqueous solutions (sorption) and as a matrix on which these sorbed wastes are subsequently degraded by chemical and microbial processes. Relatively high concentrations (5000 mg/L) of formulated chlorpyrifos and metolachlor can be removed using biobased materials of various types. Heat and carbon dioxide production were compared to evaluate the potential of some biobased materials to support an environment for pesticide (bio)degradation.

Methods currently available for aqueous pesticide waste reduction include waste minimization, rinsate recycling, on-site rinsate re-application, volume reduction using evaporation/degradation pits and carbon sorption. Inappropriate or inadequate pesticide waste disposal activities have been implicated as major contributors of soil, surface and groundwater contamination *(2, 5, 16)*. Development of appropriate methods for disposal of pesticide waste, which can be used by a variety of applicators, has historically been difficult *(3, 5 ,16, 26)*. Alternative disposal methods have been examined *(3, 26)*. Some of these are effective, but are costly or involve complicated procedures or equipment *(5, 16)*. Pesticide wastes may include concentrated materials, dilute rinsate solutions and contaminated products including soil. It is essential that pesticide disposal methods be effective, safe, inexpensive and relatively easy to understand and operate. Disposal methods which meet these criteria are more likely to be used by the public. Microbial-mediated degradation of hazardous chemicals to non-toxic by-products shows promise in terms of functioning as part of a disposal system *(7, 19, 27)*. We have found that some pesticides degrade rapidly under composting conditions, while others may be more persistent *(9, 12, 14)*. Recent reports on composting yard wastes containing pesticide residues support these findings *(6, 11)*.

A biologically-based system for clean-up of pesticide-laden wastewater is under development *(9, 13, 14)*, Figure 1. The system includes both a sorption and a disposal component. The sorbent component includes 1) a batch demulsification and sorption step where pesticide-laden waste solutions (or suspensions) are mixed with organic sorbents (lignocellulosic materials such as peat moss, processed wood products, etc.) and demulsification agents [Ca(OH)$_2$], and 2) a column sorption and filtration step where the solution is passed through a column containing a lignocellulosic sorbent. During this step, pesticides are removed from the aqueous solution by sorption processes. Degradation of alkaline-labile pesticides may also occur during the first step of the process. It has been found that demulsification facilitates pesticide removal and sorption from aqueous pesticide suspensions containing emulsifying agents *(10)*. The disposal component begins after the separation of the sorbed pesticide from the treated aqueous phase (column sorption step). The aqueous solution may then be discarded and the pesticide-laden sorbent added to bioreactors where (bio)degradation of pesticides occurs. Microbial populations used may be native to the matrix or enrichment cultures may be added.

Lignocellulosic materials (peat moss, steam-exploded wood fibers, peanut hulls, and newspaper) were examined for use as sorbents in our disposal process because they are inexpensive, can be highly sorbent and capable of supporting microbial activities associated with pesticide degradation *(13, 14)*. The feasibility of reusing peat moss as a sorbent in the disposal process following a composting cycle has been examined. We also evaluated the bioreactivity of selected biobased materials which may prove useful in terms of supporting a pesticide degrading microbial consortium.

METHODOLOGY

Solvents used in this study were pesticide grade. Analytical standards of chlorpyrifos and metolachlor were obtained from the USEPA Pesticide and Industrial Chemicals Repository MD-8 Research Triangle Park, NC. Information regarding pesticide properties and routine pesticide extraction and analytical procedures used are referenced *(8, 25)*. Aqueous samples (0.250 mL) were sonicated and extracted three times with 20 mL hexane and once with 20 mL acetone. The combined extracts were dried on sodium sulfate columns, followed by volume reduction (flash evaporation). Volume adjustments for gas chromatography analyses (column conditions: 4'4" L x 1/4" I.D.; 1.5/1.95 % OV-17/OV-210, 100/120 Chromosorb WHP [Supelco]; oven temp = 210°C; electron capture detector) were made with hexane. Recoveries for chlorpyrifos were 97.7% ± 13 and 100% ±9 for metolachlor. Sorbents which were tested included sphagnum peat moss (new and recycled), ground peanut hulls, steam-exploded yellow poplar wood fibers, peanut hulls, and newspaper *(17)*, all of which were ground in a Wiley mill using a 2 mm screen.

Two-Step Batch Demulsification, Sorption and Filtration Solution Clean-Up. One hundred milliliters of aqueous solution containing approximately 5000 mg/L of either chlorpyrifos or metolachlor were mixed with 2 grams sorbent and 1 gram Ca(OH)$_2$ in an Erlenmeyer flask for 4 hours. The solution was then placed onto 100 ml bulb columns

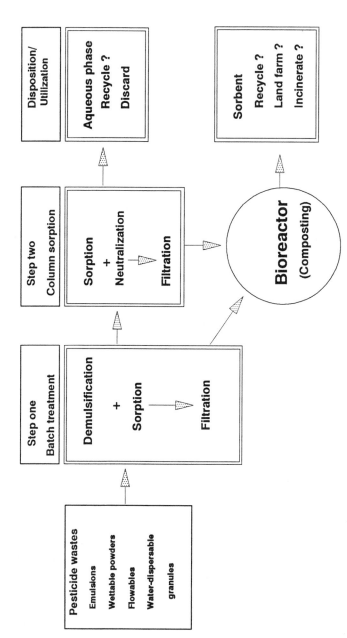

Figure 1. Model for Pesticide Wastewater Disposal using Organic Sorption and Microbial Degradation. The process consists of two main components: a batch demulsification/sorption component, and a disposal component. See text for details.

containing 2 grams of prewet sorbent. Samples (1 ml) taken at various stages during the sorption process were centrifuged (10,000 x g) to remove suspended particulates and analyzed.

Bioreactivity Potential of the Biobased Materials. Carbon dioxide production was measured in sealed small-scale bioreactors (500 ml Erlenmeyer flasks). In large-scale compost studies, temperature was monitored as a means to determine biodegradability of the lignocellulosic substrates. Seven substrates (including mixtures) were examined; including ground peanut hulls (GPH), steam-exploded peanut hulls (SEPH), ground peanut hulls + steam-exploded peanut hulls (1:1, w/w) (GPH+SEPH), peat moss (PM), peat moss + 8% vegetable oil (PM+VO), steam-exploded yellow poplar (SEW), and steam-exploded yellow poplar + 8 % vegetable oil (SEW + VO). Carbon dioxide release was used to evaluate biodegradability of the lignocellulosic substrates. Fifty grams of lignocellulosic substrate was mixed with 1 gram of a soil/straw compost innoculum and placed into a 500 ml Erlenmeyer flask. Moisture content of the lignocellulosic components was maintained between 72-75%. The flasks were closed with rubber stoppers fitted with gas sampling ports. Duplicate flask cultures were incubated at either 25 or 40°C for 48 days. The gas contents were sampled and analyzed for CO_2 concentration every 2-3 days. The percent CO_2 was determined by injecting 100 ul of gas from the flasks into a gas chromatograph (model 5890; Hewlett Packard Co.) equipped with a thermal conductivity detector. Carbon dioxide was separated on a Porapak N column (1.8 x 2.1 mm ID, 80/100 mesh). After sampling, the flasks were flushed with fresh air and closed. In the large-scale bioreactors, temperature was monitored over time. Three cubic feet of each lignocellulosic material was placed into submerged field bioreactors *(12)*. The moisture content was adjusted to approximately 75%. Temperature measurements were taken every 2-4 days at the center of the compost.

RESULTS

A two-step protocol has been developed whereby pesticides are removed from aqueous suspension. This process has been shown to be effective for a variety of pesticides and their formulations *(14)*. Research activities have now been extended to examine biologically-based materials which not only function as pesticide sorbents but which will also support high levels of microbial activity. Increased pesticide degradation is generally correlated with increases in microbial activity *(6, 19)*. Oil-treatment of sorbent may improve the hydrophobic sorptive capability of certain materials. The effects of oil-amendment of peat moss, steam-exploded wood and newspaper have been examined with respect to enhancement of pesticide sorption and their potential to support microbial activity. Ground peanut hulls and steam-exploded peanut hulls were also examined because these lignocellulosic by-products contain 2-3% lipid and represent an abundant crop residue resource in certain parts of the U.S.

Chlorpyrifos and metolachlor removal from aqueous suspensions. Table I shows the data for the removal of chlorpyrifos and metolachlor from aqueous suspensions using a two-step treatment process with several different sorbent types. Chlorpyrifos was reduced from about 4000 mg/L to low levels (1.3% to 0.003%) of the original concentrations. Oil-treatment of peat moss improved sorption of chlorpyrifos, but similar treatment of

Table I. Removal of chlorpyrifos and metolachlor from aqueous suspensions using a two step demulsification, sorption and filtration/centrifugation process

Compound	Initial Conc.	Peat Moss	Peat Moss + 10% Oil	Steam Exploded Wood Fibers	Steam Exploded Wood Fibers	Ground Peanut Hulls	Steam Exploded Peanut Hulls
				Concentration mg/L (percent of initial concentration)[1]			
Chlorpyrifos	3994 ± 86 (100%)	45 ± 8 (1.1%)	0.1 ± 0.09 (0.003%)	3.4 ± 2.3 (0.009%)	1.0 ± 0.99 (0.03%)	52 ± 20 (1.3%)	1.3 ± 0.2 (0.03%)
Statistical comparisons[2]		a	b	a	a	a	a
Metolachlor	6096 ± 391 (100%)	88 ± 18 (1.4%)	2.0 ± 0.6 (0.03%)	149 ± 14 (2.4%)	12.3 ± 0.9 (0.2%)	36 ± 3 (0.6%)	36 ± 9 (0.6%)
Statistical comparisons[2]		a	b	a	b	a	a

[1] Values expressed as means ± standard error of three replicates;

[2] Statistical comparisons: Effects of treatments between similar sorbents are not significantly different when followed by the same letter (P > 0.05, studentizied T-test).

steam-exploded wood had no effect. No differences in sorptivity of chlorpyrifos were observed between ground peanut hulls or steam-exploded peanut hulls. Peat moss and SEW with or without oil was effective in reducing metolachlor (initial concentration 6000 mg/L) to 0.03 to 2.4 % of the original concentration (Table I). Treatment of these two sorbents with oil improved sorption efficiency. As was the case for chlorpyrifos, no differences in metolachlor removal between ground peanut hulls or steam-exploded peanut hulls were observed.

Table II compares removal of metolachlor from aqueous suspensions using oil-treated and untreated steam-exploded newspaper. Oil treatment significantly improved the sorptive capability of steam-exploded newspaper in both demulsification/sorption (step one) and sorption/centrifugation (step two).

Pesticide removal from aqueous solutions using recycled peat moss. As indicated in the disposal model, composted sorbent must be dealt with once it has been removed from the bioreactors (Figure 1). The options listed are recycling, landfarming and incineration. Experiments have been conducted to evaluate pesticide sorbency using recycled peat moss and two pesticides; chlorpyrifos and metolachlor. The recycled peat moss was obtained from a bioreactor that had a total of 54,000 mg/kg diazinon applied over a three year period. One year after the final application, diazinon levels were 3.4 mg/kg *(9)*.

Very low levels of chlorpyrifos (0.002 to 0.005%) were recovered from the aqueous phase after the second step when aqueous suspensions of about 5700 mg/L chlorpyrifos were mixed with recycled peat moss from the diazinon bioreactor, (Table III). Removal of chlorpyrifos was enhanced by oil-amended peat moss during step one, but there was no difference in removal during step two. Similar results were obtained when aqueous suspensions of metolachlor (about 5100 mg/L) were mixed with the recycled peat moss (Table IV). Metolachlor removal after the two-step treatment was 0.3% of the original concentration. Sorption efficiency of the recycled peat moss was enhanced by mixing with oil-amended peat moss, but no differences were indicated in step two.

Composting Potential of Various Lignocellulosic Sorbents. Production of CO_2 from the Erlenmeyer flask incubations provides information regarding the biodegradability of the various lignocellulosic sorbents. The release of CO_2 from flasks containing ground peanut hulls, SEPH and equivalent mixtures of these two (GPH+SEPH) was about the same regardless of the incubation temperature (Figures 2 and 3). Similar amounts of CO_2 were produced in flasks containing either steam-exploded wood (SEW) or steam-exploded wood + 8% vegetable oil (SEW + VO) regardless of incubation temperatures. Peat moss (PM) was the least bioreactive, but CO_2 production increased when vegetable oil was added.

Higher composting temperatures (50 to 60°C) were observed in the large-scale bioreactors, where GPH, SEPH and GPH + SEPH served as the organic matrix (Figure 4). These data correlate well with the results obtained in the CO_2 production experiment, where the peanut hull products were comparatively more bioreactive than either SEW or PM.

Table II. Removal of metolachlor from aqueous suspensions using a two-step sorption onto steam exploded newspaper (SEN) and filtration/centrifugation procedure

| | Concentration mg/L (percent of initial concentration)[1,2] | |
| | Step One | Step Two |
Sorbent	Mixing + Centrifugation	Column Sorption + Centrifugation
SEN	1048 ± 193 a (21%)	30 ± 2 a (0.6%)
SEN + 10% oil	445 ± 16 b (8.9%)	0.1 ± 0.0 b (0.002%)

[1] Initial concentration = 5016 ± 457 mg/L; metolachor as Dual 8 E; N = mean ± standard error of 3 replicate samples

[2] Statistical comparisons: Effects of sorbent treatment (non oil-amended versus oil amended) are not significantly different when followed by the same lower case letter in a column ($P > 0.05$, studentized T-test).

Table III. Removal of chlorpyrifos from aqueous suspensions using a two-step sorption onto recycled peat moss and filtration/centrifugation procedure

| | Concentration mg/L (percent of initial concentration)[1,2] | |
| | Step One | Step Two |
Sorbent	Mixing + Centrifugation	Column Sorption + Centrifugation
Peat moss	103 ± 4 a (1.8%)	0.4 ± 0.3 a (0.005%)
Peat moss + 10% oil	69 ± 2 b (1.2%)	0.1 ± 0.0 a (0.002%)

[1] Initial concentration = 5671 ± 272 mg/L; Chlorpyrifos as Dursban 4E; N = mean ± standard error of 3 replicate samples

[2] Statistical comparisons: Effects of sorbent treatment (non oil-amended versus oil amended) are not significantly different when followed by the same lower case letter in a column ($P > 0.05$, studentized T-test).

Table IV. Removal of metolachlor from aqueous suspensions using a two-step
sorption onto recycled peat moss and filtration/centrifugation procedure

| | Concentration mg/L (percent of initial concentration)[1,2] | |
| | Step One | Step Two |
Sorbent	Mixing + Centrifugation	Column Sorption + Centrifugation
Peat moss	1593 ± 243 a (31%)	14 ± 2 a (0.3%)
Peat moss + 10% oil	536 ± 16 b (10%)	17 ± 11 a (0.3%)

[1] Initial concentration = 5080 ± 1056 mg/L; metolachor as Dual 8 E; N = mean ± standard error of 3 replicate samples

[2] Statistical comparisons: Effects of sorbent treatment (non oil-amended versus oil amended) are not significantly different when followed by the same lower case letter in a column ($P > 0.05$, studentized T-test).

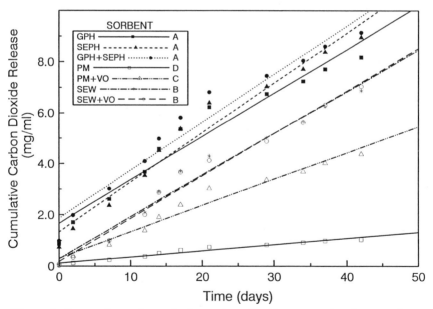

Figure 2. Comparison of cumulative carbon dioxide production from various lignocellulosic materials incubated at 25°C in Erlenmeyer flasks. Statistical comparisons: Sorbents producing similar CO_2 release levels are not significantly different when followed by the same letter. ($P > 0.05$, Co-analysis of variance, Tukey's test on the regression analysis).

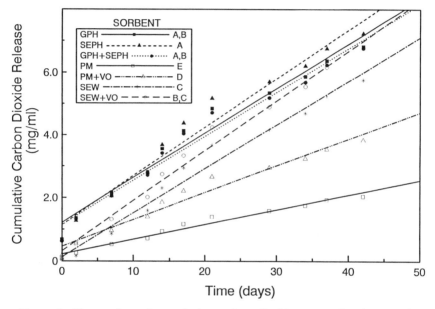

Figure 3. Comparison of cumulative carbon dioxide production from various lignocellulosic materials incubated at 40°C in Erlenmeyer flasks. Statistical comparisons: Sorbents producing similar CO_2 release levels are not significantly different when followed by the same letter. ($P > 0.05$, Co-analysis of variance, Tukey's test on the regression analysis).

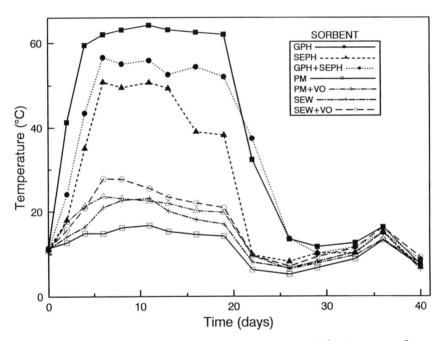

Figure 4. Comparison of temperature levels measured in the center of bioreactors containing various lignocellulosic materials.

DISCUSSION

A two-step batch treatment/column sorption/filtration procedure using several bio-based materials shows promise for removing pesticides at high concentration levels from aqueous suspensions. In most cases, removal of more than 99% of chlorpyrifos and metolachlor (initial concentration about 5000 mg/L) was achieved using this system. The results obtained from the pesticide-laden wastewater clean-up using this two-step procedure, compares quite favorably with other methods. Some examples of these include: Treatment of 400 gallons of solution containing 7 pesticides at 100 mg/L each (totalling 700 mg/L) with 45 lbs of Calgon F-400 activated carbon for 21 hours reduced the concentrations of each pesticide in the range of 0.5 to 5.6 mg/L (99.5 to 94.4% reduction) *(4)*. Pesticide rinsate treatment of 3 pesticides ranging from 17 to 82 mg/L using an ozone/bioreactive soil column treatment reduced the concentrations to levels less than 5 mg/L *(21)*. Toller and Flaim *(23)* reported greater than 99% removal of pesticides from an apple orchard pesticide spray operation (concentrations ranged from 27 to 1820 mg/L) using a peat moss/manure filtration system.

Treatment of the matrices on which pesticides have been sorbed involves placement into bioreactors (Figure 1). Although evaluation of the fate of several formulated pesticides sorbed onto lignocellulosic matrices (step one and two) during composting needs further study, the fate of several pesticides applied directly onto organic matrices has been studied *(9, 12, 18)*. Some of the pesticides tested (i.e. diazinon and carbofuran) disappeared rapidly in bioreactors containing bio-based materials enriched with a ground corn energy source. Sorbent fortification with vegetable oil enhanced their bioreactivity (Figures 2 and 3). The effects of oil addition to lignocellosic sorbents also requires examination regarding enhancement of pesticide disappearance.

The proposed pesticide disposal procedure has several advantages including: simplicity, low cost, and safety. Prototype equipment which employs a two-step demulsification, sorption and filtration process designed to treat 35-40 gallons of pesticide rinsate is undergoing field tests. Presently, certain aspects of this system are cumbersome, but equipment modifications should simplify the procedure, making it considerably easier to operate. Lignocellulosic sorbent materials which may be used in this system are relatively inexpensive. Peat moss is readily available at low cost. The steam-exploded lignocellulosic materials (wood products, crop residues, newsprint, etc.) represent potentially new sorbent resources. These studies indicate that they could be effective for use in the wastewater clean-up process. Steam-exploded materials are not yet commercially available, but cost estimates for bulk quantities of these products appear to be competitive with peat moss. Furthermore, sorbent with oil-treatment improves removal of some pesticides and increases the bioreactivity of lignocellulosic materials in compost. The use of these materials might facilitate the disposal process. It might be noted that oils are a waste byproduct of many fast food restaurants and require disposal procedures to which a cost is associated. Combining these three waste effluents, (pesticide, newspaper, and used cooking oils) could prove to be an innovative means for their disposal. A major advantage of this proposed process is in the potential safety of handling these materials. Concentration of pesticides onto a solid matrix facilitates the ease of handling and spills could be more easily managed than in a liquid form.

CONCLUDING REMARKS

There are a few important questions associated with the pesticide rinsate process which require some attention. The first of these is a need for regulating agencies to determine pesticide waste concentration levels that represent an acceptable level of minimal risk. This is a regulatory issue which needs to be addressed by the national, state and local regulatory agencies.

The second question involves the pH and conductivity (salinity) levels of the treated rinsate and their suitability for release into the environment. Demulsification with $Ca(OH)_2$ produces a high pH in the effluent (step one: pH = 12) which should be neutralized. Acid neutralization suggested previously (14) will result in an increase in salinity. However, recent experiments indicate that the use of peat moss sorbent in step two (sorption column) reduces the treated solution pH and salinity (measured as conductivity) to significantly lower levels (15). Peat moss which is acidic, apparently acts as a cation exchanger, effectively removing excess calcium ions during the neutralization process.

A third concern is the disposition of the spent sorbent following composting in the proposed disposal method. There will be about a 20% reduction in mass during composting and low levels of some pesticide residues may remain associated with the sorbent. The leachability of pesticide residues from spent compost has been quite low and should represent minimal environmental risks (1). Options for disposal of spent compost indicated in the proposed disposal model include landfarming, incineration, or recycling. Landfarming of spent compost could be an acceptable option, should further research indicate that residual pesticide leaching is insignificant. Incineration may also be acceptable. One currently acceptable method for disposal of paper pesticide containers may include incineration. Presumably the low levels of pesticide associated with the emptied containers does not pose an environmental hazard. A third option involves the reuse of spent compost as a sorbent. Data presented here indicates that this might be possible.

There are about 200 active pesticidal ingredients contained in a large number of formulations. As many as 75% are currently used as liquid suspensions of emulsifiable concentrates, wettable powders, flowables, etc. (20, 24). The system under development should be capable of providing for disposal of a wide variety of pesticides and their various formulations.

However, reassessment of formulation inert ingredients has resulted in new regulations concerning inert ingredients (20, 22). As formulation technology develops to accommodate these changes, there will undoubtedly be a need for a corresponding development of appropriate pesticide disposal strategies.

ACKNOWLEDGMENTS

This work was supported in part, by the Virginia Agricultural Foundation, USEPA, and the Virginia Center for Innovative Technology in conjunction with Birdsong Peanuts, Suffolk, Va. Appreciation is extended to Ms. Andrea DeArment for the technical assistance she provided during major portions of our work and to Mr. Keith Tignor for providing assistance with the statistical analysis. Steam-exploded newspaper was provided by Recoupe Recycling Technologies, Richmond, Va.

LITERATURE CITED

1. Berry, D. F.; et al. Unpublished data.
2. Brandt, E. T.; Harris, C.; Whitmore, R. *In: Proceedings of a Symposium on the Fate and Significance of Pesticides in Urban Environments.* ACS San Francisco. **1992** (this volume).
3. Bridges, J. S.; Dempsey,C. R. Eds. *Pesticide Waste Disposal Technology.* Noyes Data Corporation. Park Ridge, N. J. **1988**.
4. Dennis, W. H.; Kobylinski, E. A. *J. Environ. Sci. & Health* **1983**, *18*, 317-331.
5. Ferguson, T. D. Ed. *Proceedings of International Workshop on Research in Pesticide Treatment/Disposal/Waste Minimization.* USEPA. EPA 600/9-91-047, **1992**. 194pp.
6. Fogarty, A. M.; Tuovinen, O. H. *Microbiol Rev.* **1983**, *55*, 225-233.
7. Hart, S. A. 1991. *In: Biological Processes, Innovative Hazardous Waste Treatment* Series; Sfrerra, F. R. Ed., Technomic Publishing Co. Lancaster, Pa. **1991**, *3*, 7-17.
8. Hartley, D.; Kidd, H., Eds.; *The Agrichemicals Handbook.*, Royal Soc. Chem., The University of Nottingham, England, **1987**, 2nd edition.
9. Hetzel, G. H.; Mullins, D. E.; Young, R. W.; Simonds, J. M. *In:* Pesticides in *Terrestrial and Aquatic Environments.* Proc. Nat. Res. Conf, Weighman, D. L., Ed.; Richmond, Va. **1989**, 239-248.
10. Judge, D. N; Mullins, D. E.; Hetzel, G. H.; Young, R. W., *In: Pesticides in the next decade: The Challenges Ahead.* Proc. 3rd Nat. Res. Conf. on Pesticides, Weighman, D. L., Ed.; Richmond, Va., **1990**, 145-158.
11. Lemmon, C. R.; Pylypiw, H.M. Jr. *Bull. Environ. Contam. Toxicol.* **1992**, *48*, 409-415.
12. Mullins, D. E.; Young, R. W.; Palmer, C. P; Hamilton, R. L.; Sherertz, P. *C. Pestic. Sci.* **1989**, *25*, 241-254.
13. Mullins, D. E.; Young, R. W.; Hetzel, G. H.; Berry, D. F. *In: Proceedings of the International Workshop on Research in Pesticide Treatment, Disposal and Waste Minimization* Ferguson, T. D. Ed. USEPA. Cincinnati, OH. **1992**, 32-45.
14. Mullins, D. E.; Young, R. W.; Hetzel, G. H.; Berry, D. F. *In: Managing Pesticide Wastes, Proc.* ACS Symposium, New York, NY, Bourke, J; Seiber, J. N., Eds. **1991** (in press).
15. Mullins, D. E.; et al. Unpublished data.
16. Norwood, V. M. *A Literature Review of Waste Treatment Technologies Which May be Applicable to Wastes Generated at Fertilizer/Agrichemical Dealer Sites.* Tennessee Valley Authority Bulletin Y-214 Muscle Shoals. AL. **1990**.
17. Overend, R. P.; Chornet, E. *Phil. Trans. R. Soc.* Lond. A. **1987**, *321*, 523-536.
18. Petruska, J. A.; Mullins, D. E.; Young, R. W.; Collins, E. R. *Nuclear and Chem. Waste Manag.* **1985**, *5*, 177-182.
19. Sauage, G. M.; Diaz, L. F.; Golueke, C. G. *BioCycle,* **1985**, *26*, 31-34.
20. Seaman, D. *Pestic. Sci.* **1990**, *29*, 437-449.
21. Somich, C. J.; Muldoon, M. T.; Kearney, P. C. *Environ. Sci Technol.* **1990**, *24*, 745-749.
22. Thomas, B. *Pestic. Sci.* **1990**, *29*, 475-479.

23. Toller, G.; Flaim, G. M.; *Wat. Res.* **1988**, *22*, 657-661.
24. Ware, G. *The Pesticide Book*, Thomson Publications, Fresno, Ca. **1989**, 3rd ed. 340 pp.
25. Watts, R. R., *Analytical Reference Standards and Supplemental Data for Pesticides and other Organic Compounds.* 1981, USEPA-600-12-81-001.
26. Wilkinson, R. R.; Kelso, G. L.; Hopkins, F. C. Eds *State of the Art Pesticide Disposal Research.* USEPA. 600/2-78-183, 1978.
27. Williams, R. T.; Myler, C. A. *BioCycle,* **1990**, *31*, 78-82.

RECEIVED October 30, 1992

Chapter 12

Fate of an Antifoulant in an Aquatic Environment

A. Jacobson[1], L. S. Mazza[1], L. J. Lawrence[2], B. Lawrence[2], S. Jackson[2], and A. Kesterson[2]

[1]Rohm and Haas Company, Spring House, PA 19477
[2]PTRL-East, Inc., Richmond, KY 40475

RH-5287 (2-n-octyl-4,5-dichloro-1-isothiazolin-3-one) had a half-life of less than 1 hour in both an aerobic and an anaerobic aquatic microcosm consisting of marine sediment and seawater. Upon application of 0.05 ppm ^{14}C RH-5287, over 90% of the ^{14}C-activity partitioned rapidly into the sediment. Soxhlet extractions with dichloromethane:methanol (9:1) followed by methanol eluted approximately 30 - 60% of the total applied radioactivity. After exhaustive extraction of the post-Soxhlet extracted sediment with 0.25N HCl followed by 1N NaOH, 14 to 40% of the total applied radioactivity still remained bound to the marine sediment. In the aerobic microcosm, ^{14}CO$_2$ accounted for approximately 24% of the applied activity after 30 days. The production of sizable quantities of ^{14}CO$_2$ and extractable polar metabolites indicated that degradation involves cleavage of the isothiazolone ring.

RH-5287 is a member of the 3(2H)-isothiazolone class of compounds which have demonstrated biocidal activity against a wide spectrum of bacteria, fungi and algae *(1)*. RH-5287, when formulated as Sea-Nine 211™ Biocide, has been found to be an effective active ingredient in marine paint formulations to prevent buildup (fouling) of algae and invertebrate animals on submerged hulls of ships and other vessels.

Isothiazolones are known to undergo chemical hydrolysis, especially in the presence of a nucleophile *(2, 3)*. Previous studies on other 3(2H)-isothiazolones has shown that biological degradation of these compounds is very rapid *(4)*. The metabolic pathway involves cleavage of the isothiazolone ring and subsequent oxidation of the terminal methylene substituents.

0097–6156/93/0522–0127$06.00/0
© 1993 American Chemical Society

In order to assess the safety and evaluate the impact of RH-5287 in the marine environment we performed an aerobic and an anaerobic microcosm study. The microcosms, consisting of marine sediment and seawater, were monitored for volatiles, degradation kinetics, partitioning between seawater and sediment, and degradation products.

EXPERIMENTAL PROCEDURES

Chemicals. Radiolabeled RH-5287 (2-n-octyl-^{14}C(4,5)-dichloro-1-isothiazolin-3-one) and ^{13}C RH-5287 (^{13}C(4,5)-dichloro) were prepared at Rohm and Haas Company, Research Laboratories, Spring House, PA. The radiopurity was greater than 98% and the specific activity was 55.39 µCi/mg. The chemical purity of the ^{13}C material was greater than 97%. Additional chromatographic standards were also prepared at Rohm and Haas Company. All laboratory chemicals were reagent grade and all solvents HPLC grade.

Sediment and Water. The sediment and seawater used for this study were obtained from the York River near Gloucester Point, VA, and were used shortly after their collection in order to insure the viability of their natural biota. The physical properties of the sediment and seawater are listed in Tables I and II.

Aerobic Microcosm. Wet sediment (55.7 g; 20 g dry weight) and 64.3 ml of seawater were added to an autoclaved 500 ml Erlenmeyer flask equipped with a ground glass stopper and stopcock inlet and outlet tubes. The inlet and outlet tubes were used to remove volatile products while providing for replacement with fresh oxygen. Sediment and seawater were not treated in any way prior to their addition to an Erlenmeyer flask.

Six µg RH-5287 (1.5 µg ^{13}C and 4.5 µg ^{14}C) was added to each flask to yield a nominal 0.05 ppm dose. This concentration of parent compound was slightly below the minimum concentration that inhibits microbial activity and over 100 times higher than the expected environmental concentration. Dosed and control flasks were maintained in a dark incubator at 25°C and duplicate flasks were removed on Day 0, 1, 2, 5, 9, 15, 20, 26 and 30. At approximately seven day intervals oxygen was flushed through the flasks and the exiting gas passed through a series of two gas dispersion tubes containing, in order, ethylene glycol and 10% NaOH. After replacing the gas dispersion tubes/solutions, the flask was briefly flushed with oxygen and resealed. The expired ethylene glycol solutions and the $BaCl_2$ precipitated $^{14}CO_2$ from the NaOH solutions were radioassayed.

After incubation for the specified time, the seawater and sediment phases were separated by either centrifugation or filtration. The seawater phase was partitioned with dichloromethane and radioassayed. The separated sediment was extracted using a method similar to that of Rice *et al. (5)*. The entire sediment was mixed with 22 g of Na_2SO_4 and 3 g Quso G 35 (precipitated silica, Degussa Corporation, Teterboro, NJ) and subsequently placed in a cryogenic freezer. After at least 24 hours in the freezer, the sediment mixture was transferred to a Waring blender and the resulting homogeneous mixture placed in a cellulose extraction thimble. The samples were Soxhlet extracted for 48 hours with dichloromethane:methanol (9:1) followed by a 24 hour extraction with methanol alone.

The extraction solvents were individually concentrated, radioassayed and chromatographed (HPLC). The Soxhlet-extracted sediment was stored frozen until it was exhaustively extracted.

Characterization of the Soxhlet-insoluble residues followed the classical methods suggested by the U.S. Environmental Protection Agency *(6)*. The insoluble sediment was initially refluxed in 0.25 N HCl. The resulting insoluble residue was extracted overnight with 1 N NaOH to yield three fractions: 1) humic acid (precipitated from alkaline solution by acid), 2) fulvic acid (that part of the alkaline solution not precipitated by acid) and 3) humin (sediment material not soluble in alkali).

Anaerobic Microcosm. The anaerobic samples were treated identically to the aerobic samples with the following exceptions. On the river bottom, the upper layer of aerobic sediment was first swept away allowing for the sampling of the lower anaerobic layer. The Erlenmeyer flask contained 54.1 g of wet sediment (20 g dry weight) and 66 ml of water purged with nitrogen. Glucose was added to each flask and the flask was flushed with nitrogen and stored in an incubator ($25°C$) to insure anaerobic conditions. After 30 days, ^{14}C RH-5287 (5.9 µg) was added to each flask, the flasks were flushed with nitrogen, and were returned to the incubator. All manipulations were carried out in a glove box flushed constantly with nitrogen. Samples were taken on Day 0, 1, 5, 7, 29, 61 and 90. Extraction and characterization of the two phases were identical to that of the aerobic samples.

HPLC. A Spectra Physics or a Waters Associates HPLC system was utilized for chromatographic analysis. Separation of compounds was accomplished with a water/methanol gradient. System 1 employed a Supelco LC-18 column and the following linear gradient steps: a) 75% methanol from 0 to 15 minutes, b) 75 to 100% methanol over the next 5 minutes, c) 100% methanol for the next 15 minutes and d) 100 to 75% methanol over the next 5 minutes. System 2 employed a Supelco LC-18DB column and the following linear gradient steps: a) 5% methanol from 0 to 5 minutes. b) 5% to 95% methanol over the next 30 minutes, c) 95% methanol for the next 5 minutes and d) 95% to 5% methanol over the next 10 minutes. Flow rate for both systems was 1 ml/min and detection was with a radioactive flow monitor and a UV/visible (220 or 270 nm) detector.

RESULTS AND DISCUSSION

Distribution of Radioactivity. The applied ^{14}C-activity partitioned rapidly and primarily into the sediment. After centrifugation or filtration to separate the two phases, over 92% of the applied activity was present in the sediment throughout the study (Figures 1 and 2). In the aerobic sediment, the Soxhlet-extractable residues (dichloromethane:methanol and methanol extractions combined) declined from about 48% of the applied activity to 16% over the 30 days of the experiment. This decrease in extractable residues was most pronounced in the dichloromethane:methanol extraction, though the methanol extraction also decreased with time, albeit, more slowly (data not presented). There was a steady increase in $^{14}CO_2$ throughout the study and by Day 30 it comprised about 24% of the

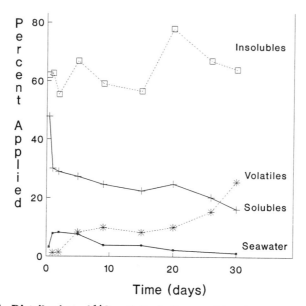

Figure 1. Distribution of ¹⁴C-activity in the aerobic microcosm over time. Seawater and sediment phases were separated and the sediment extracted yielding a Soxhlet soluble and insoluble fraction.

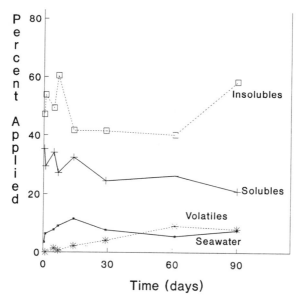

Figure 2. Distribution of ¹⁴C-activity in the anaerobic microcosm over time. Seawater and sediment phases were separated and the sediment extracted yielding a Soxhlet soluble and insoluble fraction.

applied dose. The Soxhlet-insoluble residue accounted for a majority of the applied activity, ranging between 57 to 77%. The recovery of applied ^{14}C averaged 103.6 ± 10.8% over the 30 days.

Results from the anaerobic sediment demonstrated trends similar to the aerobic sediment (Figure 2). There was a general decline in Soxhlet-extractable residue with increased incubation time. The fraction containing most of the ^{14}C-activity was the Soxhlet insoluble residue comprising between 40 to 60% of the applied activity. Volatile production was much less than in the aerobic sediment with [14]CO_2 accounting for approximately 8% of the dose by Day 90. The recovery of applied ^{14}C-activity averaged 88.1 ± 9.6% over the 90 days.

Numerous extraction solvents (both organic and aqueous), extraction techniques (e.g., homogenization, sonication, shaking), as well as extraction times were examined to achieve the highest extractability of ^{14}C residues from sediment. The double Soxhlet extraction procedure employed in this study was the most effective method; it extracted approximately 50% of the sediment-associated ^{14}C residue. When sterile sediment was spiked with ^{14}C RH-5287, approximately 90% of the dose was extracted by this method (data not presented). Thus it appears that biological degradation of RH-5287 is occurring and the degradates may be tightly incorporated into the sediment. Microbial and chemical processes can occur within the soil or sediment whereby reactive compounds are generated leading to formation of covalently bound residues *(7)*. Studies on other isothiazolones *(4)* have similarly demonstrated a tight association between ^{14}C residues of isothiazolones and sediment/soil.

The ^{14}C-activity remaining after Soxhlet extraction was further characterized by exhaustive extraction with 0.25 N HCl followed by 1 N NaOH (Table III). Acid extraction had virtually no effect on the bound residue. Treatment with base released a significant percentage of the bound residue with practically all the base-soluble ^{14}C activity associated with the humic acid fraction. However, even with this severe base treatment, over 50% of the bound residue (14.5 to 40.7% of the applied dose) was insoluble (humin). Thus a large percentage of the ^{14}C-activity is tightly associated with the sediment.

Half-life. The half-life of RH-5287 in an aerobic and an anaerobic microcosm was less than 1 hour (Figure 3, insert). Less than 6% of the extractable residue at time 0 was parent, and at subsequent sampling intervals no parent compound was detected. The small amount of parent detected at time 0 may seem illogical but it took approximately 1 hour to prepare and freeze, and thus biologically inactivate the samples. Due to the necessary sample preparation, no sampling intervals of less than 1 hour were possible. When coupled with the rapid metabolism, a more detailed kinetic analysis was impossible.

Fortification of sterile sediments with ^{14}C RH-5287 yielded extraction efficiencies approaching 90%, and chromatography of these sediment extracts showed that over 95% of the ^{14}C residues was parent compound (data not presented). Thus in the presence of a biologically active microcosm, RH-5287 degraded extremely rapidly. In biologically active natural and synthetic seawater the half-life of RH-5287 was similar to the microcosm results *(8)*. The degradation of N-methyl isothiazolones in a river die-away and an activated sludge environment was also rapid *(9)*. The N-S bond of isothiazolones

Table I. Physical-Chemical Characteristics of Aerobic and Anaerobic Sediment

Parameter	Aerobic	Anaerobic
pH	6.6	6.6
Texture Class	Silt Loam	Silt Loam
Sand	20%	13%
Silt	60%	65%
Clay	20%	22%
Organic Matter	8.1% Dry	5.3% Dry
Cation Exchange Capacity	35 meq/100 g	29 meq/100 g
Field Capacity	58%	53%
Sulfur, Total	1.18%	1.02%

Table II. Physical-Chemical Characteristics of Seawater

Total Alkalinity	84 mg/L $CaCO_3$
Total Organic Carbon	3.2 mg/L
pH	7.4
Salinity	19.62 g/Kg
Total Suspended Solids	54 mg/L
Specific Conductance	32,100 μmohs/cm
Sulfate	2,513 mg/L
Total Calcium	104 mg/L
Total Potassium	266 mg/L
Total Sodium	6,315 mg/L

Table III. Exhaustive extraction of Soxhlet extracted sediment

Day	Percent Bound	Percent HCl Soluble	Percent in Humin Fraction	Percent in Humic Acid Fraction	Percent in Fulvic Acid Fraction
Anaerobic					
0	21.0	0.1	14.5	13.4	0.2
Aerobic					
0	53.4	0.1	40.7	22.1	0.3
30	60.3	0.1	29.3	25.0	0.5

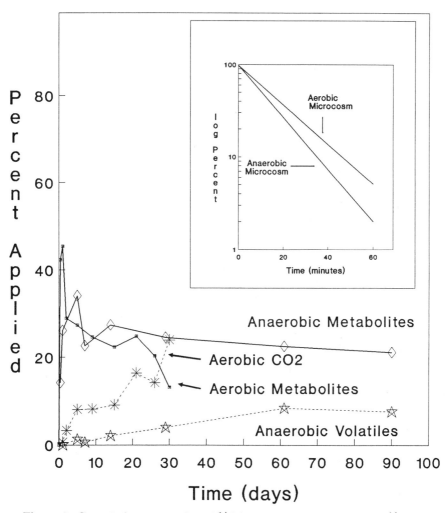

Figure 3. Cumulative production of $^{14}CO_2$ and total Soxhlet soluble ^{14}C metabolites detected by HPLC. Both the aerobic and anaerobic microcosms are presented. Insert represents the decline of parent over the first hour of the experiment.

is very labile, undergoing rapid chemical cleavage in the presence of electrophiles or nucleophiles (2, 3). Thus, degradation of RH-5287 is rapid, involving a biologically mediated attack on the N-S bond.

The rapid half-life coupled with the extraction data comparing sterile and nonsterile sediment suggests that it is the degradates of RH-5287 that are being rapidly and preferentially adsorbed to aquatic sediment. As outlined above, this adsorption is very strong.

Metabolite Characterization. By Day 30, $^{14}CO_2$ was a major degradation product of RH-5287, comprising almost 25% of the applied dose in the aerobic microcosm (Figure 3). This is an important observation since the only way to liberate $^{14}CO_2$ is by isothiazolone ring cleavage and subsequent oxidation of the labeled methylene groups. In the reducing environment of the anaerobic microcosm, a smaller quantity of $^{14}CO_2$ was produced. This environment would be conducive to the production of nucleophiles such as HS^- and electrophiles such as CN^- which will rapidly cleave the N-S bond of isothiazolones (2, 3). The production of $^{14}CO_2$ and possibly other oxidized degradates in the anaerobic environment is similar to that of alcohol and heterolactic fermentations which involve enzymatic catalysis. Figure 3 also illustrates a correlation between the decrease in total Soxhlet soluble HPLC detectable ^{14}C metabolites and an increase in $^{14}CO_2$. This is very evident for the aerobic microcosm where by Day 30 more $^{14}CO_2$ was present than Soxhlet-extractable ^{14}C metabolites.

HPLC analysis of the Soxhlet extracts is presented in Figures 4 and 5. For both aerobic and anaerobic environments, three major metabolites with retention times of approximately 3.5, 4 and 7 minutes (HPLC system 1) were detected. These metabolites were chromatographically more polar than parent compound. The correlated decrease in HPLC detectable polar metabolites and the increase in $^{14}CO_2$ over the 30 day study suggests that degradation involves successive oxidation of the ring cleaved isothiazolone (Figure 3). Co-chromatography with standards characterized these metabolites as n-octyl oxamic acid, n-octyl malonamic acid, and either n-octyl-hydroxylacetamide, n-octyl-glyoxylamide or the n-octyl-acetamide (Table IV). These are similar to the metabolites identified by Krezmenski et al. (9) for N-methyl isothiazolones in sludge effluent and river water. In addition, a series of isothiazolone compounds were demonstrated to undergo photoisomerization by cleavage of N-S bond (10).

CONCLUSIONS

When exposed to a biologically active aerobic or anaerobic microcosm consisting of seawater and sediment or seawater alone (8) RH-5287 rapidly degrades by ring opening and subsequent oxidation. A major portion of these degradates are tightly and preferentially associated with sediment. From these data it appears that when RH-5287 enters the environment as the result of leaching from marine antifoulant paints it will be rapidly degraded and the bioavailability of these degradates will be severely restricted by the rapid and covalent-like association with marine sediment.

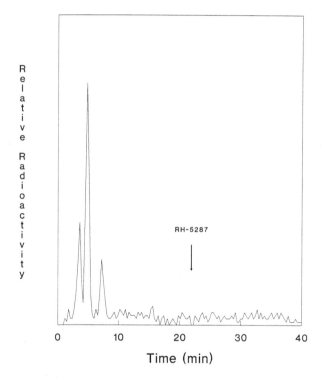

Figure 4. Chromatogram (HPLC system 1) of the Soxhlet soluble residue from the aerobic microcosm.

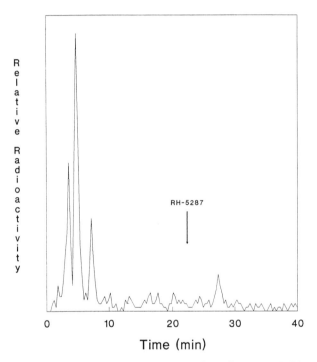

Figure 5. Chromatogram (HPLC system 1) of the Soxhlet soluble residue from the anaerobic microcosm.

Table IV. Chromatographic Analysis of Standards in HPLC System 1

Name	Structure[1]	Rt
RH-5287		23.5
RH-893		10.7
N-(n-octyl)-malonamic acid	NH-C(O)-CH$_2$CO$_2$H	3.6
N-(n-octyl)-oxamic acid	R-NH-C(O)-CO$_2$H	4.1
N-(n-octyl)-1-hydroxylacetamide	R-NH-C(O)-CH$_2$OH	7.0
N-(n-octyl)-glyoxylamide	R-NH-C(O)-CHO	6.8
N-(n-octyl) acetamide	R-NH-C(O)-CH$_3$	7.3
N-(n-octyl) chloroacetamide	R-NH-C(O)-CH$_2$Cl	8.3
N-(n-octyl)-chloropropionamide	R-NH-C(O)-CH$_2$-CH$_2$Cl	9.5

[1] R is C$_8$H$_{17}$.

ACKNOWLEDGMENTS

We gratefully acknowledge the assistance of Dr. Robert J. Huggett and his colleagues at Virginia Institute of Marine Science for providing the sediment and seawater and Dr. Sou-Jen Chang, Rohm and Haas Company for preparation of the chromatographic standards.

LITERATURE CITED

1. Miller, G.A. and Lovegrove, T., *J. Coatings Technol.* **1980**, *2,* 69.
2. Crow, W.D. and Nelson, N.J., *J. Org. Chem.* **1965**, *30,* 2060.
3. Crow, W.D. and Gosney, I., *Aust. J. Chem.* **1967**, *20,* 2729.
4. Krzeminski, S.F., Brackett, C.K. and Fisher, J.D., *J. Agric. Food Chem.* **1975**, *23,* 1060.
5. Rice, C.D., Espourteille, F.A. and Huggett, R.J., *App. Organometallic Chem.* **1987**, *1,* 541.
6. U.S. Environmental Protection Agency, *Federal Register* June **1975**, *40[123],* 26803.
7. Führ. F. In *Pesticide Science and Biotechnology;* Greenhalgh, R and Roberts, T.R., Eds.; Sixth International Congress of Pesticide Chemistry (IUPAC); Blackwell Scientific Publication: Oxford, U.K., **1987**, pp 381-89.
8. Shade, W.D., Hurt, S.S., Jacobson, A.H., and Reinert, K.H., In *Environmental Toxicology and Risk Assessment; 2nd Volume ASTM STP 1173;* Gorsuch, J.W., Dwyer, F.W., Ingersoll, C.M. and La Point, T.W., Eds; American Society for Testing and Materials, Philadelphia, PA (in press).
9. Krzeminski, S.F., Brackett, C.K., Fisher, J.D. and Spinnler, J.F., *J. Agric. Food Chem.* **1975**, *20,* 1068.
10. Rokach, J. and Hamel, P., *J.C.S. Chem. Comm.* **1979**, pp 786.

RECEIVED October 29, 1992

MOBILITY OF PESTICIDES IN URBAN ENVIRONMENTS

Chapter 13

Horizontal and Vertical Distribution of Chlorpyrifos Termiticide Applied as Liquid or Foam Emulsions

R. E. Gold, H. N. Howell, Jr., and E. A. Jordan III

Center for Urban and Public Health Entomology, Department of Entomology, Texas A&M University, College Station, TX 77843–2475

Damage due to termites now exceeds $1.7 billion annually in the United States. Termite control presently emphasizes the use of persistent pesticides which either eliminate pest populations directly or prevent their invasion into structures. An evaluation was conducted with liquid and foam formulations of chlorpyrifos termiticide. Horizontal distribution under simulated concrete slabs was enhanced through the use of foam carriers as compared to liquid emulsions applied with a subslab injector system. Vertical penetration within the soil profile was similar for both formulations with 92% and 95% of the total chlorpyrifos recovered from the first 3 cm of soil for liquid and foam emulsions, respectively.

Termites (Order Isoptera) are small, delicate insects that cause tremendous damage to wooden components of structures. While it is difficult to estimate accurately the effects of termite damages, the annual costs for control of termites and repair of their damage exceeds $1.7 billion in the United States. Termites are a problem throughout the world but are primary pests in tropical and subtropical regions which include many areas of the United States. Granovsky (1) estimated that termites cost each American $5.16 per year (in 1983 dollars), and do more damage than all tornadoes, hurricanes and wind storms combined (2, 3). He also reported that termites strike over five times as many homes each year as do fires, and that subterranean termites represent the greatest threat of damage to homes of all natural causes. Termites are of particular importance in the southern regions of the United States, where there is a direct correlation between the per cent of infestation and the age of structures. By the time a structure in the coastal regions of Texas is 40 years old, the probability of infestation with one or more of the several species of termites exceeds 90%. In colder climates such as represented by Nebraska (4), it was estimated that 5% of all structures are infested with termites at any point in time.

Termite control and prevention requires a combination of approaches as part of an integrated management system. In addition to the use of pesticides (termiticides), it has been recommended that wood-to-soil contacts be eliminated, moisture sources be reduced (repairing water leaks, changes in landscapes, and increased air circulation in structures with crawl spaces) *(5)*, and that regularly scheduled inspections be performed to locate developing infestations.

Termiticides have been used both to prevent and to control termite infestations in structures. They are used both as pre-construction (pretreatment) or post-construction (remedial) applications. The objective of the application of termiticides is to establish a continuous protective barrier between the termite colony (usually in the soil) and the wood within a structure *(6, 7)*. For best results both a horizontal and vertical chemical barrier are recommended. This protective barrier is intended either to kill the invading insects, or to repel them thus preventing their entrance into the structure. In the case of remediation treatments, the chemical is applied to reestablish the termiticide barrier or to kill insects before the infestation increases in size and spreads to other parts of the structure. In order to be most effective as a barrier to invading termites, a continuous contamination zone must be established.

The chlorinated hydrocarbon termiticides were considered ideal for the prevention and control of termite damage due to their wide spectrum of efficacy and persistence *(8)*. Chlordane and heptachlor were used for these purposes from 1952 until 1988-89, when all registrations were discontinued in the United States. It is unlikely that these termiticides will be returned to the market *(9)*. Organophosphate, carbamate, and pyrethroid termiticides are available and effective for both pre- and post construction treatments *(10)*. Results of a survey of professional pest control operators indicated that chlorpyrifos (Dursban TC) was preferred by 65.1% of those responding *(11)* .

At the present time there are questions as to how long the new termiticides will provide protection against termites, and how these products should be applied for best results *(12)*. Evaluations of various application technologies and termiticide distribution have been conducted *(8, 13-23)*. As a result of that research a number of specific recommendations have been made about specific termiticide products, application equipment (pumps, injectors, flow meters), application pressures, application rates, drill hole spacing, trenching procedures, and rodding techniques. Even with all the available information, it still appears that most termiticide applications are made "blindly" when treating beneath concrete slabs *(6)*. In these situations, it has been difficult if not impossible to insure that a continuous protective barrier is established. Different approaches to solving this problem have been taken including the use of termiticide foam formulations *(22, 23)*. These preliminary reports indicate more even distribution of termiticide under construction slabs as compared to conventional liquid injection techniques.

The purpose of this research was to evaluate the horizontal distribution and vertical penetration in soil by chlorpyrifos (Dursban TC) termiticide when applied as a liquid or foam emulsion.

MATERIALS AND METHODS

Study Site. Field studies were conducted at the Center for Urban and Public Health Entomology of the Department of Entomology, Texas A&M University, College Station, Texas. Pine dimensional lumber (5 cm X 15 cm X 4.87 m) was used to construct square soil frames of 1.22 m per side. A total of 24 frames were used in this study with all treatments replicated at least three times. After construction, the frames were placed on top of the existing terrain and leveled. Each frame was filled with soil (Lufkin Series: pH 7.1; 1.2% total organic matter; 53.7% sand; 33.7% silt; 12.5% clay) which was hand tamped and then leveled with a screen. The soil was compacted in the frame to a final depth of 10 cm. The frames were then covered with 20 mm Plexiglass which was used to simulate a concrete slab through which termiticide applications were made. The use of Plexiglass facilitated the visual confirmation of distribution patterns in these tests which were documented through videography and still photography. Injection holes (1.3 mm O.D.) were drilled in the Plexiglass cover in three locations. One hole was drilled in the center of the square (Figure 1), and two other holes were drilled 10.2 cm from one edge, 20 cm apart (Figure 2). A 2.54 cm spacer was used to maintain a gap between the top surface of the soil and the bottom surface of the Plexiglass cover. This space represented the effects of soil settling or shrinkage that takes place after concrete has been poured on grade with standard monolithic slab construction types used typically throughout Texas and surrounding states.

Chemicals. The termiticide used in this study was chlorpyrifos [O,O-Diethyl O-(3,5,6-trichloro-2-pyridinyl) phosphorothioate] sold as Dursban TC by DowElanco (Indianapolis, Indiana). Concentrate material was mixed with water to make a 1.0% active ingredient (a.i.) emulsion. Two different emulsions were prepared for these tests including a standard 1.0 % liquid which was applied as a liquid emulsion, and a 1.0 % foam emulsion which was prepared from Dursban TC concentrate, mixed with water and to which was added a foaming agent (Flexafoam, Foam Innovations Inc., Pleasanton, California). Sufficient Flexafoam was added to make a foam with an expansion factor of 8-10 (1 l of liquid yielded 8-10 l of foam).

Chemical Applications. Liquid applications were made with a standard sub-slab injector equipped with a straight, open tip (B&G Equipment Co., Model 486). Flow rate was 3.8 l/min at 172.5 kPa using a Hypro 6500NR gas engine roller pump. Foam was made with a Flexafoamer (Foam Innovations Inc.) which was inline with the Hypro 6500NR roller pump. The foam was dispensed through a custom-built sub-slab injector with a shut-off at the tip. Foam and liquid output (flow rate) was measured with an electronic digital flow meter (Digital Flowmeter Model PHL-3, Technology Management, Inc., Kalamazoo, Michigan). All mixing and application of termiticide in this study were done per commercial pest control standards by representatives of Orkin Exterminating Company, Inc., using their equipment and chemicals.

Treatment procedures involved the application of liquid chlorpyrifos at the rate of 5.0 l/m applied against one side of the soil frame (total volume divided between two injection holes). The second treatment was 3.7 l/m followed immediately by the application of 1.2 l/m liquid equivalents of foam (yield=30 l of foam). The total active ingredient applied (37 g/m) was the same for Treatment 1 as it was for Treatment 2, but the application medium (water or water plus foam) differed. Treatment three was 1.2 l/m liquid equivalents of foam which equated to 0.25% of the total chlorpyrifos active ingredient delivered in either Treatments 1 or 2. Treatments 4-6 were made in the center of the soil frame as opposed to the edge (Treatments 1-3). Treatment 4 was 4.1 l/m^2, Treatment 5 was 4.1 l/m^2 liquid equivalent as foam, and Treatment 6 was 16.3 l/m^2.

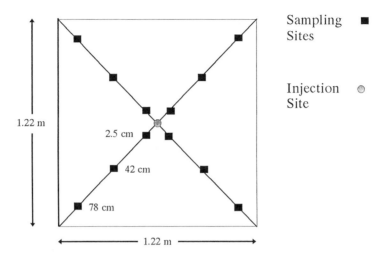

Figure 1. Sampling Scheme for Center Plots

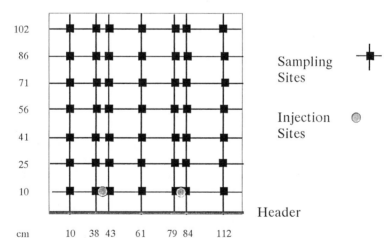

Figure 2. Sampling Scheme for Edge Treatments

Sampling Procedures. Following termiticide applications the plots were covered with plywood and plastic sheeting to minimize the effects of rain. Sampling was initiated 10 days post-treatment. Soil samples were taken by pressing glass shell vials (25 mm diam x 95 mm high), open end down, into the soil, which were then carefully removed. Soil cores were held in these glass vials and stored at -5°C until analysis.

Core samples from the edge treatments (Treatments 1-3) were taken from a grid of seven columns by six rows. The first row was along the row of injection (10 cm from the edge). The successive rows were 15 cm from the previous row. The columns were defines as follows: Column 1 was taken at 10 cm from the left side of the square with the row of injection closest; Columns 2 and 3 were taken approximately 2.5 cm on either side of the injection hole left from the application; Column 4 was midway between the injection holes (61 cm from the left side); Columns 5 and 6 were as in 2 and 3 next to the opposite side of the injection crater; and Column 7 was sampled as was column 1, only from the right side of the square (Figure 2).

For the center injection treatments (Treatments 4-6), core samples were taken along the axes of lines drawn diagonally through the plots. The first and last sample on each diagonal were taken 6 cm from the corners. The third and fourth samples were taken 2.5 cm from the crater in the center of the plots created by the injection process. The second and fifth samples were taken midway along the diagonal from the other samples (Figure 1).

Sample Preparation. Soil samples were prepared for analysis by dividing each sample into levels relating to depth below the soil surface. Each layer weighed approximately 5 g and represented a depth of approximately 1 cm. Each subsample was weighed and put into a 25 ml glass scintillation vial with 20 ml of acetone. The subsamples were shaken and then allowed to sit overnight at room temperature. An aliquot of the initial extraction was then injected into a gas chromatograph(GC).

Chemical Analysis. Analyses were performed using a Lee Scientific Supercritical Fluid Gas Chromatograph (Model 66-D) fitted with a flame ionization detector (Lee Scientific FID-3) operated in a standard GC mode. Conditions for the instrument were as follows: He carrier gas at 30 ml/min, H_2 at 35 ml/min, air at 300 ml/min, N_2 make up gas at 25 ml/min, and a column head pressure at 34.5-68.9 kPa. Temperatures were: injection port, 250°C; detector, 325°C; and oven with a ramp program starting at 75°C for 1 min and increased to 250°C at 50°C/min, held for 7 min and then cooled back to 75°C at -50°C/min. The capillary column was a J&W Scientific DB5, 0.32 mm I.D., 15 m. Autosampler was a Dynatech Precision Sampler (GC-411) with an injection volume of 2µl. Column retention time for chlorpyrifos was 2.67 min with a total run time of 15 min. Performance of the method and instrumentation was monitored through the use of spiked blanks and standardization curves. Recovery rate was 85 ± 5.3% based on extraction and analysis of replicated spiked soil samples. The limit of detection was 10 ng chlorpyrifos/on column, with an overall methods sensitivity of 5 ppm chlorpyrifos.

RESULTS

Visual Observations. It was possible to see visual evidence of the application and movement of chlorpyrifos in both the liquid and foam treatments. The liquids had a tendency to move to the lowest point in the soil frames, and there was evidence of areas that were not contacted by the chemical. Some areas were not contacted by the termiticide because there was not enough liquid or foam. The foam applications appeared to be much more thorough having fewer missed areas in both the edge and center applications. When the Plexiglass cover was removed from the soil frame, it was evident that the foam had contacted not only the soil and wooden frame, but also the underside of the slab. Applications of the foam took twice as long as the liquid applications, but there was evidence in the center treatments that the foam covered at least twice the area within the space beneath the covered slab as was covered by the equivalent liquid dilutions.

Chemical Analysis. Analysis for chlorpyrifos in the liquids used for treatments yielded an initial concentration of 0.6% a.i. for all liquid applications and 1.6% a.i. for the foams. The findings were confirmed by an independent laboratory (Office of the Texas State Chemist). The data from the applications is expressed in parts per million (ppm) (Figures 3 and 5, and Tables I, III, VI and VIII). Since termiticide concentration differed with treatments, comparisons were made on the per cent of total chlorpyrifos recovered from the soil in both horizontal and vertical dimensions (Figures 4 and 6, and Tables II, IV, V and VII).

Chlorpyrifos residue analysis provided evidence that the application method did make a significant difference in the horizontal distribution of the termiticide (Figure 3) when applied within 10 cm of a header (Figure 1). While the distribution patterns were similar for the 5.0 l/m and the 3.7 l/m plus the 1.2 l foam, there was uniform spread of the 1.2 l foam/m. The chlorpryrifos concentrations (ppm) indicated in Figure 3 were sufficient for effective termite treatments *(10, 24-31)*. When comparisons were made of the percentages of the total amount of chlorpyrifos that was deposited with increasing distances from the header (Figure 4), there were no significant advantages to the use of foams in the edge treatments.

Horizontal movement of termiticide applied in the center of each plot (Figure 2) differed with each of the three treatments (Figure 5) when concentrations (ppm) were considered. The foam only treatment (4.1 l/m²) provided uniform coverage throughout the plots as did the 16.3 l/m² liquid applications. The 4.1 l/m² liquid applications provided less horizontal coverage than either of the other application procedures. When the percentage of the total chlorpyrifos deposited was correlated with distance from the point of injection (center treatments) (Figure 6) the 4.1 l/m² foam application was as effective as the 16.3 l/m² liquid application even though only 25% as much liquid equivalent was applied, thus demonstrating the advantage of the foam formulation in terms of horizontal movement.

Results of the vertical penetration study indicated that chlorpyrifos was effectively applied throughout 7 cm of soil within 25 cm of the header (Table I) for rates of 5.0 l/m and 3.7 l plus 1.2 l foam/m. The 1.2 l foam/m was not as effective in penetrating the soil within the first 25 cm from the header as compared with the other applications. Observations at the time of treatment were that holes (approximately 5 cm across and 7

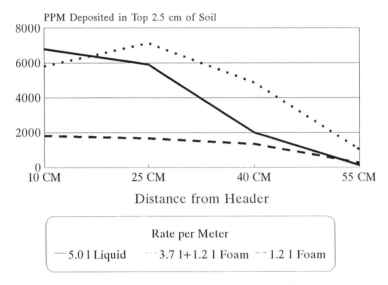

Figure 3. **Horizontal Distribution of Termiticide**

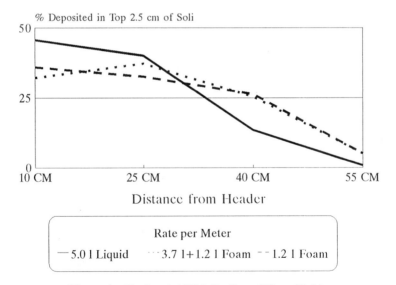

Figure 4. **Horizontal Distribution of Termiticide**

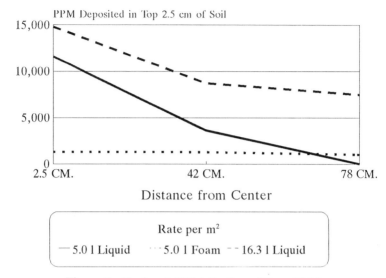

Figure 5. Horizontal Distribution of Termiticide

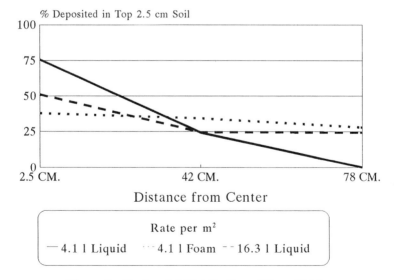

Figure 6. Horizontal Distribution of Termiticide

Table I.   Mean Concentrations in ppm of Chlorpyrifos by Formulation, Horizontal
            Distribution, and Vertical Penetration in Edge Treatments

Distance in cm	Depth in cm	FORMULATION liters/m		
		5.0 1 Liquid[a]	3.7 1 Liquid + 1.2 1 Foam	1.2 1 Foam[b]
10	0-1	3423	3694	1240
	1-2	2281	1694	425
	2-3	1086	406	139
	3-4	183	176	30
	4-5	47	48	15
	5-6	40	104	0
	6-7	95	205	0
25	0-1	3011	3758	1061
	1-2	2178	2753	459
	2-3	722	622	140
	3-4	129	103	13
	4-5	19	41	0
	5-6	77	15	0
	6-7	135	15	8
40	0-1	1083	2565	789
	1-2	676	4687	461
	2-3	242	613	89
	3-4	94	120	12
	4-5	10	7	0
	5-6	0 [c]	0	0
	6-7	0	0	0
55	0-1	87	526	194
	1-2	26	407	55
	2-3	12	94	16
	3-4	11	0	6
	4-5	0	0	0
	5-6	0	0	0
	6-7	0	0	0

[a]0.6% a.i.
[b]1.6% a.i.
[c]Limit of Detection = 5 ppm

Table II. Mean Percent Deposition of Chlorpyrifos by Formulation, Horizontal Distribution, and Vertical Penetration in Edge Treatments

Distance in cm	Depth in cm	FORMULATION liters/m		
		5.0 1 Liquid[a]	3.7 1 Liquid + 1.2 1 Foam	1.2 1 Foam[b]
10	0-1	48.9	58.4	66.9
	1-2	31.9	26.8	22.8
	2-3	15.2	6.4	7.5
	3-4	2.6	2.8	0.8
	4-5	0.7	0.8	0.0
	5-6	0.6	1.6	0.0
	6-7	1.3	3.2	0.0
25	0-1	48.0	51.4	62.9
	1-2	34.7	37.7	27.2
	2-3	11.5	8.5	8.3
	3-4	2.1	1.4	0.8
	4-5	0.3	0.6	0.2
	5-6	1.2	0.2	0.2
	6-7	2.2	0.2	0.5
40	0-1	51.3	51.3	58.0
	1-2	32.0	33.8	33.9
	2-3	11.5	12.3	6.5
	3-4	4.5	2.4	0.9
	4-5	0.5	0.1	0.3
	5-6	0.1	0.1	0.1
	6-7	0.2	0.0	0.2
55	0-1	62.6	51.1	71.6
	1-2	18.7	39.6	20.3
	2-3	8.6	9.1	5.9
	3-4	7.9	0.2	2.2
	4-5	2.2	0.0	0.0
	5-6	0.0	0.0	0.0
	6-7	0.0	0.0	0.0

[a]0.6% a.i.
[b]1.6% a.i.

Table III. Mean Concentrations in ppm of Chlorpyrifos Deposited by Formulation, Horizontal Distribution, and Vertical Penetration in Center Treatments

Distance in cm	Depth in cm	FORMULATION liters/m²		
		4.1 1 Liquid[a]	4.1 1 Foam[b]	16.3 1 Liquid
2.5	0-1	3308	1200	3418
	1-2	2418	646	2900
	2-3	1220	253	2554
	3-4	252	114	1652
	4-5	15	50	917
	5-6	0 [c]	10	279
	6-7	0	0	139
42	0-1	990	1376	2254
	1-2	778	634	2000
	2-3	409	48	969
	3-4	144	0	377
	4-5	10	0	92
	5-6	0	0	22
	6-7	0	0	0
78	0-1	11	776	1852
	1-2	0	594	1487
	2-3	0	283	1135
	3-4	0	21	730
	4-5	0	0	372
	5-6	0	0	72
	6-7	0	0	14

[a]0.6% a.i.
[b]1.6% a.i.
[c]Limit of detection = 5 ppm

Table IV. Mean Percent Deposition of Chlorpyrifos by Formulation, Horizontal Distribution and Vertical Penetration in Center Treatments

Distance in cm	Depth in cm	FORMULATION liters/m² 4.1 l Liquid[a]	4.1 l Foam[b]	16.3 l Liquid
2.5	0-1	45.9	52.8	28.8
	1-2	33.5	28.4	24.5
	2-3	16.9	11.1	21.5
	3-4	3.5	5.0	13.9
	4-5	0.2	2.2	7.7
	5-6	0.0	0.4	2.4
	6-7	0.0	0.0	1.2
42	0-1	42.5	66.9	39.4
	1-2	33.4	30.8	35.0
	2-3	17.5	2.0	17.0
	3-4	6.2	0.0	6.6
	4-5	0.4	0.0	1.6
	5-6	0.0	0.0	0.4
	6-7	0.0	0.0	0.0
78	0-1	100.0	46.3	32.7
	1-2	0.0	35.4	26.3
	2-3	0.0	16.9	20.0
	3-4	0.0	1.3	12.9
	4-5	0.0	0.2	6.6
	5-6	0.0	0.0	1.3
	6-7	0.0	0.0	0.2

[a] 0.6% a.i.
[b] 1.6% a.i.

Table V.   Mean Percent Deposition of Chlorpyrifos by Formulation and Horizontal
Distribution in Edge Treatments

TREATMENT	DISTANCE							
liters/m	10 cm		25 cm		40 cm		55 cm	
	%	S.D.	%	S.D.	%	S.D.	%	S.D.
5.0 Liquid[a]	46.3a[c]	2.4	39.3a	2.1	13.6a	3.9	0.8a	0.72
3.7 Liquid +1.2 Foam	31.8b	9.9	38.5a	5.8	24.5a	15.5	5.2a	4.14
1.2 Foam[b]	35.8ab	3.6	33.3a	1.2	26.0a	2.0	4.7a	1.76

[a] 0.6% a.i.
[b] 1.6% a.i.
[c] Means followed by the same letter not significantly different at 5% level

Table VI.   Mean Concentrations of Chlorpyrifos by Formulation and Horizontal
Distribution in Edge Treatments

TREATMENT	DISTANCE							
liters/m	10 cm		25 cm		40 cm		55 cm	
	ppm	S.D.	ppm	S.D.	ppm	S.D.	ppm	S.D.
5.0 Liquid[a]	2263a[c]	1332	2088a	1306	1181b	1327	375a	385
3.7 Liquid +1.2 Foam	2028a	1996	2378a	1949	1892a	2620	601a	737
1.2 Foam[b]	625b	831	591b	625	471c	531	221a	312

[a] 0.6% a.i.
[b] 1.6% a.i.
[c] Means followed by the same letter not significantly different at 5% level

Table VII. Mean Percent Deposition of Chlorpyrifos by Formulation and Horizontal Distribution in Center Treatments

TREATMENT	DISTANCE					
liters/m²	2.5 cm		42 cm		78 cm	
	%	S.D.	%	S.D.	%	S.D.
16.3 Liquid[a]	25.2b[c]	7.1	12.2a	7.5	12.5a	8.6
4.1 Liquid	38.5a	4.1	11.4a	10.3	0.1b	0.2
4.1 Foam[b]	18.8b	9.6	17.3a	10.3	13.9a	8.6

[a] 0.6% a.i.
[b] 1.6% a.i.
[c] Means followed by the same letter not significantly different at 5% level

Table VIII. Mean Concentrations of Chlorpyrifos by Formulation and Horizontal Distribution in Center Treatments

TREATMENT	DISTANCE					
liters/m²	2.5 cm		42 cm		78 cm	
	%	S.D.	%	S.D.	%	S.D.
16.3 Liquid[a]	3505a[c]	1288	2102a	828	3025a	728
4.1 Liquid	2127b	697	1677a	1191	64b	88
4.1 Foam[b]	601c	400	555b	414	639b	631

[a] 0.6% a.i.
[b] 1.6% a.i.
[c] Means followed by the same letter not significantly different at 5% level

cm deep) were formed immediately below the point of application. There was evidence of pesticide flow beneath the 7 cm of filled and tamped soil as indicated in Table I for the first 25 cm from the header.

When analysis of the vertical penetration was made based on the per cent of the total chlorpyrifos residue in each of the soil layers for each treatment method and rate (Table II) it was determined that 95% of the termiticide was deposited in the top 3 cm of soil. Whether or not this depth and concentration constitutes an effective barrier to invading termites is not known. Similar results were determined for the center applications (Tables III and IV) with 92% of the chlorpyrifos recovered from the first 3 cm of soil. Both the 4.1 l/m² foam and 16.3 l/m² liquid were superior to the 4.1 l/m² applications both in terms of vertical and horizontal movement of the termiticide.

DISCUSSION

The use of foam formulation for the application of chlorpyrifos termiticide (Dursban TC) had an advantage over liquid applications in situation where the termiticide must be moved beneath concrete slabs to areas that are inaccessible to drill and treat operations. The foam formulation had the advantage of uniformly filling the space between the bottom surface of the concrete slab and the upper surface of the subsoil. In these studies the application of 4.1 l/m² (liquid equivalent) foam completely filled a square soil frame of 1.2 m on a side with a 2.5 cm gap between the upper slab and the subsoil. While the horizontal distribution of chlorpyrifos was greatly increased as compared to equivalent liquid applications (4.1 l/m²), the vertical movement of the termiticide may be insufficient for effective termite control or repulsion. Approximately 92% of the total chlorpyrifos was in the top 3 cm of soil. The paradox is that while the foam formulation may move the termiticide further under the slab, the greater the horizontal distribution the less active ingredient there was per unit area in all dimensions. While it may be advantageous to have the undersurface of the slab treated along with the subsoil and headers, any pesticide not deposited in the soil would not contribute to the barrier, and will not prevent termites from invading the soil under the structure. Research is needed to develop a foam that is dense enough to travel to inaccessible areas, but is wet enough to treat soil to a depth, with a sufficient concentration of termiticide to present an effective barrier to termites. A portion of this problem could be solved through the use of more concentrated (greater than 1% a.i. Dursban TC=present label rate) liquids from which the foams were generated.

Chlorpyrifos is an effective termiticide with LC_{50} values ranging from 1.7-15.4 ppm for various termite species (10, 24, 26, 27). Concentrations of 10-50 ppm caused mortality of subterranean termites within 24 hours and 100 ppm inhibited tunneling activity completely (30). Other reports indicated that chlorpyrifos at 5,000 ppm caused termites to seal off tunnels thus avoiding treated soils (25). Jones (28, 29) determined that 500 ppm chlorpyrifos knocked down subterranean termites in 1.25 hrs, but that there was slight tunneling activity at 500 ppm. From this information, it is concluded that chlorpyrifos at between 25-500 ppm will stop tunneling activity of subterranean termites with death of individuals which contact treated soils occurring at much lower levels. Based on this research, concentrations exceeding 500 ppm were obtained within the first 3 cm of soil with all treatments, and it can be concluded that chlorpyrifos would be effective for termite control until such time as application concentrations are degraded to the point that protection is lost. Research into this paradigm is currently underway in our laboratory.

LITERATURE CITED

1. Granovsky, T. A. *Pest Control* **1983**, *50*(3), 14, 16, 20.
2. Granovsky, T. A. *Tierra Grande* **1979**, *8*, 19-21.
3. Granovsky, T. A. *Tierra Grande* **1983**, *22*, 12-15.
4. Kamble, S. T.; Gold, R. E.; Rauscher, J. D. *Distribution and Economic Impact of Subterranean Termites in Nebraska.* Agricultural Research Division, Institute of Agriculture and Natural Resources, University of Nebraska-Lincoln, Lincoln, NE, **1984**.
5. Moore, H. *Pest Control Tech.* **1990**, *18*(2), 42-43, 46, 50.
6. Sprenkel, R. J. *Pest Control Tech.* **1988**, *16*(4), 38-40.
7. Kamble, S. T. *Subterranean Termites and Their Control.* Nebraska Cooperative Extension Service (EC 91-1556-B), Institute of Agriculture and Natural Resources, University of Nebraska-Lincoln, Lincoln, NE, **1991**.
8. Hedges, S. *Pest Control Tech.* **1989**, *17*(10), 70, 74, 76-77.
9. Dysart, J. *Pest Control* **1990**, *58*(3), 56.
10. Su, N-Y.; Scheffrahn, R. H. *J. Econ. Entomol.* **1990**, *83*(5), 1918-1924.
11. Mix, J. *Pest Control* **1991**, *59*(2), 22-23.
12. Mampe, C. D. *Pest Control* **1991**, *59*(2), 28, 30.
13. Smith, M. W. *Pest Control* **1957**, *41*(7), 36.
14. O'Brien, R. E.; Reed, J. K.; Fox, R. C. *Pest Control* **1965**, 33(2), 14-15, 42-43.
15. Frishman, A.; St. Cyr, A. *Pest Control Tech.* **1988**, *16*(4), 33-34, 36.
16. Frishman, A.; St. Cyr, A. *Pest Control Tech.* **1989**, *17*(5), 42, 44.
17. Frishman, A.; St. Cyr, A. *Pest Control Tech.* **1990**, *18*(6), 70, 72-73.
18. Frishman, A.; St. Cyr, A. *Pest Control Tech.* **1990**, *18*(11), 64, 66.
19. Brehm, W. L. *Pest Control* **1991**, *59*(2), 32-33.
20. Thomas, C.; Robinson, W. *Pest Control Tech.* **1991**, *59*(10), 60, 64, 66.
21. Thomas, C.; Robinson, W. *Pest Control Tech.* **1991**, *19*(11), 38, 42-44.
22. Potter, M.F.; Hardy, J.P.; Richardson, S.E. *Pest Control* **1991**, *59*(6), 72-73, 76-77.
23. Davis, R. W.; Kamble, S. T. *Bull. Environ. Contam. Toxicol.* **1992**, *48*, 585-591.
24. Su, N-Y. *Pest Control* **1990**, 58(9), 24, 30, 34, 36.
25. Su, N-Y.; Tamashiro, M.; Yates, J. R.; Haverty, M. I. *J. Econ. Entomol.* **1982**, *75*, 188-193.
26. Hutacharern, C.; Knowles, C. O. *J. Econ. Entomol.* **1974**, *67*, 721-727.
27. Khoo, B. K.; Sherman, M. *J. Econ. Entomol.* **1979**, *72*, 298-304.
28. Jones, S. C. Pest Management **1989**, *8*(2), 16-19.
29. Jones, S. C. *J. Econ. Entomol.* **1990**, *83*, 875-878.
30. Smith, J. L.; Rust, M. K. *J. Econ. Entomol.* **1990**, *83*, 1395-1401.
31. Smith, J. L.; Rust, M. K. *J. Econ. Entomol.* **1991**, *84*, 181-184.

RECEIVED October 30, 1992

Chapter 14

Pesticide Fate in Turf

Studies Using Model Ecosystems

B. E. Branham[1], D. R. Smitley[2], and E. D. Miltner[1]

Departments of [1]Crop and Soil Sciences and [2]Entomology, Michigan State
University, East Lansing, MI 48824

The fate of DCPA and isazofos in turfgrass was studied in specially
designed model ecosystems. The effect of irrigation frequency and the
presence of thatch on the fate of DCPA was monitored over an eight week
period. Of the six soil type/irrigation frequency treatments, only the sandy
soil with thatch irrigated every fourth day had less than 50% of the applied
dose of DCPA remaining after 8 weeks. All other treatment combinations
had between 67 and 95% of the applied DCPA remaining after 8 weeks.
No volatility or evolution of $^{14}CO_2$ was detected. The principal route of
DCPA dissipation was cleavage of the methyl ester groups to the
corresponding acid and subsequent leaching of these mobile metabolites.
Between 1 and 25% of the applied DCPA was detected as metabolites in
the leachate. The fate of isazofos in two soil types with or without thatch
was compared. The presence of turf had a small but consistent effect on
the fate of isazofos. Where turf was present, isazofos degraded more
rapidly with only 5% remaining after 4 weeks with a Kentucky bluegrass
turf whereas 13% remained in the same soil without turf. Soil
unextractable material accumulated more rapidly in soils where turf was
present indicating a more active microbial biomass. The major metabolite
detected, CGA-17193, accumulated rapidly in all soil types with between
20 to 60% of the applied radioactivity detected as CGA-17193 at one week
after treatment. CGA-17193 was more mobile in soil than isazofos with 8
to 17% CGA-17193 found in the leachate compared to 1-5% of isazofos at
4 WAT.

The movement and metabolism of pesticides applied to plants and soils has been
intensively studied over the past thirty years. These studies have been expensive, time-
consuming, and often yield information that is specific to a particular site or set of
environmental conditions. To develop a comprehensive understanding of pesticide fate for
a single pesticide has turned out to be an arduous task. In order to better understand the
movement and metabolism of pesticides, many different experimental approaches have
been tried. These include using radioactively labeled pesticides in the laboratory or

0097–6156/93/0522–0156$06.00/0

greenhouse, applying non- labeled or radioactively labeled pesticides to completely enclosed cylinders in the field, or using completely enclosed systems in a growth chamber, an approach termed model ecosystems.

The use of model ecosystems for pesticide fate research can be traced to the studies of Metcalf *(1)* who used aquarium tanks to set up a small-scale food chain. Seedlings of various crops were treated with radiolabeled pesticides and seven species of insects and predators were introduced. In this way, bioaccumulation and biomagnification of the pesticide or its metabolites through a simulated food chain could be readily studied. Other investigators *(2, 3)* modified this approach to study pesticide fate in various ecosystems. Nash and Beall *(4)* developed an agroecosystem to study pesticide fate under traditional agricultural conditions. A large glass chamber was used to grow a particular crop and a radioactively labeled pesticide was applied to the soil or crop. Loss by volatilization, plant uptake, and soil degradation were easily studied using this system.

During the 1980's, the emphasis on pesticide issues began to change as reports of groundwater contamination with pesticides and nitrates appeared with increasing regularity in many areas of the country where intensive agriculture was practiced. The presumption that pesticide and nutrient applications to turf resulted in similar groundwater contamination was widely perceived by the general public and many from the scientific community. Model ecosystems represent one approach to developing a comprehensive understanding of the fate of a particular agricultural chemical.

MATERIALS AND METHODS

The model ecosystems used to perform the experiments on the fate of DCPA (dimethyl 2,3,5,6-tetrachloro-1,4-benzenedicarboxylate) and isazofos (O,O-diethyl -O-(5-chloro-1-isopropyl-1,2,4,-triazolyl)-3-thiophosphate) have been previously described *(5)*. Briefly, the model ecosystem consists of a glass atmospheric chamber, a brass base to hold the turf samples with a porous ceramic tension plate in the bottom to simulate normal soil water movement, and traps to collect ^{14}C labeled materials leaving the system.

The analytical trapping system consists of two bubbling tubes filled with 1 N NaOH to trap CO_2. In the DCPA experiment, 2 additional bubbling tubes filled with ethylene glycol were used to trap volatilized DCPA. In the isazofos study, polyurethane foam plugs were used to trap volatilized isazofos.

The model ecosystems were housed in growth chambers. The temperatures inside the model ecosystems were 24 ± 2 and $16 \pm 1°C$ for day and night cycles, respectively in the DCPA study with a 12 hour (L:D) cycle. In the isazofos study, a photoperiod of 15:9 (L:D) and a temperature cycle of 26 ± 2 and $15 \pm 1°C$ was maintained.

Pesticide Application. DCPA was applied as a 5% granule on a 40/60 mesh montmorillonite clay carrier. Technical grade DCPA was combined with uniformly ring labeled ^{14}C DCPA to produce a 5% AI granule with a specific activity of 66 Bq mg^{-1}. These granules were applied at the recommended rate of 11.8 kg AI ha^{-1} which resulted in 0.15 MBq applied to each model ecosystem. Isazofos, labeled with ^{14}C at the 3 position of the triazole ring, was supplied by Ciba-Geigy (Greensboro, NC) and had a specific activity of 0.75 TBq Kg-1. The labeled isazofos was mixed with the standard 4E formulation of isazofos so that each model ecosystem received 2.24 kg AI ha^{-1} with

0.15 MBq of [14]C. Isazofos was applied with a 1 L hand sprayer while DCPA granules were applied with a salt shaker. All treatments were irrigated with 1.0 cm of water following application.

SOILS

DCPA Experiment. Six treatments were used in the DCPA experiment:

1. Turf growing on sandy soil with a thatch layer irrigated every four days.
2. Turf growing on sandy soil without a thatch layer irrigated every four days.
3. Turf growing on mineral soil with a 25-35 mm thatch layer irrigated every four days.
4. Turf growing on mineral soil without thatch irrigated every four days.
5. Turf growing on mineral soil without thatch irrigated daily.
6. Turf growing on mineral soil without thatch, not irrigated, and held at -.3 MPa soil moisture or less.

The properties of the four soils used in this study are listed in Table I.

Isazofos Experiment. The fate of isazofos was studied in sandy and sandy loam soils with or without turf. Sandy loam soil (58% sand, 26% silt, and 16% clay) with Kentucky bluegrass was cut intact (30 cm^2 x 5 cm deep) from the Hancock Turfgrass Research Center, Michigan State University. Sandy soil (95% sand, 1% silt and 4% clay) with bermudagrass was provided from the Ciba Geigy Research Farm in Vero Beach, FL, USA. The four treatments studied were sandy loam alone, sandy loam with Kentucky bluegrass (Poa pratensis 'Touchdown'), sandy soil alone, and sandy soil with bermudagrass (Cynodon dactylon 'common'). Kentucky bluegrass thatch was thick (20-25 mm) and dense whereas bermudagrass thatch was less thick (10-15 mm) and not as dense. All treatments were placed in the model ecosystems for 48 hr prior to pesticide application.

ANALYTICAL METHODS

DCPA Experiment. In order to trap $^{14}CO_2$, two glass bubblers connected in series were filled with 350-450 ml of 1 N NaOH. Tests showed that two bubblers in series recovered 89% of the $^{14}CO_2$ released. NaOH solutions were changed daily until the end of the experiment. Aliquots (3 ml) were counted in 15 ml of Aquasol (New England Nuclear) to determine recovered radioactivity. Two additional bubbling traps were filled with ethylene glycol and placed in a dewar flask to trap volatilized DCPA; these traps were changed every 4 days. A 100 ml aliquot of the ethylene glycol solution was extracted with 2 40 ml portions of hexane. The combined hexane extracts were dried over Na_2SO_4 and the hexane removed with air. The residue was taken up in methanol and counted to determine radioactivity.

Leachate was collected prior to each irrigation event and was stored in polyethylene bottles at 2°C until analyzed. A 5 ml aliquot was counted for gross radioactivity. The remaining solution was then extracted with 2-50 ml portions of isopropyl ether. The ether extracts were combined with 0.2 ml of 2% paraffin oil in benzene, dried over anhydrous

Table I. Analysis of soils used in DCPA experiment

Treatment	pH	% Organic Matter	Cation Exchange capacity (meq/100 g)	% Sand	% Silt	% Clay	Soil Textural Class
sandy soil without thatch (trmt. 2)	7.8	0.9	5.3	94.3	2.0	3.7	Sand
mineral soil with thatch - thatch layer only (trmt. 3)	5.8						
mineral soil with thatch - underlying soil (trmt. 3)	6.9	2.3	10.3	52.3	26.0	21.7	Sandy clay loam
mineral soil without thatch (trmts. 4,5,6)	5.7	2.8	14.8	10.3	52.0	37.7	Silty clay loam
sandy soil with thatch - thatch layer only (trmt. 1)	7.0						
sandy soil with thatch - underlying soil (trmt. 1)	7.3	21.0	4.2	94.3	2.0	3.7	Sand

Na_2SO_4, and the ether removed to dryness with a gentle stream of air. The residue was taken up in 3-5 ml of methanol and stored for HPLC analysis.

Soil Analysis. Five randomly chosen soil cores were removed at 0, 1, 2, 4, 6, and 8 weeks after DCPA application. The cores were sectioned into 0-10 mm, 10-30 mm, and 30-50 mm layers and the soil from the same depth interval was combined and stored at -10 C until analysis. A portion of the soil was used to determine the percent moisture in the soil. To extract DCPA and metabolites from soil, 50 ml of acidified acetone (95:25:2.5/acetone:H_2SO_4:H_2O) were added to a flask containing 25 gm of soil which was shaken on a wrist action shaker for two hours. The soil slurry was filtered and the filter cake was washed with 2-15 ml portions of acidified acetone. The acetone was removed by air until ca. 5 mls of solution remained. 50 mls of 0.4 N $NaHCO_3$ were added to the acetone residue and this solution was extracted 3X with 40 ml isopropyl ether. The combined ether extracts were dried over Na_2SO_4 and the ether removed to dryness with air. The residue was taken up in 3-5 ml methanol, a 0.5 ml aliquot was counted to determine gross radioactivity and the remainder was reserved for HPLC analysis.

HPLC analysis was performed on RP C_{18} column (4.6 mm x 15 cm) at a flow rate of 1.0 ml min^{-1} with a mobile phase composition of 75:25 (CH_3 OH:H_2O). A Buchler LC 100 fraction collector was used to collect peaks for assay by LSC.

Isazofos Experiment. The same system was used to trap $^{14}CO_2$ as was described for the DCPA study, the only difference was that the traps were changed every 2 days instead of daily. To trap volatilized isazofos, the air stream leaving each chamber was passed through a polyurethane foam plug which effectively removed isazofos from the air stream. The foam traps were changed at 1, 2, 3, 4, 7, 14, 21, and 28 days after isazofos application. Isazofos was recovered from the foam filters by washing with 150 ml acetone through a Buchner funnel. Tests with known amounts of radioactivity showed that 89% of applied isazofos could be recovered from the foam. Radioactivity in the extract was quantified by LSC.

Leachate was collected continuously and sampled every 4 days. The model ecosystems were irrigated with 0.5 cm of water after each sample collection. The volume of leachate was recorded and a 3 ml aliquot was taken to determine gross radioactivity. Samples were stored at -20 C until analysis. Parent compound and CGA-17193 were extracted from 100 ml subsamples of the leachate with 3-50 ml portions of hexane.

Soil Analysis. Soils were sampled at 0, 7, 14, 21, and 28 days after isazofos application. The same sampling protocol as described for the DCPA experiment was used.

Analysis of the parent compound and its major metabolite CGA-17193 (5- chloro-3-hydroxy-1-isopropyl-1, 2, 4-triazole) was based upon a method supplied by Ciba-Geigy (Research Triangle Park, NC). First, 100 ml of methanol were added to 10 g of soil and refluxed for 60 min. The extract was vacuum filtered and the methanol volume reduced to 2 ml. One ml was saved for HPLC analysis and the other 1 ml was counted for total radioactivity. The soil from the methanol reflux was resuspended in 100 ml of 0.2 N HCl and refluxed again for 60 min. to remove the major metabolite, CGA-17193. The extract was filtered, an aliquot taken for total radioactivity, and the extract was then partitioned with 3-50 ml portions of hexane. The combined hexane extracts were evaporated to dryness and the residue was taken up in 1 ml of hexane for HPLC analysis.

Unextractable soil residues were determined by combusting a 0.5 g subsample of the soil after the above extraction process was completed. The soil was oxidized in a biological oxidizer (OX-400, R. J. Harvey Instruments), the $^{14}CO_2$ trapped in 5 ml Carbo-Sorb (Packard) to which was added 10 ml of Permafluor (Packard Instruments) and radioactivity was determined by LSC.

Grass plants inside the model ecosystems were clipped 2.5 cm above the soil surface 24 hr before isazofos application and every 7 days thereafter. Subsamples (0.5 gm fresh weight) were combusted in biological oxidizer and treated as described above.

HPLC analysis of isazofos. A RP C_{18} column (4.6mm x 25cm) with a mobile phase of 63:37 (CH_3 OH: H_2O) and a flow rate of 1.0 ml min^{-1} was used to separate isazofos from CGA- 17193. Retention times for isazofos and CGA-17193 were 12.8 and 4.4 min, respectively. Sample peaks were collected directly into scintillation vials, covered with 15 ml of scintillation cocktail, and counted by LSC.

Because of variability in the application of the pesticides, recovery of ^{14}C- pesticide from the soil samples did not provide good data on the quantity of ^{14}C remaining in the soil. Therefore, since the model ecosystems are closed system, the amount of radioactivity in the soil was determined by difference. The sum of all radioactivity recovered from the $^{14}CO_2$ traps, volatility traps, and the leachate traps was subtracted from the total ^{14}C applied with the remainder assumed to be in the soil. The HPLC data was used to determine the ratio of the parent to metabolites in the soil for both experiments.

RESULTS AND DISCUSSION

DCPA Experiment. In both experiments, limited amounts of radioactivity were detected in the 10- 30 and 30-50 mm layers. These data were omitted for clarity in the presentation of the data.

The degradation and movement of DCPA is very limited compared to most organic pesticides applied to soil. No volatilization of the parent compound nor $^{14}CO_2$ from the degradation of the ring structure of the compound was detected. The only movement of DCPA from the point of application was the leaching of the acid metabolites out of the soil profile (Table II). Thus, the fate of this herbicide is straightforward; it is applied to soil or turf where it exerts its herbicidal effect until metabolized to the monomethyl ester or dicarboxylic acid metabolites. The metabolites are very mobile in soil and will readily leach to groundwater. The different soil, thatch, and irrigation treatments produced differing rates of DCPA degradation, but all fit the pattern described above (Table II). Greatest degradation of DCPA was observed on a sandy soil with thatch which was irrigated every four days. The least degradation was observed on a silty clay loam soil where the soil moisture was held at or below -.3 MPa. The influence of thatch on the degradation of DCPA was variable. A sandy soil with thatch had the highest rate of DCPA degradation while a sandy clay loam soil with thatch showed little degradation, with 90% remaining after eight weeks. These results indicate that thatch, while being primarily organic matter, could have large differences in physical properties, particularly the degree of hydrophobicity, which should be characterized.

Table II. Environmental fate of DCPA applied to different soil-thatch treatments

			Percent ^{14}C detected			
	Weeks after DCPA	Cumulative Amt.			Recovery from soil and thatch 0-10mm	
Treatment	Appl.	in leachate	Volatilization	$^{14}CO_2$	DCPA	Metabolite
	2	2	ND	ND	90	8.7
sandy soil w/thatch	4	4	ND	ND	74	22.0
irrigation	6	12	ND	ND	72	15.8
every 4 days	8	19	ND	ND	47	33.5
sandy soil	2	3	ND	ND	95	1.2
without thatch	4	5	ND	ND	94	2.0
irrigation every 4 days	6	6	ND	ND	89	5.4
	8	10	ND	ND	85	4.5
sandy clay loam	2	0.5	ND	ND	98	1.6
with thatch	4	1	ND	ND	97	2.0
irrigated every	6	2	ND	ND	94	4.4
4 days	8	4	ND	ND	91	5.7
silty clay loam	2	0	ND	ND	97	2.3
without thatch	4	1	ND	ND	92	7.4
irrigated every	6	2	ND	ND	88	9.2
4 days	8	6	ND	ND	81	12.7
silty clay loam	2	1	ND	ND	98	0.8
without thatch	4	5	ND	ND	92	3.2
irrigated daily	6	14	ND	ND	81	5.3
	8	25	ND	ND	68	7.3
silty clay loam	2	0	ND	ND	98	1.9
no irrigation	4	0.3	ND	ND	96	4.0
soil moisture	6	0.3	ND	ND	94	6.2
at -0.3 MPa or less	8	0.5	ND	ND	95	4.1

Soil type and irrigation frequency seemed to play a major role in the leaching of the metabolites through the 5 cm soil profile. The silty clay loam soil without thatch was irrigated daily and most of the metabolites were found in leachate with a small fraction remaining in the soil (Table II). The sandy soil with thatch had the next highest amount of metabolites in the leachate, however, 63% of the total metabolites remained in the soil profile. It is not clear why a higher percentage of the metabolites of DCPA were retained in the sandy soil with thatch treatment. The presence of anion exchange sites within the thatch could reduce leaching, however, the likelihood of this being a significant retention mechanism is small. The sandy soil without thatch had less total leaching than the sandy soil with thatch but nearly 70% of the metabolites were found in the leachate at week 8. In the same soil and thatch type increasing irrigation frequency resulted in an increased amount of DCPA degradation with most of the metabolites moving into the leachate.

The data presented on the degradation of DCPA is the first examination of its total fate in turf. This herbicide is a relatively old product and was registered at a time when registration standards were much less restrictive. Thus there are few studies that examine the fate of the herbicide beyond using simple bioassays *(6, 7)* or examine only the degradation of the parent *(8-10)*. Thus, it was somewhat surprising to find that EPA's recently concluded survey of pesticide contamination of well water indicated that the most commonly found pesticide was the acid metabolite of DCPA. The extreme tendency of the acid metabolites to leach was not reported in the literature although it would not be unexpected based upon the structure of these metabolites. This study demonstrates that the fate of DCPA in turf is a simple process with most of the applied DCPA being degraded and leached through the soil profile. That portion that is not leached may be incorporated into soil biomass.

Isazofos Experiment. The fate of isazofos was determined by calculating the proportion of ^{14}C from radiolabeled isazofos found in grass plants, soil, leachate, and air at 7, 14, 21, and 28 days after treatment (DAT) (Table III). Isazofos was rapidly degraded in all soil-plant systems. Only 25-50% of isazofos applied remained 1 week after application and only 5-20% remained at 4 weeks after application. In both soil types, a grass sod increased the amount of isazofos degradation when compared to bare soil. At 28 DAT, isazofos was most persistent in sandy soil without turf (20% remaining) and least persistent in sandy loam soil with Kentucky bluegrass (5% remaining). While isazofos degraded rapidly, the primary metabolite CGA 17193 appeared to be more stable. Concentrations of 30-60% of the applied radioactivity were found in the soil as CGA 17193 at 1 week after application (Table III). The percent CGA 17193 found in the soil remained in this range throughout the study for all treatments. Analysis of leachate indicated some isazofos (1-5%) moved through the 5 cm of soil in the model ecosystem, but the bulk of radioactivity in leachate was from the primary metabolite, CGA 17193 (8-17%, Table III).

Throughout these experiments the largest proportion of ^{14}C was detected as CGA 17193 in soil (Table III). The relationship among relative amounts of parent compound in soil, CGA-17193 in soil, soil unextractables and CGA 17193 in leachate indicates that isazofos was converted to CGA 17193 in soil, and the CGA 17193 was continuously leached through the soil or degraded further to unextractable soil compounds. The continuous conversion of isazofos to CGA 17193 and subsequent loss of CGA 17193 resulted in relatively stable net amounts of CGA 17193 in soil over the 28 days of these

Table III. Environmental Fate of Radiolabeled Isazofos Applied to Two Soil Types and Two Turfgrass Species ANOVA

Treatment	Days after Isazofos Applied	Cumulative Plant Uptake	Cumulative Amount in Leachate CA 171 93	Cumulative Amount in Leachate Isazofos	Cumulative Volatilization	Cumulative $^{14}CO_2$	Recovery from Soil and Thatch Soil Unextractables	Recovery from Soil and Thatch CGA 17193	Recovery from Soil and Thatch Isazofos
Sandy loam with Kentucky bluegrass	7	2	1	1	4	1	12	54	25
	14	3	1	1	5	2	20	52	15
	21	4	4	1	5	3	25	48	10
	28	6	8	1	5	4	29	42	5
Sandy loam soil	7	---	1	1	2	0	6	60	31
	14	---	4	1	2	1	9	59	25
	21	---	6	2	2	1	16	60	14
	28	---	10	2	2	1	24	48	13
Sandy with bermudagrass	7	1	2	1	2	0	13	20	50
	14	1	4	1	2	1	22	30	37
	21	2	8	2	3	2	30	40	14
	28	2	12	2	3	2	39	31	10
Sandy soil	7	---	2	2	3	0	4	50	39
	14	---	8	4	3	1	4	46	34
	21	---	12	5	4	1	7	49	22
	28	---	17	5	4	1	11	42	20
Effect									
Treatment		**	**		**	**	**	**	**
Sampling date		**	**		**	**	**	NS	**
Treatment x date		**	**		**	**	NS	NS	NS
C.V. %		11.54	19.91		40.99	25.15	21.68	14.16	27.89
# of sampling dates		4	7		8	14	4	4	4

**Significant at P = 0.05   NS = Not significant

experiments. Loss of CGA 17193 in all treatments during the last 7 days suggests that it would continue to disappear from the soil through leaching or biodegradation at a constant rate, although more slowly than the rate of loss of isazofos.

Unextractable soil compounds accumulated most rapidly in sandy soil with bermudagrass and in sandy loam soil with Kentucky bluegrass (39 and 29%, respectively at 28 DAT, Table III). Accumulation of unextractables was slower in sandy loam and sandy soil alone, where 24 and 11%, respectively, were recovered 28 DAT.

A significant amount of isazofos was recovered in the leachate only when isazofos was applied to sandy soil without turfgrass (Table III). On this soil, 5% of the applied radioactivity was recovered as the parent isazofos. All other treatments showed cumulative isazofos leaching of 1-2% over the 4 weeks of the study. The major metabolite, CGA 17193 proved to be more mobile than isazofos with a maximum of 17% recovered from the leachate of the sandy soil without turf after 4 weeks. The other treatments also showed significant leaching of CGA 17193 with values ranging from 8-12%. While these values are significant, it should be recalled that the total soil depth is only 50 mm. The proportion of isazofos in leachate steadily decreased as the proportion of CGA 17193 increased during the first 14 days. At 7, 14, and 28 DAT 50-62, 75-90 and 92-95% of the ^{14}C detected in leachate form all soil-turf systems was in the form of CGA 17193.

The amount of ^{14}C detected in grass blades steadily increased during the 28 day experiment. At 28 DAT 6% of recovered ^{14}C was from Kentucky bluegrass leaf blades and 2% from bermudagrass leaf blades (Table III).

Most of the isazofos that volatilized did so in the first 4 days after application (Table III). Only in the sandy loam soil-Kentucky bluegrass system did significant amounts of isazofos continue to volatilize for an additional 11 days. After 15 days little isazofos was detected in the air of any system. The greatest amount of isazofos volatilized in the sandy loam - Kentucky bluegrass system, followed by sandy soil alone, sandy soil with bermudagrass and sandy loam soil alone (Table III).

Very little $^{14}CO_2$ was detected over the course of the experiment from any treatment (Table III). This contrasts sharply with results obtained in earlier model ecosystem studies with diazinon where 22-55% of the applied radioactivity was recovered as $^{14}CO_2$ (5). This data shows the relative stability of CGA 17193 and the triazole ring structure in soils. The greatest $^{14}CO_2$ evolution occurred in the Kentucky bluegrass-sandy loam soil system where $^{14}CO_2$ evolution peaked 8 days after application, but was still less than 4% of the total applied.

Because the fate of isazofos was studied in a model ecosystem all major avenues of pesticide loss were monitored. No previous studies of isazofos, and only one investigation of a different insecticide (5) have attempted to evaluate relative loss of an insecticide applied to turfgrass through volatilization, soil metabolism and leaching.

In previous turfgrass studies of diazinon, chlordane and chlorpyrifos less than 1% of the applied insecticides were recovered from soil below a depth of 10mm (5, 11, 12). When Sears and Chapman (11) sampled soil at a depth of 10-25 mm below the surface 0, 3, 7 and 14 DAT with isazofos, they recovered 1, 4, 1 and <1%, respectively, of applied isazofos. Niemczyk and Krueger (12) reported 9699% of all isazofos recovered from Kentucky bluegrass in silt loam soil was found in the 19 mm thatch layer.

We found isazofos to degrade, volatilize and leach from Kentucky bluegrass with sandy loam soil at such a rate that 15% remained at 14 DAT and 5% remained at 28 DAT, which agrees with the results of Niemczyk and Krueger *(12)*. They found isazofos residues in soil and thatch to decrease by 85% from 3 hr application (3.60 ppm) to 28 days after application (0.54 ppm). However, Sears and Chapman *(11)* observed even faster degradation of isazofos in an experiment on a golf course fairway where they recovered less than 2% of the applied isazofos 14 days after application.

We found 1-4% of applied isazofos in the leachate at 14 DAT. Less isazofos (0-1%) was recovered in leachate from 14 to 28 DAT. An important avenue of isazofos loss from all soil-turfgrass systems was as CGA 17193 in the leachate. The amount of CGA 17193 that leached through the 50 mm of soil and thatch depended largely on the soil texture and surface vegetation. CGA 17193 leached through sandy soil at a rate 2-fold greater than it leached through sandy loam soil (Table III). In our studies, the presence of turfgrass slowed leaching of CGA 17193 through the soil turfgrass system.

Greater volatilization of isazofos in the Kentucky bluegrass-sandy loam system compared to the other systems is difficult to explain. The amount of increased surface vegetation does not explain the increase in volatility because volatility was greater in sandy soil alone compared to sandy soil with bermudagrass. Also, soil type does not explain volatility well because sandy loam soil alone volatilized the least amount of isazofos. Thatch may be a factor because the bluegrass-sandy loam system was the only one with a significant amount of thatch. In previous studies with diazinon, thatch had no effect on the rate of diazinon volatility *(5)*.

Soil degradation of isazofos to unextractable soil compounds was two to three-fold more rapid in soil with turfgrass compared to soil alone. The amount of $^{14}CO_2$ trapped with turf present was also greater than that with soil alone, suggesting that microbial degradation of isazofos was greater when turf was present.

One purpose of this study was to evaluate the effect of turfgrass on the environmental fate of isazofos. Applications to turf resulted in a more rapid dissipation of parent isazofos when compared to the same soil without a turfgrass cover. Significantly less leaching of isazofos occurred in sandy loam soil than in sandy soil. Bermudagrass turf significantly reduced leaching compared to sandy soil alone, while bluegrass turf reduced isazofos leaching but not significantly. Both turf types increased the degradation of isazofos and CGA 17193 compared to the same for soil alone. More ^{14}C was found in the soil unextractable fraction at the conclusion of the study in the soils with turf than in soils alone, indicating a more active microbial biomass where turf was present.

CONCLUSIONS

The above data provide useful information on the environmental fate of two pesticides, DCPA and isazofos, commonly used in turfgrass management. While environmental fate data may be useful for newly registered compounds for which little published data is available, the real questions surrounding pesticide use relate to the potential for off-target movement and more specifically the potential for leaching. While the study of DCPA movement provides ample evidence for groundwater contamination, the isazofos study is much less clear-cut. Leaching of a few percent of the applied dose may or may not be enough to cause significant groundwater contamination. Data collected under natural field conditions will give the most accurate and reliable data on pesticide leaching. For all the data generated by a model ecosystem approach, the chief disadvantage is that it is not field collected data. In addition, most model ecosystems suffer from a very shallow soil profile. Our soil depth was only 5 cm but most do not exceed 15 cm.

Recently, our approach to pesticide fate issues has changed to focus on the leaching of pesticides and nutrients in the field. To carefully study this aspect of pesticide fate, large, non-weighing container lysimeters are being used. These lysimeters are termed soil monolith lysimeters to denote that they contain an intact core of soil instead of being back-filled with excavated soil as is most commonly done. Four cylindrical lysimeters 1 m^2 in surface area by 1.2 m deep have recently been installed at our research facility in E. Lansing, MI. These lysimeters will form the basis for future studies of pesticide and nutrient leaching in turf.

LITERATURE CITED

1. Metcalf, R. L.; Sangha, G. K.; Kapoor, I. P. *Environ. Sci. Technol.* **1971**, *5*, 709-713.
2. Isensee, A. R.; Kearney, E. A.; Woolson, E. A.; Jones, G. E.; Williams, V. P. *Environ. Sci. Technol.* **1973**, *7*, 841-845.
3. Gillett, J. W.; Gile, J. D. *Int. J. Environ. Stud.*, **1976**, *10*, 15-22.
4. Nash, R. G.; Beall, M. L. Jr; Harris, W. G. *J. Agric. Food Chem.*, **1977**, *25*, 336-341.
5. Branham, B. E.; Wehner, D. J.; Torello, W. A.; Turgeon, A. J. *Agron. J.*, **1985**, *77*, 176-180.
6. Cardenas, J.; Santelman, P.W. *Weeds*, **1966**, *14*, 309-312.
7. Menges, R.M.; Hubbard, J.L. *Weed Sci.*, **1970**, *18*, 247-252.
8. Walker, A. *Weed Res.*, **1978**, *18*, 305-313.
9. Hurto, K.A.; Turgeon, A.J.; Cole, M.A. *Weed Sci.*, **1979**, *27*, 154-157.
10. Choi, J.S.; Fermanian, T.W.; Wehner, D.J.; Spomer, L.A. *Agron J.*, **1988**, *80*, 108-113.
11. Sears, M. K.; Chapman, R. A. *J. Econ. Entomol.* **1979**, *72*, 272-274.
12. Niemczyk, H. D.; Krueger, H. R. *J. Econ. Entomol.* **1987**, *80*, 950-952.

RECEIVED October 30, 1992

Chapter 15

Potential Leaching of Herbicides Applied to Golf Course Greens

A. E. Smith and W. R. Tillotson

Agronomy Department, University of Georgia, Griffin, GA 30223–1797

A critical issue facing the turfgrass industry is the environmental fate and safety of pesticides used in the management of recreational facilities. The purpose of our research program was to develop a data base for the determination of the potential movement of pesticides from golf course greens into potable aquifers. Lysimeters were developed, in the greenhouse, for the measurement of herbicide leaching from simulated greens. Data were obtained from lysimeters containing 'Tifdwarf' bermudagrass maintained as simulated greens and receiving treatments of the dimethylamine salt of 2,4-D as a split application at rates of 0.56 + 0.56 kg ae ha^{-1} on a two week interval. Only minute quantities of 2,4-D were detected in the effluent from the lysimeters containing two mixtures of rooting media. These data were compared to the estimated values obtained from the GLEAMS mathematical model simulations using parameters independently determined to describe the lysimeter system. The GLEAMS model overestimated the actual data-values received from the lysimeter experiments on the potential for 2,4-D to leach through both rooting-media profiles.

Although agriculture represents the largest use of pesticides in North America, use on turfgrass is a routine part of modern living. The use of pesticides has tremendous impact on productivity and quality of turfgrass. Color, uniformity, and density may be affected adversely by incursions of weeds, disease, and insects. The public demand for high quality and uniform turf often requires the use of intensive management to maximize pest control and nutrient availability *(18)*. Pesticides promote sustained turf quality, reduced labor costs, and reduced energy expenses. Accurate estimates of the quantity of pesticides used on turfgrass are difficult to develop, since most of the pesticides produced for this market are available through a wide variety of outlets and may be applied by the owner, by a pest control operator, or by municipal or other government agencies. Probably, on an area basis, golf course greens receive more pesticides than most other turfgrass uses. Despite the obvious cultural and economic benefits, conflicts have developed over pesticide use in relation to environmental quality issues.

TURFGRASS PESTICIDES

Turfgrass is typically the most intensively managed biotic system in urban landscapes. The increasing interest by the general public for the environmental impact and human safety of certain management practices used at recreational facilities is a major concern for the research and regulatory institutions responsible for turfgrass management practices. A critical issue facing the turfgrass industry is the environmental fate and safety of pesticides used in the management of recreational facilities. The enhanced interest in nutrient and pesticide use is, in general, a response to their increased use since the 1960s and the advancements in technology allowing scientists to detect their presence at very low concentrations. Many compounds which, because of their constituents (many contain halogens or nitrogen), can be detected in sub-parts per billion. Once the part per million was the visible limit, now we commonly measure things in parts per trillion. We will achieve recognition of concentrations of a part per quadrillion in the next decade. One day, we may recognize that there is something of everything in everything else, and that a glass of water probably contains a molecule of every compound on earth. "Yesterday's zero is no longer zero, and today's zero will not be zero tomorrow" *(11)*.

Concerns for the wide-spread use of pesticides began to develop during the 1950s and 1960s. The public alarm raised about pesticides in the 1960s has been translated into legislative controls. The results have been more rigid testing of pesticides prior to their registration and attempts to restrict pesticide application to competent people. Concerns about human and environmental welfare have been an important concept behind this legislation and the growing concern will, ultimately, result in more legislated controls on the use of pesticides. Since many of the controls placed on pesticide use increases the visibility of a use (i.e. mandatory posting of the area prior to treatment), public inquiries are also increased. A common problem in the scientific community is the concern that we may not have all of the answers for these inquiries and there must be a concerted effort to develop research programs of risk assessment for pesticide uses.

A major concern for the impact of pesticides on the environment is their potential entrance into drinking water sources which is facilitated by movement in surface water and groundwater from the treated site. Although the preponderance of the drinking water for rural areas comes from groundwater, much of the drinking water in urban areas is derived from surface water containments such as reservoirs. It is estimated that as much as 95% of the drinking water for some major metropolitan areas comes from reservoirs. Nutrients and pesticides are transported to surface water containments in runoff water and eroded sediment. Erosion and surface runoff processes in relation to water quality and environmental impacts have been examined by Anderson et al. *(1)*, Leonard *(12)*, and Stewart et al. *(22)*. Although conclusive evidence of health effects from long-term exposure to pesticides has yet to be established, there is intense public perception of risk concerning pesticides in drinking water *(19)*. The EPA is currently working to establish drinking water standards of reference doses for surface and groundwater *(10)*. Standards will be based on the same toxicological research used to establish reference doses (formerly called Acceptable Daily Intake, or ADI) for food. These standards will be the maximum contaminant levels (MCLs) allowed for pesticide concentrations in potable water. The MCLs for only a few pesticides used on turfgrass have been recommended. The recommended MCL for 2,4-D is 70 ppb. In addition to federal efforts to alleviate environmental quality concerns, state governments are in the process of developing water quality regulations *(5, 14)*. State governments recognize the need to protect valuable surface and groundwater resources through both education and enforcement. Some states, such as California, New York, Nebraska, and Wisconsin have selected a regulatory approach to water quality issues *(14)*. Others, including Iowa, are legislating a combined approach of education, research, and demonstration *(9)*.

The initial distribution of the chemical applied to turfgrass ultimately determines the amount of pesticide reaching the intended target and the amount of pesticide that will be lost from the turf ecosystem before reaching the intended target. There are many obstacles that a molecule must maneuver following application before reaching a point of concern in the environment. A pesticide that is primarily distributed in the turf canopy may undergo significant volatilization and/or photo-oxidation. These initial losses of applied chemical will result in insufficient pesticide concentrations to affect the intended target pest. A pesticide that is initially distributed in the thatch layer may be strongly adsorbed. Sequestering of a pesticide in the thatch may reduce its efficacy and possibly delay degradation. The pesticides may form complexes with water soluble organic compounds which are susceptible to leaching losses. The initial distribution of a pesticide in the turf system is a function of the type and rate of pesticide applied, the method used to apply the pesticide, and the rate and timing of subsequent watering or irrigation. Available information on the mobility and potential for contaminating ground water of pesticides used on turf is limited. Cohen et al. *(4)* sampled and analyzed water from 16 monitoring wells on golf courses and found chlorpyrifos, 2,4-D, dicamba, isofenophos, and trichloropyridinol in one of the wells, chlorothalonil in 2 wells, DCPA in 3 wells, heptachlor epoxide in 4 wells, chlordane in 7 wells and DCBA in 9 wells. Eighty percent of the compounds were found in concentrations less than 5.0 ppb. In a comprehensive review of turf pesticides, Walker et al. *(25)* concluded that "Quantitative data on national or regional pesticide use for pest and disease management on golf courses is currently not available".

Currently, there are over 14,000 golf courses in the United States. Assuming an average size of 120 acres per course *(2)*, there are over 1.68 million acres of turfgrass in the golf course industry. Assuming that 2% of these acres are managed for putting greens there are 31.2 thousand acres of greens in the United States. The National Golf Foundation estimates that a golf course will need to be opened every day, during the 1990's to keep pace with the projected increase in the number of golfers *(15)*.

Many golf course greens are constructed for maximum infiltration and percolation of water through the rooting media. Root zone mixture composition generally includes at least 85% by volume (97% by mass) sand allowing for rapid water percolation and an extremely low cation exchange capacity. Additionally, soil sterilization is recommended during construction for weed and disease management *(24)*. The sterilization ultimately influences the soil microbial decomposition of applied pesticides. These characteristics of the root zone mixture could allow for the rapid movement of pesticides through the rooting mixture allowing for a potential source of contamination of the effluent water from the greens into surface water drainage channels. However, the tight thatch overlying the rooting media is very important in the retention and degradation of most pesticides.

Studies by several investigators *(3, 6 ,16, 20, 21)* showed that the chlorinated hydrocarbon insecticide chlordane and several organophosphorus pesticides were retained in large amounts (>90%) by bluegrass thatch and that only small amounts (<10%) leached below the thatch zone. Gold *(7)*, in studies with dicamba and 2,4-D, however, found 1.0 and 0.4 percent, respectively, of the total amounts applied to pass through the turf thatch.

The objective of our research program is to develop a data base for the determination of the potential movement of pesticides from urban landscapes into potable aquifers. The information included in this report is a summary of our research program designed to determine the potential for pesticide movement from golf course greens containing 'Tifdwarf' bermudagrass and 'Penncross' bentgrass.

MATERIALS AND METHODS

Construction of Lysimeters for Measuring Herbicide Leaching from Simulated Greens. Thirty-six lysimeters were constructed,in the greenhouse, by placing turfgrass growth boxes (40 X 40 X 15 cm deep) on top of a base. The bottom of the wooden growth boxes was perforated steel and at the inside-center of the growth boxes a 13 cm length of polyvinyl chloride (PVC) tubing (15 cm diam.) was fastened to the bottom with acrylic caulk. The base of the lysimeter consisted of a 60 cm length of PVC tubing (15 cm diam.) with a cap over one end (bottom) of the tube. The cap had a drain tube placed in the bottom for the collection of aqueous effluent in 1-L black glass bottles. The growth boxes were designed to be removed from the bases to allow for the pesticide application to the turfgrass sod using a spray chamber at a location separate from the greenhouse in order to minimize contamination to the greenhouse.

Prescribed rooting mixtures (sand and sphagnum peat moss) are based on the percolation rate as determined for the sand used in the mixture. The proportions were selected to give percolation rates of 39 and 33 cm hr^{-1} which are prescribed for bentgrass and bermudagrass greens, respectively. The rooting-media mixture of sand and sphagnum peat moss at v:v ratios of 85:15 and 80:20 (2.26 and 3.17% organic carbon by weight, respectively) resulted in the respective percolation rates. The rooting media were steam sterilized prior to use. The lysimeter bases were filled with sized gravel (10 cm), coarse sand (7.5 cm), and rooting mix (42.5 cm) in ascending sequence from the bottom simulating USGA specifications for greens construction *(14)*. The layers were carefully packed, using a vibrating table, which gave the rooting mix horizon a total porosity of 0.49 cm^3 cm^{-3}. The 85:15 mixture had a field capacity of 0.13 cm^3 cm^{-3}, a wilting point of 0.03 cm^3 cm^{-3} and an effective saturated conductivity of 39.6 cm hr^{-1}. The 80:20 mixture had a field capacity of 0.15 cm^3 cm^{-3}, a wilting point of 0.50 cm^3 cm^{-3} and an effective saturated conductivity of 33.5 cm hr^{-1}.

The lysimeter base was located against the bottom of the growth box aligned with the PVC tube on the inside of the box for direction of the aqueous percolation from the center of the growth box into the base of the lysimeter. The depth of the rooting mix in the combined PVC tubes was 55.5 cm. Although the total growth box was sodded and treated to minimize edge effects, the only area of concern for effluent movement was the area directly above the lysimeter base (182.3 cm^2). 'Tifdwarf' bermudagrass was sodded in all lysimeters allowing for the determination of the influence of the two organic matter contents in the rooting media on pesticide movement. The bases of the lysimeters were enclosed and cooled by an air conditioner in order to maintain the soil temperature between 18-21°C. The lysimeters were housed in a greenhouse covered with Lexan[R] thermoclear sheet glazing. The glazing has approximately 90% the light transmission of monolithic glass and a transmission of 80% for the wavelengths between 400 and 1200 nm. The ambient temperature was monitored and controlled (27-30°C) with a steam heating system and water cooled pads.

An automatic track-irrigation system was developed for controlling the rates and times for irrigation. The watering nozzles traversed a horizontal track located above the growth boxes at a speed of 2.9 m min-1. The flow rate of the water was adjusted to a rate of 1.82 ml sec-1 at 20 psi. The daily irrigation of 0.625 cm of water and a weekly rain event of 2.54 cm were controlled with an automatic timer. These conditions were chosen to simulate management practices and average rainfall events for golf course greens in central Georgia. During watering the coefficients of variation (CV) were less than 8.0% across the boxes laterally and on the length of the track.

Our program was recently initiated and the past year was devoted to developing the greenhouse lysimeters and methods for herbicide analyses. A single treatment was conducted under the described conditions in the greenhouse lysimeters. The dimethylamine salt (DMA) of 2,4-D was applied to 'Tifdwarf' bermudagrass established on the two rooting mixes (85:15 and 80:20). The herbicide was applied as a split application at rates of 0.56 + 0.56 kg ae ha-1 on a two-week interval. The treatments were applied in 4 replications to lysimeters containing both rooting mixes and the first application was made on November 5, 1991. Effluent samples were collected weekly for a 77-day period to quantify the herbicide passing through the lysimeters.

Future treatments will include the herbicides registered by the Environmental Protection Agency for use on golf course greens (Table I) and all treatments will be applied in 3 replications on May 1, 1992 to approximate a standard time of treat for these post emergence herbicides.

Table I. Herbicide Treatments to be Applied to Greenhouse Lysimeters

Herbicide	Rate (kg ha-1)	
	'Penncross' bentgrass	'Tifdwarf' bermudagrass
greenhouse		
2,4-D DMA[1]	0.3	0.56 + 0.56 (2 wk)
2,4-D BEE[2]	0.3	0.56 + 0.56 (2 wk)
dicamba	0.067	0.28
mecoprop	0.56	1.25
dithiopyr	0.56	0.56

[1]DMA = dimethylamine salt formulation
[2]BEE = butoxyethyl ester formulation

Extraction and Analysis of Pesticides in the Lysimeter Leachates. Methods for herbicide extraction from the effluent samples and analytical methods utilized for the 2,4-D, mecoprop, and dicamba were adapted from published procedures *(23)* and procedures developed in our laboratory. Subsamples of 100 mL are transferred from the storage bottle into a 250 mL beaker. An internal standard (2,4,5-T) was added to the beaker and the mixed solution is acidified to a pH of 2 with 0.2M HCl. The herbicides are extracted from the acidified solution by liquid-liquid partitioning into 200 mL diethyl ether. The diethyl ether is evaporated, the herbicides are esterified with diazomethane *(22)*, and the methyl esters are quantified by gas chromatography using an electron capture detector (ECD). The diazomethane is prepared fresh each day. The gas chromatograph is equipped with a capillary column (30 m X 0.50 mm i.d. Rtx-35 fused silica megabore, 0.5 μm thickness, Restek Corporation). Inlet, oven and detector temperatures were 220, 210, and 325°C, respectively. The helium carrier gas head pressure is adjusted until a 1 μL head space sampling from methylene chloride has a retention time of 2.5 min. Nitrogen is used for make-up and purge gas at flow rates of 10 and 50 mL min^{-1}, respectively. The extraction and quantification systems were established to give a lower limit of herbicide concentration detection at 7 μg L^{-1} in the aqueous effluent. This lower limit was determined as adequate considering that the concentration is 10-fold less than the MCL (70 μg L^{-1}) established for 2,4-D *(17)*.

Dithiopyr will be analyzed according to the method developed in our laboratory *(8)*. Dithiopyr is extracted from the aqueous phase and concentrated on LC-18 solid phase extraction tubes (Supelco, Inc.), elutriated from the solid phase with toluene, and analyzed by ECD gas chromatography on a Rtx-35 megabore column. The operation temperatures for the GC inlet, oven, and detector are 250, 200, and 325°C, respectively. Metribuzin is used as an internal standard. This system yielded recovery levels near 99% dithiopyr in aqueous-solution volumes ranging from 4 to 80 mL containing concentrations ranging from 1 to 100 μg L^{-1}.

The treatments, sampling, and laboratory analyses are conducted according to the Good Laboratory Practice Standards as established in Federal Register 40 CFR part 160 and in compliance with standards established by USGA.

Mathematical Predictions. A relative potential for selected turfgrass pesticides to leach has been estimated by Weber *(27)* and is termed the Herbicide Leaching Potential (HLP). The HLP ranged from 0.01 for chemicals with a very high potential to contaminate groundwater to 893 for chemicals with extremely low potential to contaminate ground water. The assumption is made that half of the pesticide applied to established turf reaches the soil. The leaching potential of a soil depends on many characteristics, but ones that are of greatest importance to herbicide movement are texture, organic matter, and pH *(27)*. In order to develop a Soil Leaching Potential index (SLP), Weber *(27)* assigned weighted factors of 3, 10, and 4 to the above characteristics, respectively. Dissolved chemicals move most readily through sand and silt and least readily through clay to muck. Thus the rating scheme for various soil textures progresses from 1 for clay or muck and 10 for sand, loamy sand, sandy loam, loam, silt-loam, or silt. Adsorption increases and mobility decreases as soil organic matter content increases, thus the rating scheme for various organic matter levels are assigned from 1 for soils with high organic matter content to 10 for soils with low organic matter content. The rating scheme for various soil pH levels ranges from 1, for soils with pH levels less than 5, to 10, for soils with pH levels greater than 7.0. The SLP is the sum of the products of the rating and the weighted factors for texture, organic matter content, and pH of the soil. Using a matrix for the SLP and HLP allows one to determine the Ground Water Contamination Potential (GWCP). The GWCP ratings range from "hazardous" for the case where the herbicide has a high HLP and it is to be used on a soil with a high SLP to "safe" for cases where herbicides with low SLPs are considered for use on soils with high, moderate or low SLPs (27).

The GLEAMS (Groundwater Loading Effects of Agricultural Management Systems) mathematical model (13) was used to aid in an initial identification of significant chemical and soil properties, and plant and meteorological factors influencing the leaching of herbicides applied to golf course greens. Experimental observations of herbicide leaching for evaluating the GLEAMS model were derived from the 'Tifdwarf' bermudagrass simulated greens in the greenhouse lysimeters described earlier.

For the GLEAMS model simulations, model parameters were independently determined when possible to describe the greenhouse lysimeter system. The 'Tifdwarf' bermudagrass provided a dense and uniform vegetative surface with a leaf area index assumed to be 2.5 and which intercepted all of the herbicide during application. Herbicide properties were obtained from Wauchope et al. (26) (Table II). The 2,4-D application was split with 0.56 kg ae ha^{-1} being applied on simulation days 4 (Tuesday, November 5, 1991) and 19 (Wednesday, November 20, 1991) of a 120 day simulation. All of the 2,4-D on the vegetative surface was assumed to be available to washoff from the daily overhead water applications of 0.625 cm except on Friday of each week when there was a 2.54 cm rainfall simulation. No other water was received by the lysimeters and no water was applied on the days of herbicide application. The washoff threshold for herbicide on the vegetative surface was 0.25 cm of water as computed by the GLEAMS model. A net first-order foliar degradation parameter for 2,4-D was considered (Table II). The monthly maximum and minimum air temperatures required for the GLEAMS model were calculated from values measured daily in the greenhouse where the lysimeter system was located. The monthly solar radiation values corresponded to averages for the Atlanta, GA area.

Table II. Properties of herbicides used in the GLEAMS model

Herbicide	Water Solubility	K_{oc}	Foliar Half-Life	Soil Half-Life
	(mg/L)	(ml/g)	(days)	(days)
2,4-D (DMA)	8.0×10^5	20	8.3	10
2,4-D (BEE)	100	100	0.8	10
dicamba (DMA)	4.0×10^5	2	8.3	14
MCPP (DMA)	6.6×10^5	20	5.0	21
dithiopyr	1.38	1638	8.3	18

SOURCE: Adapted from ref. 26

The bermudagrass-covered soil profiles with a depth of 55.5 cm consisting of a single horizon (rooting media) containing either 85:15 or 80:20 (v:v) sand:sphagnum mixture. A single value for the net first-order soil degradation of herbicides was used for the entire profile (Table II). No transformation products were assumed to result from the soil degradation of the herbicides.

To examine the influence of the bermudagrass thatch on herbicide transport through golf course greens the surface of the existing rooting media was modified in the GLEAMS model to include a thin surface horizon. This horizon extended from the surface to a depth of 1.40 cm and had an organic matter content of 5.80% (mass basis) (personnel communication with R. N. Carrow). The surface horizon was identical in all other characteristics to the subtending horizon.

RESULTS AND DISCUSSION

Pesticides begin to disperse from the target area, upon application. Partitioning of the pesticides in the environment and potential loss of pesticides to groundwater and surface water is determined by innumerable interacting factors and conditions. The potential for pesticides to leach to groundwater depends on the: 1) properties of the chemical, 2) properties of the soil, 3) application conditions, and 4) climatic conditions *(25)*. Chemicals found most often in groundwater had many of the following characteristics: 1) highly mobile in soil leaching studies (high Rf values), 2) low retention by soil in adsorption studies (low K_{oc} values), 3) applied at moderate to high rates over large acreage, and 4) moderate to long lived in the environment (half-lives of 30 days or longer) *(22)*. We used a mathematical equation *(27)* and the GLEAMS model to predict the potential for pesticides to move through bermudagrass and bentgrass greens, and compared the predictions with data from the lysimeter experiments.

When using the groundwater contamination potential (GWCP) classification proposed by Weber *(27)* as a criterion for determining herbicide use on golf course greens, DMA formulations of 2,4-D, dicamba, and mecoprop would be considered as Risky (Table III). These herbicides are commonly applied as the DMA formulation in which the molecules have a high water solubility and a low K_{oc} (<50 mL g^{-1}) resulting in a high HLP rating. Golf course greens that are constructed according to USGA specifications *(24)* have a sandy texture, 2-4% organic matter, and a pH of 6-7 resulting in an SLP rating of moderate. The combined effect from the high HLP and moderate SLP ratings is a GWCP of Risky for these herbicides. Dithiopyr, MSMA, and fenarimol have low HLPs and GWCPs that are classed as safe.

Only minute quantities of 2,4-D were detected in the effluent from the lysimeters containing the two rooting media (Figures 1 and 2). The extraction and analytical methods were developed to give a minimum-dependable sensitivity for 2,4-D at 0.005 mg L^{-1} and the peak areas were comparable to 0.002 mg L^{-1} or less indicating that only a trace of 2,4-D leaches through the rooting media and the aqueous concentration is several orders of magnitude less than the MCL standard of 70 µg L^{-1} established by the Office of Drinking Water U.S. EPA *(17)*. It would appear that this concentration of herbicide in the effluent water is probably not deserving of the risky rating for the GWCP (Table III). There is no question that the GWCP rating system is good for a general indication of herbicide leaching potential. However, our data indicate that the equation overestimates

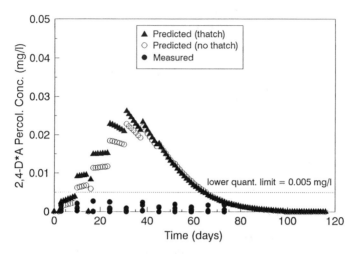

Figure 1. Predicted (using the GLEAMS model) and measured 2,4-D concentration (percol. conc.) in effluent from greenhouse lysimeters containing sand:peat (80:20%) over 120 days following applications of 0.56 kg ae ha⁻¹ 2,4-D (DMA) on simulation days 4 and 19.

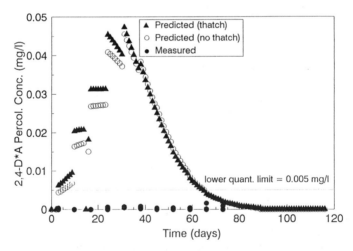

Figure 2. Predicted (using the GLEAMS model) and measured 2,4-D concentration (percol. conc.) in effluent from greenhouse lysimeters containing sand:peat (85:15%) over 120 days following applications of 0.56 kg ae ha⁻¹ 2,4-D (DMA) on simulation days 4 and 19.

the actual water contamination level. It must be realized that greenhouse conditions are much more amenable to herbicide degradation prior to movement from the thatch layer than the conditions assumed by Weber *(27)*.

Table III.   Herbicide leaching potential index (HLP) and groundwater contamination potential for herbicides commonly used on golf course greens [soil leaching potential (SLP) for greens mix is 114 (moderate)]

Herbicide	HLP	GWCP
2,4-D	H	RISKY
dicamba	H	RISKY
mecoprop	H	RISKY
MSMA	L	SAFE
dithiopyr	L	SAFE
fenarimol	L	SAFE

SOURCE:Adapted from ref. 27.

Additionally, the GLEAMS model overestimated the actual data-values received from the lysimeter study for the potential of 2,4-D to leach through both rooting-media profiles (Figure 1 and 2). The GLEAMS model data infers that the increased level of sphagnum peat in the rooting medium reduced the 2,4-D concentration in the aqueous effluent. Since the observed levels of 2,4-D were below the lower limit of quantification, it was impossible to determine an influence of the increased organic matter content in the rooting media on the 2,4-D concentration in the aqueous effluent. The inclusion of the thatch layer in the GLEAMS model did not alter the concentration of 2,4-D in the aqueous effluent from lysimeters containing the rooting media compared to noninclusion (Figure 1 and 2). Even though the GLEAMS model greatly overestimates the observed herbicide load, the maximum predicted concentration of 0.048 mg L^{-1} is less than the MCL standard (70 ppb) established for 2,4-D. Differences between the measured and predicted leaching of 2,4-D can partially be accounted for by the lack of quantitative understanding of herbicide fate on the vegetative surface and in the turfgrass thatch horizon. Specific processes needing attention are volatilization, sorption, and degradation. The identification of these processes is supported by the reasonable agreement of predicted and measured average daily percolation values (Figures 3 and 4). Future research efforts should evaluate GLEAMS and additional mathematical models for their ability to predict herbicide fate in turfgrass.

For both the 85:15 and 80:20 rooting media the predicted daily percolation out of the bottom of the 55.5 cm profiles exceeded the average daily percolation calculated from measured values (Figures 3 and 4). Differences between the measured and predicted average daily percolation values could partially result from the inability of the GLEAMS

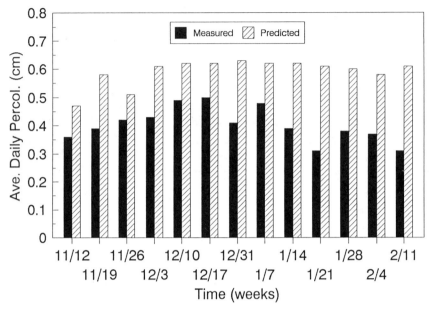

Figure 3. Predicted (using the GLEAMS model) and measured average (ave.) daily water percolation (percol.) through greenhouse lysimeters containing sand:peat (80:20%) following water applications of 6.29 cm during the week.

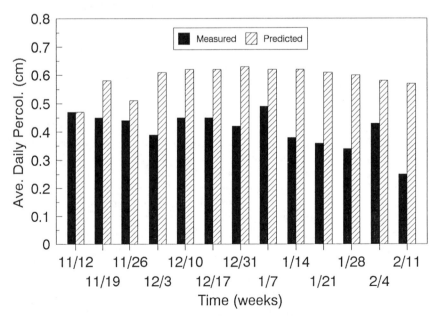

Figure 4. Predicted (using the GLEAMS model) and measured average (ave.) daily water percolation (percol.) through greenhouse lysimeters containing sand:peat (85:15%) following water applications of 6.29 cm during the week.

model to accurately predict hourly or daily evapo-transpiration from the limited climatological data entered into the model. Precautions were taken to restrict the evaporation of the collected percolate from the collection device over the sampling period.

The use of the GLEAMS model for the prediction of the transport of herbicides through the simulated greens in the lysimeters indicated that the potential for high concentrations of the DMA formulations of 2,4-D, dicamba, and mecoprop to exit the lysimeters with both rooting media was higher than the BEE formulation of 2,4-D and dithiopyr (Table IV). The higher organic matter content in the rooting media decreased the herbicide transport. The predicted increased quantity of dicamba and mecoprop to exit the lysimeters compared to the DMA formulation of 2,4-D is probably due to the lower K_{oc} and higher soil half-life for dicamba and the higher water solubility and soil half-life for mecoprop.

Table IV. Predicted transport of selected herbicides below 55.5 cm after 116 days

Herbicides	85% Sand-15% Peat		80% Sand-20% Peat	
	(g/ha)	(% applied)	(g/ha)	(% applied)
2,4-D (DMA)	93.0	8.3	52.8	4.7
	[97.8]	[8.7]	[58.5]	[5.2]
2,4-D (BEE)	0.9	0.1	0.1	0.0
	[1.1]	[0.1]	[0.08]	[0.0]
dicamba (DMA)	42.7	38.8	37.5	34.1
	[43.3]	[39.3]	[38.1]	[34.6]
MCPP (DMA)	298.4	21.3	209.6	15.0
	[302.0]	[21.6]	[216.7]	[15.5]
dithiopyr	0.0	0.0	0.0	0.0
	[0.0]	[0.0]	[0.0]	[0.0]

[ ] = values corresponding to presence of thatch; 1.40 cm depth and 5.80% organic matter by weight.

ACKNOWLEDGMENTS

We express gratitude to A. Lee, N. Mantripragada, B. Nicholls, H. Peeler, L. Robicheaux, and W. Slaughter for their assistance. Funding for this research is furnished by the United States Golf Association and the Georgia Golf Course Superintendents Association.

LITERATURE CITED

1. Anderson, J. L., J. C. Balogh, and M. Waggoner. *State Nutrient and Pest Management Workshop Proc.* USDA SCS St. Paul MN, **1989**; 453 pp.

2. Beard, J. B. *Turf management for golf courses*; Macmillan Pub. Co.: New York, NY, 1982; 642 pp.
3. Braham, B. E.; Webner, D. J. *Agron. J.* **1985**, *77*, 101-104.
4. Cohen, S. Z.; Nickerson, S.; Maxey, R.; Dupay, A.; Senita, J. A.; *Ground Water Monit. Rev.* **1990**, *10*, 160-173.
5. Fairchild, D. M. *Ground water quality and agricultural practices.* Lewis Publ.Co.: Chelsea, MI, **1987**; 273-294.
6. Goh, K. S.; Edminston, S; Maddy, K. T.; Meinders, D. D.; Margetich, S. *Bull. Environ. Contam. Toxicol.* **1986**, *37*, 27-32.
7. Gold, A. J.; Morton, T. G.; Sullivan, W. M.; McClory, J. *Water Air Soil Poll.* **1988**, *37*, 121-129.
8. Hong, S.; Smith, A. E. *J. Agric. and Food Chem.* **1992**, In Press.
9. Johnson, P. W. *Agricultural chemicals and groundwater protection: Emerging management and policy.* Freshwater Foundation: St. Paul, MN, **1988**; 167-170.
10. Kimm, V. J.; Barles, R. *Agricultural chemicals and groundwater protection: Emerging management and policy.* Freshwater Foundation: St. Paul, MN, **1988**; 135-145.
11. Lehr, J. H. *J. Prod. Agric.* **1991**, *4*, 282-290.
12. Leonard, R. A. In; *Environmental Chemistry of Herbicides*; Grover, R., Ed.; CRC Press: Boca Raton, FL, **1988**, Vol. 1.
13. Leonard, R. A.; Knisel, W. G.; Still, D. A.; 1987. *Trans. ASAE* **1987**, 30, 1403-1418.
14. Morandi, L. *Agricultural chemicals and groundwater protection: Emerging management and policy.* Freshwater Foundation: St. Paul, MN, **1988**; 163-166.
15. National Golf Foundation. *Golf Market Today*; **1991**, March/April: 2-3.
16. Niemzcyk, H. D.; Filary, A.; Krueger, H. R. *Western Views Magazine.* **1988**, Jan.-Feb. p. 7.
17. Office of Drinking Water USEPA. *Drinking water regulations and health advisories.* U. S. Printing: Washington, D. C. **1990**. H04-IID-PESTI.
18. Potter, D. A.; Cockfield, S. D.; Morris, T. A. *Ecological side effects of pesticide and fertilizer use on turfgrass.* 1989-625-030 U.S. Environmental Protection Agency: Washington, D.C. **1989**, 33-44.
19. Pratt, P. F. *Council for Agricultural Science and Technology.* **1985**, Cast Report No. 103. 62 pp.
20. Sears, M. K.; Bowhey, C.; Braun, H.; Stevenson, G. R. *Pestic. Sci.* **1987**, M. K.; Chapman, R. A. *Advances in Turfgrass Entomology*; Hammer Graphics, Inc.: Piqua, OH; **1984**; 57-59.
22. Stewart, B. A. et al. *U. S. EPA and USDA ARS.* EPA 600/2-75-026: **1984**. Vol. I. 111 pp.
23. U.S. EPA. In *Determination of chlorinated acids in water by gas chromatography with an electron capture detector.* Graves, R. L., Ed.; EPA Methods. U.S. Environmental Protection Agency: Washington D.C. **1989**, 221-253.

24. USGA Green Section Staff. *Specifications for a method of putting green construction.* Bengeyfield,W. H. Ed.; United States Golf Assoc. Golf Hills, Far Hills, NJ. **1989**, 1-24.
25. Walker, W. J.; Balogh, J. C.; Tietge, R. M.; Murphy, S. R. *Environmental issues related to golf course construction and management: A literature search and review.* Spectrum Research, Inc., Duluth, MN. **1990**.
26. Wauchope, R. D.; Buttler, T. M.; Hornsby, A. G.; Augustijn-Beckers, P.W.M.; Burt, J. P. In *Reviews of Environmental Contamination and Toxicology.* Ware, G. W., Ed.; The SCS/ARS/CES pesticide properties database for environmental decision-making. U.S. Environmental Protection Agency: Washington D.C. **1992**, 1-35.
27. Weber, J. B. *North Carolina Turfgrass.* **1990**, *9(1)*: 24-29.

RECEIVED December 3, 1992

Chapter 16

Leaching of Agrichemicals from Suburban Areas

A. J. Gold[1] and P. M. Groffman[2]

[1]Department of Natural Resources Science, University of Rhode Island, Kingston, RI 02881
[2]Institute of Ecosystems Studies, Box AB, Millbrook, NY 12545

Groundwater leaching losses from home lawns of the herbicides 2,4-D and dicamba and the nutrient nitrate (NO_3^-) were found to be quite low in a multiple year study using application rates recommended for residential lawn care. Annual geometric mean concentrations of both 2,4-D and dicamba were less than 1 µg L^{-1}. The annual flow-weighted mean concentration of NO_3^--N never exceeded 5 mg L^{-1} and was typically less than 2 mg L^{-1} during 5 years of monitoring. When compared to silage corn plots monitored at the same location over the identical time period, home lawns generated approximately 15% of the NO_3^- lost to groundwater when comparable fertilization and irrigation practices were used. Levels of microbial biomass were found to be significantly higher in home lawns than in silage corn plots and were associated with higher rates of herbicide dissipation and potentially with higher rates of N immobilization. Higher rates of these microbial processes and the perennial nature of lawns may contribute to lower leaching losses of N and other agrichemicals from suburban lawns than those reported from many agricultural crops.

Leaching of agrichemicals applied to croplands is the result of the interaction of a number of processes including: 1) plant and microbial activity, which influence dissipation and residence time in the soil; 2) hydrology, particularly the timing and quantity of precipitation, evapotranspiration and the export of percolation water from the root zone; and 3) management of the crop, specifically the coupling of the timing and application rate of agrichemicals with planting and harvest activities. Integrated analysis of these diverse factors requires an ecosystem approach. Ecosystem analysis characterizes the structure, function and interactions between physical, chemical and biological components of a system. Structure refers to the characteristics of the organisms within the ecosystem, while function refers to system inputs, internal transformations and outputs.

0097–6156/93/0522–0182$06.00/0
© 1993 American Chemical Society

Ecosystem analysis is particularly useful for comparing different land uses such as home lawns and silage corn when a number of ecosystem factors that affect agrichemical dynamics are strikingly different (Table I). On home lawns of the northeast United States, turfgrass has a dense, perennial growth form that actively photosynthesizes and transpires throughout much of the year. Whereas cool season turfgrass is biologically active from late March through early November in Rhode Island, row crops, such as silage corn, are planted in June and harvested in September. Even relative to deciduous forests of New England, turfgrass has a longer period of biological activity, often an additional 4-6 weeks in the spring and fall. Soil disturbance is a routine event for row crop agriculture usually occurring at least annually, while home lawns generally have minimal physical disturbance. With row crop agriculture the soil can be bare for the majority of the year which increases infiltration and percolation, while diminishing plant related activity within the soil.

In addition to the differences between turf and row crop ecosystems listed above, the frequency and application rate of agrichemicals can be quite different between turfgrass on home lawns and row crops such as silage corn. While annual applications of a given chemical may be comparable, row crops typically receive one large application, often within a 2-4 week period around planting, while on home lawns chemical inputs are often split into 3-5 small applications. Multiple applications to actively growing turfgrass lowers the intensity of input and can match application rates to changing requirements that occur throughout the long growing season. In most row crops the time surrounding planting and chemical application of fertilizer is the period with the highest potential to generate offsite losses of agrichemicals due to low plant uptake and high soil moisture at these times.

While the importance of plants as modulators of agrichemical dynamics are relatively well studied, the importance of microbial processes has received less attention. Microbial populations can take up or "immobilize" significant quantities of fertilizer nutrients, and are responsible for the degradation of many pesticides. There have been very few comparative studies of microbial processes in different rural and suburban land use types.

Conceptually, ecosystem analysis suggests that the fate and transport of agrichemicals in turfgrass managed as home lawns should differ from row crops. The purpose of this paper is to compare leaching losses of nitrate-nitrogen (NO_3^--N), 2,4-D and dicamba from home lawns and silage corn and to relate those losses to ecosystem properties.

This chapter incorporates the results of several field studies conducted on the same set of research plots at the University of Rhode Island, including studies on leaching of NO_3^--N, 2,4-D and dicamba *(1, 2)*, and a study on microbial processes and dissipation of 2,4-D and dicamba *(3)*.

METHODS

Site Description. All studies were conducted on field plots located on well drained soils characterized by a silt loam or sandy loam mantle overlying a 2C horizon of highly permeable sands and gravels. The NO_3^--N leaching studies reported here were conducted from January 1987 to December 1988 on: home lawns, silage corn, mature forest lands and a septic system leaching field. Table II describes each of the treatments. The herbicide leaching study was conducted in 1985 and 1986 and was restricted to the home lawn plots. The herbicides 2,4-D and dicamba were applied in a manufactured mixture of TRIMEC (marketed by PPI Gordon, Kansas City, MO) in the amine salt form. The herbicide was applied three times per year (April, June, September) at a rate of 1.1 kg ha[-1] and 0.11 kg ha[-1] per application of 2,4-D and dicamba, respectively. Annual precipitation ranged from 109 cm in 1986 to 127 cm in 1988.

As described in Gold et al. *(1)*, soil water percolate from the home lawns, silage corn and forest treatments was collected with ceramic lysimeter plates 27.4 cm in diameter connected to subsurface PVC vacuum reservoirs. All plates were located below the root zone at the point where an abrupt texture change between sandy/silt loam and gravelly coarse sand occurred. The plates were placed at a depth of 0.2 m in the home lawns and 0.5 m in the silage corn and forest treatments. A suction of 0.01 MPa was imposed on each lysimeter to simulate field capacity. For a given precipitation event, samples were removed from the reservoirs at intervals of 24 to 48 hours until drainage ceased, then composited and stored at 4°C pending analysis.

Septic system leachate was monitored with ceramic suction cup lysimeters (5 cm diameter) located 1 m below the bottom of the constructed leaching trench. Septic system leachate was monitored monthly. A minimum of 3 lysimeters were monitored for all leaching studies.

The dissipation study of 2,4-D and dicamba was conducted in August, 1989 on the silage corn and home lawn treatments. At the inception of the study the herbicides in a TRIMEC mixture were applied at a rate of 1.1 and 0.11 kg ha[-1] of 2,4-D and dicamba, respectively, to 3 replicate 1 m^2 plots within each treatment. Soil samples were collected at 5, 10, 20, 40 and 80 days following herbicide application. Soils were sampled at three depths: 0-5 cm, 5-25 cm, and 25-50 cm. Herbicide residues were extracted from the soil samples and concentrations determined using a high performance liquid chromatograph following the methods of Arjmand et al. *(4)* and Hardy (personal communication).

Soil microbial biomass nitrogen of the upper 50 cm of soil was determined on the silage corn and home lawn treatments on April, 1988, December 1988, and 5 separate dates during August 1989 by the chloroform fumigation-incubation method *(5, 6)*. For the leaching study, NO_3^- was analyzed by ion chromatography. For the microbial study, mineral nitrogen was analyzed on an Alpkem RFA 300 Rapid Flow Analyzer using a cadmium reduction method. For the herbicide leaching study lysimeter samples were extracted with diethyl ether *(7)*, esterified with diazomethane followed by solvent exchange with hexane *(8)*, and then analyzed with a Shimadzu gas chromatograph equipped with a ^{63}Ni electron capture detector.

RESULTS

Nitrate Leaching Study. The concentrations of NO_3^--N in leachate during the two year study are displayed in Figure 1. Septic system leachate consistently had the highest concentrations of NO_3^--N with a two-year mean of 59 mg L[-1] while the forest treatment generated leachate concentrations near the detection limit of 0.2 mg L[-1]. Although the annual rate of N fertilization was comparable for the home lawn and silage corn treatments, concentrations of NO_3^--N in leachate from home lawns were markedly lower than from silage corn. In over 60 leaching events during the two year study, leachate from the turfgrass had ranged from 5.0 mg L[-1] NO_3^--N to less than 0.2 mg L[-1]. During extended periods each year, leachate concentrations from the fertilized home lawns were comparable to those from the forest. In contrast, the silage corn plots had NO_3^--N leachate concentrations from 3-50 mg L^{-1}. Leachate concentrations from the silage corn treatments followed a seasonal pattern, rising dramatically each fall following harvest and lowering by the early spring.

Herbicide Leaching Study. Concentrations of 2,4-D and dicamba in leachate from the root zone of the home lawn treatments were quite low. As shown in Table III, 98% of all leachate samples had concentrations of < 5 µg L^{-1} for both 2,4-D and dicamba. Although 2,4-D was applied at 10 times the rate of dicamba, the geometric mean concentration of 2,4-D was roughly twice that for dicamba, suggesting more rapid dissipation of 2,4-D. Both these herbicides have been found to leach in sandy soils and in soils low in organic matter *(9)*. The home lawn treatment plots had sandy loam soils (85% sand) with relatively low organic matter, yet generated little herbicide in leachate from the rootzone.

Dissipation Studies. The home lawn treatments showed more rapid dissipation of 2,4-D and dicamba than the silage corn plots (Figures 2 and 3). Differences in dissipation of 2,4-D were most pronounced; after 5 days 4 fold greater residues of 2,4-D remained in soil from the silage corn soil versus the home lawn treatment. In both treatments, no residues of either herbicide were detected 20 days following application. A large rainfall event (> 5 cm) occurred on day 19.

Microbial Biomass N. Soil microbial biomass N was consistently higher in the home lawn treatments than in the silage corn treatments (Figure 4). In the silage corn treatments there was considerable temporal variability, with soil microbial biomass N at a low in December, roughly 10 weeks after harvest, and rising to a high in April, after more than 6 months without disturbance. During the August 1989 herbicide dissipation study, soil microbial biomass N was nearly twice as high in the home lawn treatments than the silage corn treatments.

DISCUSSION

The striking contrasts in NO_3^--N leachate concentration and the dissipation rate of 2,4-D and dicamba between home lawns and silage corn are the product of the major differences in ecosystem properties between these land uses. The extended period of plant growth and the small, frequent applications of fertilizer to the turfgrass maximized the opportunity for grasses to absorb applied N. The silage corn treatment had a substantial rise in NO_3^--N leaching and a decline in soil microbial biomass N in the fall, following harvest. At harvest, silage corn roots undergo rapid decomposition and mineralization. Without plant uptake, a rapid increase in leachable inorganic N occurs. Finally, the frequent disturbance by tillage, and the removal of plant residues by harvest reduces the level of soil microbial biomass in silage corn ecosytems relative to home lawns. High levels of soil microbial biomass facilitate storage of N in non-leachable organic forms and dissipation of organic compounds such as 2,4-D and dicamba.

Table I. Ecosystem Comparisons: Home Lawns versus Silage Corn

Home Lawn	Silage Corn
Perennial	Annual
Dense permanent cover with organic thatch layer	Extended periods of bare ground
Active growth at >5°C (in R.I. late March to early November)	Active growth June 1 - September 15
Soil undisturbed for years	Mechanical disturbance of soil at least annually
Agrichemicals applied incrementally throughout season	Most agrichemicals applied around planting

Table II. Description of Treatments in Leaching Studies

Treatment	Nitrogen Source	Application Rate kg N ha^{-1} y^{-1}	Time of Application
Home lawns (established 1981, thatch not removed, irrigated only to avoid drought stress)	50% Urea plus 50% UREAFORM (liquid)	344	Split over 5 applications (J, J, A, S, N)
Silage corn (no cover crop; plowed each spring; continuous corn since 1982)	Urea	202	June (34 kg ha^{-1}) July (168 kg ha^{-1})
Forest (mixed oak-pine 80-120 years old)	Natural deposition		
Septic system (3 person home; occupied 1985)	Household wastewater		Continuous

Table III. Frequency Distribution of 2,4-D and dicamba concentrations (μg L^{-1}) in soil water leachate from home lawns. Data from Gold et al. 1988 *(1)*

Herbicide	< 1.0	1.0 - 5.0	5.0 - 10.0	> 10.0
2,4-D (n=47)	72%	26%	2%	0%
Dicamba (n=44)	95%	3%	0%	2%

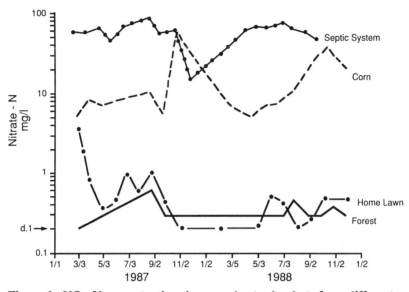

Figure 1: NO$_3$-N concentrations in groundwater leachate from different landuses in Rhode Island. Data from Gold et al. *(2)*.

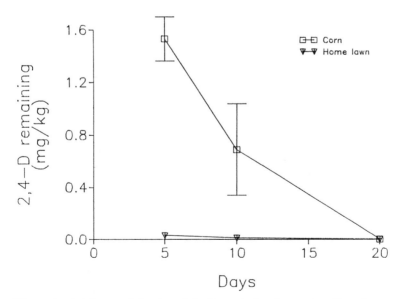

Figure 2: 2,4-D remaining in soil in field dissipation study. Data from Groffman and Voos *(3)*. Values are mean ± standard error.

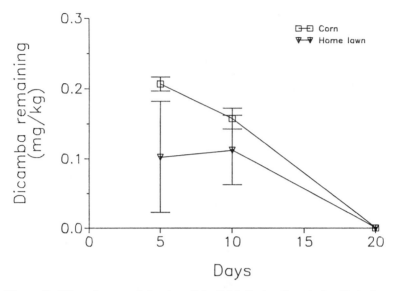

Figure 3: Dicamba remaining in soil in field dissipation study. Data from Groffman and Voos (3). Values are mean ± standard error.

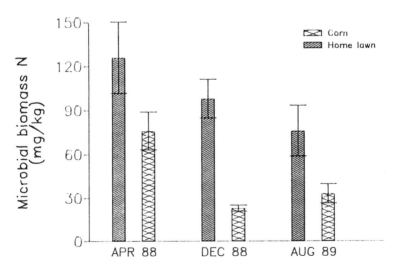

Figure 4: Soil microbial biomass N in corn and home lawn soils. Values are mean ± standard error.

Septic system leachfields are major contributors of nitrogen to groundwater. Within a septic system leachfield, nitrogen-rich wastewater is introduced to the soil below the rootzone at extremely high rates per unit area (~ 0.2 kg m^{-2} yr^{-1}). The large influx of N exceeds the capacity of the microbial pool to efficiently cycle the nitrogen, resulting in substantial percolation losses. Denitrification is not a large sink for N in septic system leachate, due to an absence of available carbon and anaerobic conditions following initial filtration and nitrification within the first 100 cm of the soil.

In suburban developments lacking sewers the extent of NO_3^--N contamination to groundwater will largely depend on housing density rather than the area of home lawns. At low densities, NO_3^--N contributions from septic systems will be diluted by percolating water from other permeable land covers such as home lawns or forests. The NO_3^--N concentrations in leachate from the home lawn treatments are comparable to other studies where urea and urea formaldehyde have been used as the source of N fertilizer; however, much higher concentrations of NO_3^--N have been found when inorganic forms of N such as NH_4NO_3 are used as fertilizer. Most commercial lawn care companies use a formulation and rate of application similar to that reported in this study, so our estimates may be widely applicable. For the studies reported here, the home lawn plots were carefully managed and had no notable problems with disease, excessive traffic or establishment. In residential situations, agrichemicals may be applied to dead or dormant patches of turf which may have less potential for dissipation and immobilization. In addition, mechanical disturbance of home lawns may result in significant leaching losses of N accumulated in thatch and soil organic fractions.

There is concern that after many years of fertilization, N losses from home lawns may increase. Whether such an increase occurs will depend on where fertilizer N inputs are being stored in the ecosystem. If soil organic N levels are building up, or if high gaseous losses are occurring, then hydrologic losses may not increase for many years. Research on the fate of fertilizer N added to home lawns is continuing.

The results of the leaching and dissipation studies suggest that significant differences exist in the fate of agrichemicals applied to turfgrass managed as home lawns versus silage corn. Many simulation models of the fate of agrichemicals do not account for differences in structure and function between these ecosystems and without calibration of field data, these models may not accurately depict leaching of chemicals from home lawns.

ACKNOWLEDGMENTS

This research was supported by grants from the USDA-SCS and the Northeast Pesticide Impact Assessment Program. Journal article #2783 of the Rhode Island Agricultural Experiment Station.

LITERATURE CITED

1. Gold, A.J.; Morton, T.G; Sullivan, W.M.; McClory, J. *Water, Air and Soil Pollution* **1988**, *37*:121-129.
2. Gold, A.J.; Deragon, W.R.; Sullivan, W.M.; Lemunyon, J.L. *J. Soil Water Conserv.* **1990**, *45*:305-310.
3. Groffman, P.M.; Voos, G. Microbial degradation and leaching of phenoxy herbicides in a heterogeneous landscape, unpublished report, **1990**.

4. Arjmand, M.; Spittler, T.D.; Mumma, R.O. *J. Agric. Food Chem.* **1988**, *36*:492-494.
5. Jenkinson, D.S.; Powlson, D.S. *Soil Biol. Biochem.* **1976**, *8*:209-213.
6. Voroney, R.P.; Paul, E.A. *Soil Biol. Biochem.* **1984**, *16*:9-14.
7. Nicholaichuk, W.; Grover, R. *J. Environ. Qual.* **1983**, *12*:412.
8. Cessna, A.J.; Grover, R.; Kerr, L.A.; Aldred, M.L. *J. Agric. Food Chem.* **1985**, *33*:504.
9. Bailey, B.W.; White, J.L. *Residue Reviews* **1970**, *32*:29-90.

RECEIVED November 9, 1992

Chapter 17

Nutrient and Pesticide Concentrations in Water from Chemically Treated Turfgrass

S. A. Harrison, T. L. Watschke, R. O. Mumma, A. R. Jarrett, and G. W. Hamilton, Jr.

Department of Agronomy, The Pennsylvania State University, University Park, PA 16802

Turfgrass was established on sloped (9 to 14%) plots by sodding with Kentucky bluegrass or seeding with one of two commercial mixtures. After establishment, the plots were identically treated with pesticides (pendimethalin, 2,4-D ester, 2,4-DP ester, dicamba, and chlorpyrifos) and fertilizers (N, P, and K) in a maintenance program similar to those employed by professional turfgrass managers in the northeastern United States. Irrigation was applied to the plots several days before and after each chemical application at an initial rate of 75 mm hr^{-1} and 150 mm hr^{-1} thereafter, for the hydrologic characterization of the slopes and to produce runoff and percolate samples for chemical analyses. Natural precipitation did not produce detectable levels (> 0.6 mm hr^{-1}) of runoff during the course of the study, although several events produced nondetectable flows that were sampled for chemical analyses. Irrigation applied at the rate of 75 mm hr^{-1} was not sufficient to produce runoff from the newly sodded plots. Irrigations of 150 mm hr^{-1} x 60 min produced average runoff volumes of 0.8%, 13.4%, and 11.6% of that applied to the sodded and two seeded treatments, respectively. No residues of pendimethalin, chlorpyrifos, or the esters of 2,4-D and 2,4-DP were detected in any sample. Mean concentrations of 2,4-D acid, 2,4-DP acid, and dicamba for individual events ranged as high as 312, 210, and 252 ug L^{-1}, respectively. Nondetections for these same compounds accounted for 63%, 64%, and 51% of the analyses, respectively, and another 30%, 25%, and 47%, respectively, were below 70 ug L^{-1}. Highest concentrations were observed in those samples that were collected within several days of application. Nutrient concentrations remained rather constant and generally reflected the nutrient concentration of the irrigation water. Results of this study suggest that runoff quantities and mean concentrations of dissolved pesticides and nutrients in turfgrass runoff and percolate are generally low.

0097–6156/93/0522–0191$06.00/0

Contamination of surface and groundwater by agrichemicals (pesticides and fertilizers) can occur through the processes of runoff and leaching from treated areas. Chemical transport by these mechanisms is a function of the product chemistry, soil type, rainfall or irrigation, other climatic factors, topography and geology, application rate and timing, and the biological system into which the chemical is introduced. Most water quality studies in agriculture have focused on food and fiber production systems which account for about 80% of U.S. pesticide use (1). However, the use of pesticides and fertilizers for turfgrass management and the continuing growth of this economic sector (2,3) has increased the need to understand the impact of these chemical applications on associated water quality. Unfortunately, the dissimilar conditions that exist under perennial turfgrass culture versus most conventional agricultural production systems suggest that extrapolation of data between the two is inappropriate.

Turfgrass management practices (including chemical inputs) can vary widely, ranging from low maintenance utility rights-of-way to highly managed golf putting green surfaces. The bulk of acreage, however, is dedicated to "medium-input" stands for uses such as home lawns, parks, athletic fields, and golf course fairways (4). In his review, "The Fate of Nitrogenous Fertilizers Applied to Turfgrass," Petrovic (5) noted that losses of N to leaching were highly variable across studies, ranging between 0 and 84% of the amount applied. These differences between studies reflect variation among factors that influence the N-leaching process.

Studies of chemical losses in runoff from turf have been severely lacking, largely due to the fact that most grassed areas have not produced sufficient runoff for sampling purposes. Kelling and Petersen (6) determined nutrient losses in runoff from private lawns using simulated rainfall. They observed N losses totaling 0.3 to 15.2% of the amount applied, with concentrations ranging between nondetectable and 18.5 mg L^{-1}. Phosphorous losses were from 0.4 to 11.7%, with concentrations between nondetectable and 8.5 mg L^{-1}; and K losses were 0.6 to 18.4%, with concentrations between 0.5 to 23.0 mg L^{-1}. Gross et al. (7) studied nutrient and sediment losses from sodded turf plots receiving five scheduled applications of urea fertilizer per year. Natural precipitation produced such low levels of runoff and nutrient or sediment losses that a separate study was conducted to determine leaching losses. Nitrate-nitrogen concentrations in percolate averaged below 3.5 mg L^{-1} during the course of the study. Researchers at the University of Rhode Island investigated nitrogen (8) and pesticide (9) losses from sloped experimental lawns maintained under high and low input irrigation and chemical management. Runoff from this site was also a rarity. Mean flow-weighted, inorganic-N concentrations in soil water ranged between 0.2 and 5.6 mg L^{-1}. Total inorganic-N losses in percolate averaged from 3.1 to 13.1% of the amounts applied. Concentrations of the herbicides 2,4-D and dicamba ranged from nondetectable to 15 and 38 ug L^{-1}, respectively. Distribution of the concentrations was skewed toward lower values, with the vast majority of samples below 1 ug L^{-1}. Total amounts of 2,4-D and dicamba recovered in percolate from the highest loading treatment were 0.4% and 1.0%, respectively, of the amounts applied.

In a recent monitoring study of four Cape Cod golf courses, Cohen et al. (10) analyzed groundwater for 17 pesticides and related compounds that are commonly applied to golf courses in the region. Seven of the compounds, including two of which there was no record of use, were never detected. With two exceptions, the remainder were detected infrequently, with concentrations near or below 1 ug L^{-1}. The exceptions were chlordane

[1,2,4,5,6,7,8,8-octachlor-2,3,3a,4,7,7a-hexahydro-4,7-methanoindane], of which there was also no record of use and which was suspected to be a contaminant during well construction; and DBCA (2,4-dichlorobenzoic acid), a compound of unknown origin which may have been an impurity of several pesticide products.

The historical lack of water quality data addressing runoff from turfgrass receiving chemical inputs was the major impetus for this research. The objective was to determine the concentration of nutrients and pesticides in runoff and percolate from treated turf.

METHODS AND MATERIALS

This research was conducted at the Landscape Management Research Center at the University Park campus of The Pennsylvania State University. The site, located on a 9 to 14% slope, was formerly utilized for soil erosion research and was left undisturbed and unattended for nearly 40 yr before being renovated to accommodate this project. The soil is a Hagerstown series (Typic Hapludalf) originating from limestone residuum and typical of the karst topography found in the ridge and valley province of central Pennsylvania *(11)*. The surface soil was classified as clay (23% sand, 36% silt, 41% clay). This textural feature is most typical of subsurface horizons in the Hagerstown series, suggesting that significant erosion of the surface horizon(s) had occurred at the site. Bulk density of the top 15 mm of soil was gravimetrically determined to be 1.24 g cm^{-3}, in the approximate middle of the common range for fine-textured soils as reported by Brady *(12)*. Depth to bedrock was variable and ranged from 5 to 60 cm.

Turfgrass Plot Preparation. Surface preparation for turfgrass establishment consisted of rototilling (10 cm depth), stone removal, leveling by hand raking, and rolling the 6.5 m by 19 m plots. Plots were separated by a plastic edging material (Edg-King, Oak Brook, IL) that extended 10 cm into the soil to eliminate interplot surface and near surface movement of water or applied chemicals. Each plot contained 21 Weathermatic (Garland, TX) pop-up sprinkler irrigation heads fitted with #520 nozzles. At the bottom of each sloped plot was an epoxy-coated concrete weir that intercepted runoff water. Runoff from individual plots was directed through galvanized steel chutes into buildings that housed the flow monitoring and subsampling apparatus. Inside each building, water from the chute flowed through a polyethylene splitting chamber (for subsample collection) and into a partitioned, 0.6 m by 1.2 m by 0.3 m deep steel tank. A length of corrugated plastic pipe (20 cm diameter) was suspended below the splitter to act as a baffle to minimize wave formation in the tank. Water accumulating in the receiving side of the tank flowed into the exit chamber via a 90 degree V-notch in the partition wall and was pumped to a storage/disposal tank. A float and counterweight assembly was positioned in the receiving side of the partitioned tank and was banded to a pulley mounted on a potentiometer. The potentiometer produced a voltage signal that was read every 60 seconds by a microprocessor-equipped datalogger (ACUREX Autocalc Data Acquisition System, Mountainview, CA) in an adjacent laboratory. The water level in the tank was maintained at the bottom of the V-notch so that changing water levels in the tank (a function of runoff flow rate) turned the potentiometer and altered the voltage signal. The datalogger was programmed to convert the voltage signal into a flow rate and record it on a computer tape. The data collection system could be activated manually, or automatically by the detection of rainfall at an adjacent weather station.

Prior to seedbed preparation, four pan-lysimeter-type subsurface sampling devices were installed 150 mm below the soil surface to capture percolating water. Two of the samplers were located in the upslope portion and two in the downslope portion of the plots. The subsurface samplers consisted of cylindrical polyethylene containers (265 mm diameter by 150 mm depth) that were filled with 16 mm diameter glass marbles. Their water holding capacity was equivalent to a depth of 38 mm. Polyester geotextile fabric separated the glass ballast from the overlying soil and prevented sedimentation in the samplers. Polyethylene fittings installed at the top and bottom of the containers allowed venting and emptying of the samplers.

Three turfgrass types (experimental treatments) were established in June of 1985: "CLASSIC," a seed mixture of perennial turfgrass species consisting of 25% 'Merit' Kentucky bluegrass (Poa pratensis L.), 25% 'Julia' Kentucky bluegrass, 20% 'Shadow' chewings fescue (Festuca rubra ssp. commutata Gaud.), and 30% 'Citation' perennial ryegrass (Lolium perenne L.); "CONTRACT," a seed mixture containing 60% annual ryegrass (Lolium multiflorum Lam.), 20% common Kentucky bluegrass, and 20% creeping red fescue (Festuca rubra L.); and "KBG SOD," a three-year-old Pennsylvania Certified Kentucky bluegrass sod grown on a similar silt loam soil in southeastern Pennsylvania from the following seed mixture: 'Adelphi' (25%), 'Baron' (25%), 'Fylking' (25%), and 'Nassau' (25%). Seed was applied at the rate of 19.6 gm m^{-2} (CONTRACT) or 14.9 gm m^{-2} (CLASSIC) with a drop spreader and mulched with clean straw. All treatments received a complete fertilizer (according to soil test recommendation) at planting at a rate of 48.6, 190.3, and 40.6 kg ha^{-1} of N, P, and K, respectively. Approximately 90 percent of the P component was applied as superphosphate (46% P_2O_5) and incorporated during the rototilling operation. The remaining P and the N and K were added as a 15-15-15 (N -P_2O_5-K_2O) fertilizer (N source: ammonium nitrate). The fertilizer was applied and raked into the soil surface just prior to seeding or sodding. Soil pH was 7.0 and no lime was applied.

Turf Maintenance Practices. The turf management program employed was typical of professionally treated lawns in the northeastern United States. Plots were mowed weekly to a height of 5 cm and clippings were removed. Irrigation was not employed as a routine maintenance practice, however, scheduled irrigations were used to produce runoff and percolate samples. To avoid disruption of the soil surface and subsequent effects on runoff characteristics, mechanical cultivation techniques such as core aeration, slicing, or spiking were not practiced. The area was not subject to foot or wheel traffic (compaction factors) beyond that required for the maintenance of the plots and experimental procedures.

Pesticides included in the study were pendimethalin [N-(1-ethylpropyl)-3,4-dimethyl-2,6-dinitrobenzenamine]; 2,4-D butoxyethanolester [(2,4-dichlorophenoxy) acetic acid]; 2,4-DP butoxyethanolester [2-(2,4-dichlorophenoxy) propionic acid]; dicamba [2-methoxy-3,6-dichlorobenzoic acid]; and chlorpyrifos [O,O-diethyl O-(3,5,6-trichloro-2-pyridyl)-phosphorothioate]. Beginning in 1986, pesticides and fertilizers were applied to the plots with a Chemlawn (Columbus, OH) spray gun delivering 1640 L ha^{-1}. Applications were made four times annually as follows:

SPRING - Pendimethalin (1.68 kg ha[-1]) for preemergence control of annual grassy weeds, plus a complete, soluble fertilizer (36.5, 4.2, and 8.0 kg ha[-1] of N, P, and K, respectively); (fertilizer analysis (N only): 8.8% nitrate-N, 1.0% ammoniacal-N, 10.2% urea-N)

EARLY SUMMER - 2,4-D ester, 2,4-DP ester, and dicamba (1.12, 1.12, and 0.28 kg ha[-1]) for postemergence control of broadleaf weeds, plus urea fertilizer (36.5 kg N ha[-1]);

LATE SUMMER - 2,4-D ester, 2,4-DP ester, and dicamba (1.12, 1.12, and 0.28 kg ha[-1]), plus chlorpyrifos (1.12 kg ha[-1]) for the control of insect pest species, plus urea (36.5 kg N ha[-1]);

FALL - 2,4-D ester, 2,4-DP ester, and dicamba (1.12, 1.12, and 0.28 kg ha[-1]), plus urea (36.5 kg N ha[-1]).

Irrigations were generally conducted one week prior to and two days after each chemical application. Irrigation duration was 90 minutes for pre-application events and 60 minutes for post-application events. In addition, all natural precipitation events were monitored for the occurrence of runoff and percolate.

Sampling and Analysis. Runoff water for quality analyses was subsampled continuously from the splitting chamber during each runoff event. Water was transferred at a rate of 16 mL min[-1] to a Nalgene (Rochester, NY) one liter high density polyethylene bottle through 0.635 mm diameter Tygon tubing via a peristaltic pump (Masterflex Model No. 7017, Cole Palmer Instrument Co., Chicago, IL). Percolate samples were withdrawn from the subsurface basins through Tygon (Norton Performance Plastics, Akron OH) tubing, located in a 10 cm access tube adjacent to and downslope from the samplers, with a centrifugal pump. No effort was made to characterize the adsorption of pesticides or nutrients onto the various components of the runoff or percolate collection system.

Runoff and percolate were collected immediately following irrigation or within 12 hr of natural precipitation events. A 250 mL aliquot was filtered through a Millipore (Bedford, MA) 0.45 um membrane filter and refrigerated at 4 C until nutrient determinations were completed. The remainder of each sample was frozen until pesticide concentrations were determined by the Pesticide Research Laboratory at Penn State University.

Nutrient concentrations were determined colorimetrically with a Hach (Loveland, CO) DR/3000 spectrophotometer. Nitrate- and nitrite-N were determined using a cadmium reduction procedure, and soluble phosphorus as orthophosphate via amino acid reduction of molybdophosphoric acid. Both procedures are standard methods *(13)* adapted for the Hach apparatus, and are described in the instrument reference manual *(14)*. Potassium was determined via the tetraphenylborate method as described in the Hach *(14)* reference manual.

A procedure was developed by the Pesticide Research Laboratory *(15)* for the analyses of seven pesticides in two high pressure liquid chromotography (HPLC) runs. The compounds were solid-phase (C_8) extracted from 100mL of sample water and adjusted to pH 2.2. Dicamba and the parent acids of 2,4-D and 2,4-DP were analyzed by ion-pair HPLC utilizing a mobile phase of methanol-water and UV detection at 230 nm.

Pendimethalin, chlorpyrifos, and the two esters 2,4-DIOE and 2,4-DPBEE were quantified with HPLC utilizing a C_{18} column, methanol-water mobile phase, and UV detection at 230 nm.

Total vegetation and weed cover were visually estimated to determine whether stand quality was related to runoff response. Vegetative cover was determined as a percent of the total area and reflects the amount of exposed soil. Weeds were also assessed as a percent of the total area.

Statistical Design. The three treatments were arranged in a randomized complete block design with three replications. The three physically fixed water sampling locations (upper and lower lysimeters and runoff) did not allow randomization of this main effect, and resulted in a "split-block type" statistical arrangement of these data. Mean separations for hydrologic data were determined using Fisher's lsd *(16)*.

RESULTS AND DISCUSSION

Hydrology. During the period November 1985 to December 1988, natural precipitation did not result in detectable levels (> 0.6 mm min^{-1}) of runoff. This observation concurs with recent experiments in Maryland *(7)* and Rhode Island *(8,9)*. However, those studies were conducted on sandy loam soils with moderate slopes of 5 to 7% and 2 to 3%, respectively. In contrast, the site used in this study was located on a borderline clay-textured soil with slopes of 9 to 14 percent, and the scarcity of runoff from natural events was unexpected. Several natural events did produce runoff sufficient for sampling purposes, however, the flow rates were below the detection limit of the equipment.

Initial testing of the irrigation system, originally designed to deliver 75 mm hr^{-1}, on the bare plots (prior to turfgrass establishment in 1985) produced quantities of runoff that exceeded the capacity of the data collection system. However, this irrigation intensity was not sufficient to produce runoff from newly sodded plots, and the system was refitted to double the original intensity. According to a statistical treatment of historical Pennsylvania rainfall data by Aron et al. *(17)*, the simulated events of 1985 (75 mm hr^{-1} x 1 or 1.5 hr) had a return frequency of >100 years in State College, PA, a town neighboring the experimental site. The dissimilar droplet patterns and subsequent impact energies of sprinkler irrigation versus natural rainfall could have been considered in determining the statistical significance of these simulated events or in predicting runoff from such storms. However, since no sediment was present in either the natural or irrigated runoff samples, it was assumed that the turfgrass canopy absorbed most of the water droplet impact energy, thus eliminating this concern.

Statistical analyses were conducted for individual irrigated events only (Table I). Varying irrigation intensities and durations and environmental conditions precluded analysis across dates. Significant differences in runoff volume between cover types (seed versus sod, generally) most commonly occurred when runoff volumes were highest. A seasonal pattern was noted with highest runoff volumes most prevalent during the months of September, October, and November.

Hydrologic trends and comparisons among treatments were evaluated using data from the 1 hr x 150 mm hr^{-1} events. The statistical frequency of a natural storm of this magnitude is not well defined by Aron *(17)* or other available sources, however, a storm

Table I. Runoff volumes for irrigated events conducted between November 1985 and December 1988

DATE OF EVENT	IRRIGATION mm/hr	hr	RUNOFF VOLUME % of total applied CLASSIC	CONTRACT	KBG SOD	AVG	
1985:							
13-Nov	75	1.5	19.3	2.0	0.0	7.1	ns#
25-Nov	75	1.0	21.0 a##	19.4 a	0.0 b	13.4	
		avg	20.2	10.7	0.0	10.3	
1986:							
25-Aug	150	0	8.0	6.5	0.0	4.8	ns
08-Sep	150	1.0	9.1 a	6.7 a	0.0 b	5.3	
08-Oct	150	1.0	16.4 a	18.2a	0.4 b	11.7	
23-Oct	150	1.0	18.4 a	15.4 a	2.0 b	11.9	
		avg	13.0	11.7	0.6	8.4	
1987:							
03-Jun	150	1.0	1.5	5.8	0.0	2.5	ns
25-Jun	150	1.5	3.6	5.2	0.1	3.0	ns
10-Jul	150	1.0	4.8	5.7	0.0	3.5	ns
22-Sep	150	1.0	11.7 a	11.1 a	0.5 b	7.8	
01-Oct	150	1.0	12.5 a	13.4 a	2.2 b	9.4	
04-Nov	150	1.5	3.3 ab	8.9 a	0.0 b	4.1	
16-Nov	150	1.0	13.8 a	12.4 a	4.9 b	10.4	
10-Dec	150	1.5	12.9 a	11.9 a	4.7 b	9.8	
		avg	8.0	9.3	1.6	6.3	
1988:							
23-May	150	1.3	8.7 a	7.4 a	0.0 b	5.4	
05-Jul	150	1.5	0.3	1.2	0.1	0.5	ns
11-Jul	150	1.0	0.6	0.0	0.0	0.2	ns
22-Aug	150	1.3	0.7	0.7	0.0	0.5	ns
27-Aug	150	1.0	1.0	1.1	0.0	0.7	ns
10-Oct	150	1.5	1.5	2.3	0.0	1.3	ns
19-Oct	150	1.0	32.4	49.4	0.0	27.3	ns
03-Dec	150	1.5	8.9 a	2.6 b	0.2 b	3.9	
		avg	6.8	8.1	0.04	5.0	

\#   Treatment means are not different at the (.10) level of significance

\## Treatment means in the same row followed by the same letter are not different at the (.10) level of significance (Fisher's lsd)

delivering the same depth in 24 hours has a return frequency of approximately 100 years in this region *(18)*. The 1.5 hour events were conducted for the sole purpose of ensuring runoff for sampling. They were not incorporated into the hydrologic analyses because their magnitude and return frequency were on the scale of a natural disaster. In addition, the 60-minute, post-application events were usually conducted 7 to 10 days after the pre-application (90 minute) irrigations, providing more uniform antecedent soil moisture conditions under which to make comparisons.

In general, lowest runoff volumes were associated with the sodded plots and seasonal effects that we attributed to soil moisture conditions. Nearly equivalent runoff volumes from the seeded treatments in both years, despite a 100% increase in irrigation intensity and volume, suggest that a substantial increase in the infiltration capacity of these plots occurred between the spring of 1985 and fall of 1986. This corresponds to a rapid increase in vegetative cover in the seeded plots during the two growing seasons following establishment of the plots.

Turfgrass cover and weed competition were noticeably different between the two seeded treatments until mid-1987. The CONTRACT treatment was quicker to establish than CLASSIC and competed more effectively with annual weeds in 1985 because of the high percentage of annual ryegrass in the mixture. The situation reversed in the following year, however, when the perennial species in the CLASSIC mixture aggressively competed with weeds but the CONTRACT plots suffered a loss of plant density from winter kill of the annual ryegrass component. KBG SOD, on the other hand, provided an "instantaneously" stable perennial grass population of very high density. The effect of establishment method on overland flow patterns was such that average runoff volumes from 1 hr irrigations in 1986-7 were 0.8%, 13.4%, and 11.6% for KBG SOD, CLASSIC, and CONTRACT, respectively. Differences in runoff volume reflect a higher infiltration capacity for the sodded plots compared to those that were seeded. This result was probably related to the superior vegetative cover provided by the Kentucky bluegrass sod, especially during the two years following establishment. However, differential runoff responses continued after the vegetative stand on the seeded plots stabilized (August 1987), suggesting that turf type or establishment method influenced the runoff process in some manner beyond the effect of areal vegetative ground cover. Two possibilities are stand density and thatch development. Although we did not quantify plant density, the rhizomous growth habit of the mature Kentucky bluegrass sod produced a densely matted tangle of plants and thatch that completely covered the soil. The seeded plots contained large proportions of noncreeping, bunch-type grasses and never reached this level of plant density. Even after 5 yr of development bare soil was evident on these plots when the turf foliage was separated by hand. KBG SOD possessed an average 9 mm of compressed thatch at installation and 11.5 mm in 1987, while the seeded plots averaged 4.4 mm in 1987. Thatch was practically nonexistent on much area of the seeded plots, except where sample cores happened to dissect a plant crown. It is likely that these treatments differentially affected soil physical properties which influence the infiltration process. Most notably, sodding completely protected the soil from the impact energy of rainfall and irrigation. Conversely, the essentially bare soil of the seeded plots was subject to structural degradation which typically results in the formation of a surface crust that impedes infiltration *(19)*. No experimental measurements were made to confirm this notion.

In each of the 3 yr, runoff volumes tended to be higher in the fall, particularly during the months of October and November. The seasonal variation in runoff volumes may have been associated with increases in antecedent soil moisture levels resulting from seasonal decreases in evapotranspiration rates (20), however, neither evapotranspiration rates or soil moisture conditions were measured. The pattern was especially evident in 1988. Under the severe drought conditions of the summer months, very low levels of runoff were observed from all treatments. In October, when a substantial natural event left the soil in a very wet condition, an irrigated event conducted the following day produced the highest levels of runoff observed during the course of the study.

Runoff volumes were substantially lower than anticipated. Introduction of the experimental conditions (land use, soil type, and antecedent soil moisture) into the widely adapted SCS Soil-Cover-Complex method (18) yielded runoff depth estimates of 75 to 90 mm for a 150 mm rainfall (Curve Numbers of 70 to 80), as opposed to the 1.2 to 20.1 mm (Curve Numbers of 30 to 40) observed in the study. The differences between predicted and observed data are even more acute when one considers that the SCS method assumes an S-shaped mass rainfall distribution pattern and a 24-hour storm duration. In this research, a constant intensity, one hour duration irrigation pattern was used, which should have increased the observed runoff depth over the predicted. SCS Curve Numbers reflect site conditions that affect runoff including soil infiltration rate, vegetative cover type, soil conservation practices, and antecedent soil moisture levels. Tables of CN values available in the literature (18,20,22) for common field conditions have been empirically derived from watershed studies of rainfall-runoff relationships and were intended for predicting watershed level impacts of land use/management changes on basin runoff characteristics (23). The results of this experiment support the contention of Rallison and Miller (23) that the use of CN's for less-than-watershed-scale applications is inappropriate, and a more site specific, infiltration based method of determining them is needed for runoff event simulation in field scale applications.

Rallison and Miller (23) also noted the inherent weakness of using the CN method in karst regions and other areas of similar subsurface permeability. Ritter (24) described a subcutaneous zone of highly weathered limestone that commonly exists between the soil and the intact bedrock. This zone generally exhibits even greater porosity and permeability than the underlying bedrock, and is very conducive to subsurface storage and transmission of water. Average runoff retention data for these plots suggests that such a zone may have existed at this site. Retention curves for the 60 min events of 1986-7, while significantly higher for KBG SOD than either of the seeded treatments, indicate that steady-state infiltration conditions were approached but often not established for any of the treatments.

Water Quality Analyses. A total of 540 samples from the 1986 and 1987 growing seasons were analyzed for pesticides and 648 samples from the 1986, 1987, and 1988 growing seasons were analyzed for nutrients.

Pesticides. Detection limits for the seven pesticides were as follows: 6.0 ug L^{-1} for 2,4-D acid; 6.0 ug L^{-1} for 2,4-DP acid; 20.0 ug L^{-1} for 2,4-D IOE; 10.0 ug L^{-1} for 2,4-DP BEE; 2.4 ug L^{-1} for dicamba; 5.0 ug L^{-1} for pendimethalin; and 5.0 ug L^{-1} for chlorpyrifos. No residues of pendimethalin, chlorpyrifos, or the esters of the 2,4-D and 2,4-DP were detected in any sample. The first two pesticides are strongly adsorbed to soil particles and organic matter, exhibit marginal water solubility, and are relatively stable in the soil (half-lives greater than 30 days) *(25,26)*. Under the conditions of this experiment, there was no effective mechanism for aqueous transport. The esters of 2,4-D and 2,4-DP are strongly adsorbed to organic matter *(25,26)* and are readily converted to the parent acids within plant tissue *(27)*, so their absence was not unexpected.

Mean concentrations of 2,4-D acid, 2,4-DP acid, and dicamba for individual events ranged as high as 312, 210, and 252 ug L^{-1}, respectively. Such high concentrations were not common, however. Nondetections accounted for 63%, 64%, and 51% of the 2,4-D acid, 2,4-DP acid, and dicamba analyses, respectively. Another 30%, 25%, and 47% of the 2,4-D acid, 2,4-DP acid, and dicamba analyses results, respectively, were below 70 ug L^{-1}. We arbitrarily note this concentration level because it is the U.S. Environmental Protection Agency's enforceable Maximum Contaminant Level for 2,4-D in public drinking water, and the most limiting of legal standards for the 3 compounds. The conditions under which most of these samples were produced represent an almost unimaginable event. All things considered, it is highly unlikely that the number and concentration of these samples is indicative of what might be expected from a similar lawn under natural conditions.

Statistical analyses (Fisher's lsd) of the data for these compounds and the three fertilizer nutrients revealed that significant concentration differences between treatments (turf cover types) or sample locations (runoff, percolate) were not common. Of the 29 dates for which nutrient data were available, significant effects were noted on a total of eight dates when all three of the nutrients were considered and on no more than four dates for any individual nutrient. For pesticide data, significant effects were noted on a total of six of 21 dates, and on three dates for each individual compound. No clear trends of preferential chemical movement into runoff or percolate, or from any cover type, were evident from those data where significant effects were noted. Thus, these main effects are not addressed in the remaining discussion.

Chemical application dates and treatment-averaged sample concentrations in runoff and percolate are plotted in Tables II, III, IV, and V. Because of the continuous sampling method, runoff concentrations reflect averages for entire events. The 38 mm depth capacity of the subsurface samplers limited observations to this initial flush of percolate. Any additional percolate was assumed to have passed around the sampling units. Generally, highest concentrations of pesticides were observed in samples collected from events occurring within several days of an application. A similar trend was noted by Wauchope *(26)* in his review of pesticides in agricultural runoff. To date, no other runoff data from highly managed turf are available for comparison to these results. Gold et al. *(9)* reported their percolate data as flow-weighted, geometric annual mean concentrations rather than individual events, again making comparisons impossible. However, they noted that over 90% of their samples were of concentrations below 5 ug L^{-1}, regardless of watering practices or pesticide application rate. Although significant concentrations of dicamba and the acids of 2,4-D and 2,4-DP were occasionally observed in our samples, dissipation of these chemicals appears to have been fairly rapid and in line with predicted soil life expectancy *(28)*.

Nutrients. Nutrient concentrations did not exhibit any specific patterns in relation to application dates. In fact, they remained rather constant and generally reflected the nutrient content of the water supplying the irrigation system. Average concentrations of

Table II. Application dates and rates of active ingredient *(italicized)* of 2,4-D acid, 2,4-DP acid, and dicamba, and mean concentrations (ug L^{-1}) in runoff

EVENT (I = irrigated, N = natural)	2,4-D	2,4-DP	DICAMBA
02-Aug-86	*1.12 kg ha^{-1}*	*1.12 kg ha^{-1}*	*0.28 kg ha^{-1}*
09-Sep-86 (I)	46	24	12
09-Oct-86 (I)	ND	ND	ND
21-Oct-86	*1.12 kg ha^{-1}*	*1.12 kg ha^{-1}*	*0.28 kg ha^{-1}*
24-Oct-86 (I)	196	130	24
10-Nov-86 (I)	40	21	19
05-Dec-86 (I)	ND	ND	ND
15-May-87 (I)	ND	ND	ND
03-Jun-87 (I)	ND	ND	ND
15-Jun-87 (N)	ND	ND	ND
25-Jun-87 (I)	ND	ND	4
06-Jul-87 (N)	ND	ND	ND
07-Jul-87	*1.12 kg ha^{-1}*	*1.12 kg ha^{-1}*	*0.28 kg ha^{-1}*
10-Jul-87 (I)	45	48	11
27-Jul-87 (N)	ND	ND	5
22-Sep-87 (I)	ND	ND	ND
28-Sep-87	*1.12 kg ha^{-1}*	*1.12 kg ha^{-1}*	*0.28 kg ha^{-1}*
30-Sep-87 (I)	ND	ND	4
05-Oct-87 (N)	ND	ND	-
04-Nov-87 (I)	ND	ND	ND
10-Nov-87	*1.12 kg ha^{-1}*	*1.12 kg ha^{-1}*	*0.28 kg ha^{-1}*
17-Nov-87 (I)	12	40	6
10-Dec-87 (I)	ND	ND	ND

ND = Nondetectable

Table III. Application dates and rates of active ingredient *(italicized)* of 2,4-D acid, 2,4-DP acid, and dicamba, and mean concentrations (ug L^{-1}) in percolate

EVENT (I = irrigated, N = natural)	2,4-D	2,4-DP	DICAMBA
02-Aug-86	*1.12 kg ha^{-1}*	*1.12 kg ha^{-1}*	*0.28 kg ha^{-1}*
09-Sep-86 (I)	35	34	11
09-Oct-86 (I)	ND	ND	ND
21-Oct-86	*1.12 kg ha^{-1}*	*1.12 kg ha^{-1}*	*0.28 kg ha^{-1}*
24-Oct-86 (I)	114	102	21
10-Nov-86 (I)	11	12	4
05-Dec-86	ND	ND	ND
15-May-87 (I)	ND	ND	ND
03-Jun-87 (I)	ND	ND	ND
15-Jun-87 (N)	ND	ND	ND
25-Jun-87 (I)	ND	22	3
06-Jul-87 (N)	ND	ND	ND
07-Jul-87	*1.12 kg ha^{-1}*	*1.12 kg ha^{-1}*	*0.28 kg ha^{-1}*
10-Jul-87 (I)	84	89	22
27-Jul-87 (N)	ND	ND	ND
22-Sep-87 (I)	ND	ND	ND
28-Sep-87	*1.12 kg ha^{-1}*	*1.12 kg ha^{-1}*	*0.28 kg ha^{-1}*
30-Sep-87 (I)	71	105	118
05-Oct-87 (N)	6	10	52
08-Oct-87 (N)	ND	ND	26
04-Nov-87 (I)	ND	ND	ND
10-Nov-87	*1.12 kg ha^{-1}*	*1.12 kg ha^{-1}*	*0.28 kg ha^{-1}*
16-Nov-87 (N)	12	41	57
17-Nov-87 (I)	26	81	51
08-Dec-87 (N)	ND	ND	41
10-Dec-87 (I)	ND	ND	ND

ND = Nondetectable

Table IV.   Dates and rates of applied nutrients (*italicized*), **and mean concentrations (mg L⁻¹) in runoff**

EVENT (I = irrigated, N = natural)	N	P	K
02-Aug-86	*36.5 kg ha⁻¹*	-	-
09-Sep-86 (I)	1	1	3
09-Oct-86 (I)	2	ND	3
21-Oct-86	*36.5 kg ha⁻¹*	-	-
24-Oct-86 (I)	2	2	5
10-Nov-86 (I)	2	6	4
05-Dec-86 (I)	2	1	1
15-May-87 (I)	2	ND	1
01-Jun-87	*36.5 kg ha⁻¹*	*4.2 kg ha⁻¹*	*8.0 kg ha⁻¹*
03-Jun-87 (I)	2	1	4
15-Jun-87 (N)	ND	5	3
25-Jun-87 (I)	1	1	4
06-Jul-87 (N)	2	1	1
07-Jul-87	*36.5 kg ha⁻¹*	-	-
10-Jul-87 (I)	2	1	2
27-Jul-87 (I)	4	2	3
22-Sep-87 (I)	2	ND	1
28-Sep-87	*36.5 kg ha⁻¹*	-	-
30-Sep-87 (I)	2	1	2
05-Oct-87 (N)	ND	ND	1
24-May-88 (I)	2	1	6
25-May-88	*36.5 kg ha⁻¹*	*4.2 kg ha⁻¹*	*8.0 kg ha⁻¹*
27-May-88 (I)	5	3	19
05-Jul-88 (I)	3	1	7
07-Jul-88	*36.5 kg ha⁻¹*	-	-
11-Jul-88 (I)	3	2	6
22-Aug-88 (I)	5	3	5
25-Aug-88	*36.5 kg ha⁻¹*	-	-
27-Aug-88 (I)	4	3	8

ND = Nondetectable

Table V. Dates and rates of applied nutrients *(italicized)*, and mean concentrations (mg L^{-1}) in percolate

EVENT (I = irrigated, N = natural)	N	P	K
02-Aug-86	*36.5 kg ha^{-1}*	-	-
09-Sep-86 (I)	3	1	3
09-Oct-86 (I)	1	ND	2
21-Oct-86	*36.5 kg ha^{-1}*	-	-
24-Oct-86 (I)	3	1	2
10-Nov-86 (I)	ND	ND	1
05-Dec-86 (I)	1	ND	1
15-May-87 (I)	1	ND	1
01-Jun-87	*36.5 kg ha^{-1}*	*4.2 kg ha^{-1}*	*8.0 kg ha^{-1}*
03-Jun-87 (I)	2	1	3
15-Jun-87 (N)	ND	2	3
25-Jun-87 (I)	1	1	2
06-Jul-87 (N)	ND	ND	2
07-Jul-87	*36.5 kg ha^{-1}*	-	-
10-Jul-87 (I)	2	1	1
27-Jul-87 (N)	1	1	3
22-Sep-87 (I)	2	ND	1
28-Sep-87	*36.5 kg ha^{-1}*	-	-
30-Sep-87 (I)	2	1	3
05-Oct-87 (N)	2	1	2
08-Oct-87 (N)	2	ND	2
10-Nov-87	*36.5 kg ha^{-1}*	-	-
08-Dec-87 (N)	ND	ND	1
10-Dec-87 (I)	2	1	2
24-May-88 (I)	1	1	1
25-May-88	*36.5 kg ha^{-1}*	*4.2 kg ha^{-1}*	*8.0 kg ha^{-1}*
27-May-88 (I)	10	2	12
05-Jul-88 (I)	3	1	3
07-Jul-88	*36.5 kg ha^{-1}*	-	-
11-Jul-88 (I)	4	2	3
19-Jul-88 (N)	4	2	3
22-Jul-88 (N)	4	ND	2
22-Aug-88 (I)	4	2	3
25-Aug-88	*36.5 kg ha^{-1}*	-	-
27-Aug-88 (I)	2	2	3
30-Aug-88 (N)	4	2	4

ND = Nondetectable

N, P, and K in the laboratory tap water (same water supply as irrigation) were 2.1, 0.4, and 0.4 mg L^{-1}, respectively, and ranged between nondetectable and 4.1, 3.7, and 4.0 mg L^{-1}, respectively. Water quality standards have not been established for P and K, thus the low concentrations we measured are not discussed further. Unlike nitrate-N, dissolved P and K are not generally considered to be a health hazard to humans or wildlife, although elevated levels of phosphate can cause algal blooms and eutrophication of surface water bodies.

The absence of elevated concentrations immediately after application is interesting, particularly for N which was applied four times annually. Detection of N would have hinged on the conversion of urea-N (applied form) to the NO_3^-- or NO_2^--N for which we analyzed. It is likely that a significant amount of the urea was either absorbed by foliage or lost due to NH_3 volatilization during the first two or three days following application. Wesely et al. *(29)* applied urea-N (2.5 g N m^{-2}) to eight N-deficient turfgrasses grown under controlled conditions and observed an average of 38.5% absorption of the applied urea by foliage in the first 48 hours. Volatilization of urea is the result of its hydrolysis to NH_3 in the presence of the enzyme urease. High levels of urease activity in turfgrass thatch and foliage under summer-like conditions have been documented *(30)*. Titko et al. *(31)* observed volatilization losses from turfgrass grown under simulated field conditions to be as high as 31.4% of dissolved urea applied at the rate of 73 kg N ha^{-1}. Nitrification of NH_4^+ to NO_2^- or NO_3^- by soil microbes, however, did not likely occur in the initial two days following our applications, since the delivery volume was sufficient to wet the foliage and exposed thatch but not to incorporate the spray solution into the soil. Since neither urea-N or NH_4^+-N were analyzed for in our procedure, the amount remaining is unknown. The fate of these surface-resident N forms under the extreme irrigations conducted in the study is also unknown. The apparent absence of NO_3^--N at later dates could be due to plant uptake of NH_4^+ or NO_3^-, leaching of dissolved urea below the detection zone (150 mm), or a combination of both. Denitrification may also have played a part. However, the irrigation events that would have favored denitrification conditions were isolated and short-lived.

CONCLUSIONS

In this study, very low levels of runoff were measured, regardless of the method of turfgrass establishment. Quantities of dissolved nutrients and pesticides in runoff or percolate were also quite small for all treatments. The data reported here are meant to be representative of root zone and "curbside" levels that might be found in a similar suburban yard. They ignore the continued cycling of nutrients and degradation of pesticides, and the dilution effect of other urban and suburban stormwaters that can influence the environmental impact of these compounds on the watershed. These data suggest that under normal rainfall conditions the quantities of dissolved pesticides and fertilizer nutrients in runoff and percolate that are transported from turfed sites are low.

It is not clear how well these data reflect the response of turfgrass that is subjected to the cultural and physical stresses common to intensively used or highly trafficked areas, or that is improperly established or poorly managed. According to Aron's *(17)* treatment of Pennsylvania rainfall data, the 100-year-frequency storm of 60-minute duration has a depth of 58 mm. On this site, a 75 mm depth from an irrigation of the same duration did not produce detectable runoff from sodded slopes. It is the experience of this author that such extreme events can produce surface ponding and runoff from turfed areas. The effects of construction practices, athletic wear, foot and wheel traffic, pest infestations, and the hydrologic condition of adjacent areas all impact the hydrologic character of a given site. Further research into the characterization of home lawns, golf courses, athletic fields, and other turfgrass areas is critical to understanding the implications of these and similar research data.

ACKNOWLEDGMENTS

This work was supported in part by the U.S. Department of the Interior, U.S Geological Survey Grant No. 14080001G in cooperation with the Environmental Resource Research Institute, The Pennsylvania State University. The mention of trade names does not constitute their endorsement by the authors or by The Pennsylvania State University.

LITERATURE CITED

1. Nielsen, E. G.; Lee, L. K. Agricultural Economic Report Number 576. USDA/ERS. **1987.**

2. Anonymous. *American Lawn Applicator.* **1988,** *9(10).*

3. *Lawn Inst. Harvests;* Roberts, E. C., Ed.; The Better Lawn and Turf Institute, Pleasant Hill, TN, **1986.**

4. Roberts, E. C.; Roberts, B. C. *Lawn and sports benefits;* The Better Lawn and Turf Institute. Pleasant Hill, TN, **1988;** p. 28.

5. Petrovic, A. M. *J. Environ. Qual.* **1990,** *19(1):*, pp. 1-14.

6. Kelling, K. A.; Peterson, A. E. *Proc. Soil Sci. Soc. Am.* **1975,** *39*, pp. 348-352.

7. Gross, C. M.; Angle, J. S.; Welterland, M. S. *J. Environ. Qual.*, **1990,** *19(3)*, pp. 663-668.

8. Morton, T. G.; Gold, A. J.; Sullivan, W. M. *J. Environ. Qual.* **1988,** *17(1)*, pp. 124-130.

9. Gold, A. J.; Morton, T. G.; Sullivan, W. M.; McClory, J. *Water, Air, and Soil Pollution.* **1988,** *37* , pp. 121-129.

10. Cohen, S. Z.; Nickerson, S.; Maxey, R.; Dupuy Jr., A.; Senita, J.A. *Ground Water Monitoring Review.* **1990,** *10(4)* , pp. 160-173.

11. National Cooperative Soil Survey. Soil survey of Centre County, Pennsylvania. Soil Conservation Service, Wash. D.C., **1981.**

12. Brady, N. C. *The nature and properties of soils.* 8th ed. Macmillan, NY, **1974;** pp. 58-62.

13. American Public Health Administration. *Standard methods for the examination of water and wastewater.* 16th ed. American Public Health Association, NY, **1985.**

14. Hach Company. *D/R 3000 spectrophotometer instrument manual.* 3rd ed. Hach Company, Loveland, CO, **1986.**

15. Bogus, E.; Watschke, T. L.; Mumma, R. O. *J. Agric. Food Chem.* **1990,** *38(1)* , pp. 142-144.

16. Steel, R. G. D.; Torrie, J. H. *Principles and procedures of statistics: A biometrical approach.* 2nd ed. McGraw-Hill, NY, **1980.**

17. Aron, G.; Wall, D. J.; White, E. L.; Dunn, C.N. *Water Resour. Bull.* 23(3), **1987**.
18. U.S. Department of Agriculture. *Urban hydrology for small watersheds.* 2nd ed. Soil Conserv. Serv. Tech. Rel. 55. Soil Conserv. Serv., Wash. D.C., **1986**.
19. Jennings, G. D.; Jarrett, A. R.; Hoover, J.R. *Trans. Am. Soc. Agric. Eng.* **1988**, *31(3)*, pp. 761-768.
20. Schwab, G. O.; Frevert, R. K.; Edminster, T. W.; Barnes, K.K. *Soil and water conservation engineering.* 3rd ed. John Wiley and Sons, NY, **1981**, pp. 68-71.
21. Leonard, R. A.; Knisel, W. G.; Still, D. A. *Trans. ASAE.,* **1987**, *30(5)* , pp. 1403-1418.
22. Viessman, W.; Harbough, T. E.; Knapp, J. W. *Introduction to hydrology.* Educational Publishers, NY, **1972**.
23. Rallison, R. E.; N. Miller. In *Rainfall-runoff relationships;* Singh, V. P., Ed., Proc. International Symposium on Rainfall-Runoff Modeling. Water Resources Publications. Littleton, CO, **1982**, pp. 353-364.
24. Ritter, Dale F. *Process geomorphology.* 2nd edition. Wm. C. Brown Publishers, Dubuque, IA, **1986**.
25. Goss, D.; Wauchope, R. D. In *Pesticides in the next decade: The challenges ahead;* Weigmann, D. L., Ed., Proc. of the Third National Research Conference on Pesticides. Virginia Water Resources Research Center. Blacksburg, VA, **1990**, pp 471-493.
26. Wauchope, R. D. *J. Env. Qual.* **1978**, *7(4)* , pp. 459-472.
27. Menzie, C. M. Bur. of Sport Fisheries and Wildlife Special Scientific Report - Wildlife No. 127. U.S. Fish and Wildlife Service. Washington, D.C., **1969**, p. 109.
28. Weed Science Society of America. Herbicide handbook. 6th ed. Champaign, IL, **1989**.
29. Wesely, R. W.; Shearman, R. C.; Kinbacher, E. J. *J. Amer. Soc. Hort. Sci.* **1985**, *110(5)*, pp. 612-614.
30. Torello, W. A.; Wehner, D.J. *Agron. J.* **1983**, *75(3)*, pp. 654-656.
31. Titko, S., III; Street, J. R.; Logan, T. J. *Agron. J.* **1987**, *79(3)*, pp. 535-540.

RECEIVED December 2, 1992

Chapter 18

Field and Model Estimates of Pesticide Runoff from Turfgrass

W. D. Rosenthal[1] and B. W. Hipp[2]

[1]Texas Agricultural Experiment Station, Temple, TX 76502
[2]Texas Agricultural Experiment Station, Dallas, TX 75252

Environmental awareness of surface runoff water quality is increasing. A study was conducted to analyze the impact of different turfgrass fertilizer and pesticide management systems on runoff water quality. A hydrologic and water quality model, Erosion Productivity Impact Calculator (EPIC), was used to estimate pesticide and nutrient concentrations in runoff from turfgrass on a Houston Black Clay. Nutrient and pesticide concentrations in the surface runoff increased significantly for highly maintained turfgrass systems. A larger fraction of the amount applied was observed in runoff for the moderate application rate treatments. Simulated results are being validated from measured runoff of turfgrass plots at Dallas, TX.

Pesticide and nutrient pollution in surface runoff from urban landscapes is becoming an increasingly important environmental issue. There has been an increase in the number of reports of urban surface runoff with detectable levels of pesticides and nutrients (1). Highly maintained turfgrass areas, as found on golf courses, may have surface runoff with detectable amounts of pollutants (2). In addition, common rules associated with fertilizing lawns (e.g. watering immediately after fertilizer application) may in fact be detrimental to runoff water quality. As a result, management practices to reduce surface runoff nutrient and pesticide concentrations need to be evaluated.

Two ways to evaluate management practices are monitoring and simulation modeling. Numerous research projects have been conducted evaluating the effect of urban cultural practices on surface water quality (3, 4). Evaluations of different management treatments through monitoring will take time and money. In addition, several models (e.g. SWRRB-WQ, EPIC, QUAL-TX) have been developed to simulate surface water quality for extreme events (5). However, a combination of monitoring and modeling has not been used to evaluate management practices in different soil and climatic environments. Our objective was to (1) develop and monitor surface runoff water quality from turfgrass plots subjected to different management levels, and (2) simulate extreme runoff conditions for the above management scenarios. The EPIC (Erosion Productivity Impact Calculator)

0097–6156/93/0522–0208$06.00/0
© 1993 American Chemical Society

model was developed to monitor erosion from plots and small fields. This model was selected because it can simulate the fate of many pesticides simultaneously and quantify runoff magnitude for small areas.

MATERIALS AND METHODS

Model Description. A detailed description of the EPIC model and its capabilities was given by Williams et al. *(5, 6)*. The model simulates hydrologic processes, plant growth, and pesticide/nutrient fate based on tillage, environment, and other management practices. The pesticide fate components were recently incorporated from the GLEAMS model *(7)*. A mass balance approach accounts for pesticide fate. Key pesticide inputs into EPIC include pesticide name, application date and rate, effective killing efficiency, adsorption coefficient for organic carbon, half-life in the soil and foliage, water solubility, and washoff fraction. Pesticide fate output information includes pesticide quantities in surface runoff, adsorbed to the plants and each soil layer, degraded on the plant and in the soil, leaching out of the root zone, and lost in eroded sediment. The amount and concentration in surface runoff is primarily a function of the half-life of the pesticide, soil adsorption, chemical characteristics, chemical placement, and application amount.

Turfgrass Plot Description. Twenty-four 2.5 X 3.7 m turfgrass plots were installed in 1990 at the Texas Agricultural Experiment Station in Dallas. Four management treatments were imposed on the plots and replicated six times. These included a highly maintained, medium-high maintenance, medium-low maintenance, and xeriscape (low) maintenance systems (Table I). Ornamental plants with a bark mulch surface were installed on 1/3 of the area in each plot. Bermudagrass *(Cynodon dactylon)* was planted in the medium and highly maintained treatments; whereas, Buffalograss *(Buchloe dactyloides)* was planted in the low maintenance plots. The plots were mowed every 7-14 days. Each plot was on a 2% slope of Houston Black clay soil and fitted with gutters on the downslope side that funnelled runoff water to collection samplers. Water quality could be monitored through periodic sampling during a runoff event. The amounts of chemicals applied to the plots for each treatment are given in Table I and are representative of common practices on turfgrass. Surface runoff was collected and sampled for NO_3^- and PO_4^{-2}, but Diazinon (Spectracide), which was applied once in 1991, was not analyzed in the surface runoff.

Model Simulation. The same four treatments and nutrient and pesticide application amounts and dates were simulated using the EPIC model (Table I). Additional insecticides and pesticides were simulated. Application dates and amounts were inputs into the model (Table II). The model was run under one scenario: using the model weather generator to simulate 30 years of representative weather data for Dallas, TX. Other inputs were representative of soil, plant, and atmospheric conditions for Dallas, TX.

RESULTS

Field. Nitrate concentrations were significantly different for the various treatments. Surface runoff from early irrigations had higher NO_3^- concentrations in the runoff than later irrigations. Irrigations on the same day as fertilizer applications on 3 June had

Table I. Experimental Design of Turfgrass Runoff Study Treatment

	Low Maintenance	Medium-Low Maintenance	Medium-High Maintenance	High Maintenance
Irrig. (mm)	0	150	250	975
Fertilizer (kg/ha)	0	73	145	290
# Fertilizer App.	0	2	3	6
Insecticides (kg/ha)	None	Chlorpyrifos (2.2) or Carbaryl (1.1) or Diazinon (6.0)	Chlorpyrifos or Carbaryl (1.1) or Diazinon (6.0)	Chlorpyrifos or Carbaryl (1.1) or Diazinon (6.0)
# Insecticide App.	0	1	1	3
Herbicides (kg/ha)	None	None	2,4-D (1) or Dicamba (.5) or Atrazine (1.5)	2,4-D (1) or Dicamba (.5) or Atrazine (1.5)
# Herbicide App.	0	0	1	1

Table II. Peak Diazinon Concentrations (ppb) for May-October

Treatment	May	June	July	August	September	October
High	102	40	70	3	4	3
Medium High	400	335	60	5	3	2
Medium Low	400	390	72	16	12	0.7

average NO_3^- levels of 15-16 ppm for the highly and medium high maintained treatments, which is above the recommended EPA threshold level. Subsequent irrigations had decreasing NO_3^- levels (Figure 1).

Another scenario was to determine the nitrogen concentration in a runoff producing storm late in the growing season. On 22 October 1991, ten cm of water was applied to all plots. The mean runoff for the highly maintained treatment was 2.47 cm; the low maintenance treatment had only 0.25 cm of runoff ($LSD_{.05}$=1.5 cm). Concentrations of nitrate in the runoff were 5 ppm for the highly maintained treatment and 0.3 ppm for the low maintenance treatment. Additional runoff had lower NO_3^- concentrations in runoff for the highly maintained treatment. The low maintenance treatment had a consistent 0.3-0.4 ppm NO_3^- ($LSD_{.05}$=2.2 ppm) concentration in the runoff throughout these irrigations (Figure 1). This level represents background N concentrations in the surface soil layer and organic matter. These were the only two runoff events during 1991.

Model. Nitrogen and pesticide concentrations were highest for the highly maintained and medium-high treatment (Tables II, III). These values were significantly higher for precipitation amounts immediately after application. Concentrations for medium low treatments were even greater than the high and medium high treatments. Of the six pesticides analyzed, atrazine and diazinon had the longest continuous period with concentrations above the EPA Lifetime Health Advisory Level (Diazinon--0.6 ppb; Atrazine 3 ppb). Atrazine had a maximum surface runoff concentration of 919 ppb; diazinon concentrations in surface runoff were as high as 400 ppb. Ranges of monthly quantities of atrazine and diazinon were 1 to 47 g ha^{-1} and 1 to 26 g ha^{-1}, respectively. Monthly nitrate levels averaged 1 ppm to 390 ppm for the highly and low maintained treatments (Table III). These results contradict those of Watschke (2). He found that the concentration of pesticides did not exceed the EPA threshold the majority of the time. The difference could be explained by the differences in soil type. Watschke (2) used sand as the soil medium. In the present study, the soil was Houston Black clay, which has a slow infiltration rate (0.1 cm hr^{-1}). With the slower infiltration rate, measurable surface runoff is more likely to occur.

DISCUSSION

In spite of the fact that simulated results indicate there may be occasions when nutrient and pesticide concentrations in surface runoff from a single lawn exceed the EPA threshold level, the combined water concentration within the urban system may be diluted to the point of having combined concentrations less than the threshold. The EPA found that pesticides and nutrients were present in urban runoff, but were not as prominent as metals such as lead (1). Further studies are needed using other pesticides to determine the degree of dilution and fate in the urban system. Additional studies with the turfgrass plots will be conducted in the future. Volatilization of the pesticide is one factor not accounted for in EPIC. Thatch may also serve as an adsorption medium for the pesticide. This may account for some quantity of pesticide lost for these pesticides.

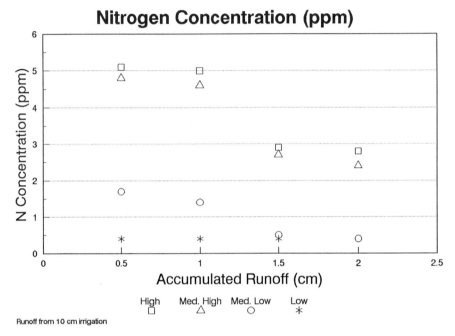

Figure 1. Nitrogen concentration as a function of accumulated surface runoff from the turfgrass plots at Dallas.

Table III. Peak Nitrate Concentration (ppb) in Runoff

	Treatment			
	High	Medium High	Medium Low	Low
January	18	2	1	1
February	19	13	8	5
March	14	9	8	6
April	142	131	3	2
May	226	18	88	4
June	63	59	39	4
July	70	14	309	2
August	137	276	11	1
September	44	1	636	1
October	9	1	1	1
November	5	3	2	1
December	10	5	3	2

LITERATURE CITED

1. U. S. Environmental Protection Agency. **1983.** Final Report of the Nationwide Urban Runoff Program.
2. Watschke, T. L., S. Harrison, and G. W. Hamilton. USDA Green Section Record. **1989,** (May/June), 5-8.
3. Morton, T. G. A. J. Gold, and W. M. Sullivan. *J. Environ. Qual.* **1988,** *17,* 124-130.
4. Petrovic, A. M. *J. Env. Qualit.* **1990,** *19,* 1-14.
5. Williams, J. R., C. A. Jones, and P. T. Dyke. *Trans. ASAE.* **1984,** *27,* 129-144.
6. Williams, J. R., C. A. Jones J. R. Kiniry, and D. A. Spanel. *Trans. ASAE.* **1989,** *32,* 497-511.
7. Leonard, R. A., W. G. Knisel, and D. A. Still. *Trans. ASAE.* **1987,** *30,* 1403-1418.

RECEIVED October 30, 1992

Chapter 19

Groundwater and Surface Water Risk Assessments for Proposed Golf Courses

S. Z. Cohen, T. E. Durborow, and N. L. Barnes

Environmental & Turf Services, Inc., 11141 Georgia Avenue, Suite 208, Wheaton, MD 20902

Proposed golf course developments usually require environmental impact statements in the U.S. Concerns about ground water, surface water, and near-shore coastal water quality and wetlands often require state-of-the-art risk assessments and complex computerized simulation modeling. It is extremely important to obtain site-specific data for these risk assessments. Thus soil sampling, test borings, stream surveys, and coastal surveys are often done. Daily weather records are obtained or generated. The new PRZM-VADOFT model pair is used for leaching assessments, even though nonlinear adsorption isotherms cannot be used. The SWRRBWQ model is difficult to use but it is appropriate for the modeling of complex drainage patterns at the basin and sub-basin scale, as with golf courses. Annual and storm-event runoff values are computed for pesticides, nutrients, runoff water, and sediments. It is best used for areas expected to experience appreciable runoff. EXAMS II provides useful predictions of stream water quality. An uncertainty analysis is a critical but often overlooked part of modeling. These results help fine tune proposed turf management programs and may indicate the need for design changes. Risk assessments in Hawaii are especially complex; they often indicate the need for detention basins.

There are over 14,100 golf courses in the United States. It is a growing sport with approximately 27,000,000 participants. Over 1200 new golf courses were in the planning or construction phase as of February, 1992 (1).

Golf courses require the use of pesticides and fertilizers to maintain healthy turf and suitable playing surfaces. Increasingly, turf managers are using the principles of Integrated Pest Management (IPM). IPM includes more of a reliance on spot treatments than broadcast applications, and limits a majority of fungicide use to greens and tees. IPM requires the establishment of pest infestation thresholds for triggering pesticide applications.

0097–6156/93/0522–0214$06.00/0

Questions about potential turf pesticide and fertilizer impacts on ground water, surface water, wetlands, and nearshore water quality are frequently raised during the local permitting process. Sometimes the concerns are genuine. Sometimes they are a strawman for anti-development sentiment. The attacks frequently degenerate into anti-pesticide hysteria, where the basic principles of risk assessment are not understood. Further, the attackers frequently dismiss the heavily regulated FIFRA framework as ineffective.

The best way to respond to these concerns is with responsible turf management and state-of-the-art risk assessment. The turf management program takes the form of an integrated golf course management program (IGCMP), using IPM. The basic philosophy of the IGCMP is that one minimizes the need for pesticides by growing in quickly and maintaining a healthy stand of turf. A variety of chemical and non-chemical management techniques are included, e.g., aerification, proper irrigation, and use of parasites.

The next step is a risk assessment based on a reasonable worst-case scenario of possible pest infestations and turf chemical usage. Computer simulation modeling is often required. The ultimate goal of this risk assessment process, described in this paper, is to fine tune the IGCMP and/or suggest changes to the golf course design to minimize or eliminate any impacts on water quality.

Thus the purpose of this paper is to:

1) describe this risk assessment process;
2) point out potential pitfalls and uncertainties;
3) provide examples where this process has recently been applied in Hawaii; and
4) compare some modeling results with monitoring data.

RISK ASSESSMENT PROCESS OVERVIEW

A draft of the IGCMP is developed by turf agronomists and given to the environmental scientists charged with conducting the ground water and surface water risk assessment. Parallel to this effort, the environmental scientists are visiting the site, sampling the subsurface, and reviewing whatever relevant data are available. One of the most important parts of the risk assessment process is the identification of potentially significant exposure pathways. The relevance of the risk assessment will be reduced if any potentially significant exposure pathways to sensitive receptors are missed. Thus the following pathways of offsite migration of turf chemicals are evaluated to determine whether they should be included in the quantitative risk assessment:

• leaching to ground water that lies within the zone of influence of current or future drinking water wells;
• discharge of potentially contaminated ground water to nearshore coastal waters, including possible impacts on nearshore coral reef communities;
• runoff to perennial streams or ponds containing sensitive aquatic organisms; and
• runoff to gulches/intermittent streams that discharge to the shoreline and/or promote rapid infiltration to ground water.

In addition, if offsite transport of turf applied chemicals in aerial drift is an issue, outside expertise is retained to address the issue. Currently, the AGDISP model (2) is used to simulate drift from tractor boom application under varying conditions of wind speed, boom height and relative humidity (e.g., (3)).

Following are more specific descriptions of the ground water and surface runoff risk assessment process. It is important to note that this is not a "how-to" treatise about computer simulation modeling. Rather, minimal discussions about modeling methods and results are presented to adequately describe the role of computer modeling in the risk assessment process. More detail can be found in the references cited.

EVALUATING GROUND WATER CONTAMINATION POTENTIAL

Site Evaluation. Soil samples are collected from 0-15 cm (0-6 in) and 15-30 cm (6-12 in) depths from several locations so that different soil types are represented at the site. The number of locations is dependent upon the availability and reliability of soil mapping data for the site and soil chemistry analysis for the particular soil series, as well as the apparent homogeneity across the area. The samples are analyzed for organic carbon, pH, field capacity (moisture content at 0.1 bar), sand/silt/clay content, bulk density, porosity, infiltration rate, and available water capacity. Geophysical surveys are sometimes needed to help characterize soil thickness and subsurface geology.

The site is also evaluated carefully for the presence or likelihood of ground water discharges from the site to nearby sensitive surface water bodies, e.g. pristine streams or nearshore coral reef environments. As an extension of this evaluation, marine and freshwater biologists are usually included on the team as appropriate.

Pesticide and Nitrogen Evaluations. The literature is reviewed and evaluated carefully for information on mobility, persistence, human toxicity and aquatic toxicity of all pesticides. Significant metabolites are considered as well. Pesticide chemistry evaluations are similar to those done by Cohen, et al. (4). That is, key mobility and persistence data are evaluated for their relevancy for the particular site. Data sources include the open, peer-reviewed literature, EPA's NPIRS on-line data base, and the environmental fate data bases of Syracuse Research Corporation. Nitrogen leaching data from lysimeters are also evaluated for relevance to the particular turf/soil mix anticipated at the site (e.g., (5)). The greatest difficulty is encountered when trying to extrapolate pesticide degradation data to specific sites. This is especially true for Hawaii with its unique geophysical and climatological setting. When possible, relevant data available from studies done in Hawaii, e.g., Miles (6), Miles and Doerge (7), and Glynn et al. (8), are used.

Computer simulation modeling costs significant amounts of time and money, typically 50-100 person-hours or more, not including the site investigation, pesticide characterizations, etc. Consequently, a simple ranking scheme was developed to identify the best candidates for modeling, i.e., the pesticides and metabolites within a set that have the greatest potential to leach to ground water at toxicologically significant concentrations. The chemicals are ranked according to their GUS Index, which combines Koc and t1/2 data (9); total pounds of active ingredient anticipated to be applied in a reasonable worst case scenario; and the Health Advisory Level (HAL), which usually must be calculated. The HAL is calculated using EPA's methods: it is based on the Acceptable Daily Intake or carcinogenic potency factor, as appropriate, and assumes 2 liters of water per day consumption for adults and 1 liter of water per day for toddlers. The Attenuation Factor by Rao, et al. *(10)* can be used in place of the GUS Index. The ranks are combined linearly, and the pesticides with the lowest total rank scores are modeled. [The approach is simplistic. A linear combination of HAL and pound variables makes sense, but it is unclear whether a better approach could be developed for integrating the GUS Index or the Attenuation Factor.]

An example is presented in Table I which was created for a golf course proposed on Maui. Thus, as a result of this computation, mancozeb and its metabolite ETU were among the highest priority candidates for modeling. We are considering supplementing the scheme for considerations of phytotoxicity, especially if irrigation water may impact wetland areas or sensitive ornamental plants.

Table I. Ranking Chemicals for Unsaturated Zone Modeling (Leaching) for a Proposed Golf Course on Maui

Chemical	Ranks			
	GUS Index	Pounds	HAL	Total
mancozeb	11	1	3	1
ETU (metab.)	12	3	1	2
DDVP (metab.)	10	5	2	3
metalaxyl	1	11	6	4
•				•
•				•
•				•
glyphosate	13	14	13	16

Selection of Leaching Model and Model Description. The selection of the appropriate computer simulation model is based on scientific and nonscientific criteria. There are several models that, upon further examination, may be shown to meet our scientific requirements (e.g., LEACHMP *(11)* and Boesten's model *(12)*). The main scientific concerns are field verification, a realistic or conservative representation of solute transport, and the ability to track metabolites. The nonscientific criteria are the ability to model more than one chemical simultaneously, user friendliness, user support, and EPA endorsement. The latter criterion is especially important in contentious, emotional public hearings. Thus, PRZM-VADOFT (referred to as PRZM2) is our primary choice.

Use of PRZM. The Pesticide Root Zone Model (PRZM) coupled with the Vadose Zone Flow and Transport Model (VADOFT) *(13-15)* is a one dimensional, compartmental, numerical solution modeling system that performs daily computations to simulate the fate and transport of pesticides below the root zone to ground water. It also can calculate erosion loss in surface runoff. The PRZM model has two major components: hydrology and chemical transport. Two input files are required to run PRZM, a meteorological file and the PRZM parameter file. More detailed descriptions of the PRZM2 modeling system, its components and input files can be found in the literature cited above.

It is important to note that in the risk assessment results presented below, the PRZM2 concentration profile is not used due to concerns about its consistent accuracy. Smith, et al. (16) found that PRZM predicted peak pesticide and tracer concentrations fairly well, but Pennell, et al. (17) noted that PRZM did not reliably predict solute concentration distributions. It was, however, reasonable in predicting the pesticide center of mass and the mass remaining in the soil profile. In our assessments, the estimated pesticide mass loss from the vadose zone is diluted into the water flux at the bottom of the vadose zone on a monthly time step to yield concentrations in micrograms per liter. These concentrations can then be compared with HALs as criteria for evaluating potential risks. Specifically, the computed values were based on a 30-day period of pesticide leachate accumulating in a 'stagnant' aquifer, a conservative assumption. The year with the highest mass lost from the profile was selected for each pesticide and divided by 12 to yield an average monthly mass loss. The highest year was chosen to represent the reasonable worst case for a conservative assumption.

Some Simulation Results. Table II shows a comparison between two areas in Hawaii that receive significantly different amounts of rainfall and how results from PRZM2 simulations of turf-applied pesticides in these areas compare with HALs. The values in Table II represent estimates of the highest average daily mass loss from the vadose zone during a five year simulation. These estimates were calculated by dividing the highest monthly mass loss by the number of days in that particular month. The wet site receives approximately 132cm/yr (52 in/yr) of rainfall and the dry site receives approximately 30 cm/yr (12 in/yr) of rainfall (18). Although the rainfall amounts are

Table II. Comparison of PRZM-VADOFT Results Between Wet and Dry Sites in Hawaii (all concentrations in μg/L)

Pesticide + Metab.	Wet	Dry	HAL
2,4-D	0.33	0.001	70
Mancozeb	$1.4 * 10^{-7}$	$2 * 10^{-18}$	21
ETU	0.01	0.004	0.2

HAL (Health Advisory Level) for this chemical has been multiplied by 0.2 as an additional safety factor to allow for the possibility of significant food tolerances and/or dietary residues.

significantly different, the rainfall distributions throughout the year for the two areas modeled are similar. The areas are otherwise fairly comparable in terms of soils and geology, despite the significant differences in rainfall.

Two pesticides and one metabolite were modeled for both the wet and dry areas. Soil water concentrations of both pesticides and the metabolite were at least one order of magnitude greater for the wet site compared to the dry site. The concentrations were, however, considerably lower than the respective HALs for both sites.

The modeling results in Table II are what one may have expected -- sites with more rainfall have more water available to leach solutes to ground water, resulting in higher predicted concentrations. However, these results are contradicted by two completely different studies, but supported by a third. EPA *(19)* recently found that the county-level recharge measure from the DRASTIC scoring scheme was <u>inversely</u> related to frequency of pesticide detections in its national survey for pesticides in drinking water wells (although other precipitation measures did not correlate with pesticide detections). Similarly, Gold, et al. *(20)* found that the turf lysimeters treated with higher amounts of water and herbicides (2,4-D and dicamba) actually generated <u>lower</u> herbicide concentrations in the leachate than those with less water and herbicides. But in agricultural studies, Lorber, et al. *(21)* found that higher rates of water input (rainfall plus irrigation) correlated with <u>higher</u> concentrations of aldicarb residues below the root zone. This is an area that definitely needs more research.

Table III shows a comparison of PRZM2 results between mean values and an assumed 95% confidence interval that was calculated as part of an uncertainty analysis which is explained below.

Table III. Comparison of Upper 95% Confidence Interval With Mean Values of Concentration Predictions

Pesticide	Wet		Dry	
	Mean	95% C.I.	Mean	95% C.I.
2,4-D	0.013	0.412	0.006	0.068
Mancozeb	$5 * 10^{-19}$	$2 * 10^{-6}$	$2 * 10^{-19}$	$4 * 10^{-7}$
ETU	$4 * 10^{-4}$	0.012	$3 * 10^{-4}$	0.003

All values are in μg/l for a 30-day period, assuming ground water flow velocity = 0 for the 30 days.
Wet = an area which receives 132 cm/yr (52 in/yr) of rain
Dry = an area which receives 30.5 cm/yr (12 in/yr) of rain

The two areas modeled had significant differences in rainfall. The wet area receives 132 cm/yr (52 in/yr) of rainfall while the dry area only receives 30.5 cm/yr (12 in/yr). The aquifers were assumed to be the same size as the golf course acreage (90 acres for wet, 228 acres for dry-2 golf courses). Mean values of predicted concentrations range between one to 13 orders of magnitude below the 95% confidence interval (95% CI).

The 95% CI is estimated for the uncertainity analysis by subtracting one standard deviation from the degradation rate constant, adding one s.d. to the saturated hydraulic conductivity, and subtracting one s.d. from the K_d. The standard deviations are calculated based on information contained in the following two key references. Rao and Davidson (22) critically reviewed the literature and obtained coefficients of variation (CV) of rate constant (k) and (Koc) values for 31 and 42 pesticides, respectively. These CVs were combined and it was found that the average CV for k was 73% and for Koc it was 62%. The K_{sat} CV, calculated in a similar manner, was determined to be 200% based on data presented in Dean, et al. (15). (We plan to include soil- moisture retention properties in future analyses.) Combining these CVs in the manner described above generates predicted concentrations that are assumed to be worst case. The difference between this worst case value and the mean/expectation value is taken to equal approximately four standard deviations, following the statistician's rule-of-thumb (23). The assumed 95% CI is calculated as the mean plus two s.d.'s. These values replace previous values and the model is run again.

Table IV is a comparison of the PRZM2 computer simulation and analytical results of five pesticides from a ground water monitoring study of four golf courses on Cape Cod (24). The numbers in the table show that the PRZM2 model yields results similar to the analytical results. Table IV PRZM2 results are also based on an approximation of the 95% CI.

Table IV.   Comparison of Computer Simulation and Analytical Results from the Cape Cod Study[H]

Pesticides	AA[+]	PRZM[++]	Analyte	MDL[***]
Chlorothalonil	G,T,	$5 * 10^{-5}$	ND[**]	
	F	$1 * 10^{-5}$	ND	0.015
Chlorpyrifos	G,T	$2 * 10^{-11}$	ND	0.05
2,4-D	F	0.002	ND	0.05
MCPP	F	0.0009	ND	0.05
Isofenphos	G	0.012	0.57[+++]	0.75

[H] All results in $\mu g/L$
[**] ND = Non-detect
[***] MDL = Method Detection limit
[+] AA = application area: G = greens, T = tees, F = fairways
[++] Upper 95% confidence interval
[+++] Average of one detection at 1.17 ppb and 3 x ND, where ND = 1/2 MDL (MDL = 0.75 $\mu g/L$, as described in Cohen, et al. (25)). A log-probit analysis would be more appropriate if there were more detections.

EVALUATING SURFACE RUNOFF POTENTIAL

Site Evaluation. Soil samples are collected and analyzed as described in the ground water section above. Drainage patterns and subbasin boundaries are delineated from the site visit, USGS 7.5 minute topographic contour maps, and aerial photographs.

Pesticide Evaluations. Pesticides are evaluated as described in the ground water section above. Significant differences are that a greater focus is placed on application timing in relation to 'wet' seasons, and great care is taken to review the literature and calculate one-tenth of the LC_{50} of the most sensitive aquatic species even remotely relevant to the project site.

A chemical ranking procedure is done to help select three to six pesticides for runoff modeling. The criteria are Koc, pound of use, HALs, application timing relative to rainy periods, and aquatic vertebrate and invertebrate toxicity. (Nitrogen, phosphorus, and sediment runoff are usually also modeled.) HALs usually must be calculated using EPA's standard procedures.

Selection of Runoff Model and Model Description. Several computer models are available for the estimation of surface runoff losses of water, sediment, and chemicals. SWRRBWQ (Simulator for Water Resources in Rural Basins, Water Quality Model *(25)*) and GLEAMS (Groundwater Loading Effects from Agricultural Management Systems *(26)*) have both been validated against field studies for runoff and chemical transport *(27-29)* and are widely used by government, research, and private sector scientists for assessing water quality management options. The SWRRBWQ model was used for the Hawaii golf course assessment described below. SWRRBWQ was developed to model sites that are hydrologically complex and large scale such as those encountered in Hawaii. The SWRRBWQ model also allows for the simulation of nitrogen and phosphorus transport. This option has only recently been released for GLEAMS (September 16, 1992) and was not available at the time this work was done.

The major relevant components are weather, hydrology, erosion, pesticides, and nutrients. Irrigation can be simulated based on soil moisture stress. The hydrology component employs the SCS curve number technique *(30)* driven by the daily weather input. Erosion losses are predicted with the Modified Universal Soil Loss Equation (MUSLE) *(31)* and a simple flood routing component. A complete description of SWRRBWQ can be found in Arnold, et al. *(25)* and Arnold, et al. *(32)*.

ETS evaluated the potential for leaching and runoff losses of a list of 21 pesticides and one metabolite suggested for use on a proposed golf course located in Hawaii. The 300-400 acre area that would include the 18-hole golf course is characterized by forested slopes. Localized erosion exists presently in areas where a dense, deep mat of long pine needles has washed-out. The SWRRBWQ model was used to evaluate potential losses of pesticides in runoff and subsequent impacts to aquatic organisms in the nearshore coastal environment. The final step was comparison of acute aquatic toxicity criteria (action levels) with conservatively predicted pesticide runoff concentrations. The assessment revealed that potential chlorpyrifos concentrations in runoff could exceed the EPA established water quality criteria. Consequently, alternative pesticides with minimal potential for aquatic impacts were recommended. Selected results are presented in Table V.

The runoff losses are from statistically significant storm events of 24 hour duration. Rainfall amounts for these events, a 1-year return, 2-year return, 10-year return, 50-year return, and 100-year return, 24-hour duration storms were estimated from isopluvial maps prepared by the U.S. Weather Bureau for the Hawaiian Islands (33). Each storm event was modeled within an annual simulation to allow for realistic antecedent moisture conditions. They were added to site-specific rainfall data input file within one to two days following the application of the pesticides. (One day for the 1-year through 10-year return storms and two days for the 50-year and 100-year return storms.)

Table V. SWRRBWQ Runoff Modeling - Storm Event Results - Developed Condition - Pesticides

(all values expressed in: dissolved = μ/l; sorbed = μg/kg)						
Runoff Losses	1-Yr	2-Yr	10-Yr	50-Yr	100-Yr	Aquat Tox
Bendiocarb						47.0
-dissolved-	0.03	0.02	0.01	0.01	0.01	
-sorbed-	0.35	0.35	0.04	0.02	0.01	
Chlorothalonil						3.2
-dissolved-	1.40	1.12	0.91	0.80	0.71	
-sorbed-	57.9	51.7	15.4	10.0	7.7	
Chlorpyrifos						0.011
-dissolved-	0.06	0.05	0.04	0.04	0.03	
-sorbed-	8.7	8.1	2.8	1.9	1.6	
Isazofos						0.6
-dissolved-	0.005	0.003	0.001	0.001	0.000	
-sorbed-	0.00	0.00	0.00	0.00	0.00	
Mancozeb						160.0
-dissolved-	1.84	1.40	0.98	0.79	0.63	
-sorbed-	31.7	26.4	6.2	3.4	2.2	

IN-STREAM MODELING

It is beyond the scope of this paper to discuss in-stream modeling in detail, but a few statements are required to complete the description of the risk assessment process.

The Exposure Analysis Modeling System (EXAMS II; version 2.94) is the model that appears to be most appropriate and user-friendly for these applications (36). It treats the water in ponds, lakes, or streams as discrete but linked water column constructs in the areas of geometry, flow, dispersion, sediment content, solar intensity, nonpoint source flow, etc. EXAMS II can be run in the steady state or pulse modes. It is a validated model that is used and supported by the EPA.

COMPARISON OF MODELING AND MONITORING RESULTS

Smith, et al. *(16)* recently tested PRZM and GLEAMS simulation results with a Bahiagrass test plot in Georgia. A bromide ion tracer and atrazine and alachlor were added and tracked over time with soil solution samplers and monitoring wells. Both models did a good job of predicting time-to-peak concentrations at 0.61 m (2 ft) and 1.22 m (4 ft) depth, and produced fair to good predictions of the peak concentrations.

Squillace and Thurman *(34)* recently reviewed the literature and reported new data on herbicide runoff from agricultural field plots and watersheds. They noted that the proportion of the herbicides that run off from these environments typically varies from 0.3% to 5% of the amount applied, on an annual basis. This compares well with the SWRRBWQ predictions for the herbicides 2,4-D of 0.03% and 1.83% for the fungicide mancozeb at sites in Hawaii. These predictions are for turf, which tends to generate less runoff than corn, soybeans, etc.

Arnold, et al. *(35)* demonstrated a significant decrease in sediment loss from a rural area after it was urbanized. Sediment loss was reduced from 2.9 to 1.2 tons per acre after a lakeside area in Texas became 77% urbanized. This urbanization included the replacement of much undeveloped land by turf and impervious surfaces. The SWRRB model was used to simulate runoff and sediment losses in the watershed. The erosion, sediment delivery ratio, and reservoir sedimentation results compared well with the data from the SCS erosion studies on the reservoir watershed.

Computer Simulation of a Golf Course Runoff Monitoring Study. A limited runoff water quality monitoring study was conducted in the spring and summer of 1991 on a portion of a Florida golf course. A longer-term ground water monitoring study was also done. The studies were performed by Camp Dresser & McKee, Inc., Sarasota, Florida as a component of the Sarasota Bay National Estuary Program Point and Non-point Source Loading Assessment, a federal, state, and local funded project (Camp Dresser & McKee, Sarasota, Florida unpublished data). Runoff water was sampled during select storm events and analyzed for basic water quality parameters: total phosphorus, total Kjeldahl nitrogen, NO2-NO3 nitrogen, NH4 nitrogen, and total suspended solids. Three sampling sites were established. Results from site 1 were simulated for this paper. Site 1 collected overland runoff from a drainage basin of approximately 4.6 acres. Each basin included portions of the more intensively managed turf areas as well as areas that were not fertilized, irrigated, or treated with pesticides.

Simulation of the Monitoring Study Using SWRRBWQ. The drainage area of site 1 was selected for the comparison of runoff modeling results with actual monitoring data for two storm events. The SWRRBWQ model was chosen for this exercise based on two primary considerations: SWRRBWQ simulates nitrogen and phosphorus transport in runoff in addition to water and sediment yield; and different management areas within the drainage basin can be represented individually as sub-basins.

The objective of this exercise was not to calibrate the model to the field results, but rather to evaluate its performance in comparison with field results based on reasonable application of the model from a user point-of-reference. Site-specific data were input where available. Otherwise, reasonable assumptions and values recommended in the model documentation were used.

Key SWRRBWQ Model Input Parameters. The 4.6 acre drainage area of the golf course was divided into 6 sub-basins that were delineated based on management intensity. Climatological data were generated for a one year period and combined with measured rainfall for the period of the monitoring study. Rainfall data for the site were not available outside of the period of the runoff study (April to July, 1991). The predominant soil is a Pomello fine sand. The slopes throughout the basin, including the drainage channel, on the average are very gentle (<1%). The drainage channel was maintained with the same practices as the surrounding areas and showed no evidence of erosion (Kaminski, personal communication, 1992). The superintendent of the golf course made a single spring fertilizer application on fairways with Par-Ex 16-4-8 which contains water-soluble and slow-release nitrogen sources. Irrigation on the fairways was simulated based on moisture stress.

Results and Discussion of the Simulation. The two dates corresponding to sampling events in the monitoring study were June 6 and July 20. Measured and simulated runoff water quality results are given in Table VI. No water or sediment loss was simulated to occur on the June 6 event. Water yield from the July 20 event compares well with the measured amount. No sediment loss was predicted, however. This may explain underestimation of organic nitrogen and total phosphorus. The lack of sediment loss may be a factor of model sensitivity rather than accuracy. Sediment yield is presented in terms of metric tonnes per hectare (T/ha). The smallest unit would be 0.01 T/ha. If the model were in fact accurately predicting sediment yield, the July 20 runoff concentration of 10.5 mg/l back-calculates to 0.0007 T/ha. The general failure of the model to predict the June 6 results is probably due to the very low amount of water and sediment runoff that was generated from the generally flat, sandy site. Parenthetical values represent what might be considered detection limits for the model.

Table VI. Comparison of Measured vs. Simulated Runoff

	Measured		Simulated	
	6/6	7/1	6/6	7/1
Rainfall, in	0.48	1.89	0.48	1.89
Water Yield, cf	179	4455	(<7)	5239
Sediment Conc., mg/l	9.5	10.5	(<106)	(<106)
NO2-NO3 N, mg/l	0.035	0.094	(<0.1)	1.74
Total P, mg/l	4.76	2.29	(<0.1)	1.49

Thus the results of this model testing exercise demonstrate the lower limits of SWRRBWQ to predict turf runoff. Basically, SWRRBWQ does not do a good job of predicting runoff at sites with minimal runoff, and is more appropriate for sites that may experience significant losses, which is where the focus should be anyway.

CONCLUSIONS

Questions about potential impacts of turf chemicals on water quality must be answered with risk assessments. In cases of proposed golf courses when citizen and/or regulatory concerns are great, and/or the potential for impacts on humans or aquatic organisms are significant, the risk assessments should be quantitative. Currently, the most rigorous way to conduct quantitative risk assessments for pesticide leaching potential or turf chemical runoff potential is via use of computer simulation models. But modeling results are inexact, i.e., one cannot use modeling results to predict precise concentrations in ground water or surface runoff. The ultimate uses of the risk assessment results are to help develop environmentally responsible Integrated Golf Course Management Plans and golf course designs. This process provides useful information to regulators, developers, and others during the permitting process.

LITERATURE CITED

1. National Golf Foundation. *Golf Market Today*, 32(2), March- April, 1992.
2. Bilanin, A.; Teske, M.; Barry, J.; Ekbald, R., *Trans. ASAE*, **1989**, *32*, 1, 327-334.
3. Honeycutt, R.D.; Tolle, J., "Estimation of Pesticide Drift from Groundboom Application to Golf Courses-Use of the AGDISP Model," In "Environmental Risk Assessment and Integrated Golf Course Management Plan for The Proposed Golf Courses at Maui Wailea 670," Environmental & Turf Services, Inc., Wheaton, MD, **1992**, Appendix F, unpublished report.
4. Cohen, S.Z.; Carsel, R.F.; Creeger, S.M.; Enfield, C.G., In *Treatment and Disposal of Pesticide Wastes*, Krueger, R.F. and J.N. Seiber, Eds., Am, Chem. Soc., Wash. D.C., **1984**, 297-325.
5. Petrovic, A.M., *J. Environ. Qual.*, **1990**, *19*, 1-14.
6. Miles, C.J., In *Pesticide Transformation Products Fate and Significance in the Environment*, Somasundaram, J. and J.R. Coasts, Eds., Am. Chem. Soc., Wash., DC, **1991**, 61-74.
7. Miles, C.J.; Doerge, D.R., *J. Agric. Food Chem.*, **1991**, *39*, 214-217.
8. Glynn, P.W.; Howard, L.S.; Corcoran, E.; Freay, A.D., *Marine Pollution Bull.*, **1984**, 15, 370-374.
9. Gustafson, D., *J. Environ. Tox. Chem.*, **1989**, *8*, 339-357.
10. Rao, P.S.C.; Hornsby, A.G.; Jessup, R.E., *Soil and Crop Sci. Soc. Florida*, **1985**, *44*, 1-8.
11. Wagenet, R.J.; Hutson, J.L., *LEACHM: A Finite Difference Model for Simulating Water, Salt and Pesticide Movement in the Plant Root Zone. Continuum. Vol. 2, Version 2.0*, New York State Water Resour. Inst., Cornell Univ., Ithaca, NY, 1989.
12. Boesten, J.J.T.I., *Pestic. Sci.*, **1991**, *31*, 375-388.
13. Carsel, R.F.; Smith C.N.; Mulkey L.A.; Dean J.D.; Jowise P., *User's Manual for the Pesticide Root Zone Model (PRZM): Release 1*, EPA 600/3-84-109, U.S. EPA, Athens, GA, 1984.

14. Dean, J.D.; Huyakorn, P.S.; Donigian, Jr., A.S.; Voos, K.A.; Schanz, R.W.; Meeks, Y.J.; Carsel, R.F., *Risk of Unsaturated/Saturated Transport and Transformation of Chemical Concentrations (RUSTIC) Volume I: Theory and Code Verification*, EPA/600/3-89/048a, U.S. EPA, Athens, GA, 1989.

15. Dean, J.D.; Huyakorn, P.S.; Donigian, Jr., A.S.; Voos, K.A.; Schanz, R.W.; Carsel, R.F., *Risk of Unsaturated/Saturated Transport and Transformation of Chemical Concentrations (RUSTIC) Volume II: User's Guide*, EPA/600/3-89/048b, U.S.EPA, Athens, GA, 1989.

16. Smith, C.M.; Bottcher, A.B.; Campbell K.L.; Thomas D.L., *Trans. ASAE*, **1991**, *34*(3), 838-847.

17. Pennell, K.D.; Hornsby, A.G.; Jessup, R.E.; Rao, P.S.C., *Water Resourc. Res.*, **1990**, *26*(11), 2679-2693.

18. Giambelluca, T.W.; Nullet, M.A.; Schroeder, T.A., *Rainfall Atlas of Hawaii*, Report R76, State of Hawaii, DLNR, DOWALD, Honolulu, HI, 1986.

19. EPA, Office of Pesticide Programs and the Office of Drinking Water, *Another Look: A National Survey of Pesticides in Drinking Water Wells Phase II Report*, EPA 579/09-91-020, NTIS, Springfield, VA, 1992.

20. Gold, A.J.; Morton, T.G.; Sullivan, W.M.; McClory, J., *Water, Air and Soil Pollution*, **1988**, *37*, 121-129.

21. Lorber, M.N.; Cohen, S.Z.; Noren, S.E.; DeBuchananne, G.D., *Ground Water Mon. Rev.*, **1989**, *9*, 109-125.

22. Rao, P.S.C; Davidson, J.M., In *Environmental Impact of Nonpoint Source Pollution*, Overcash, M.R. and J.M. Davidson, Eds., Ann Arbor Science Publishers, Ann Arbor, MI, **1980**, 23-66.

23. Parrish, R., Personal communications, 1991, Statistician, Computer Sciences Corporation, Environmental Research Laboratory, EPA, Athens, Georgia.

24. Cohen, S.Z.; Nickerson, A.; Maxey, R.; Dupuy, Jr., A.; Senita, J., *Ground Water Mon. Rev.*, **1990**, *10*, 160-173.

25. Arnold, J.G.; Williams, J.R.; Griggs, R.H.; Sammons, N.B., *SWRRBWQ A Basin Scale Model for Assessing Management Impacts on Water Quality*, USDA, ARS, in cooperation with Texas Agricultural Experiment Station, Texas A&M University, Temple, TX, 1991.

26. Leonard, R.A.; Knisel, W.G.; Still, D.A., *Trans. ASAE*, **1987**, *30*(5), 1403-1418.

27. Arnold, J.G.; Williams, J.R., *J. Water Resour. Plan. and Manag.*, ASCE, **1987**, *113*(2), 243-256.

28. Leonard, R.A.; Knisel, W.G.; Davis, F.M.; Johnson, A.W., *J. Irrig. Drainage Eng.*, **1990**, *116*(1), 24-35.

29. Knisel, W.G.; Leonard, R.A.; Davis, F.M.; Sheridan, J.M., *J. Soil and Water Conserv.*, **1991**, Nov-Dec.

30. USDA, SCS, *Urban Hydrology for Small Watersheds*, U.S. Dept. of Agriculture, Soil Conserv. Service, Washington, D.C., 1986.

31. Williams, J.R.; Berndt, H.D., *Trans ASAE*, **1977**, *20*(6), 1100-1104.

32. Arnold, J.G.; Williams, J.R.; Nicks, A.D.; Sammons, N.B., *SWRRB: A Basin Scale Simulation Model for Soil and Water Resources Management (1ˢᵗ ed).*, Texas A&M University Press, College Station, TX, 1990.

33. US Dept. of Commerce, *Rainfall-Frequency Atlas of the Hawaiian Islands for Areas to 200 Square Miles, Durations to 24 Hours, and Return Periods from 1 to 100 Years*, U.S. Dept. of Commerce, Weather Bureau, Washington, D.C., 1962.

34. Squillace, P.G.; Thurman, E.M., *Environ. Sci. Technol.*, **1992**, *26*(3), 538-545.

35. Arnold, J.G.; Bircket, M.D.; Williams, J.R.; Smith, W.F.; McGill, H.N., *Water Res. Bull.*, **1987**, *23*, 1101-1107.

36. Burns, L.A., *Exposure Analysis Modeling System: User Guide for EXAMS II Version 2.94*, EPA 600/3-89/084, U.S. EPA, Athens, GA, 1990.

RECEIVED November 23, 1992

Chapter 20

Two Small-Plot Techniques for Measuring Airborne and Dislodgeable Residues of Pendimethalin Following Application to Turfgrass

J. J. Jenkins[1,3], A. S. Curtis[1], and R. J. Cooper[2]

[1]Massachusetts Pesticide Analysis Laboratory, Department of Entomology and [2]Department of Plant and Soil Sciences, University of Massachusetts, Amherst, MA 01003

Airborne and dislodgeable residues were determined following application of the dinitroaniline herbicide pendimethalin to Kentucky bluegrass field plots at the University of Massachusetts Turf Research Farm in South Deerfield, Massachusetts. Two small plot techniques were used to investigate the diurnal flux of airborne residues as well as the decline in daily flux over a two-week period following application. In the first technique, airborne residues were measured using field chambers consisting of 19 L Pyrex bottles with the bottoms removed and fitted with Teflon cartridges containing 25 g of XAD-4 porous polymer resin. The second technique utilized the Theoretical Profile Shape method. This technique employs a circular plot 20 meters in radius, sampling the air at a single height in the center of the plot. For both techniques, turf samples were collected to determine the daily decline in foliar dislodgeable residues. The results of these two techniques were compared to estimate pendimethalin airborne loss from turfgrass.

Concern over the release of pesticides into the air in urban environments has increased over the past few years. Application of pesticides to turfgrass constitutes a major urban use. Human exposure via dermal as well as inhalation routes should be considered in assessing the risk of pesticides applied to turfgrass. A previous study *(1)* examined the use of chambers placed in the field to directly monitor airborne residues of the dinitroaniline herbicide pendimethalin following application to turfgrass. This technique was investigated for the study of pesticide loss from turfgrass as it allowed for a replicated

[3]Current address: Department of Agricultural Chemistry, Oregon State University, Corvallis, OR 97331

small plot design (<40 m²), requiring relatively few measurements. In addition, pendimethalin airborne loss was compared to foliar dislodgeable residues. The determination of foliar dislodgeable residues has traditionally been used to estimate the potential for human dermal exposure. However, foliar dislodgeable residues may also be characterized as those residues most available for airborne loss or movement to other parts of the canopy with infiltrating water or dry deposition (1). Presented here is a second technique, the Theoretical Profile Shape method. This technique also allows for a small plot design (<1300 m²), and requires relatively few measurements. These two methods for estimating pendimethalin airborne loss from turfgrass are compared.

EXPERIMENTAL DESIGN

Field Chamber Method. Pendimethalin airborne residues were measured using field chambers as described in Jenkins et al. (1). Pendimethalin was applied as the 60 WDG formulation at 3.4 kg a.i./ha to Kentucky bluegrass field plots at the University of Massachusetts Turf Research Farm in South Deerfield, Massachusetts. Plot design consisted of 7 strips (0.4 x 3.4 meters) treated with pendimethalin, separated by walkways with similar dimensions, and 1 untreated strip. Each strip was designed to accommodate three chambers. Chamber design is shown in Figure 1. Chambers were moved to a new strip for successive diurnal sampling periods. This minimized the impact of sampling method on the "natural environment."

Pendimethalin airborne residues were trapped by drawing air at 30 liters/minute through Teflon cartridges containing 25 g (50 ml) of Amberlite XAD-4 polymeric resin. A similar amount of resin was placed at the inlet to remove any pendimethalin airborne residues from the incoming air. Resin cartridges were collected at the end of each sampling period and the chambers were disassembled and rinsed with acetone/hexane 1:1 to determine airborne residues on the chamber surfaces.

Air and foliar dislodgeable residue samples were collected over a 15-day period in May 1988. Air sampling began at 0700 hour immediately following application. Samples were collected continuously for the first two days at 2-hour intervals between 0700 and 1900 hours, followed by a continuous overnight sample. Two-hour air samples were collected between 0900 and 1700 hours following application on days 4, 5, and 15.

Temperature was monitored at the grass surface both inside and outside the chambers at the beginning, middle, and end of each sampling period. In addition, ambient temperature, relative humidity, rainfall, and total daily solar radiation were recorded.

Three replicate foliar dislodgeable residue samples of 91.5 cm² were collected from an area adjacent to each chamber. The turfgrass was separated from the thatch and soil and foliar dislodgeable residues analyzed as described in Jenkins et al. (2).

Theoretical Profile Shape Method. The Theoretical Profile Shape (TPS) method, which uses the trajectory-simulation (TS) model of Wilson et al. (3), was also used to estimate pendimethalin airborne loss from turfgrass. Previous work by Majewski and co-workers (4-6) has show this method to be comparable to other micrometeorological techniques for estimating evaporative flux of a number of pesticides from soil. Details of the TPS method and the TS model are described in Wilson et al. (3,7) and Majewski et al. (4-6). Briefly, the TPS method employs the TS model, a 2-dimensional dispersion model to estimate source strength [$F_z(0)$] from a single measurement within the vertical profile of the horizontal flux at the center of a circular plot. Where:

$$F_z(0) = (uc)^{measured} / \Phi$$

$F_z(0)$ = source strength determined as the actual vertical flux rate (mg/m²hr)
$(uc)^{measured}$ = product of the measured wind speed and air concentration
Φ = normalized horizontal flux predicted from the TS model.

The measurement height (ZINST) is chosen based upon plot radius, roughness length (z_0), and Monin-Obukhov atmospheric stability length L. For a given radius and z_0, height ZINST is chosen to minimize the effect of L. The TS model uses a constant value of Φ for specified conditions of atmospheric stability expressed in terms of L. L = ± 5 m for very stable and unstable conditions and L = ∞ for neutral conditions. Values of Φ were determined for stable/unstable, neutral, and intermediate conditions of atmospheric stability as described in Wilson et al. (*3,7*). For L = ∞, defined as periods of daytime cloudiness, early in the morning or late in the afternoon on clear days, and clear nights if the wind speed is > 2.0 m/s at 2.5 m, Φ = 9.4. For L = ± 5 m, defined as clear nights if the wind speed at 2.5 m is < 2.0 m/s and also during the day when wind speeds are < 2.0 m/s at 2.5 m, Φ = 9.0. For intermediate conditions of atmospheric stability Φ = 9.2. All categories of atmospheric stability occurred during the study, and the wind speed at ZINST never exceeded 5 m/s.

    Airborne residue and wind speed were measured at a height ZINST of 73 cm chosen according to plot radius of 20 meters and surface roughness length of 0.2 cm, as described in Wilson et al. (*3*). Pendimethalin airborne residues were collected with a Staplex TF1A high volume air sampler containing 130-140 ml of Amberlite XAD-4 polymeric resin. Air was drawn through the resin trap at a rate of 0.8 m³/minute. The air sampler was mounted on a CM10 weather instrument tripod (Campbell Scientific). This tripod also contained instrumentation for the measurement of wind speed (at a height of 73 cm), wind direction, solar radiation, and temperature (at the foliar surface and heights of 73, 123, and 173 cm). Rainfall data was obtained from a LI-1200S Data Logger (LI-COR, Inc.).

    Pendimethalin was applied as the 60 WDG formulation at 3.4 kg a.i./ha to a Kentucky bluegrass field plot at the University of Massachusetts Turf Research Farm in South Deerfield, Massachusetts. Air and foliar dislodgeable residue samples were collected over a 14-day period beginning in late April 1989. Air sampling began at 0700 hours immediately following application. Samples were collected continuously for the first two days at 2-hour intervals from 0700 to 1900 hours, followed by an overnight sample from 1900 to 0700 hours the following day. This sampling regime was also used for sampling on days 5, 8, and 14.

    Four replicate foliar dislodgeable residue samples were collected at approximately 1300 hour on each air sampling day. Samples were collected using a 10.8 cm diameter golf cup as described in Jenkins et al. (*1*).

Residue Analysis. Preparation of the XAD-4 resin and sample analysis is described in Jenkins et al. (*2*). Pendimethalin was extracted from XAD-4 resin by shaking for one hour in 250 ml of acetone/hexane (1:1) on a Wrist-Action shaker. The extract was filtered and concentrated by rotary evaporation at 45°C, taken to dryness under nitrogen, and dissolved in toluene for analysis. Field chamber/funnel rinsate samples were dried over anhydrous sodium sulfate, concentrated by rotary evaporation at 45°C, taken to dryness with N_2, and dissolved in toluene for analysis. Distilled water was added to the foliar dislodgeable residue methanol extract to obtain 10% methanol in water solution. Samples were loaded onto 6 ml C18 columns at 20 ml/minute and the eluant discarded. Pendimethalin residues were eluted with 4 ml acetone/hexane (1:1). The eluant was taken to dryness under nitrogen and dissolved in toluene for analysis. The turfgrass was separated from the thatch and soil and foliar dislodgeable residues prepared as described in Jenkins et al. *(2)*. All samples were analyzed by capillary gas liquid chromatography using a Hewlett-Packard 5890A GC equipped with a N-P detector.

Limits of detection and method recovery data for the chamber method are reported in Jenkins et al. *(2)*. For the chamber method, the overall limit of detection for pendimethalin airborne flux was approximately 8μg/m²hr. For the TPS method, the limit of detection for pendimethalin airborne flux was approximately 14 µg/m²hr for the 2-hour sampling periods and 0.7 µg/m²hr for the overnight sampling periods. In both studies, the limit of detection for the dislodgeable foliar residue samples was 1 µg/sample. Turfgrass leaf area ranged from approximately 300 to 500 cm²/sample, giving a limit of detection on a leaf area basis (single-sided) of approximately 2.5 µg/cm². The procedure for determining turfgrass leaf surface area from sample weight is given in Jenkins et al. *(1)*.

For the TPS method, to determine method recovery, 250 ml XAD-4 resin extracts were fortified at 4 µg and 200 µg per sample. Recovery from samples fortified at 4 µg and 200 µg was similar. Overall recovery was 81% (SD=6, n=17).

RESULTS AND DISCUSSION

Field Chamber Method. Total airborne loss of pendimethalin on the day of application was 17.1 mg or 5% of the 340 mg a.i./m² application. Pendimethalin source strength for days 1 and 2 is shown in Figure 2.

Diurnal variation in pendimethalin source strength, or airborne flux, was most pronounced on day 1, and was well correlated with solar radiation (r=0.86) and chamber canopy temperature (r=0.94). Day 2 of the study was overcast, resulting in daily solar radiation 5-6 times lower than other sampling days. On day 2 pendimethalin source strength was equally well correlated to chamber canopy temperature (r=0.94) as compared to day 1. However, the correlation with daily solar radiation was much lower (r=0.53). The stronger correlation of source strength to chamber canopy temperature as compared to solar radiation is thought to be due to the "greenhouse effect" inside the chambers, resulting in higher afternoon temperatures inside the chambers as compared to ambient. This effect was most apparent under the prevailing weather conditions on day 2. Over the course of the study, however, pendimethalin source strength was most closely correlated to chamber canopy temperature.

For the remaining sampling days the correlation between chamber canopy temperature and source strength was not as strong as for days 1 and 2 (day 4, r=0.49; day 5, r=0.84; day 15, r=0.73). This suggests that as pendimethalin foliar deposits become depleted, and as residues are redistributed with rainfall (26 mm between days 2 and 12) to a variety of

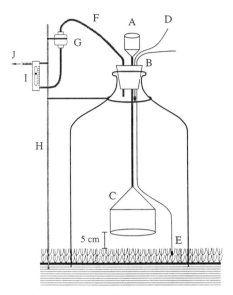

Figure 1. Diagram of field chamber. (A) intake resin trap, (B) aluminum foil-covered stopper, (C) air dispersion funnel, (D) chamber ambient temperature thermistor, (E) chamber canopy temperature thermistor, (F) Teflon tubing, (G) Teflon resin cartridge, (H) support rod, (I) flow meter, (J) connection to vacuum pump.

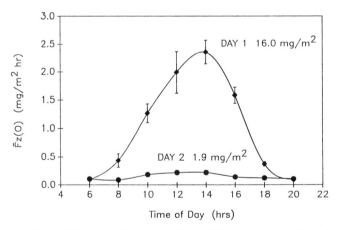

Figure 2. Diurnal flux of airborne residues following application of pendimethalin 60 WDG at 3.4 kg a.i./ha to turfgrass. Average source strength (n=3), represented by $F_z (0)$, measured by the Field Chamber method for the day of application (Day 1) and the following day (Day 2).

sites with differing sorption properties and microclimates, there is no longer a simple relationship between solar radiation (as it affects chamber canopy temperature) and source strength.

Pendimethalin daily airborne loss and foliar dislodgeable residues are shown in Figures 3 and 4, respectively. The decline in both daily airborne loss and foliar dislodgeable residues can be characterized as bilinear, with an initial period of rapid decline ending 5-7 days following application, followed by a period of slower decline for the remainder of the study. The natural break in both sets of data between 5 and 7 days supports the observation that dislodgeable residues are most available for airborne loss.

Theoretical Profile Shape (TPS) Method. In the TPS study, total airborne loss on the day of application was 7.0 mg or 2% of the initial application. Pendimethalin source strength for days 1 and 2 of the TPS study is shown in Figure 5. Pendimethalin source strength varied diurnally, correlating equally well with both canopy temperature and solar radiation on days 1, 2, 5, and 8, with correlation coefficients for canopy temperature of 0.96, 0.91, 0.87, and 0.93 respectively. While the pattern of diurnal variation of pendimethalin source strength on day 14 was similar to that on preceding days, the correlation between source strength and canopy temperature (r=0.63) was much lower than for the preceding sampling days. As described earlier, the weaker correlation most likely reflects the attenuation and redistribution of foliar dislodgeable residues following 67 mm of rainfall between days 10 and 13.

Daily airborne loss and foliar dislodgeable residues for the TPS study are shown in Figures 6 and 7. Under the weather conditions that prevailed for this study, both daily airborne loss and foliar dislodgeable residues declined more uniformly as compared to the Field Chamber study. The slower initial decline in foliar dislodgeable residues in the Theoretical Profile Shape study is most likely due to the absence of rainfall until 10 days following application, as compared to the 18 mm of rainfall that occurred by day 5 in the Field Chamber study.

Estimate of Daily Airborne Loss. The diurnal variation of hourly flux exhibited in both studies allows for the estimate of total daily airborne loss based on the following assumptions:

1. Peak flux occurs during the sampling period between 1300 and 1500 hr.
2. Airborne loss occurs only during daylight hours (0600-2000 hr).
3. The loss rate varies linearly between the endpoints and peak flux.

Using these assumptions total daily airborne loss is estimated by integrating the area under the triangle formed. The use of this procedure to estimate daily airborne loss using the Field Chamber method is given in Jenkins et al. *(1)*. The estimated and measured daily airborne loss for the Theoretical Profile Shape study are compared in Table I. Measured daily airborne loss was determined by summing the airborne loss for the 2-hour sampling periods from 0600 to 2000 hr. Estimated daily airborne loss was determined from the peak loss during the 1300-1500 hr sampling intervals using the simple integration technique described above. Overnight loss (2000-0600 hr) is assumed to be negligible. Measured overnight airborne loss for the first two days of the study averaged 0.1 $\mu g/m^2$ (SD=0.07). Estimated daily airborne loss values were in close agreement with the

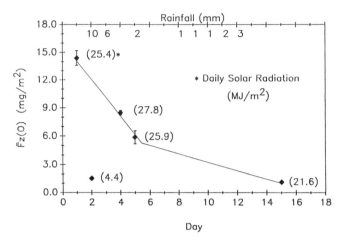

Figure 3. Daily airborne loss following application of pendimethalin 60 WDG at 3.4 kg a.i./ha to turfgrass. Average source strength (n=3), represented by F_z (0), estimated by the Field Chamber method as the sum of the 2-hour sampling intervals from 0900 to 1700 hr. Daily solar radiation (MJ/m^2) from 0900 to 1700 hr is shown in parenthesis.

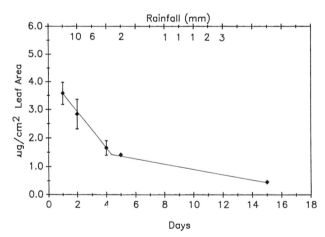

Figure 4. Average foliar dislodgeable residues (n=3), expressed as μg/cm^2 single-sided leaf area, following application of pendimethalin 60 WDG at 3.4 kg a.i./ha to turfgrass, Field Chamber study.

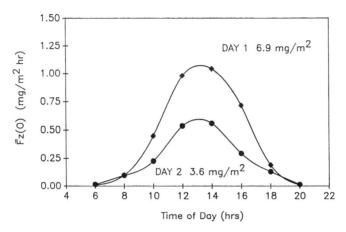

Figure 5. Diurnal flux of airborne residues following application of pendimethalin 60 WDG at 3.4 kg a.i./ha to turfgrass. Source strength, represented by F_z (0), measured by the Theoretical Profile Shape method for the day of application (Day 1) and the following day (Day 2).

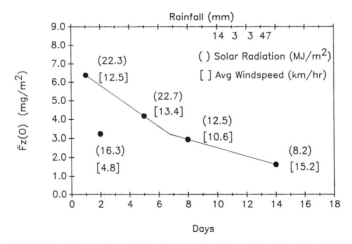

Figure 6. Daily airborne loss following application of pendimethalin 60 WDG at 3.4 kg a.i./ha to turfgrass. Source strength, represented by F_z (0), was estimated by the Theoretical Profile Shape method as the sum of the 2-hour sampling intervals from 0900 to 1700 hr. Daily solar radiation (MJ/m²) from 0900 to 1700 hr is shown in parenthesis. Average wind speed (km/hr) from 0900 to 1700 hr is shown in brackets.

measured values, differing by an average of 11% (SD=6). These results suggest that under conditions that result in diurnal airborne flux patterns similar to those shown in Figure 1, estimates of pendimethalin daily airborne loss from turfgrass may be obtained from a single midday airborne residue sample.

Table I. Pendimethalin Daily Airborne Loss Measured by the Theoretical Profile Shape Method and Estimated Based on Peak Flux

Sampling Interval (Days)	Peak Flux (mg/m^2hr) (1300-1500)	Daily Airborne Loss (0600-2000)[a] (mg/m^2)	
		Measured	Estimated
1	1.042	6.9	7.3
2	0.559	3.6	3.9
5	0.783	4.6	5.5
8	0.520	3.4	2.1
14	0.303[b]	1.8	2.1

[a]Average overnight airborne loss (2000-0600 hr) 0.1 mg/m^2 (SD=0.07).
[b]1100-1300 hr sampling period.

Relationship Between Temperature and Source Strength. Temperature affects pesticide source strength primarily as it affects vapor pressure (Vp) *(8)*. For ideal conditions, the affect of temperature on vapor pressure is described by the Clausius-Clayperon equation:

$$Log\ Vp = b - [(dH_{vap}/2.303R) \times 1/T]$$

For ideal conditions, plotting log Vp versus reciprocal temperature gives a linear relationship. This relationship was applied to the effect of canopy temperature on source strength for data obtained for sampling days 1, 2, 5, and 8 of the Theoretical Profile Shape study as shown in Figure 8. To investigate the affect of temperature only, source strength determined for each 2-hour sampling interval was normalized to the mean wind speed for the study using the relationship shown in Figure 9. The good fit of the data (r^2=0.91) in Figure 8 suggests source strength at the foliar surface is controlled, in part, by the affect of temperature on vapor pressure. Conceptually, this would suggest that for conditions where there is complete coverage of the foliar surface (i.e., the pesticide is layered on the surface and is in effect volatilizing from itself), source strength is controlled primarily by the temperature at the foliar surface, which determines the rate of vapor formation and diffusion through the stagnant air layer closely surrounding the surface *(1)*. For this reason, data from day 14 was not included in Figure 8 as the 67 mm of rainfall that occurred between day 8 and day 14 resulted in redistribution of dislodgeable residues from the foliar surface (see Figure 7).

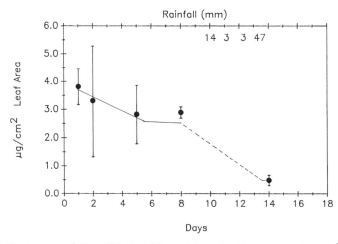

Figure 7. Average foliar dislodgeable residues (n=4), expressed as µg/cm² single-sided leaf area, following application of pendimethalin 60 WDG at 3.4 kg a.i./ha to turfgrass, Theoretical Profile Shape study.

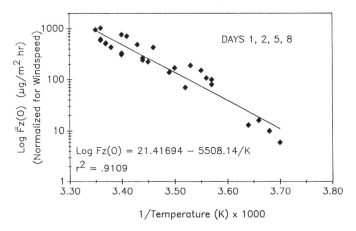

Figure 8. Relationship between temperature and wind speed normalized pendimethalin source strength (F_z (0)) for each 2-hour sampling interval (0600-2000 hr) for days 1, 2, 5, and 8 of the Theoretical Profile Shape method study. F_z (0) was normalized to the mean wind speed determined from the average wind speed during each 2-hour sampling interval using the relationship shown in Figure 9.

Relationship Between Wind Speed and Source Strength. The effect of wind speed on airborne loss of pesticide surface residues is discussed in greater detail in Jenkins et al. *(1)*. This discussion is summarized as follows: assuming that diffusion across the stagnant air layer is rate limiting, wind speed will affect source strength as it affects the depth of the stagnant air layer. Increased wind speed will reduce the depth of the stagnant air layer, resulting in increased source strength *(9)*. However, the relationship between source strength and wind speed has rarely been demonstrated. The laboratory data of Farmer and Letey *(10)* and Phillips *(9)* are shown in Figure 9. These data show the relationship between wind speed and dieldrin flux from a "non-adsorbing" surface. The data of Farmer and Letey *(10)* represent dieldrin flux from quartz sand at 30°C. The data of Phillips *(9)* represent dieldrin flux from glass treated at 4-9 µg/cm², adjusted by Spencer and Claith *(8)* for differences in vapor pressure between 30°C and temperatures used by Phillips. These data suggest that between wind speeds of 0.0033 and 4.8 km/hr, there is an exponential relationship between wind speed and dieldrin source strength. This relationship was used to determine the normalized wind speed values shown in Figure 8.

Effect of Temperature and Wind Speed on Field Chamber Results. A detailed discussion of the affect of temperature and wind speed on results of the Field Chamber method is given in Jenkins et al. *(1)*. Field chamber results are affected by the modification of the environment during sampling as compared to the natural conditions outside of the chambers, particularly with respect to temperature and wind speed. To minimize the affect of the chambers on the natural environment, no area was sampled for more than two hours in any sampling day (except for overnight samples taken during the first 48 hours following application).

Although temperatures inside the chambers were as much as 11°C greater than outside, chamber temperatures never exceeded 38°C. Higher canopy temperatures inside chambers should result in increased source strength. A number of researchers have reported a three to fourfold increase in pesticide volatilization for each 10°C increase *(8, 11, 12)*. These data suggest that the Field Chamber method will *overestimate* source strength by three to fourfold when the temperature inside the chamber is 10°C greater than outside the chamber.

Low wind speed inside the chambers during sampling must also be considered. Wind speed in the chambers during sampling (0.03 km/hr) is well below what might be found in the field under all but "still air" conditions. Using the relationship shown in Figure 9, extrapolating from 0.03 to 4.8 km/hr wind would result in approximately a threefold increase in source strength; a 25 km/hr would be required for a fourfold increase. Whether the relationship shown in Figure 9 holds for wind speeds above 4.8 km/hr is not known. Phillips *(9)* concluded that the effect of increasing wind speed on increasing source strength must ultimately reach a limiting value. Taking this into consideration, the Field Chamber method will *underestimate* source strength by three to fourfold compared to "natural conditions" for a range of wind speeds of 3 to 25 km/hr.

The major disadvantage of the Field Chamber method is that air sampling is conducted under artificial conditions. However, it appears that for pendimethalin, under the chamber conditions that prevailed during this study, the effects of the chamber environment on two of the critical parameters that control airborne loss from foliar surfaces, wind speed and temperature, were offsetting.

The use of the Field Chamber technique to estimate pesticide airborne loss under conditions other than those experienced during this study may require that the airborne flux values determined be adjusted for effects of higher temperatures and lower wind speeds within the chamber as compared to the "natural environment."

Errors associated with TPS method. Wilson et al. *(3,7)* discuss sources of error associated with the TS model that contribute to uncertainty of airborne flux values determined. They estimate that the inherent error in the model for a plot with a 20 m radius and roughness length of 0.2 cm is 4%. In addition, they estimate error due to horizontal turbulence is less than ±10% of the total horizontal flux. The accuracy for the TPS method also depends on the correct choice of the roughness length z_0, which is used to select the sampling height ZINST. Roughness length (z_0) can be determined experimentally by measuring wind speed at various heights (z_n). Roughness length z_0 is determined from the intercept of a plot of wind speed vs. ln z_n. The roughness length of 0.2 cm used in the present study was derived from data published in Linsley et al. *(13)* for grass cut to 1.5 cm. At the initiation of the study grass length was close to 1.5 cm, however the grass length changed over the course of the study. Linsley et al. *(13)* report values for z_0 for a range of grass lengths from 1.5 cm (z_0=0.2 cm) to 4.5 cm (z_0=1.7 cm). Using correction factors given in Wilson et al. *(3)* to account for an incorrect z_0, the difference in grass length between 1.5 cm and 4.5 cm would result in <10% error in the airborne flux determination using the TPS method. Finally, there is some uncertainty in the determination of Φ associated with how atmospheric stability is described. The procedure of Wilson et al. *(3)* was used is the present study. However, Majewski et al. *(6)*

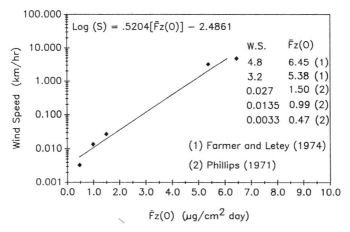

Figure 9. Relationship between wind speed and dieldrin flux from a "non-adsorbing" surface at 30°C. Data of Farmer and Letey (*10*) represent dieldrin flux from quartz sand at 30°C following treatment at 1000 μg/g. Data of Phillips (*9*) represent dieldrin flux from glass treated at 4-9 μg/cm². Data of Phillips (*9*) was adjusted by Spencer and Claith (*8*) for differences in vapor pressure between 30°C and temperatures used by Phillips.

chose to use the Richardson number (Ri), determined from on site measurements of thermal stability, to define atmospheric stability conditions which determine Φ. Because of differences in site characteristics (plot radius, z_0, ZINST) a direct comparison of values of Φ determined by Majewski et al. *(6)* with the present study is not possible. However, for the values of Φ chosen Majewski et al. *(6)* estimate error in determining Φ at ±6.5%.

Comparison of Methods. Foliar dislodgeable residues, airborne loss between 0900-1700 hr, and 2 hour average canopy temperatures for the Field Chamber and Theoretical Profile Shape studies are shown in Table II.

Foliar dislodgeable residues were similar for both studies. For comparable sampling days in each study *(1, 2, 5, 14/15)* foliar dislodgeable residue levels days were not significantly different at the 95% confidence level, except for day 5.

Estimates of airborne loss from 0900-1700 hr for the two studies were in good agreement, never differing by more than a factor of 2. The average canopy temperature data suggests that differences in the results may be partially explained by differences in canopy temperature on comparable sampling days. For example, on the day of application (day 1) average canopy temperatures interior and exterior to the chambers were 13.2 and 4.5°C greater than those observed on the day of application in the Theoretical Profile Shape study. Correspondingly, the pendimethalin source strength in the Field Chamber study was 2 times greater on the day of application. Conversely, on day 2 of the Field Chamber study, chamber interior and exterior canopy temperatures were 4.7 and 6.5°C

Table II. Comparison of Pendimethalin Airborne Flux, Foliar Dislodgeable Residues, and Canopy Temperature Between Theoretical Profile Shape and Field Chamber Methods

Day[a]	Airborne Loss[b] $F_z(0)$ (mg/m²)		Avg. Canopy Temp.[c] (°C)			Foliar Dislodgeable Residues (µg/cm²)	
				Chamber			
	TPS	Chamber	TPS	In	Out	TPS	Chamber
1	6.8	14.4	21.5	34.7	26.0	3.8	3.6
2	3.2	1.5	21.8	17.1	15.3	3.3	2.8
5	4.2	5.9	20.1	35.0	27.2	2.8	1.4
14/15	1.7	1.1	12.8	33.9	35.2	0.5	0.5

[a] Number of days following application of Pendimethalin 60 WDG at 3.4 kg a.i./ha. Day 1 indicating the day of application.

[b] Sum of pendimethalin airborne loss measured for consecutive 2-hour sampling periods from 0900 to 1700 hr each sampling day. TPS-Theoretical Profile Shape method, Chamber-Field Chamber method.

[c] Average canopy (foliar surface) temperature for hourly measurements between 0900 and 1700 hr. For field chambers, temperature is given for both inside (In) and outside (Out) the chambers.

lower than the corresponding canopy temperatures for day 2 of the Theoretical Profile Shape study. Likewise, for day 2, pendimethalin source strength was 2 times less in the Field Chamber study than that determined in the Theoretical Profile Shape study.

CONCLUSIONS

Both the Field Chamber and Theoretical Profile Shape methods provide an estimate airborne loss rather than an absolute measurement. Provided above is a comparison of two estimates. Both methods utilize a small plot design and require relatively few measurements to determine pesticide source strength. In contrast, more "conventional" techniques, such as the aerodynamic method *(14)*, typically require a uniform fetch on the order of 300 meters, and multiple measurements of pesticide concentration, wind speed, temperature, and relative humidity over a common range of heights. In addition, the Field Chamber method allows for a replicated experimental design and provides a direct measurement of pesticide source strength under relatively controlled conditions. However, these controlled conditions will often result in increased temperatures and decreased wind speeds as compared to the natural environment. We have provided empirical evidence that will allow correction of the temperature and wind speed differences to estimate airborne loss under actual environmental conditions. The accuracy of the TPS method is dependent on the various sources of error associated with the TS model. An attractive feature of the TPS method is that research reported here suggests that this technique will allow estimation of daily pendimethalin airborne loss from turfgrass based upon a single measurement of airborne flux at the peak of the diurnal solar radiation cycle.

   As was reported earlier for the Field Chamber study *(1)*, the meteorological conditions during the course of the TPS study afforded the opportunity to observe the direct relationship between solar radiation (as it effects canopy temperature) and pendimethalin airborne loss from the foliar surface. In addition, weather conditions during the TPS study demonstrated the effect of wind speed on pendimethalin airborne loss from turfgrass. As is the case with most field research, the results presented are unique to the weather patterns which developed, both diurnally and over the two week course of both studies. Additional field research, under a variety of environmental conditions, is necessary to develop a better understanding of the relationships among the various environmental factors which influence pendimethalin airborne loss from turfgrass. In addition, the sources of error in the TS model need to be further defined so that field studies can be designed to minimize their effect and thereby more accurately estimate pesticide airborne loss.

LITERATURE CITED

1.   Jenkins, J. J.; Cooper, R. J.; Curtis, A. S. In *Long Range Transport of Pesticides*; Kurtz, D. A., Ed.; Lewis: Chelsea, MI, **1990**; pp 29-46.
2.   Jenkins, J. J.; Cooper, R. J.; Curtis, A. S. *Bull. Environ. Contam. Tox.* **1991**, *47*, 594-601.
3.   Wilson, J. D.; Thurtell, G. W.; Kidd, G. E.; Beauchamp, E. G. *Atmos. Environ.* **1982**, *16(8)*, 1861-1867.

4. Majewski, M. S.; Glotfelty, D. E.; Seiber, J. N. *Atmos. Environ.* **1989**, *23(5)*, 929-938.
5. Majewski, M. S.; Glotfelty, D. E.; Paw, K. T.; Seiber, J. N. *Sci. Technol.* **1990**, *24*, 1490-1497.
6. Majewski, M. S.; McChesney, M. M.; Seiber, J. N. 1991. *Environ. Toxicol. Chem.* **1991**, *10*, 301-311.
7. Wilson, J. D.; Catchpoole, V. R.; Denmead, O. T.; Thurtell, G. W. *Agric. Meteorol.* **1983**, *29*, 183-189.
8. Spencer, W. F.; Cliath, M. M. In *Fate of Pollutants in Air and Water Environments*; Suffet, I. H., Ed.; John Wiley and Sons: New York, 1977, Part I; pp 107-126.
9. Phillips, F. T. *Pestic. Sci.* **1971**, *2*, 255-266.
10. Farmer W. J.; Letey, J. Volatilization Losses of Pesticides from Soils; U.S. Environmental Protection Agency. U.S. Government Printing Office: Washington, DC, 1974; Environ. Prot. Tech. Series. EPA-660/2-74-054.
11. McCall, P. J.; Stafford, L. E.; Gavit, P. D. *J. Agric. Food Chem.* **1986**, *34*, 229-234.
12. Burkhard, N.; Guth, J. A. *Pestic. Sci.* **1981**, *12*, 37-44.
13. Linsley, R. K.; Kohler, M. A.; Paulhus, J. L. H. *Hydrology for Engineers*, 2nd ed.; McGraw-Hill: New York, 1975; pp 42-44.
14. Parmele, L. H.; Lemon, E. R.; Taylor, A. W. *Water Air Soil Pollut.* **1972**, *1*, 433-451.

RECEIVED November 4, 1992

Chapter 21

Effect of Spray Adjuvant on Off-Site Airborne and Deposited Parathion from Cranberry Bogs Treated by Aerial Application and Chemical Irrigation

J. M. Clark, J. R. Marion, and D. M. Tessier

Massachusetts Pesticide Analysis Laboratory, Department of Entomology, University of Massachusetts, Amherst, MA 01003

Cranberries are the number one agricultural cash crop in Massachusetts, yet their cultivation occurs in significantly populated coastal areas that show continuing trends toward urbanization. With the development of residential and business properties adjacent to cranberry bogs, conflicts between growers and non-growers have arisen as persons with no experience in agricultural practices are confronted with the realities of pesticide use. The major issue is "chemical trespass," the deposition of pesticides outside the target area, and the corresponding potential for adverse acute and chronic health effects. Because of this, the effectiveness of using spreader/sticker spray additives (adjuvants) in reducing airborne pesticide residues from cranberry bogs was studied. Ethyl parathion (Aqua 8, FMC) was applied to a 4 hectare section of bog by both aerial and chemical irrigation (chemigation) methods, with and without adjuvant in the spray mixture. Collection sites for airborne and deposited residues were established around the periphery of the bog at distances up to 200m, and sampling occurred for up to 48 hours post application. Aerial application resulted in approximately 3 to 4-fold higher drift residues than chemigation. Overall residue levels were reduced by approximately 80% by the use of adjuvant in both application strategies.

Substantial quantities of agriculturally applied pesticides have been shown to leave the treatment area during and after application operations. This unwanted feature of pesticide usage, referred to as off-site pesticide drift, results not only in loss of pest control but may result in potential exposure to workers and other individuals near agricultural sites (1). This has produced a wave of public concern and in many cases a very negative opinion of pesticide chemicals. The concern of both public and regulatory agencies about the deposition of pesticides outside the target area and the potential health effects due to this exposure situation has been termed "chemical trespass". In the northeastern United

0097–6156/93/0522–0243$06.00/0

States, the problem of chemical trespass has been amplified due to the rather limited areas used for agricultural purposes and to the relatively high population densities which exist around them *(2)*.

Although cranberries are produced commercially in the United States in a number of different states (e.g., Massachusetts, New Jersey, Oregon, Washington and Wisconsin), the cultivation of this crop occupies a unique position in Massachusetts. Cranberries are the number one agricultural cash crop produced in Massachusetts. Their cultivation is situated in coastal areas which are already heavily populated and where this trend towards urbanization is increasing at an alarming rate. When property adjacent to cranberry bogs becomes developed for residential and business use, individuals with no past personal experience with agricultural practices are confronted with realities such as the application of pesticides and consequent drift. One of the major issues which increases conflict between growers and non-growers in this situation is the contamination of adjacent off-site areas by airborne pesticide drift in the form of pesticide aerosols, vapors or dusts *(1)*. Besides the acute and chronic toxicological implications of exposure to airborne pesticide residues, both human health consequences and various effects to non-target organisms, there are also problems associated with noise and odors from application, inadvertent killing of bees and other beneficial insects and loss of "organic" status of organically grown produce.

Because the average bog size in Massachusetts is relatively small and the topography of the cranberry-producing coastal areas rather non-uniform, many growers rely on aerial application of pesticides and other agrochemicals for crop protection and increased yields. There is much information concerning the increased level of off-site pesticide residues due to aerial application compared to various ground application strategies including chemigation. The use of helicopters in place of fixed-wing aircraft have greatly reduced the amount of off-site drift in cranberry cultivation but this type of application is almost always noticed by adjacent property owners. Also, the complete suppression of pesticide drift during aerial application is very difficult, if not impossible at this time. The conversion of a large number of bogs to chemigation as a standard procedure for pesticide application in the cranberry industry indicates a movement away from aerial application towards a method which helps suppress pesticide drift. The following experiments were designed to compare the amount of off-site airborne and deposited residues due to aerial and sprinkler application (chemigation) of parathion to a cranberry bog and the mitigation of off-site residues by the use of a spreader/sticker agent (i.e., adjuvant).

Cranberry Cultivation in Massachusetts. Massachusetts produces more cranberries than any other area in the United States. The production of approximately 90,000 tons of cranberries annually is a $100 million agricultural industry in Massachusetts. It is second in value only to the greenhouse/nursery green industry (approx. $120 million) and almost doubles the combined values of fruit ($32 million) and vegetables ($36 million) grown in the state. The total Massachusetts revenue generated when production, packaging, processing, advertisement and marketing are included is $390 million *(3)*. To accomplish this, Massachusetts has approximately 12,400 acres dedicated to cranberry production which represents about 46% of the national total. This allows Massachusetts to produce approximately 1,811,874 barrels (100 lbs./barrel) or about 49% of the total national annual production. This level of production and the importance of cranberries to the

Massachusetts economy has resulted in a rather intense type of cultivation restricted to bogs located in the southeastern part of the state, Cape Cod, Nantucket and Martha's Vineyard.

Massachusetts is a small but densely populated state, particularly so in its eastern third. This situation is further perturbated because Cape Cod and the Islands serve also as a major recreational and vacationing area during the summer months when cranberry cultivation is most active. Moreover, most Massachusetts growers (58%) operate small bogs of less than 10 acres which results in many occurences of bogs in close proximity to residential and business areas. Thus, cranberry cultivation in Massachusetts offers an unique situation to study the impact of various agricultural practices on urban/suburban environments. This information can then be used to devise ways to mitigate these impacts in order to sustain agriculture in an increasingly urbanized nation and world.

METHODS AND MATERIALS

Study Sites and Participants. The study site (i.e., test plot, heavy hatched area) consisted of a 3.96 hectare section of Long Pond Bog, located in Rochester, MA, and was made available by the Decas Brothers Cranberry Company, Inc., Figure 1. The study site section was central to a larger complex of bogs (marked with irrigation ditch outlines) which in turn was surrounded by secondary growth and scrub forest to the east, south and west and Long Pond to the north. This entire bog complex remained inactive for the 1986-1987 growing seasons during the period over which this study was performed. Parathion was applied only to the study site section and the nearest working bog was 0.2 km away and separated by second growth forest.

Application of Pesticide. Ethyl-parathion (Aqua 8 Parathion emulsion concentrate, 76.35 % 0,0-diethyl-0-p-phosphorothioate, FMC, Ag Chem Group, Philadelphia, PA 19103) was applied with a Bell 47 helicopter flying crosswind 0.9 to 1.5 meters above the bog at an air speed of 72 km/h. The spray boom (3.85 meters each side) consisted of 32 D-6 (46 core) nozzles and gave a swath width of 9.6-11.5 meters. The per hectare pesticide mixture was 0.88 liters Aqua 8 parathion to 46 liters of water (840.9gm/hectare) and, when a spreader/sticker adjuvant was tested, 0.88 liters Bivert (Stull Chemical Co., San Antonio, TX 78265) was added to the pesticide-water mixture. The volume rate for aerial application was 37.7 liters/min. The adjuvant, Bivert, is a positively charged inverted emulsion which encapsulates the pesticide in a water-filled macro-droplet. Chemically, it consists of amine salts of vegetable fatty acids, organic aromatic acids, aromatic and aliphatic petroleum distillates. The larger droplet size that forms reduces off-site drift during application. Subsequent evaporation from the site of application is also decreased due to its positively-charged spreader/sticker characteristics which binds to the negative changes on the leave surface. Four aerial applications were made; two with and two without adjuvant.

For chemigation, 0.88 liters/hectare of Aqua 8 parathion was injected into the pressure main between the water pump and the first row of sprinklers in the study site. Initial tests with 0.88 liters/hectare of a visible dye indicated that all sprinkler heads received the dye, the system delivered the dye completely in 10 min, and the system delivered dye to the entire study site. The volume rate for chemigation application was 1296 liters/min. The application rate for parathion was the same as during aerial appliations (840.9gm/hectare).

The chemigation system in the study site consisted of a pressurized main irrigation line (327 liters/hectare/min) which divided the study site in half (northwest to southeast, Figure 1). Five booms were spaced equidistant from each other (approximately 30 meters) and alternated side to side at a 90° angle with the main irrigation line. Each boom had four sprinkler heads spaced 23 meters apart. The top of each sprinkler head was 0.38 meters high. Two chemigation applications were made, one with and one without adjuvant.

Sampling of Airborne Parathion Residues. Air sampling *(4)* was performed with high-volume air samplers (Staplex, Brooklyn, NY 11232) calibrated to sample surrounding air at a rate of 0.71 m^3/min. Two collecting media (i.e., collectors) were used. A 102 mm diameter glass- fiber filter (Gelman Sciences, Ann Arbor, MI 48106) backed by 100 ml volumes of Amberlite XAD-4 polymeric adsorbent resin (Rohm and Haas, Philadelphia, PA 19105). Air sampling was conducted at the following times: 12 to 10 hrs prior to the spray, during the spray (i.e., a 5 min sampling period for aerial application and a 10 min sampling period for chemigation), and 1 to 3, 8 to 10, 22 to 24, and 46 to 48 hrs post-spray. Four high-volume air samplers were used, one located 30 meters upwind of the bog perimeter, and the others located 50, 100, and 200 meters downwind of the bog perimeter. The actual sampler sites were adjusted prior to each sampling period to account for changed wind direction.

Pesticide fallout (i.e., deposition) was sampled with cellulose collector discs (Whatman 33 cm diameter P4 cellulose filter paper discs, Fisher Scientific) placed on horizontal aluminum foil-covered plywood platforms at a height of 6 inches above the bog surface. These were positioned permanently along north (N), south (S), east (E) and west (W) axes, at 75', 150', and 300' from the perimeter of the bog. Sampling periods were: 12 to 10 hrs pre-spray, during the spray application and 1 to 3, 3 to 8, and 8 to 24 hrs post-spray.

A total of six field trials were made during the summer months of 1986 and 1987, four were aerial applications, two with (9/7-10/86 and 7/16-19/87) and two without (8/12-15/86 and 8/25-28/86) adjuvant, and two chemigation applications, one with (7/27-30/87) and one without (7/22-25/87) adjuvant.

Meteorological Conditions and Instrumentation. To insure applications were made during appropriate meteorological conditions as recommend by the Pesticide Bureau, MA Dept. of Food and Agriculture (see below), weather data was continuously monitored over the 3.5 days of each experiment. Wind speed and direction was monitored with a Skyvane W102-P Wind Sensor, WTB102-H4-540 Wind Translator, and 338 Recorder (Weather Measure Corp., Sacramento, CA 95841). Temperature and relative humidity were monitored with a hydrothermograph (Qualimetrics model 4021, Weather Measure Corp., Sacramento, CA 95841). Location of the weather station is given in Figure 1. Instruments were placed 1.0 meters above the bog surface. Care was given only to make applications when wind speed conditions were approximately 3.2-6.4 km/h but not when in excess of 16 km/h. Application equipment was adjusted to deliver an average droplet size of not less than 100 microns. Aerial applications by helicopters were not to exceed a maximum altitude of 3.8 meters. Applications were made early in the day (4-6 am) when

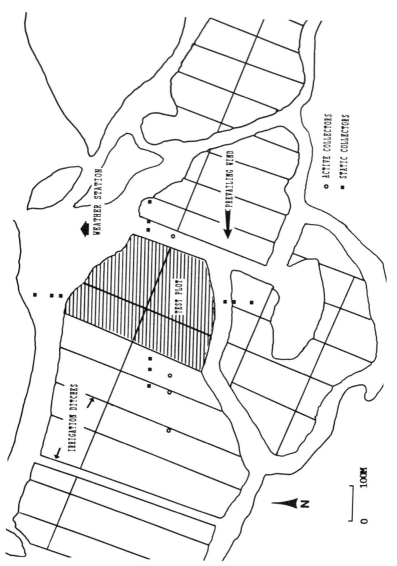

Figure 1. Cranberry bog study site.

low temperatures and high humidity condition existed. No application was made under inversion temperature conditions.

During and after helicopter applications without adjuvant, the average temperature over the 49 hr collection periods was 19.8 ± 4.5°C (14-26°C range). Average wind speed was 9.9 + 7.1 km/h (0-32.2 km/h range) and average relative humidty was 62 ± 17.4% (32-82% range). With adjuvant, the average temperature over the 48 hr collection period was 18.3 ± 5.0°C (13-26°C range). Average wind speed was 8.0 ± 3.9 km/h (0-16 km/h range) and average relative humidity was 61.7 ± 23.3% (33-82% range).

During and after chemigation application without adjuvant, the average temperature was 21.8 ± 3.9°C (18-28°C range). Average wind speed was 8.5 ± 3.1 km/h (0-16 km/h range) and average relative humidity was 79.5 ± 15.1% (62-95% range). With adjuvant, the average temperature was 22.8 ± 4.9°C (15-29°C range). The average wind speed was 8.2 ± 4.3 km/h (0-16 km/h range) and average relative humidity was 63.2 ± 20.6% (40-95% range).

Analytical Procedures. XAD-4 resin was cleaned prior to field collection in order to reduce analytical interferences. The resin was acid washed for 1 hr with equal volumes of resin and distilled, deionized water (DDW) at pH 5 with HCl by mechanical stirring. The acidified washing solution was decanted and the resin returned to neutral pH with repeated rinsings of DDW. The resin was then washed with pesticide-grade acetone (Fisher Scientific) to remove water, and Soxlet extracted for 4 hr (minimum 20 cycles) with 300 ml acetone. After air drying, 100 ml volumes of the resin were stored in amber sample bottles with Teflon-lined caps until field use.

Residues of parathion were extracted from the resin and cellulose filters by 4 hr of Soxhlet extractions (minimum 20 cycles) using 250 ml technical hexanes (Fisher Scientific). The extract was dried over Na_2SO_4 and the final volume for quantification was adjusted to 10 ml with hexane by concentration under nitrogen. The glass-fiber filters were extracted three times (each consisting of a 5 min extraction using a wrist-action shaker) with three 50 ml aliquots of technical hexanes. The combined extracts were dried, concentrated and prepared for quantification as above.

Quantification of parathion residues was by a gas-liquid chromatograph (Varian model 3400) equipped with a thermionic-specific detector. A 10 meter DB1 capillary column (J&W Scientific, Rancho Cordova, CA 95670) was used with a temperature program beginning at 160°C (1 min) and ramping at 10°C/min to a final temperature of 220°C. The injection port was at 250°C, and the detector at 300°C. The carrier gas was He at a flow rate of 3 ml/min. The limit of detection was 250 ppb. Parathion standards were obtained from EPA (Research Triangle Park, NC) at 99% purity. Structural confirmation of parathion residues was by gas-liquid chromatography - mass spectral analysis (GC/MS Center, Mass. Experiment Station, Univ. of Mass. Amherst 01003).

Peak areas of parathion residues were determined using a Spectra-Physics model 4290 integrator interfaced to the chromatograph. Quantification of insecticide residues extracted from field samples was by direct comparison of integrated peak areas from standard curves for parathion (0.5 ppm-10.0 ppm concentration range). For each 10 field samples analyzed, a group of 3 standard concentration were evaluated (0.5, 1, 10 ppm). If standards included in sample run deviated from the standard curve by more than 5%, the analysis was repeated.

RESULTS

Recoveries from Active and Passive Collectors. The extraction efficiencies over a range of parathion concentrations from the three collecting media (i.e., glass-fiber filters, resin and cellulose filters) are given in Table I. Extraction efficiencies at these concentrations were 89% or more. In order to assure that breathrough of parathion residues did not occur during the high-volume air samplings, simulated field recoveries were conducted to assess mass balance (Table II). This was done by fortifying the collecting media at two levels of parathion and operating the high-volume air samplers for a standard 2 hr collection period. Residues on each medium were assessed by the standard extraction and analytical procedures. While it is apparent that parathion residue applied to the glass-fiber filter ultimately were trapped primarily on the XAD-4 resin, this process did not occur in the opposite direction. This indicates that particulate residues collected initially onto the glass-fiber filter subsequently resulted in parathion vapors which were translocated to the resin during the air sampler operation and trapped there. Moreover, the 100 ml volumes of XAD-4 resin appears adequate to trap sub-milligram levels of parathion without loss due to breakthrough during a standard 2 hr collection period.

Table I. Recovery of parathion from fortified collectors: Laboratory application

Substrate	Fortification range	Recovery (% + S.D.)[a]		
Glass-Fiber Filter	1-450 ug	88.83	±	9.87
XAD-4 Resin (100ml)	1-450 ug	90.33	±	4.73
Cellulose Filter	1-100 ug	115.00	±	13.36

[a] Values represent mean percentages of integrated peak areas of extracted samples compared to parathion standards ± standard deviation (n=3). Glass-fiber filters and XAD-4 resin were dosed with 1, 50, 250 and 450 ug parathion in n-hexane. Cellulose filters were dosed with 1, 50, 100 ug parathion in n-hexane.

Off-Site Residues from Aerial Applications. Measured airborne residues are presented in Figure 2. The majority of parathion residues collected by the air samplers were associated with the resin as vapor phase residues. However, as indicated by the mass balance results presented in Table II, the glass-fiber filters were not efficient in trapping the parathion residues. Thus, it should not be assumed that residues collected by this system were principally vapor versus particulate. The highest concentrations of residues were collected during the 5 min spray application and the subsequent 2 hr collection period (i.e., 1-3 hrs post-spray). More residues were collected on the downwind samplers than on the upwind samplers with the greatest residue concentration (0.823 ug/m^3) associated with the resin collector at the 200 m downwind sampler during the 1-3 hr post-

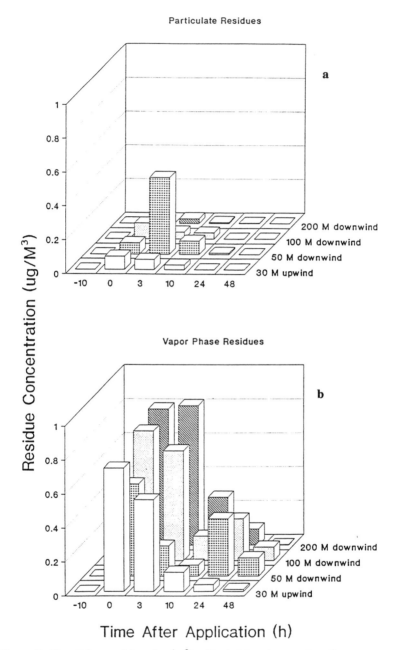

Figure 2. Parathion residues (ug/m³) collected by air samplers from
helicopter applications without adjuvant. Panel a (top) represents
particulate residues collected on glass-fiber filters. Panel b (bottom)
represents vapor phase residues collected by resin. Data represents the mean
values of two collections made 8/12-15/86 and 8/25-28/86.

spray collection period (Figure 2b). The highest concentration of particulate residues (0.453 ug/m³) was associated with the 50 m downwind sampler during the 1-3 hrs post-spray collection period (Figure 2a). No residues were detected at any of the air sampler sites during the pre-spray collection period. By 48 hrs post-spray, particulate residues were below detection levels and the highest vapor phase residue concentration (0.107 ug/m³) was associated with the nearest downwind sampler (i.e., 50 m downwind).

Table II.   Simulated field recovery of parathion from high-volume air samplers: Mass balance, laboratory application

| Fortification Level (ug) | | | Recovery (%)[a] | | |
G. F. Filter	XAD Resin	Operation Time (hr)	Filter	XAD Resin	Total
1	0	2	10.1	119.8	129.9
0	1	2	n.d.	111.4	111.4
100	0	2	0.29	112.3	112.3
0	100	2	n.d.	102.4	102.4

[a] Percentage values of parathion residues have been corrected for extraction efficiencies given in Table I.

The effect of the addition of adjuvant on airborne residues from aerial applications of parathion are illustrated in Figure 3. Overall off-site residues concentrations were greatly reduced by the addition of adjuvant. This is particularly evident in the spray and 1-3 hrs post-spray collection periods. The greatest residue concentration was associated with the particulate residues on the glass-fiber filter collector (0.368 ug/m³) of the 30 m upwind sampler during the spray collection period (Figure 3a). The highest concentration of vapor phase residues (0.168 ug/m³) was associated with the 30 m upwind sampler during the 1-3 hrs post-spray collection period (Figure 3b). No airborne residues were detected at any air sampler site during the pre-spray collection periods. By 24 hrs post-spray, both particulate and vapor phase residue levels were below or at detection limits (Note: The vapor phase residues, collected at the 200 m downwind sampler during the 22-24 hr post-spray collection period (7/18/87), are assumed to be due to an aerial application of parathion to an adjacent working bog 0.2 km from the SSE quadrant of the Long Pond bog).

Residue concentrations due to deposition of parathion onto cellulose discs are given in Figure 4. Similar to the air sampler data, the majority of residues collected onto cellulose disc were found during the 5 min spray collection period. However, in contrast to air sampler collections, the greatest residue concentration due to deposition (769.2 ng/cm²) was associated with the East-75' cellulose disc during the spray collection periods in the presence of the adjuvant (Figure 4b). A similarly high residue concentration (209.7 ng/cm²) was also associated with the South-75' disc. Although detectible residues were

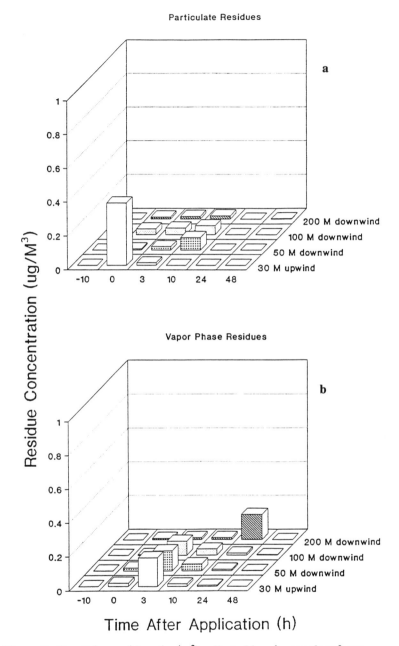

Figure 3. Parathion residues (ug/m³) collected by air samplers from helicopter applications with adjuvant. Panel a (top) represents particulate residues collected on glass-fiber filters. Panel b (bottom) represents vapor phase residues collected by resin. Data represents the mean values of two collections made 9/7-10/86 and 7/16-19/87.

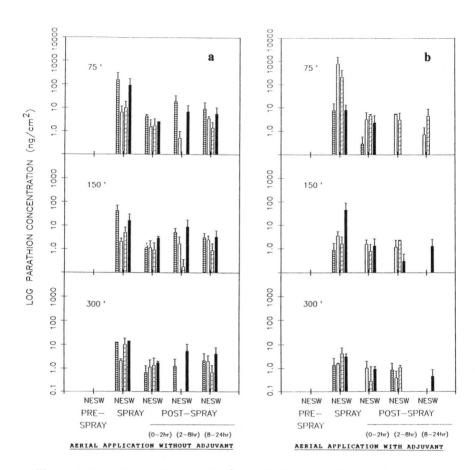

Figure 4. Parathion residues (ng/cm^2) on cellulose discs (i.e., passive deposition) due to off-site airborne drift from helicopter applications without (panel a) and with (panel b) adjuvant. Values represent means of residue concentrations from two separate collections without adjuvant (8/12-15/86 and 8/25-28/86) and two separate collections with adjuvant (9/7-10/86 and 7/16-19/87).

still found on the discs 24 hr post-spray with both types of applications, the total residues collected during the 8-24 hrs post-spray period was 5.6-fold less in the presence of adjuvant compared to those found in the absence of adjuvant (6.8 vs. 38.7 ng/cm^2, respectively).

Off-Site Residues from Chemigation Applications. As with aerial applications without adjuvant (Figure 2), the majority of residues collected by the air samplers from a 10 min chemigation application without adjuvant were associated with the resin as vapor phase residues (Figure 5). The greatest residue concentration (0.25 ug/m^3) was associated with the resin at the 30 m upwind sampler during the 1-3 hrs post-spray collection period (Figure 5b). The highest concentration of particulate residues (0.042 ug/m^3) was associated with the 30 m upwind sampler during the 8-10 hrs post-spray collection period (Figure 5a). No residues were detected at any active sampler site during the pre-spray collection period. By 24 hrs post-spray, particulate residues were at or below detection limits. In contrast, vapor phase residues were detectable at all active sampler sites at 48 hrs post-spray and ranged from 0.047 to 0.125 ug/m^3 in concentration.

The effect of the addition of adjuvant to the chemigation application are illustrated in Figure 6. As with aerial applications, the addition of adjuvant greatly reduced overall off-site residues. This was particularly true for particulate residues where there were only three collections with residue levels above detection limits (0.023 ug/m^3 at the 30 m upwind sampler during spray, 0.014 ug/m^3 and 0.016 ug/m^3 at the 30 m upwind and 50 m downwind samplers, respectively, during the 8-10 hrs post-spray periods) (Figure 6a). Except for a suspicious result obtained at the 50 m downwind sampler during the 48 hrs post-spray period, vapor phase residues were similarly reduced with the highest concentration (0.026 ug/m^3) reported at the 50 m downwind sampler during the 8-10 hrs post-spray period (Figure 6b). The 0.110 ug/m^3 residue concentration at the 50 m downwind sampler during the 46-48 hrs post-spray period is assumed to be due to a laboratory contamination.

Residue concentrations due to deposition of parathion onto cellulose discs are given in Figure 7. Similar to the aerial collections (Figure 4), the majority of residues deposited on discs occurred at the 75' collectors which were nearest to the periphery of the study site. However, in contrast to aerial collections, the greatest residue concentration due to passive deposition occurred without adjuvant and during the 2-8 hr post-spray collecting period (25.18 ng/cm^2) (Figure 7a). It should be noted, however, that this level of parathion was accumulated over a 6 hr period. The highest concentration achieved with adjuvant was 5.58 ng/cm^2 at the South 75' collector during the 0-2 hrs post-spray period (Figure 7b). Both these residue levels are substantially below those found during aerial applications. Although detectible residues were still found on discs 8-24 hrs post-spray with and without adjuvant, the total residues collected during period was 2.4-fold less in the presence of adjuvant than in its absence (5.03 vs. 11.89 ng/cm^2, respectively). Most notable, however, is the complete lack of detectible residues during the 10 min spray application period when adjuvant was included.

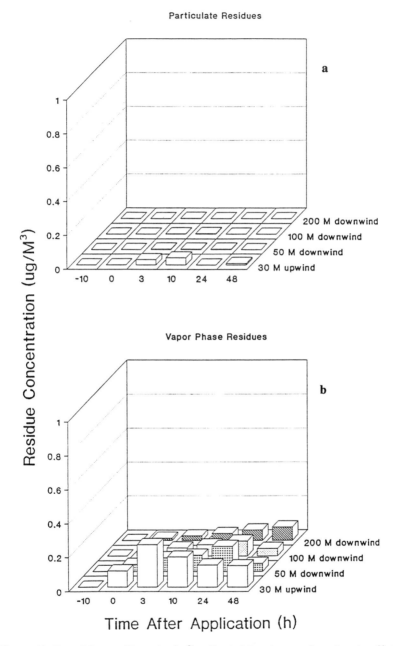

Figure 5. Parathion residues (ug/m³) collected by air samplers due to off-site airborne drift during a chemigation application without adjuvant. Panel a (top) represents particulate residues collected on glass-fiber filters. Panel b (bottom) represents vapor phase residues collected by resin. Data represents values from a single collection made 7/22-25/87.

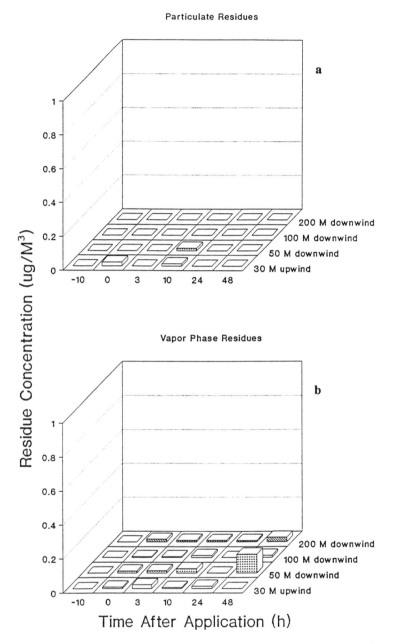

Figure 6. Parathion residues (ug/m^3) collected by air samplers due to off-site airborne drift during a chemigation application with adjuvant. Panel a (top) represents particulate residues collected on glass-fiber filters. Panel b (bottom) represents vapor phase residues collected by resin. Data represents the values from a single collection made 7/27-30/87.

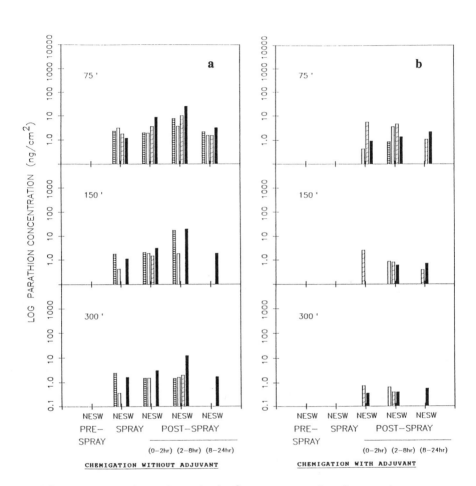

Figure 7. Parathion residues (ng/cm²) on cellulose discs (i.e., passive deposition) due to off-site airborne drift from chemigation application without (panel a) and with (panel b) adjuvant. Values represent residue concentrations from two separate collections (7/22-25/87 without adjuvant, and 7/27-30/87 with adjuvant).

DISCUSSION

Total residues associated with each collector type over the entire sampling period are summarized in Table III. Overall, chemigation without adjuvant resulted in a 76% reduction in total actively collected residues compared to aerial application without adjuvant. In the presence of adjuvant, chemigation resulted in a 72% reduction of total actively collected residues compared to aerial application. Aerial application with adjuvant resulted in 82% less airborne residues compared to aerial application without adjuvant. Likewise, chemigation with adjuvant produced 79% less airborne residues than chemigation without adjuvant.

Table III. Summation of total off-site parathion residues due to airborne drift from a treated cranberry bog

Application Type	Adjuvant	Summation of Parathion Residues[a]			
		Air Sampler collectors (ug/m^3)			Fallout collectors ng/cm^2
		Particulate Vapor		Total	Total
Aerial	-	1.036 (13.7)[b] + 6.55 (86.3) =		7.586	478.85
Aerial	+	0.659 (47.9) + 0.716 (52.1) =		1.375 [-81.9][c]	1092.79 [+ 128.2]
Chemigation	-	0.10 (5.6) + 1.692 (94.4) =		1.792	160.73
Chemigation	+	0.053 (14.0) + 0.326 (86.0) =		0.379 [-78.9]	30.01 [-81.3]

[a] Values given are means of two aerial applications and single values for chemigation applications.
[b] Values in parentheses are percentages of total air sampler or deposited residues.
[c] Values in brackets are percent increases (+) or decreases (-) of total residues due to the presence of adjuvant compared to application without adjuvant.

Total deposited residues (i.e., cellulose disc collectors) in the absence of adjuvant were reduced 66% by chemigation compared to aerial application. With adjuvant, chemigation resulted in 97% less total passively collected residues compared to aerial application. Chemigation with adjuvant produced 81% less total passive residues compared to chemigation without adjuvant. However, aerial application with adjuvant caused an increase in deposited residues compared to aerial application without adjuvant (128 % above aerial without adjuvant). This occurred primarily due to a large amount of residues (1462 ng/cm^2) found on the East-75' cellulose collector during the spray period of the 9/7/86 aerial application with adjuvant (Figure 4b). The above finding is substantiated by a concurrent high level of particulate residues (0.368 ug/m^3) found on the glass-fiber filter of the 30 m upwind high-volume air sampler during spray periods of the same application (Figure 3a). Both these two collectors were the closest to the periphery of the study site and indicates the most likely scenario for the exposure to parathion residues when applied aerially with adjuvant. Apparently, the large macro-droplets formed in the presence of adjuvant are available for transport by airborne drift to only nearby off-site locations (<50 meters from study site periphery) when applied by helicopter. Thus, a recommendation for a boundary zone buffer around cranberry bogs using this type of application technology would seem appropriate.

In conclusion, aerial application of parathion to a cranberry bog, by helicopter resulted in substantial airborne residues being collected over a 200 m downwind distance from the target site. This was most evident during the actual spray application and continued over the next 10 hr period. Both actively and passively collected residues could be substantially reduced by application with chemigation, application using an adjuvant or a combination of both.

ACKNOWLEDGMENTS

This work was supported by the Cape Cod Cranberry Grower's Association, the Massachusetts Department of Food and Agriculture (Pesticide Bureau), and the University of Massachusetts (CFNR/MAES), Hatch grant No. NE115. The Authors wish to thank the Decas Brothers Cranberry Company, Inc., for allowing this study to be conducted on their bog site.

LITERATURE CITED

1. Seiber, J.N.; Ferreira, G.A.; Herman, B.; Woodrow, J.E. In *Pesticide Analytical Methodology*; Harvey Jr., J; Zweig, G., Ed.; ACS Symposium Series: Vol. 136, Washington, D.C. **1980**, p. 177.
2. Van Driesche, R.G.; Carlson, J.; Ferro, D.N.; Clark, J.M. In *Sustaining Agriculture Near Cities*; Lockevetz W., Ed.; Soil and Water Conservation Soc. **1987**, pp. 49-63.
3. Annual Report, Cape Cod Cranberry Growers' Association, East Wareham, MA. **1990**, pp. 1-15.
4. Kilgore, W.; Fisher, C.; Rivers, J.; Akesson, N.; Wicks, J.; Winters, W.E.; Winterlin, W. *Residue Rev.* **1984**, *91*, 71-77.

RECEIVED October 30, 1992

URBAN PESTICIDES AND HUMANS

Chapter 22

Applicator and Bystander Exposure to Home Garden and Landscape Pesticides

K. R. Solomon, S. A. Harris, and G. R. Stephenson

Centre for Toxicology, University of Guelph, Guelph, Ontario N1G 1Y3, Canada

Exposure to 2,4-D was measured (as total body dose) in home gardeners applying the herbicide and in bystanders living within the household, but not applying the herbicide. Analyses of urine collected from homeowners for 96 hours following applications found total body doses ranging from non-detectable to 0.0071 mg/kg of body weight. The highest exposures were consistently associated with spills of the liquid concentrate or excessive contact with the dilute mixture on the hands or forearms. Residues of 2,4-D were not detected in urine samples supplied by bystanders to home applicators. Total dose in professional applicators applying 2,4-D and bystanders receiving a professional application of 2,4-D to their properties was measured. Professional applicators received a geometric mean dose of 0.154 mg/kg/day over a 14 day period with 96 and 99 percentiles of 1.56 and 4.95 mg/kg/day respectively. Daily excretion was poorly correlated with total amount of active ingredient (A.I.) applied. Personal work habits appeared to be the major factors affecting exposure. Residues of 2,4-D were not detected in air or urine samples supplied by 10 bystanders who received a professional application of 2,4-D to their property. Total dose of 2,4-D determined in volunteers following 1 hour exposure to a 2 by 15 m area of sprayed turf 1 and 24 hours following application. Dislodgeable residues of 2,4-D declined from 8% 1-hour after application to 1% 24-hours following application. No residues of 2,4-D were found in 96 hr urine samples supplied by volunteers except for 3 people who were barefoot and wearing shorts and contacted the turf 1 hour following 2,4-D application. The highest dose was measured was 0.005 mg/kg of body weight.

"The dose makes the poison" is one of the oldest dogmas in toxicology. Thus the assessment of hazard requires a knowledge of both the exposure and the inherent toxicity of the chemical. Users and bystanders may be exposed to pesticides through residues in food, water, and air and contact with treated surfaces, including vegetation. Pesticides

0097–6156/93/0522–0262$06.00/0

may enter the body through the oral and inhalation routes; however, the dermal route has been shown to be the most important in applicators (Figure 1). Once absorbed, the pesticide may be excreted, metabolized and excreted or, in the case of some compounds, stored in fat tissues (Figure 1).

The phenoxy herbicide 2,4-dichlorophenoxyacetic acid (2,4-D) is used for broadleaf weed control in agriculture, forestry, rights-of-way, turf and for aquatic weed control. Of the 5.1 million kg used in Canada in 1986, 85% was used in agriculture and 6% in home and garden and turf *(1)*. The acute toxicity of 2,4-D is low to moderate *(2)* but this herbicide has been the subject of scientific and public controversy because of contamination with dioxins *(3)* and recent epidemiological studies *(4, 5, 6, 7)*. Although a number of studies on exposure to 2,4-D have been carried out in ground sprayers *(8, 9, 10, 11, 12)*, aerial applicators *(13, 14, 15)*, forestry workers *(16)*, farmers *(17)* and lawn sprayers *(18)*, exposure of homeowner applicators had not been measured. In addition, exposure of bystanders to 2,4-D following domestic or professional applications had not been measured.

Measurement of exposure. A number of techniques have been used to monitor exposure to pesticides. These include passive dosimetry, fluorescence video imaging, and biological monitoring (Table I; *19, 20*). Each of these techniques has specific advantages and disadvantages. A combination of both direct and indirect measurements is best to identify routes of exposure and calculate total body dose. Where resources are limited, these are usually devoted to biological monitoring since the absorbed dose, as contrasted to dermal exposure, is of greatest human health significance.

Following occupational exposure to 2,4-D amine or ester in humans, 90 to 100% of the compound is excreted in the urine with a half-life of 10 to 28 h *(21, 22)*. Exposure to 2,4-D has been measured via this method in a number of published studies *(14, 17, 13, 16, 10, 11, 18)*. These studies suggested that, in workers who use 2,4-D regularly, the amount excreted in the urine over a 24-hour period is a reliable measure of the absorbed systemic dose, provided that they have achieved steady state pharmacokinetics. Extraction of 2,4-D from urine is relatively easy and only a single analysis is needed for the period of observation. Because of the relevance of the absorbed dose and the reduced number of analyses, biological monitoring was used in our studies.

MATERIALS AND METHODS

Study Groups and Application. For homeowner studies, 22 applicators and bystanders volunteered to participate. Bystanders were persons living within the household but not applying the pesticide. Applicators and bystanders were split randomly into two groups (non-protective and protective apparel). Each applicator applied a commercial weed-and-feed fertilizer (10:6:4 with 1% 2,4-D) in the spring and a liquid formulation of 2,4-D amine (250 g/L) in the fall. Volunteers in the protective group were instructed on measuring, mixing, application, disposal of containers and cleaning of equipment prior to and during application. Clean overalls, gloves and rubber boots were worn for the entire application. The non-protective group wore clothing of their own choice (typically long pants, running shoes and short sleeved shirt) and were allowed to apply the pesticide as they normally would. Where required, a 90 cm and a 60 cm drop spreader was supplied

Table I. Comparison of Techniques for Measuring Pesticide Exposure

Technique	Measurement	Best Use, Advantages and Disadvantages
Passive Dosimetry (Direct)	Dermal deposition (patches, sections of clothing and solvent rinses of the skin). Inhalation (air sampling) Parent pesticide analysis.	Exposure in relation to: Discrete work activities resulting in exposure. Identifying the most vulnerable body areas. Analysis is easy. Separate assessment of dermal deposition and inhalation exposure is possible. Use of patches may increase variability of measurements. Dermal penetration must be known to calculate dose *(19)*.
Fluorescence Imaging (Direct)	Dermal deposition of fluorescent tracer.	Exposure in relation to: Discrete work activities resulting in exposure. Identifying most vulnerable body areas. Estimation of total dermal deposition. Useful in education and training. Requires knowledge of dermal penetration to calculate dose. Requires calibration to account for differential penetration of dye and pesticide through clothing *(20)*.
Biological Monitoring (Indirect)	Excreted portion of dose in body (urine, faeces, sweat, etc). Pesticide and metabolite analysis required.	Exposure in relation to: Measurement of exposure via sum of inhalation, dermal and oral routes. No need to know dermal absorption rates. No assumption of clothing penetration needed. Gives closest estimate of total body dose. Does not allow identification of vulnerable areas or important routes of exposure *(19)*.

for large and small properties, respectively. Liquid formulations were applied with a hose-end sprayer. All measuring, mixing and portions of spreading or spraying were videotaped for later review.

For professional applicators, a lawn care company in Ontario was asked to participate in the study for a 14 day period. Five lawn care technicians from one area and seven technicians (including one mixer/loader) from another location volunteered. Records of the amount of 2,4-D (g A.I.) sprayed were kept for each technician throughout the period. Applicators from group 1 sprayed a mixture of 2,4-D amine/mecoprop (118:125 g/L) while those from group 2 applied a mixture of 2,4-D amine/mecoprop/dicamba (200:10:18 g/L). Ten bystanders to professional applications volunteered for the study.

Faculty, staff and students at the University of Guelph volunteered for the controlled exposure studies. The ten volunteers were split into two groups. One group wore long pants, a t-shirt, socks and shoes. The others wore shorts and a t- shirt and were barefoot. The area of turf used for exposure was cut three days before each study. Exposure plots (2 by 15 m) and dislodgeability plots were marked out. A mixture of 2,4-D amine/mecoprop/dicamba (190:100:18 g/L) was used at a rate of 1.0 kg acid equivalent/ha. Volunteers were randomly assigned to plots and, on two separate occasions (at midday, 1 and 24 h post application), undertook a 60 minute exposure session. The volunteers alternated walking and sitting on the turf for periods of 5 minutes. Each person covered the largest area possible in the plot while walking and exposed as much of their legs to the turf while lying or sitting on the plot. Volunteers sat on six different areas of the plot to facilitate maximum exposure. During the exposure period, residues dislodgeable from the turf were determined using the technique described by Thompson *et al. (23)*. The whole exposure period was videotaped. Following exposure, volunteers washed their hands but did not shower or otherwise decontaminate their skin until evening (6 h post-exposure).

Sampling. For the homeowner and professional bystander studies, air samples were collected at a height of 1.5 m, one in the house and one outside the home, downwind of the application site. Sampling pumps (Gilian Model HFS 113A) were connected to absorption tubes *(14)* containing 2 g of fluorosil (60 mesh) and set to a rate of 1 L/min. Pumps were run from 10 minutes before to 30 minutes after each application. Field spikes were conducted to check for recovery.

Urine Collection. Pre-exposure urine samples were used to confirm that prior exposure to 2,4-D had not occurred. An aliquot of this sample was used as a field spike check for recovery for each volunteer in all the studies. Volunteers stored the spiked samples with their day-1 urine samples. Starting after the application, applicators and the bystanders collected all urine for 96 h. Samples were collected daily, volumes measured and 1 ml sub-samples taken for urinary creatinine analysis as an index of completeness of urine collections. Urine from professional applicators was collected daily for 14 days.

Analysis. Subsamples (50 mL) of the combined 96 h urine collections (home applicators, bystanders or controlled exposure group) or daily urine samples (professional applicators) were hydrolysed with 250 mL of 0.1 N NaOH for 40 min at 70°C and washed three times with 50 mL of dichloromethane/hexane (20:80, v/v). The aqueous phase was acidified to pH < 1 with H_2SO_4 and extracted twice with 50 mL of diethyl ether. Ether extracts were combined, dried with Na_2SO_4 and evaporated to dryness.

Residues were esterified with boron trifluoride in methanol (14% BF_3) at 90°C for 30 min.) Methyl esters were extracted with three x 5 ml petroleum ether and washed with 25 ml distilled water. Isooctane (1 mL) was added as a keeper, the extracts dried with anhydrous Na_2SO_4 and the total volume adjusted to 5 mL by evaporation in a stream of dry nitrogen.

Gas chromatography was conducted on a glass column, 2 mm I.D. x 2 m in length, packed with 3% OV 17 on GasChrom Q. The oven was kept isothermal at 180°C, the detector at 300°C and the injector at 200°C. An electron capture (^{63}Ni) detector was used to quantitate residues using peak heights in comparison to a standard. The limit of detection for urine varied from 2 to 4 µg/L in different individuals and the limit of quantification was 5 µg/L. The limit of detection for the air samples was 0.1 µg/m³ and the limit of quantification was 0.2 µg/m³. For urine samples, storage conditions had a significant effect of recovery. Highest recovery was obtained from samples stored in a freezer, lowest for those kept in a foam cooler with an ice pack *(24)*. Recovery corrections were applied on the basis of the results of these field spikes.

RESULTS AND DISCUSSION

Compliance with collection protocols was good. For all exposed volunteers, creatinine values were above or fell within the normal range for adult males or females and were consistent on a daily basis.

Exposure to a Liquid Formulation in Homeowners. The detection of excretion of 2,4-D in the protective apparel group was infrequent (Figure 2). One of the two detections of 2,4-D in urine in these applicators probably resulted from the fact that he removed his gloves three or more times during application. He may have directly contacted 2,4-D on the outside of his gloves at these times. On the assumption that all exposures in the protective group occurred on the day of application, exposures of volunteers resulted in doses of 0.0015 and 0.00079 mg/kg/day respectively. These values represent 1/190 and 1/380 of the World Health Organization acceptable daily intake (ADI) which is 0.3 mg/kg/day or 21 mg/day for a 70 kg person *(25)*.

The six cases of positive detection in the non-protected group were directly related to spills of liquid concentrate on the bare hands or forearms or, in one case, deliberate spraying of the hands. Although most volunteers tried to avoid directly spraying the hose while spraying the lawn, the hose inevitably came into contact with 2,4-D spray on the grass. Most applicators rolled the hose in by hand which may have contributed to the measured exposure. One volunteer (744 µg total dose) spilled approximately 20 ml of concentrate directly on his hands when pouring the liquid concentrate into the hose-end sprayer and closing the sprayer. Assuming the worst case that this exposure occurred in the first day and given that this person weighed 105 kg, this would be equivalent to about 1/42 of the ADI suggested by the World Health Organization. No significant correlation was observed between the amount of 2,4-D applied and amount excreted in the urine of the protected group (r^2 for linear regression = 0.05) or the non-protected group (r^2 = 0.002).

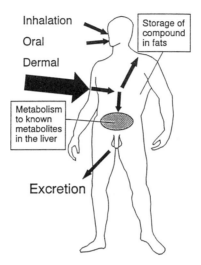

Figure 1. Routes of entry, metabolism, storage and excretion of pesticides in humans.

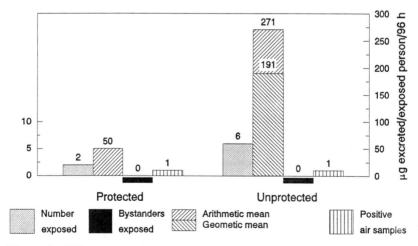

Figure 2. Urinary detection and excretion of 2,4-D in home applicators and bystanders to an application of liquid formulation.

Exposure to a Granular Formulation in Homeowners. Exposure to 2,4-D was detected in one volunteer in the protected group (Figure 3). Despite instructions, this person removed his gloves to cut open and pour the bags of fertilizer into the spreader and then replaced them to apply the material in the spreader. Exposure to 2,4-D was detected in only one volunteer in the non-protected group.

No bystanders in any group showed detectable exposure to 2,4-D. Although 2,4-D was detected in air samples inside and outside the house, levels were low (0.006, 0.01, 0.02 and 0.01 mg/m³) and none of these resulted in measurable exposure of the bystander. These positive samples may, in fact, have been as a result of accidental contamination during handling.

Highest excretion of 2,4-D was consistently associated with spills or accidental contamination of the skin. Other studies (26) have shown that 85% of potential exposure to diazinon during yard applications could be eliminated by protecting the hands. It appeared that the use of protective apparel for application of a granular formulation of 2,4-D did not reduce the frequency of exposure in the applicator. The use of rubber gloves, overalls and rubber boots, when pouring, applying and cleaning the equipment reduced the frequency and extent of exposure when using liquid formulations of 2,4-D.

Exposure in Professional Applicators. Daily excretion of 2,4-D followed a consistent pattern in most of the applicators. Using creatinine excretion as a correction factor did not change the pattern of excretion of 2,4-D to a large extent (Figure 4). In both groups, 2,4-D excretion showed two peaks. When the data were analyzed in relation to the daily amount of 2,4-D excreted in the urine and the amount of 2,4-D used each day, the peaks of excretion lagged behind the amounts of A.I. used on each day by a period of 2-4 days (Figure 5). Due to high variability between individuals in the groups, linear regression analysis failed to show high correlations between the total amount of 2,4-D sprayed and the total excreted, either on a daily basis or over the entire period of the study.

The relationship between the total amount of 2,4-D excreted by individual sprayers and the amount of 2,4-D applied was variable. This is contrary to results in farmers (17) where a better correlation was observed. Creatinine analyses suggested some incomplete samples, but, on the whole, compliance with collection protocols was good. It was not possible to observe each sprayer during all of their regular operations for the 14 day period, but it is likely that 2,4-D excretion was consistent with work practices, personal hygiene and precautions taken to decrease exposure. In other words, poor technique led to higher exposures.

The highest single-day excretion of 2,4-D in any of the sprayers was 1.108 mg. This is an exposure of about 1/19 of the ADI suggested by the World Health Organization (25). In all other applicators, excretion was lower and, over the two week period of the study, gave higher safety factors when compared to the ADI. Average excretion of 2,4-D fell within the range reported for professional applicators in the USA (18). Our results suggest that work habits and personal hygiene may be the major factors which affect exposure. Good training, consistent use of personal protective equipment and adherence to a code of good spray practice should reduce exposure still further.

A frequency distribution analysis of the daily excretion data from the professional applicators showed an approximately normal distribution of the log of the amount excreted (Figure 6). The distribution of the log of the amount applied also approximated

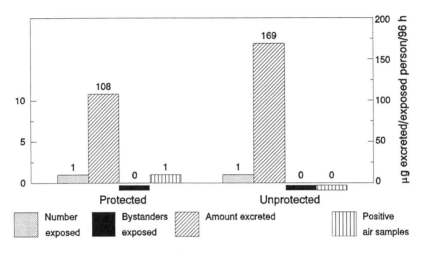

Figure 3. Urinary detection and excretion of 2,4-D in home applicators and bystanders to an application of granular formulation.

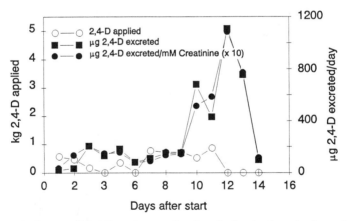

Figure 4. Daily use of 2,4-D and excretion in relation to time during a 14 day period in a professional applicator.

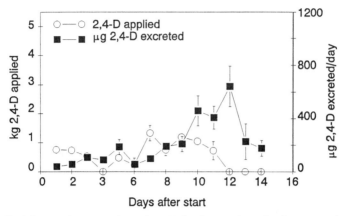

Figure 5. Mean daily excretion of 2,4-D in Group 1 professional applicators
in relation to amount of A.I. used. Vertical lines indicate the SE of the mean
(N=5).

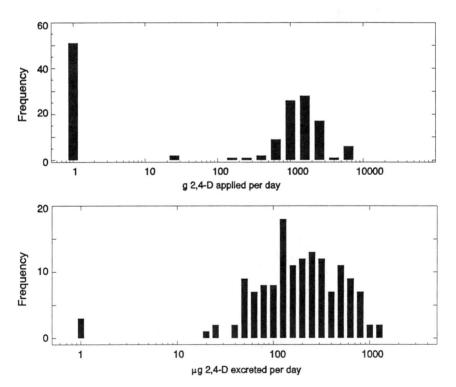

Figure 6. Frequency distribution of log-tranformed daily 2,4-D use and
excretion in all professional applicators over a 14-day period.

normality if the zero values were excluded. The geometric mean of the amount applied was 1.02 kg/day and the geometric mean of the amount excreted was 0.154 mg/person/day. The 96th and 99th percentiles for the amounts excreted per day were 1.56 and 4.95 mg/person/day. This latter amount is higher than the maximum daily amount observed in our study but is still below the WHO ADI.

Bystanders to Professional Applications. Excretion of 2,4-D was not detected in volunteers who had a professional application of 2,4-D to their lawns. Creatinine values showed good compliance with sample collection. Air samples taken both inside and outside the home downwind of the application did not show detectable residues of 2,4-D.

Controlled Exposure. Residues of 2,4-D dislodgeable from turf 1 h (8.4 ± 0.9 mg/m^2) and 24 h (1.1 ± 0.03 mg/m^2) after spraying were similar to those reported previously *(23)*. Creatinine values for the volunteers in this study were above or fell within the normal range for adult females and males and showed little variation on a daily basis, indicating good compliance with sample collection procedures. The highest excretion measured was in a volunteer exposed to the turf 1 h following spray application. Excretion in this volunteer was more than 2-fold greater than other volunteers also wearing shorts (either on a total dose or a mg/kg body weight basis). No 2,4-D was detected in urine samples from volunteers wearing long pants and closed footwear or in any volunteer 24 hours following application (Figure 7). The area of skin exposed to treated surfaces could have affected total dose absorbed. However, this did not explain differences in the 1 hour exposure group wearing shorts. Absorption of pesticides through human skin may occur at different rates, in different individuals.

CONCLUSIONS

As determined by excretion in urine, none of the measured exposures to 2,4-D was higher than the acceptable daily intake established by the World Health Organization. This ADI was based on a NOEL of 31 mg/kg/day observed in a chronic feeding study in rats *(25)*. A more recently derived NOEL in rats of 1 mg/kg/day has been suggested from the data on the long-term feeding study conducted by the Hazleton Laboratories *(27)*. Margins-of-safety (MOS = NOEL (mg/kg/day) / Exposure (mg/kg/day)) were calculated from the NOEL of 1 mg/kg/day in rats and the mean urinary excretion of 2,4-D in the exposed individuals in our study (assuming a body mass of 70 kg). These results are shown in Table II.

Home applicators can reduce exposure by using rubber gloves, overalls and rubber boots, when pouring, applying and cleaning spray equipment. Bystanders to homeowner and professional applications showed no detectable exposure to 2,4-D. Results from exposure measurements in volunteers exposed to sprayed turf indicate that these should present little risk to humans. However, people can reduce exposure to non-detectable levels by remaining off treated turf for a period of 24 hours or until after rainfall or irrigation so that dislodgeable residues, and therefore potential exposure, are essentially zero.

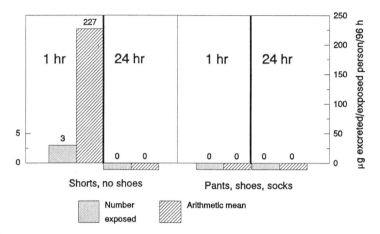

Figure 7. Urinary detection and excretion of 2,4-D in volunteers exposed to turf 1 and 24 hours after application of a liquid formulation.

Table II. Exposure Expressed as the Margin of Safety and as a Fraction of the ADI on a Daily and Life Time Basis

	Exposure dose (mg/kg/d)	Fraction of WHO ADI (daily)	Margin of safety (one day, NOEL of 1 mg/kg/day)
Commercial applicator geometric mean daily exposure	0.0022	0.0073	454
Commercial applicator 96th percentile daily exposure	0.022	0.073	45
Commercial mixer/loader mean daily exposure	0.002	0.007	500
Homeowner geometric mean total exposure	0.0027	0.009	370
Homeowner highest total exposure	0.007	0.023	143

ACKNOWLEDGMENTS

The authors would like to thank Jennifer Jupp and Kim Sayers for their enthusiastic support with the field work and Ms. C. Bowhey for technical assistance in the laboratory. We also express our appreciation to the Hazardous Contaminants Branch, Ontario Ministry of the Environment, and to the Ontario Ministry of Agriculture and Food for funding the research. Finally, although it is impossible to individually thank the more than one hundred volunteers who participated in these studies, it was they who made this project possible. Their time, co-operation, humour, enthusiasm, and dedication to science are greatly appreciated.

LITERATURE CITED

1. Deloitte, Haskins and Sells. In *An economic assessment of the benefits of 2,4-D in Canada.* Deloitte, Haskins and Sells, Guelph, Ontario **1988**.
2. WHO. In *World Health Organization, Environmental Health Criteria* 29. Geneva, **1984**.
3. Cochrane, W.P.; Singh, J.; Miles, W.; Wakeford, B. J. Chromatog **1981**, *217*, 289-299.
4. Hoar, S. K.; Blair, A.; Holmes, F. F.; Boysen, C. D.; Robel, R. J.; Hoover, R.; Fraumani, J. F. *J. Am. Med. Assoc.* **1986**, *256*, 1141-1147.
5. Hoar-Zahm, S. K.; Weisenburger, D. D.; Babbit, P.A.; Saal, R. C.; Vaught, J. B.; Cantor K. P.; Blair, A. *Epidemiolo,* **1990**, *1*, 349-356.
6. Wigle, D. T.; Semenciw, R. M.; Wilkins, K.; Riedel, D.; Ritter, L.; Morrison, H. I.; Mao, Y. *J. Nat. Cancer Inst.* **1990**, *82*, 575-582.
7. Hayes, H. M.; Tarone, R. E.; Cantor, K. P.; Jensen, C. R.; McCurnin, D. M.; Richardson, R. C. *J. Nat. Cancer Inst.* **1991**, *83*, 1226-1231.
8. Taskar, P. K.; Das, Y. T.; Trout, J. R.; Chattopadhyay, S. K.; Brown, H. D. *Bull. Env. Contam. Toxicol.* **1982**, *29*, 586-591.
9. Draper, W. M.; Street, J. C. *J. Env. Sci. Hlth. B* **1982**, *17*, 321-339.
10. Libich, S. *Ontario Hydro,* Report #SSD-81-1 **1981**, Ontario Hydro, Toronto.
11. Libich, S.; To, J. C.; Frank R. C.; Sirons, G. J. *Am. Ind. Hyg. J.* **1984**, *45*, 56-62.
12. Nigg, H. N.; Stamper, J. H. *Chemosphe,* **1983**, *12,* 209-215.
13. Lavy, T. L.; Walstad, J. D.; Flynn, R. R.; Mattice, J. D. *J. Agric. Food Chem.* **1982**, 30, 375-381.
14. Frank, R.; Campbell, R. A.; Sirons, G. J. *Arch. Env. Contam. Toxicol.* **1985**, *14*, 427-435.
15. Franklin, C. A.; Grover, R.; Markham, J. W.; Smith, A. E.; Yoshida, K. *Trans. Am. Conf. Gvmt. Ind. Hyg.* **1982**, *43*, 97-117.
16. Lavy, T. L.; Norris, L. A.; Mattice, J. D.; Marx, D. B. *Env. Tox. Chem.* **1987**, *6*, 209-224.
17. Grover, R.; Franklin, C. A.; Muir, N. I.; Cessna, A. J.; Riedel, D. *Toxicol. Letters* **1986**, *33*, 73-83.
18. Yeary, R. A. *Appl. Ind. Hyg.* **1986**, *3*, 119-121.

19. Bristol, D. W.; K. E. MacLeod, and R. G. Lewis. In *Determination and Assessment of Pesticide Exposure.* Siewierski, M., Ed.; Elsevier, Amsterdam **1984**, 79-119.

20. Fenski, R. A. In *Pesticide Science and Biotechnology: Proceedings of the Sixth International Congress of Pesticide Chemistry, Ottawa, Canada, 10-15 August, 1986.* Greenhalgh, R. and Roberts, T. R. Eds.; Blackwell Scientific Publications: Oxfordshire **1987**, 579-582.

21. Feldmann, R. J.; Maibach, H. I. *Toxicol. Appl. Pharmacol.* **1974**, *28,* 126-132.

22. Sauerhoff, M. W.; Braun, W. H.; Blau, G. E.; Gehring, P. J. *Toxicology,* **1977**, *8,* 3-11.

23. Thompson, D. G.; Stephenson, G. R.; Sears, M. K. *Pesticide Sci.* **1984**, *15,* 353-360.

24. Harris, S. A.; Solomon, K. R.; Stephenson, G. R. *J. Environ. Sci. Health,* **1992**, *B27,* 23-38.

25. WHO. *World Health Organization, Environmental Health Criteria 29* **1984**, WHO, Geneva.

26. Davies, J. E.; Stevens, E. R.; Staiff, D. C.; Butler, L. C. *Environ. Monitor. Assess.* **1983**, *3,* 23-38.

27. Hazleton Laboratories. *Combined toxicity and oncogenicity study of 2,4-dichlorophenoxyacetic acid in rats.* Volume 1. Hazleton Laboratories America Inc., Vienna, Virginia **1986**.

RECEIVED October 23, 1992

Chapter 23

Measurement of Pesticides in Air During Application to Lawns, Trees, and Shrubs in Urban Environments

R. A. Yeary and J. A. Leonard

ChemLawn Services Corporation, Columbus, OH 43235

Airborne levels of pesticides and formulation ingredients were measured during and following the mixing, loading, or application of pesticides and fertilizers. Air sampling was conducted according to procedures described in the OSHA Industrial Hygiene Technical Manual. Samples consisted of breathing zone air of pesticide applicators, indoor air of pesticide warehouse facilities and offices, indoor air of residential properties and ambient air of residential properties. Approximately 500 samples were taken in 14 cities in the United States and Canada. Breathing zone airborne pesticide measurements were made for 200 pesticide applicators. Indoor air measurements were made in 82 homes and outdoor ambient air measurements were made at 55 of the homesites. The analytes measured were; acephate, atrazine, ammonia, carbaryl, chlorpyrifos, 2,4-D, diazinon, dicofol, MCPA, pendimethalin and xylene. Monitoring results indicated that most samples (80 percent) were below detectable limits of .001 mg/M^3. Where analytes were detected, the time-weighted average concentration was less than 10 percent of any established standard.

Many pesticide products have odors (e.g., solvents, impurities) that are detectable at trace quantities. Detection of odor commonly leads to the assumption that there is significant exposure from airborne pesticides. This belief is further heightened by the additional assumption that during spray applications of pesticides to lawns, trees, and shrubs, airborne aerosols or mists are generated. To address the issue of inhalation exposure from application of pesticides in urban environments, the ChemLawn Services Corporation has conducted air sampling studies for measurement of pesticides at various locations throughout the United States and Canada. These studies were conducted over a period of three years. We have previously reported on worker exposure during urban application of pesticide to trees and ornamental shrubs [1].

0097–6156/93/0522–0275$06.00/0

MATERIALS AND METHODS

Air Sampling And Analysis. Air sampling was conducted according to procedures described in the OSHA Industrial Hygiene Technical Manual *(2)*. Samples for measurement of analytes were collected using preloaded cassettes (SKC Inc., Eighty Four, Pa.) with glass fiber filters, an absorbent layer and support pads through which air was drawn. Charcoal was used as the absorbent medium for pesticides and xylene. Silica gel was used as the absorbent medium for ammonia. Controls included field-spiked and blank filter cassettes.

The filter cassettes were analyzed for selected analytes by an accredited industrial hygiene laboratory using high pressure liquid chromatography, gas liquid chromatography or ion selective electrode as appropriate. Recovery rates for spiked media were at least 90 percent.

Analytes. The analytes measured were atrazine, acephate, ammonia, carbaryl, chlorpyrifos, 2,4-D, diazinon, dicofol, MCPA, pendimethalin and xylene. Selection of the analytes to be measured at each worksite was dependent on the agronomic program in use at the time of the site-specific study. The Occupational Exposure Limit for each analyte is shown in Table I.

Table I. Occupational Exposure Limits

Analyte	Source	TWA (Mg/M^3)
Acephate		NE
Atrazine	ACGIH	5.0
Ammonia	OSHA	35.0
Carbaryl	OSHA	5.0
Chlorpyrifos	OSHA	0.2
2,4-D	OSHA	10.0
Diazinon	OSHA	0.1 (skin)
Dicofol	Rohm & Haas	1.0
MCPA		NE
Pendimethalin		NE
Xylene	OSHA	435.0

NE - Not Established

Residential Indoor Air And Outdoor Ambient Air. Residential sampling was performed in and around the homes of company employees at the time of a pesticide application to their lawns, trees or shrubs. Battery operated, high-flow pumps calibrated at a flow of two liters per minute were placed inside the residence in the approximate center of a ground floor room prior to a pesticide application. The pumps were usually placed on a piece of furniture. They were operated continuously beginning approximately 15 minutes prior to the application and for a period of about six to seven hours. The pumps were calibrated before and after the sampling period using a Buck Calibrator. Where flow rate deteriorated significantly (>1%), the sample was discarded.

An additional pump was placed outside the residence approximately 15 feet from the building at ground level or within three feet of the ground.

Applicator Breathing Zone Air Monitoring. High-flow (2.0 L/min) sampling pumps were attached to the waistband of the applicators' pants. The collecting filter cassette was attached to the applicators' shirt collar. Sampling began prior to the morning tank mixing and loading activity and continued until the applicator returned to the operating facility at the end of the workday. Each participant maintained an activity log to record actual spray time. The time weighted average (TWA) was calculated on the basis of the total number of hours worked at all activities by dividing the amount of analyte measured by the total number of minutes the sample was collected.

Worksite Location. The studies were conducted in 14 cities of wide geographic and climatic diversity. These included:

Baltimore, Maryland	Monmouth, New Jersey
Buffalo, New York	Montreal, Canada
Chicago, Illinois	Orlando, Florida
Columbus, Ohio	Philadelphia, Pennsylvania
Dallas, Texas	Tampa, Florida
Fort Wayne, Indiana	Toronto, Canada
Los Angeles, California	Washington, D.C.

Office, Operations Room and Warehouse. The warehouse and/or office measurements were made during the period that mixing and loading of pesticides and fertilizers was taking place and continued during the same day. The sampling equipment was placed in the immediate proximity to a designated containment area for the mixing and loading process. An area adjacent to the office and separated by walls from the warehouse where pesticide applicators have a work station for making telephone calls and reviewing their daily records is designated the operations room for the purpose of this paper.

RESULTS AND DISCUSSION

Residential Indoor Air Monitoring. The results of the residential indoor air monitoring are shown in Table II. Indoor air monitoring was conducted in 82 homes. Sampling time was approximately 7 hours. The analytes were below detectable limits in 198 of the 224 samples. Carbaryl was the most frequently detected pesticide. The average TWA for the 16 positive carbaryl samples was 0.26 percent of the permissible exposure limit. Dicofol has a pungent odor that is often detected after application to ornamental plants but was detectable in only 1 of 63 homes. Xylene is a solvent in the chlorpyrifos product and diazinon product purchased and was not detected. It is very likely that xylene, which is diluted with water by a factor of 700 and is subsequently agitated in a tank vented to the atmosphere, evaporated rapidly following the mixing and loading procedure.

Table II. Residential Indoor Air Monitoring

Analyte	Number of Homes	Mean Sampling Time (Min.)	Detection Limit Mg/M^3	BDL[1]	TWA[2] Mg/M^3
Acephate (T/S)[3]	17	414	.001	16	.032 (1)
Carbaryl (T/S)[3]	38	414	.001	22	.013 (16)
Chlorpyrifos	10	438	.001	10	--
2,4-D	26	438	.001	18	.034 (6)
Diazinon	34	414	.001	34	--
Dicofol (T/S)[3]	63	414	.001	62	.002 (1)
Xylene	36	418	4.35	36	--

[1]BDL   =   Below Detectable Limits.
[2]TWA   =   Time Weighted Average. The number of positive samples from which the TWA was calculated are shown in parentheses.
[3]T/S   =   Tree and Ornamental Shrub Applications.

Residential Outdoor Ambient Air. The results of monitoring of residential ambient air are shown in Table III. Monitoring was conducted at 55 homesites. Sampling time was approximately 7 hours. Ammonia was measured in residential ambient air inasmuch as lawn care applications contained fertilizers with urea as a source of nitrogen. Urea may hydrolyze to ammonia depending upon pH and available moisture.

Neither ammonia, malathion nor xylene were detected. Carbaryl was detected at 13 of 28 homesites monitored, and the average TWA was 0.013 mg/M^3. Both the indoor detections and ambient air detections of carbaryl were made on the same day and from operations out of the same service center. The outdoor temperature was approximately 20°C and the relative humidity was above 90 percent. Eight residences had detectable levels of carbaryl in both indoor air and ambient air. It is unlikely that this was operator error in that the plants on these properties also received applications of dicofol and diazinon which were not detected.

Applicator Breathing Zone Air. Approximately 200 pesticide applicators were monitored during a workshift of at least eight hours. As shown in Table IV, pesticides were not detected in the breathing zone of 75 percent of the applicators at a sensitivity of 0.001 mg/M^3. None of the TWA values approached the permissible exposure levels suggested for workers in indoor environments. There are no applicable standards for agricultural operations. The Department of Labor has only recently proposed air contaminant standards for agriculture *(3)*.

Table III. Residential Outdoor Ambient Air Monitoring

Analyte	Number of Homesites	BDL[1]	TWA[2] Mg/M³
Acephate	17	16	.032 (1)
Ammonia	12	12	--
Carbaryl	28	15	.013 (13)
Dicofol	53	52	.006 (1)
Diazinon	34	32	.004 (2)
Malathion	5	5	--
2,4-D	16	11	.025 (5)
Xylene	30	30	--

[1]BDL = Below Detectable Limits (.001 mg/M³).
[2]TWA = Time Weighted Average for Sampling Period. The number of positive samples from which the TWA was calculated are shown in parentheses.

Table IV. Applicator Breathing Zone Air Monitoring

Substance	Number Monitored	BDL[1]	TWA[2] Mg/M³	Average Time Application/ Work Shift (Min.)
Atrazine	22	16	.001 (6)	163 /509
Bensulide	10	10	--	142 /497
Chlorpyrifos	17	9	.005 (8)	155 /581
2,4-D	76	61	.004 (15)	180 /493
Dacthal	2	2	--	215 /493
Diazinon	20	7	.014 (13)	152 /501
MCPA	25	25	--	147 /490
Pendimethalin	8	8	--	
Total	201	154		

[1]BDL = Below Detectable Limits (.001 mg/M³).
[2]TWA = Time Weighted Average. The number of positive samples from which the TWA was calculated are shown in parentheses.

Diazinon was detected in samples from seven of 20 applicators, the highest value being 0.032 mg/M³. Both diazinon and chlorpyrifos are cholinesterase inhibiting insecticides. All participants in the study were also monitored for blood cholinesterase activity at three-week intervals. All erythrocyte cholinesterase values were within 70 percent of the baseline control value for each individual and thus within the range of normal variation.

Though 2,4-D was detected in 15 of 76 samples, the average TWA was barely above the limit of detection and was only 0.04 percent of the OSHA standard. The results for 2,4-D were in general agreement with the finding of Harris and coworkers (4) who found 2,4-D in 5 of 76 air samples taken during home applications of 2,4-D. Two of these coincided with measurable applicator exposure.

The overall results for lawn care pesticide applicators were similar to those reported for workers spraying pesticides on trees and shrubs. Of 151 pesticide applicators monitored, 243 of 299 samples (80%) did not have detectable levels of pesticides in breathing zone air samples, and where detectable, levels of pesticides were generally less than 10 percent of the permissible exposure level (1).

Office, Operations Room And Warehouse. Eighty two samples were taken either in the office (22), operations room (27) or the warehouse (33) at the 14 cities where these studies were conducted. Only 5 of the 82 samples contained detectable levels of pesticides at a sensitivity of 0.001 mg/m³ when measured over a period of 8-10 hours (Table V).

The highest level of detection was diazinon (0.079 mg/M³) in a warehouse fill area in a makeshift glove box for weighing diazinon in a powder formulation.

Table V. Office, Operations Room and Warehouse Air Monitoring

Analyte	Number of Facilities	Mean Sampling Time (Min.)	Office	TWA (Mg/M³)[1] Operations	Warehouse
Atrazine	1	647[3]	ND[2]	ND	ND
Carbaryl	5	558[3]	ND	ND	ND
Chlorpyrifos	4	596[3]	.005 (1)	ND	ND
2,4-D (Office)	8	559	ND	--	--
(Warehouse)	10	588	--	--	.005 (1)
(Operations)	7	574	--	.003 (1)	--
Diazinon	3	596	ND	.025 (1)	.073 (2)
MCPA	3	416[3]	ND	ND	ND
Pendimethalin	1		--	ND	.0063 (1)
Xylene	7	583[3]	ND	ND	ND

[1]TWA = Time Weighted Average. The number of positive samples from which the TWA was calculated are shown in parentheses.

[2]ND = Below Detectable Limits (.001 mg/M³).

[3]Sampling Time Given is for Warehouse.

CONCLUSIONS

These data demonstrate that airborne concentrations of pesticides following applications in urban environments for control of weeds, insects and diseases of lawns, trees and shrubs are quite low with respect to existing standards for occupational exposures.

Pesticides were not detectable (<.001 mg/M^3) in approximately 80 percent of the 500 samples collected. When detected, the TWA values were generally less than 10 percent of any established or suggested standard. The data supports the pesticide label requirements for personal protective equipment wherein respiratory protection is not required for these general use pesticides.

LITERATURE CITED

1. Leonard, J.A.; Yeary, R.A., *Am. Ind. Hvg. Assoc. J.* **1990**, *51*, 605-609.
2. United States Department of Labor; *Industrial Hygiene Technical Manual* (OSHA Instruction CPL 2-20A), Washington, D.C., **1984,** I-3-7; II-6-6; IV-1-8; V-1-21.
3. Occupational Safety and Health Administration, *Federal Register*, **1992**, 26002-26601.
4. Harris, S.A.; Solomon, K.R. and Stephenson, G.R., *J. Environ. Sci. Health*, **1990**, *B27* (1), 23-38.

RECEIVED December 18, 1992

Chapter 24

Exposure Levels to Indoor Pesticides

R. B. Leidy[1], C. G. Wright[2], and H. E. Dupree, Jr.[2]

[1]Pesticide Residue Research Laboratory, Department of Toxicology, and
[2]Department of Entomology, North Carolina State University,
Raleigh, NC 27695–8604

The last twenty years have seen an increased awareness of insecticide residues in air, food and on surfaces within structures following treatments for control of indoor pests. Studies conducted at North Carolina State University have focused on determining the environmental fate of pesticide residues in air, food, soil and on surfaces following controlled or monitored applications. The objectives of these studies were: 1) to determine methodologies to quantitate residues in air and on surfaces; 2) to follow the movement of insecticides in air and on target and non-target sites; 3) to quantitate residue levels in pest control offices, warehouses, vehicles and on personnel; and 4) to quantitate residue levels of termiticides in air and soils of homes following application. These data will be summarized in this chapter.

For some twenty five years, personnel in the Department of Entomology and Pesticide Residue Research Laboratory have collaborated to determine the environmental fate of pesticides applied to structures to control insect pests. Such data are of interest to state regulatory personnel and toxicologists to make accurate determinations of whether applications were performed properly or if there were potential risks associated with insecticide residues found in air, food or on surfaces. Today's homeowner, business employee and pesticide applicator are exposed to a myriad of chemicals, including pesticides. This chapter will summarize the work conducted at North Carolina State University over the last two decades by focusing on the following studies: 1) methods to determine insecticide residues in air and on surfaces; 2) residue levels in air and movement to non- target sites following different application methods; 3) residues in pest control offices, storage facilities, vehicles, and on personnel; and 4) termiticide levels in air and soils following application.

0097–6156/93/0522–0282$06.00/0

MATERIALS AND METHODS

All pesticides used in the studies were commercial formulations diluted and used according to label. The pesticides are shown in Table I. If pressurized containers were used to apply the appropriate insecticide, the material was applied according to label recommendations. Commercial pest control firms, licensed by the state of North Carolina, did all termiticide applications. Treatment records were furnished, and the applications were observed by at least one of the authors. Degradation and movement studies were conducted in vacant apartments, vacant dining facilities at Fort Bragg, and institutional kitchens or vacant dormitories at North Carolina State University. Surface samples were taken with a metal template. Amounts of insecticide used, temperatures, humidities and other conditions (e.g., fans running) affecting residue levels were described and measured. All samples were collected in glass jars, tagged and stored on either solid carbon dioxide or ice for transport to the laboratory.

Laboratory Procedures. Samples were logged in and stored at -20°C until analyzed. Good Laboratory Practices were followed from methods development to data analysis including fortification of untreated sample matrices, the use of blanks, analytical grade standards, pesticide grade solvents and data review. Analyses were performed by GLC or HPLC using ECD, FPD, N/P or UV/Vis detectors. All GLC analyses were run on U-shaped packed glass columns whereas HPLC analyses were done on Waters-Millipore Radial Compression Separation Systems using Radial-Pak Cartridges. Solvent systems for HPLC analyses were HPLC grade filtered through a 0.2 µm membrane filter prior to use. Data were quantitated against analytical standards of known concentration, with standards being injected between every three to five samples. Residue levels were not corrected to reflect extraction efficiency.

RESULTS AND DISCUSSION

Method Development Studies. Different methods and materials were used in early studies to determine the movement of insecticides following application. China saucers and aluminum pie pans were used initially as a repository to catch settling aerosols (1-4). This was followed by the use of 2-methyl-2,4,-pentanediol to measure residues in air (5). Because of the difficulty in obtaining reproducible recoveries from this material, a switch was made to polyurethane foam (PUF) based on a USEPA study (6). Fortified PUF plugs were extracted easily and recovery values from fortified plugs averaged ca.10% higher than the fortified glycol samples used previously. Other adsorbents were used to trap pesticides in air, so two studies were done to compare extraction efficiencies of these materials against PUF (7, 8). In the first study, four commercial preparations, Carbowax 20m, Chromosorb 102, Porpak C_{18} and Tenax GC (2mL ea), were placed in polypropylene columns and efficiencies compared to PUF using 5 insecticides (7) (Table II). There were no significant differences between retention and sampling efficiency of the 5 sorbents although Tenax GC gave consistently lower efficiencies. As commercial adsorbent tubes became available, a study was undertaken to measure the efficiency of 5 adsorbents, used routinely by government and private laboratories, to acephate, chlordane, chlorpyrifos, diazinon, heptachlor and propoxur (8) (Table II). There

Table I. Insecticides Used in Indoor Air and Surface Studies

Common	CAS No.	Composition
Abamectin	65195-55-3	Mix of Avermectins containing >80% avermectin B_{1a} and <20% avermectin B_{1b}
Acephate	30560-19	0,S-Dimethyl acetylphosphoramidothioate
Bendiocarb	22781-23-3	2,2-Dimethyl-1,3-benzodioxol-4-yl methylcarbamate
Carbaryl	63-25-2	1-Naphthyl N-methylcarbamate
Chlordane	57-74-9	1,2,4,5,6,7,8,8-octachloro-2,3,3a,4,7a-hexahydro-4,7-methanoindane
Chlorpyrifos	2921-88-2	0,0-Diethyl 0-(3,5,6-trichloro-2-pyridinyl)phosphorothioate
DDVP	62-73-7	2,2-Dichlorovinyl dimethyl phosphate
Diazinon	333-41-5	0,0-Diethyl 0-(2-isopropyl-6-methyl-4-pyrimidinyl)phosphorthioate
Fenitrothion	122-14-5	0,0-Dimethyl 0-4-nitro-m-tolyl phosphorothioate
Heptachlor	76-44-8	1,4,5,6,7,8,8-Heptachloro-3a,4,7,7a-tetrahydro-4,7-methanoindene
Malathion	121-75-5	0,0-Dimethyl phosphorodithioate of diethyl mercaptosuccinate
Propoxur	114-26-1	2-(1-Methylethoxy) phenyl methylcarbamate
Resmethrin	10453-86-8	([5-(Phenylmethyl)-3-furanyl]methyl 2,2-dimethyl-3-(2-methyl-1- propenyl) cyclopropanecarboxylate

Table II. Sampling Efficiency of Seven Adsorbents to Seven Pesticides[a]

Compound	Amount Used (µg)	Adsorbent[b] Efficiency						
		Carbowax 20m (%)	Porpak C$_{18}$ (%)	Chromosorb 102 (%)	Orbo 42[c] (%)	Orbo 44[c] (%)	Puf (%)	Tenax GC (%)
Acephate	4	-	-	87	85	-	89	82
Chlorpyrifos	4[d]	-	-	98	98	-	98	95
	9[e]	86	101	95	-	-	92	75
Chlordane	8[d]	-	-	87	-	92	87	92
	9[e]	58	100	104	-	-	89	81
Diazinon	8[d]	-	92	91	92	-	93	87
Heptachlor	10[e]	44	-	92	-	-	86	73
	5	-	-	82	-	83	89	88
Propoxur	5[d]	-	-	84	85	-	83	85
	10[e]	85	33	100	-	-	85	83
Resmethrin	10	56	94	83	-	-	79	53

[a] Efficiency based on amounts found on adsorbent after amount found in impinger subtracted from total added
[b] Adsorbents purchased from commercial vendors and those from ref. 7 precleaned prior to use
[c] ORBO tubes purchased from SUPELCO, INC., Bellefonte, PA.
[d] Adapted from ref 8; (5 replications)
[e] Adapted from ref 7

were no differences in collection efficiency of the pesticides on the adsorbents although it was found that a 150 mg Tenax tube prevented breakthrough into the rear portion of the adsorbent compared to a 45 mg adsorbent tube.

Because pesticides move in air after application, it seemed reasonable to assume that they would settle onto non-treated sites throughout the structure. It was felt that two critera had to be met to conduct non-target surface testing: that the sampling material and solvent be readily available and be nondestructive to the surface being sampled. Commercially available cotton balls and 2-propanol were selected and tested using four surfaces and three insecticides (Table III).

Insecticide Residues in Air, Food, and on Surfaces. Residue studies at this institution have focused on the airborne concentration and movement of insecticides throughout a structure and their deposition onto non-target sites following different application methods. This section will summarize projects conducted in controlled environments (e.g. vacant university apartments and dormitories).

Application Techniques. Insecticides are applied to kitchens, including cabinets, to control insect pests without a thorough knowledge of what residue levels might be found on china and food. Two early studies *(1 and 11)* measured residue levels on china saucers in cabinets and on food present during and after a crack and crevice application. Cabinets containing porcelain china saucers were sprayed at the interior juncture of the two sides and back wall with chlordane (2.0%), diazinon (1.0%) and propoxur (1.1%), and residues were measured on the saucers for 28 days *(1)*. Thirty min. after application, residue levels of chlordane, diazinon and propoxur averaged 281, 325 and 570 µg/saucer, respectively, and decreased to 23, 0.7 and 56 µg/saucer 28 days after application. Calculations indicated that the maximum amounts of insecticides present were less than 1/1000 of the oral LD_{50} for white rats.

When chlorpyrifos (0.5 or 1.0%) and diazinon (1.0 or 2.0%) were applied as aerosol-type crack and crevice applications to rooms containing sliced potatoes and TV dinners, residues of chlorpyrifos were <0.02 ppm and diazinon residues varied from 0.01 to 0.05 ppm *(11)*. The same food products placed in the rooms 4.5 h after application and removed at 5.0 h showed no detectable levels of either insecticide.

Until crack and crevice applications became a routine method to minimize indoor insecticide levels, fogging of structures often was used routinely to control insect pests. An experiment was conducted to compare residues of diazinon (1.0%) on aluminum plates at various locations in rooms following these two application methods *(2)*. Residue levels on the plates (22.9 cm diam/plate) in the fogged apartments were higher than those from the crack and crevice application 30 min after application (466 vs 0.6 µg) (avg of 3 locations/room). At 4 days residue levels on plates in all rooms were below detectable levels of 0.35 ppm.

With an increasing public awareness of potential hazard resulting from indoor application of insecticides, industry efforts focused on minimizing exposure levels. Whitmire Research Laboratories, Inc. (St. Louis, MO) developed an aerosol-type, self-pressurized sprayer for applying the insecticide into cracks and crevices. A study was performed to compare this method to a compressed air sprayer by following the movement of chlorpyrifos (0.5 and 1.0%) and diazinon (1.0 and 2.0%) to non-target sites for 8 days *(3)*. There was significantly less movement of both insecticides to the floor and

Table III. Recovery of Three Insecticides from Four Surfaces[a]

Compound	Amount Added		Material[b]			
			Formica	Plywood (unfinished)	Stainless Steel	Vinyl Tile
					Recovery[c]	
	(µg)		(%)	(%)	(%)	(%)
Acephate	15		95	63	59	95
Chlorpyrifos	20		107	63		
Diazinon	10		95		98	
Diazinon	15		89		115	

[a] Adapted from ref. 9
[b] Materials size, 5.0 by 35.6cm; stainless steel template to sample surfaces had a 2.5 by 31cm slot cut from the center.
[c] Recovery based on sum of residues from two cotton balls

ceiling sites from rooms where the aerosol-type sprayer was used as compared to the compressed air sprayer throughout the 8 days (Table IV). A similar study was performed to determine the effects of forced air movement on residue levels of chlorpyrifos (0.5 and 1.0%) and diazinon (1.0 and 2.0%) and to determine the mortality of houseflies at floor and ceiling levels for 48 h *(4)*. Residue levels of both insecticides were higher in rooms with no forced air movement, and no residues were detected at 48 h after application. Houseflies in cages suspended from the ceilings of rooms with forced air movement exhibited a greater mortality than those in cages on the floor while the reverse was found in rooms with no forced air movement.

Movement in Air. None of the previous studies measured residues in air, so an experiment was conducted to compare airborne residues of chlorpyrifos (0.5 and 1.0%) applied to cracks and crevices using the aerosol-type spray or compressed-air sprayer *(5)* Immediately after application, less chlorpyrifos was found in air in rooms treated with the compressed-air sprayer than from rooms treated with aerosol-type sprayers (0.4 vs 1.5 $\mu g/m^3$, respectively). However, 1, 2, and 3 days after application the reverse was found. This was probably due to the greater movement of the smaller particles generated by the aerosol spray than those from the compressed-air sprayer which remained in the treated rooms for greater periods of time.

Other insecticides were gaining popularity for inside use, and an experiment was conducted to determine airborne concentrations of 5 insecticides for 3 days *(12)* (Table V). With the exception of bendiocarb, measurable amounts of all insecticides were seen at three days. Based upon the previous studies, it was apparent that insecticides not only remained in air for considerable periods of time, but probably moved between rooms through cracks and crevices. To test this hypothesis, a study was initiated to measure residue levels of diazinon, applied as a 1.0% emulsion to cracks and crevices, for 21 days *(13)*. Residue levels were highest in treated rooms (38 $\mu g/m^3$) immediately after application followed by adjacent (1 $\mu g/m^3$) and upper and lower rooms (ca. 0.4 $\mu g/m^3$). Residue levels were found in appreciable concentrations at 21 days in all rooms (treated, 7.0; adjacent 1.0; upper, 0.6 and lower 0.4 $\mu g/m^3$).

A similar study was performed in which the vertical distribution of diazinon in air was measured for 35 days after a 1.0% emulsion was applied to cracks and crevices in vacant dormitory rooms *(14)*. Residue levels were higher at floor level than at chest and ceiling heights in treated rooms on day 0 but tended to equalize by 7 days. Concentrations were greater at chest and ceiling levels at 21 days but were equivalent 35 days after application. Residue levels at 1.2m above the floor in adjacent, upper and lower rooms generally were equivalent at all sampling positions and maximum residues occurred in these and in three other rooms on the same floor as the treated room, 3 days after application. These data indicate that a relatively nonpersistent insecticide will remain within structures protected from direct sunlight and ventilation for several weeks.

Residues in Commercial Establishments. Employees of commercial firms are exposed to pesticides in offices as well as manufacturing or storage facilities. Studies were conducted to monitor residues in pest control offices and warehouses, restaurant kitchens, a supermarket and a tobacco storage warehouse.

Table IV. Chlorpyrifos and Diazinon Residues in Non-Target Sites Following Crack and Crevice Application[a]

	AI %	Day	Aerosol		Sprayer Location		Compressed Air	
			Floor	Ceiling	Floor	Ceiling	Floor	Ceiling
Chlorpyrifos	0.5	0	0.2	0.2	1.0	0.2	1.4	
		1	<0.2	<0.2	0.3	<0.2	0.2	
		8	<0.2	<0.2	0.2	<0.2	0.2	
Diazinon	0.1	0	0.4	0.3	2.2	0.3	1.5	
		1	<0.1	<0.1	0.5	<0.1	0.3	
		8	<0.1	0.5	0.1	0.5		

[a]Adapted from ref 3, (3 replications).

Pest Control Firms. Large quantities of pesticides are stored in pest control firm facilities, and in the 1970's it was not unusual to find an office and storage facility located in the same building. A study was performed to determine what organophosphate insecticides were present in six North Carolina pest control firms and to measure residues in air in both the storage facility and office *(15)*. Airborne residues of chlorpyrifos, DDVP, diazinon and malathion were found in all storage areas and, with the exception of malathion, in offices (Table VI). One office contained high levels of insecticides which were traced to a duct which had a direct air flow between the storage area and office.

Pest Control Firm Vehicles. Both concentrated and diluted formulations of pesticides are transported to treatment sites in vehicles, therefore, two studies were conducted to determine residues in the ambient air of these vehicles. Six sedans, six vans and nine pickup trucks were inventoried for the presence of organophosphate insecticides, and the ambient air was sampled while the pest control technician was present *(15)*. Significant residue levels of chlorpyrifos were detected in the cab of pickup trucks when compressed-air sprayers were kept in the cab compared to trucks in which sprayers were placed in the truck bed. Residues of diazinon were found in all vans sampled and in 5 of 6 sedans. DDVP was detected in the cabs of pickups containing a sprayer and in 2 of 6 vans. A second study was performed to determine differences in residue levels in air of chlorpyrifos and diazinon in pickup trucks while moving and stationary *(16)*. Residues of insecticides from both studies were well below the Threshold Limit Values (TLV's) and data for chlorpyrifos in pickup trucks are shown in Table VII.

Food Handling Establishments. Restaurants and supermarkets are treated routinely to control pests. Studies performed in these facilities have focused on the effects of forced air movement on insecticide residues in air and on their deposition on surfaces after application. Six institutional kitchens were treated with a crack and crevice application of 0.5% chlorpyrifos applied as a pinpoint stream and airborne concentrations were measured for 4 h after application and at 24 h *(15)*. The three facilities in which air conditioners or fans were running had higher residue levels at both sampling periods than those with no forced air movement (0.7 vs 0.4 $\mu g/m^3$, 4 h; 0.2 vs 0.05 $\mu g/m^3$, 24 h) indicating that air flow has a considerable influence on chlorpyrifos and other insecticide residues in ambient air. Since insecticide residues will settle on surfaces, a hotel kitchen, restaurant kitchen and supermarket were sampled on 18-stainless steel, formica and ceramic tile surfaces at 2-month intervals for 6 months following a prescribed crack and crevice application of 0.5% chlorpyrifos *(9)*. The greatest residues were found along the clay tile baseboard (9.0 ng/cm^2 at 2 mo) in the restaurant kitchen. At 6 months, 19 ng/cm^2 were found on the tile baseboard. Measurable amounts were found in four of the six sites (<3.0 ng/cm^2) in the hotel kitchen and supermarket at 2 months, and residues were below the detectable limit of 1.0 ng/cm^2 at 4 and 6 months.

Avermectin Residues. A new class of insecticides, the avermectins, are closely related, complex 16-membered macrocyclic lactones. Abamectin, a commercial formulation of avermectin, was labeled for cockroach control in the United States in 1990. A study was performed in three vacant dining facilities at Fort Bragg, NC to measure abamectin residues, after application, in air, food and on surfaces over a 3-month period (Wright and

Table V. Airborne Concentrations of Insecticides in Rooms[a]

Insecticide	AI (%)	Pre (µg/m³)	0 (µg/m³)	1 (µg/m³)	2 (µg/m³)	3 (µg/m³)
			Day			
Acephate	1.0	ND	1.3	2.9	0.5	0.3
Bendiocarb	0.5	ND	7.7	1.3	ND	ND
Carbaryl[b]	5.0	ND	1.3	0.2	0.1	0.01
Chlorpyrifos	0.5	0.1	1.1	1.1	0.8	0.3
Diazinon	1.0	0.2	1.6	0.6	0.5	0.4
Fenitrothion	1.0	ND	3.3	1.1	0.8	0.5
Propoxur	1.1	ND	15.4	2.7	1.8	0.7

[a]Adapted from ref 12; Four replications
[b]Applied as a 5% dust

Table VI. Insecticides in Air in Storage and Office Rooms in Pest Control Firms[a]

Insecticide	No.[b]	Storage (µg/m³)	Office (µg/m³)
		Residue	
Chlorpyrifos	5	0.2	0.1
DDVP	4	0.6	<0.1
Diazinon	6	0.3	0.2
Malathion	2	0.1	<0.1

[a]Six firms; adapted from ref. 15.
[b]Number of storage facilities containing the insecticide.

Table VII. Residues of Chlorpyrifos in Ambient Air of Pest Control Firm Pickup Trucks[a]

Location of Sprayer	No Sampled	Moving (µg/m³)	Stationary (µg/m³)
		Residue	
CAB	3	0.2	-
CAB[b]	2	0.8	0.2
Bed	9	0.2	0.3[c]

[a]Converted to 2 h sampling; adapted from ref 15, 16.
[b]Sprayer left in cab overnight
[c]n=4 These data indicate that residues present in vehicles probably result rom both residual material present on the technician and air movement due to the configuration of the vehicle.

Leidy, in press). Residues were found in air over the 3-month period, but no surface residues were found after 7 days (Table VIII). Low levels were found on bread at 3 days and lettuce at 1 day.

Spot Application. Not all insecticides are applied into cracks and crevices to control pests. Acephate can be applied along and behind baseboards as a low pressure spot spray. It is not unusual for a pest control technician to apply acephate to baseboards, but maximum control is not seen and small children and pets can contact these surfaces. A study was performed to determine levels of acephate on baseboards in 5 dining facilities following a direct application and to determine movement to non-target sites *(17)*. The highest residues of acephate were found on the wall immediately above the treated baseboard during the two-week sampling, but no residues were found on stainless steel surfaces at one week, indicating that a considerable amount of material was splashed onto areas above the baseboards. In addition, the data showed that little acephate moved into the air and to other non-target surfaces.

DDVP in Air. Fumigants are used routinely to minimize loss of stored products to pests. Tobacco storage warehouses are fumigated with DDVP at rates of 0.5 to 1.0 g/100m^3 to control insects. Airborne concentrations of DDVP were measured in air at different locations in a 26,197 m^3 tobacco storage warehouse to which 21L of a 10% solution of DDVP were applied in three different experiments *(18)*. In the three experiments, residue levels were highest initially in the center of the warehouse compared to a corner, but tended to equalize after 4 h. The data indicated that workers entering the warehouse 4 h after application would not encounter residue levels above the TLV of 0.8 mg/m^3 *(19)*.

Applicator Exposure. Pest control technicians are exposed to insecticides while traveling to treatment sites and during application through dermal exposure or inhalation. Federal regulations mandate the use of gloves, protective clothing and respirators to minimize exposure, yet a few applicators probably will not use this equipment. Two studies were conducted to determine what an individual might be exposed to during an inside application of diazinon and *(13)* while applying a termiticide formulation of chlorpyrifos *(20)*. Based upon a 15-min Short Term Exposure Level (STEL), the applicator applying a 1.0% formulation of diazinon was exposed to a residue level of 20.3 µg/m^3, well below the published TLV-STEL of 200 µg/m^3 in 1978 *(21)*. Applicators applying a 1.0% formulation of chlorpyrifos to houses to control termites averaged higher concentrations when applications were made to crawl space-constructed homes compared to either slab or a combination crawl space/slab-constructed home *(20)*. The average exposure from all applications averaged 8% of the TLV for airborne concentrations of chlorpyrifos.

Termiticide Application. The chemical nature of materials used to treat homes and businesses to control termites has changed in the last four years. With the removal of chlordane from the market in 1988, organophosphate and pyrethroid insecticides have been introduced to replace the cyclodiene termiticides. Prior to the removal of chlordane, two studies were performed to determine residues in air following a prescribed application and to determine if construction and soil type had an effect on residue levels in air *(22, 23)*. Six houses were treated with a 1.0% of technical chlordane (0.97 Kg AI/L) and three with a combination chlordane (0.5%) + heptachlor (0.25%)(0.5 + 0.25 Kg AI/L, respectively) and residues in air were measured immediately before and after application, and after 1 day, 1 week, 1 and 6 months and 1 year in six of the houses treated *(22)*. Residues of the 1% application of chlordane averaged 3.3 $\mu g/m^3$ (range 0.3 to 5.0) and 3.2 $\mu g/m^3$ (range 1.6 to 5.8) from the combination chlordane/heptachlor formulation over the 12-mo sampling period. Heptachlor residue averaged 1.1 $\mu g/m^3$ from the combination application. Because of the large variation of residues within each home over time, no firm conclusions could be drawn as to what influenced residue levels, although construction and soil type, temperature, humidity and air movement probably influenced the levels found. A second study was done to see if construction and soil type influenced termiticide levels *(23)*. Houses, treated for termites with chlordane or chlordane plus heptachlor over a 5-year period between 1979 and 1983, were divided into four groups of 15, based on soil and house type. The groups were: 1) sand, slab construction; 2) sand, crawl construction; 3) clay, crawl construction; and 4) clay, crawl/ slab contruction. Termiticide residues were measured in the soil and ambient (breathing space) air of a bedroom and kitchen in each house. Chlordane residues averaged 1475 and 1052 ppm in soils from clay and sand regions, respectively. Residues in air averaged 3.1 $\mu g/m^3$ (range 0.05 to 9.9) from all rooms in houses from clay regions and 2.8 $\mu g/m^3$ (range 0.05 to 7.2) from sand regions. Five of 15 slab-constructed houses had no detectable residue levels in air. Heptachlor levels averaged 0.5 $\mu g/m^3$ (range ND to 2.0 $\mu g/m^3$ in bedrooms and kitchens from all houses sampled. The data indicated that homes properly treated with chlordane by label directions would fall below the interim guideline of 5.0 $\mu g/m^3$ (chlordane) and 2.0 $\mu g/m^3$ (heptachlor) established in 1979 by the National Academy of Sciences *(24)*. This guideline has not changed, because additional data have not been obtained.

Chlorpyrifos has been formulated as a termiticide and used widely over the last 8 to 10 years. Residues in air were measured over a 4-year period (Table IX), and soil samples were taken at 4 years and concentrations of chlorpyrifos were determined *(24, 25)*. House construction and soil type were used to see if they affected residue levels in air. Levels in air varied over the 4-year period but none were above the National Academy of Sciences proposed guideline level of 10.0 $\mu g/m^3$ *(26)*. Soil residue levels varied widely from non-detectable to 1685 ppm *(25)*. We have no good explanation other than that application methods (trenching vs rodding), sampling technique and soil characteristics might have contributed to this variation in soil residue levels.

SUMMATION AND FUTURE RESEARCH

Studies have indicated detectable quantities of several insecticides in the ambient air and on surfaces in various building types and pest control service vehicles. Residues produced by various insecticide formulations and applications techniques were determined. Soil and food monitoring after insecticide application using approved treatment procedures were conducted. Data indicate that very small quantities of the insecticides are often detected, especially in the ambient air and on surfaces in structures even when label instructions for dilution and application are followed. Maximum levels detected were usually far less than recommended threshold limit values. Research continues on determining residues of new insecticides (e.g., cypermethrin and cyfluthrin) in air and on surfaces inside structures. A long term study is being done to follow the degradation of termiticides in soils. Other

Table VIII. Residues of Abamectin in Air, Food and on Surfaces[a]

Sample	Day After Application							
	Pre	0	1	3	7	30	60	90
Air[b]	<0.0005	0.9	0.3	0.1	0.002	<0.0005	<0.0005	<0.0005
Surface[c]								
Formica (H)[d]	<0.02	3	1	<0.02	<0.02	<0.02	<0.02	<0.02
S.Steel (H)[e]	<0.02	42	3	3	3	<0.02	<0.02	<0.02
S.Steel (V)[f]	<0.02	<0.02	1	<0.0	<0.02	<0.02	<0.02	<0.02
Bread[g]	<0.2	8	4	3				
Lettuce[g]	<0.2	7	3	-				

[a]n=3
[b]µg/m^3
[c]ng/100cm^2
[d]horizontal surface
[e]horizontal surface, stainless steel
[f]vertical surface, stainless steel
[g]ppb

Table IX. Chlorpyrifos in the Ambient Air of Houses Treated for Termites[a]

	Soil Type			
	Clay		Sand	
	Construction			
Time After Application	Slab/Crawl (µg/m^3)	Crawl (µg/m^3)	Crawl (µg/m^3)	Slab (µg/m^3)
pre	0.1	0.2	0.1	0.1
0	1.2	2.4	0.8	1.1
1wk	0.7	1.3	0.5	0.6
1mo	1.0	0.7	1.6	1.0
3mo	0.5	0.8	2.0	2.5
6mo	0.6	0.7	0.6	1.0
1yr	2.8	1.4	3.1	3.0
2yr	1.7	1.3	1.8	1.6
4yr	3.0	2.0	5.0	5.0

[a]Avg of 4 houses/construction type, 2 rooms/house; adapted from ref 24, 25.

studies will measure insecticide levels in offices and pesticide-storage areas of pest control buildings, in pest control service vehicles, and on carpets following their treatment with insecticides labeled for flea control. It is believed that data generated from studies of this type aid in understanding and determining the environmental fate of pesticides when applied indoors, and provide information to those scientists who perform risk assessments for determination of "safe" levels of pesticides in indoor environments.

ACKNOWLEDGMENTS

We wish to thank the following for their financial support: Whitmire Research Laboratories, Inc.; The North Carolina Pest Control Association; The Dow Chemical Company; The Pesticide Impact Assessment Committee, USDA; The National Pest Control Association, The North Carolina Tobacco Foundation; The American Tobacco Company; Brown and Williamson Tobacco Corporation; P. Lorillard Corporation; R. J. Reynolds Company; and The Tobacco Advisory Committee (United Kingdom). The authors wish to express their appreciation to the North Carolina Pest Control Companies who agreed to participate in some of the studies and to W. L. Jones who assisted in some of the analyses.

LITERATURE CITED

1. Wright, C. G.; Jackson, M. D. *J. Econ. Entomol.* **1971**, *64*, 457-459.
2. Wright, C. G.; Jackson, M. D. *Bull. Environ. Contam. Toxicol.* **1974**, *12*, 177-181.
3. Wright, C. G., Jackson, M. D. *Bull. Environ. Contam. Toxicol.* **1975**, *13*, 123-128.
4. Wright, C. G.; Jackson, M. D. *Arch. Environ. Contam. Toxicol.* **1976**, *4*, 492-500.
5. Wright, C. G.; Leidy, R. B. *Bull. Environ. Contam. Toxicol.* **1978**, *16*, 340-344.
6. Lewis, R. G.; Brown, A. R.; Jackson, M. D. *Anal. Chem.* **1977**, *49*, 1668-1672.
7. Roper, E. M.; Wright, C. G.; *Bull. Environ. Contam. Toxicol.* **1984**, *33*, 476-483.
8. Leidy, R. B.; Wright, C. G.; *J. Environ. Sci. Health.* **1991**, *B26*, 367-382.
9. Leidy, R. B.; Wright, C. G.; Dupree, H. E., Jr. *Environ. Monitoring Assessment.* **1985**, *9*, 47-55.
10. Wright, C. G.; Leidy, R. B.; Dupree, H. E., Jr. *Bull. Environ. Contam. Toxicol.* **1984**, *32*, 259-264.
11. Jackson, M. D.; Wright, C. G. *Bull. Environ. Contam. Toxicol.* **1975**, 13, 593-595.
12. Wright, C. G.; Leidy, R. B.; Dupree, H. E., Jr. *Bull. Environ. Contam. Toxicol.* **1981**, *26*, 548-553.
13. Leidy, R. B.; Wright, C. G.; Dupree, H. E., Jr. *J. Environ. Sci. Health.* **1982**, *B17*, 311-319.
14. Leidy, R. B; Wright, C. G.; Dupree, H. E., Jr. *J. Environ. Sci. Health.* **1984**, *B19*, 747-757.
15. Wright, C. G.; Leidy, R. B. *Bull. Environ. Contam. Toxicol.* **1980**, *24*, 582-589.
16. Wright, C. G.; Leidy, R. B.; Dupree, H. E., Jr. *Bull. Environ. Contam. Toxicol.* **1982**, *28*, 119-121.
17. Wright, C. G.; Leidy, R. B.; Dupree, H. E., Jr. *Bull Environ. Contam. Toxicol.* **1989**, *43*, 713-716.

18. Leidy, R. B.; Sheets, T. J.; Wright, C. G. *Environ. Monitoring Assessment.* **1987,** *9,* 263-268.

19. American Conference of Governmental Hygienists. *Threshold Limit Values for Chemical Substances and Physical Agents and Biological Exposure Indices.* Cincinnati, OH. **1991-1992;** 128 pp.

20. Leidy, R. B.; Wright, C. G., Dupree, H. E., Jr. *Bull. Environ. Contam. Toxicol.* **1991,** *47,* 177-183.

21. American Conference of Governmental Hygienists. *Threshold Limit Values for Chemical Substances in the Workroom Environment with Intended Changes for 1979.* Cincinnati, OH. **1978,** 94 pp.

22. Wright, C. G.; Leidy, R. B. *Bull Environ. Contam. Toxicol.* **1982,** *28,* 617-623.

23. Leidy, R. B.; Wright, C. G.; Dupree, H. E., Jr.; Sheets, T. J. *In Dermal Exposure Related to Pesticide Use*; Honeycutt, R. C.; Zweig, G.; Ragsdale, N., Eds. ACS Symposium Series No. 273; American Chemical Society: Washington, DC, **1985,** pp 265-277.

24. National Academy of Sciences. *Chlordane in Military Housing,* **1979.**

25. Wright, C. G.; Leidy, R. B.; Dupree, H. E., Jr. *Bull. Environ. Contam. Toxicol.* **1991,** *46,* 686-689.

26. National Research Council. *An Assessment of the Health Risks of Seven Pesticides Used for Termite Control.* Comm. Toxicol, Board Toxicol Environ. Health Hazards, Comm. Life Sci, Nat. Res. Council; Nat. Acad. Press. Washington, D C. **1982,** 72 pp.

RECEIVED October 30, 1992

Chapter 25

Risks Associated with Exposure to Chlorpyrifos and Chlorpyrifos Formulation Components

J. R. Vaccaro

Health and Environmental Sciences, The Dow Chemical Company, 1803 Building, Midland, MI 48674

Chlorpyrifos is a widely used organophosphate insecticide. It finds utility in control of a wide variety of household pests and has an important use in the agricultural arena. Numerous evaluations have been conducted in homes to determine residual airborne and surface concentrations following application of insecticides inside dwellings. Studies involving termiticide applications, crack and crevice application for cockroaches, broadcast applications for fleas, fogger use for a myriad of target pests and even insecticidal paints, have been conducted to determine residual air and surface concentrations. This chapter summarizes research on human exposure to chlorpyrifos and chlorpyrifos formulation components (e.g., solvents, impurities) following urban pesticide applications.

The concern over indoor air quality has become a major health issue not only in the United States but throughout the more progressive societies. Radon gas, off-gassing of household items such as insulation and carpeting, as well as volatile organic compounds (VOC) are of major interest. Although pesticides are not high on the list of concerns, they are on the list. In addition, by-products and so-called inerts associated with pesticide formulations, when in a vapor or aerosolized state, are also of interest as a perceived health risk. With a growing population of individuals "sensitive" to a host of unrelated chemicals, other routes of exposure such as the dermal route have also received some attention as having potential for chemical absorption by the body.

CHLORPYRIFOS PROPERTIES AND TOXICITY

Chlorpyrifos, the common name for O,O-diethyl-O (3,5,6- trichloro-2-pyridyl) phosphorothioate is a solid at room temperature, melting at about $41\,°C$. The acute oral LD50 in rats, ranges from 97-296 mg/kg, based on various literature references. The acute dermal LD50 in rats is greater than 2000 mg/kg in rats and 1500-1800 mg/kg in rabbits *(25)*.

0097–6156/93/0522–0297$06.00/0

Subchronic studies in animals include three-generation reproduction studies in rats, teratology studies in rats and rabbits, a multitude of mutagenicity studies, neurotoxicity studies in hens, both single and repeated doses and several 90-day feeding studies in other laboratory species. Chronic (i.e. 2-year) two species investigations have been conducted in rats and mice for determination of carcinogenicity potential.

Conclusions from sub-chronic and chronic animal studies were chlorpyrifos does not cause reproductive effects, is not a teratogen, does not cause Organophosphate Induced Delayed Neuropathy [OPIDN] in hens, is not mutagenic and does not cause cancer at doses that cause illness in test animals due to cholinesterase inhibition.

No Observable Effect Levels. No discussion of risk is complete without a discussion of No Observable Effect Levels [NOEL]. Unlike most pesticides, chlorpyrifos has had an extensive testing regimen in human volunteers. Coulston *(1)* et al conducted feeding studies with human volunteers who received doses of 14 μg/kg, 30 μg/kg, and 100 μg/kg. Twenty-eight daily doses at 14 μg/kg did not cause plasma cholinesterase depression or erythrocytic cholinesterase depression. Twenty one daily doses at 30 μg/kg caused very slight depressions in plasma cholinesterase. At 100 μg/kg, nine daily doses produced a 66% depression in plasma cholinesterase; however, it took three doses before any plasma cholinesterase depression was observed. There was no depression in erythrocytic cholinesterase and no clinical signs of cholinesterase depression. The NOEL established for repeated doses of chlorpyrifos was 30 μg/kg /day. This dose level is the basis for the current threshold limit value (TLV) of 200 μg/m^3.

In a later study by Nolan et al, *(2)* single oral doses of 500 μg/kg were given to human volunteers. This dose produced an 85% depression in plasma cholinesterase, but no depression in erythrocytic cholinesterase activity. There were no clinical signs of toxicity. In addition, single dermal doses of 5000 μg/kg were applied to human volunteers. No plasma or erythrocytic cholinesterase depression was observed. Nolan determined through biomonitoring that approximately 3% of the dermal dose was absorbed based on elimination of the metabolite as 3,5,6 trichloro-2-pyridinol (TCP) in the urine.

HUMAN CHLORPYRIFOS EXPOSURE STUDIES

A large number of exposure evaluation studies have been conducted involving chlorpyrifos use. A few years ago EPA conducted the non-occupational pesticide exposure study (NOPES) *(3)*. This non-occupational pesticide exposure study was conducted to determine the presence of a myriad of pesticides and pesticide breakdown products in Jacksonville, Florida and Springfield, Mass. Two hundred and sixteen homes were sampled for the presence of 32 different airborne materials. Airborne chlorpyrifos, because of its popularity as an indoor insecticide, was determined in each location. In Jacksonville, chlorpyrifos was found in 100% of the households. In summer, spring and winter, maximum airborne chlorpyrifos was found as high as 2.2, 4.4 and 1.04 μg/m^3, respectively. In Springfield, the highest concentrations in spring and winter were 0.25 and 0.29 μg/m^3, respectively. The study indicated the presence of older chlorinated hydrocarbon or cyclodienes was related to the age of the home.

Termite Applications. Wright *(4)* et al found between 1 and 9 $\mu g/m^3$ [0.070 and 0.630 ppb] of chlorpyrifos in the air of four dwellings (two slab construction and two crawl-space type construction) four years post-application. The proposed National Academy of Sciences [NAS] guideline *(5)* for residual chlorpyrifos following termiticide applications is 10 $\mu g/m^3$ (0.7 ppb). This guideline was established in 1982 and was specified as an interim guideline to be reviewed within three years. Wright found that sandy soils showed a tendency to lead to higher airborne chlorpyrifos concentrations than dwellings built on clay type soils. In an earlier study, Wright *(6)* et al sampled 16 dwellings for residual airborne chlorpyrifos up to 104 weeks (2 years) following a termiticide application. The highest air concentration observed was 3.13 mg/m^3. This was in a crawl-space dwelling 52 weeks post-application. Variations from sampling period to sampling period were likely due to increased vapor pressure resulting from higher ambient temperatures. Sandy soils appeared to enhance airborne chlorpyrifos concentrations.

Vaccaro *(7)* et al sampled air for chlorpyrifos vapor in 32 dwellings for up to one year following application of Dursban TC (trademark of DowElanco) insecticide for control of subterranean termites. Four types of structured dwellings were used in the study. The highest levels observed were 30 days post-application in plenum dwellings which have a unique crawl-space type structure with no duct work. The highest observed air concentration of chlorpyrifos was 6.8 $\mu g/m^3$ (0.48 ppb). The maximum airborne chlorpyrifos concentration in crawl-space dwellings was 0.7 $\mu g/m^3$ (0.05 ppb), in slabs 4.6 $\mu g/m^3$ (0.32 ppb) and in basements 5.5 $\mu g/m^3$ (0.39 ppb), all at 30 days post-application. The maximum airborne level at one year was 2.0 $\mu g/m^3$ (0.14 ppb) in a single plenum dwelling. One would expect that a termiticide application might produce the highest residual airborne chlorpyrifos concentrations for two reasons. First, the active ingredient is labeled at 1%, and second, the volume of treatment mixture may be as much as 250 gallons. By comparison, broadcast applications are about half as concentrated (0.5%) and only a gallon or so of the material is actually dispersed. The major controlling factors in the treatment with termiticides are the construction type and type of soil. A major factor precluding high airborne concentrations is that the treatment mixture is injected deep into the soil. Treatment under a slab also restricts the vapor from entering the living area of the dwelling.

Crack and Crevice Applications. A second major application technique is the use of crack and crevice treatments for the control of cockroaches. This is a baseboard treatment, but treatments may include cupboards and around food handling equipment. Generally, a pin spray from a compressed air sprayer is used to contact areas frequented by cockroaches. Wright *(8)* et al conducted crack and crevice applications, using chlorpyrifos, with an aerosol type sprayer and a compressed air sprayer. The initial air concentration of chlorpyrifos using the aerosol type was 1.5 $\mu g/m^3$ (0.1 ppb) and using the compressed airsprayer was 0.37 $\mu g/m^3$ (0.03 ppb). By doubling the active ingredient concentration in the treatment mixture to 1%, initial air concentrations were 2.7 $\mu g/m^3$ and 0.6 $\mu g/m^3$ for the aerosol type and compressed air sprayer, respectively. Air concentrations of chlorpyrifos fell rapidly on days 2 and 3 following the application. In another study conducted by Wright *(9)* et al, airborne chlorpyrifos concentrations immediately after application to cracks and crevices in several food handling areas ranged from 0.02 $\mu g/m^3$ to 1.4 $\mu g/m^3$. Within 24 hours, airborne chlorpyrifos concentrations ranged from 0.36 $\mu g/m^3$ to 4 $\mu g/m^3$. Gold (10) et al conducted crack and crevice application studies with dichlorvos and concluded "that there was not a significant risk, in terms of acute toxicity, to either the pesticide applicators or the residents of treated structures when DDVP was used for cockroach control". This was quite a surprising conclusion, however sound, considering that DDVP has a vapor pressure 100 times that of chlorpyrifos.

Broadcast Applications. Broadcast applications for fleas appear to offer the greatest potential for exposure to a homedweller. In this case, application is made to a broad surface, such as carpeting. The concentration of the treatment mixtures will be between 0.25% and 0.5%. This will put down an amount of active ingredient equal to about 12.7 $\mu g/cm^2$. This surface then offers the potential for higher airborne concentrations as well as potential for dermal exposure to crawling infants. Currie (11) et al treated both furnished and unfurnished offices with diazinon, bendiocarb and chlorpyrifos and measured both airborne insecticide levels and deposition levels following the application. Airborne diazinon, bendiocarb and chlorpyrifos peaked at 163 $\mu g/m^3$, 2.7 $\mu g/m^3$ and 27 $\mu g/m^3$, respectively. These airborne levels fall in line with the individual vapor pressures of the insecticides. The amount of chlorpyrifos on the floor ranged from 0.2 - 4.9 ng/cm^2, 24 hours post-application. Naffziger (12) et al conducted broadcast applications with chlorpyrifos using a B&G compressed air-sprayer at two concentrations; 0.25% and 0.5%. The highest one-hour airborne chlorpyrifos concentrations were 17 $\mu g/m^3$ and 35 $\mu g/m^3$ for the 0.25% and 0.50%, respectively. When using wipe testing (hand wipes) for measuring dislodgeable residue, Naffziger found a transfer coefficient of 3.5% at one-hour post-application, 0.88% at 24 hours post-application, and 0.5% at 48 hours post-application. It is very likely that the one-hour post-application wipe was conducted on a wet floor. Drying studies (13) on actual carpet samples, at 50% relative humidity, indicated that it took at least three hours before carpet sample weights began to stabilize after treatment with a 0.5% chlorpyrifos-based spray. Labeled directions are clear that contact with treated surfaces must take place only after the floor is dry. Fenske (14) published results of a study conducted in a series of rooms in a New Jersey apartment. Airborne chlorpyrifos and dislodgeable residues (hand wipes) from treated surfaces were used to estimate a dose for a 10 kg child. Both ventilated and unventilated rooms were used to assess conditions. In this study, wipe testing for determination of dose was begun 0.5 hours following completion of the application. Therefore, it is questionable whether the floor was dry in accordance with labeled directions. Transfer coefficients were about 5% on day one in the ventilated rooms and 11.4% in the unventilated rooms. On day 2, the transfer coefficients were still at 2% in the ventilated rooms and 3.5% in the unventilated rooms. Air concentrations of chlorpyrifos peaked about eight hours post-application and indicated the presence of about 94 $\mu g/m^3$ in the unventilated room and about 50 $\mu g/m^3$ in the ventilated room, when measured close to the floor. Estimated doses to a 10 kg child, based on the unventilated condition was 158 $\mu g/kg$ and for the ventilated condition 75 $\mu g/kg$. This study would indicate that under poor conditions of drying and ventilation, estimates of exposure may be quite high.

A somewhat different study *(15)* was conducted by The Dow Chemical Company Industrial Hygiene Laboratory. In this study, to assess doses of chlorpyrifos to crawling infants, six adult male volunteers were used to simulate the movement of children on treated surfaces. Both physicochemical measurements and urinary biomonitoring for the metabolite of chlorpyrifos, 3,5,6-trichloro-2-pyridinol [TCP], were used to arrive at separate assessments of dose for the crawling infant. Air monitoring was conducted to estimate the inhalation dose, dislodgeable residues were determined to assess dermal dose, and hand rinses of the volunteers, post-exposure, were conducted to determine an oral/hand component because of the tendency for crawling infants toward hand/finger sucking. Biomonitoring of urine [for TCP] and blood (for cholinesterase activity) was conducted prior to the study and following the activity phase (4-hours of crawling, sitting, walking, and lying on the treated surface). The adult volunteers wore only bathing trunks. The highest measured airborne concentration of chlorpyrifos was 28 $\mu g/m^3$ at about eight hours post-application. Dislodgeable residues ranged below 40 $\mu g/ft^2$ (43 ng/cm^2). Transfer coefficients ranged from 0.03% to 0.68% with significant decline in transfer coefficients from two hours post-application to four-hours post-application. The most significant route of exposure was the hand/oral route which contributed about 56% of the dose assessed by the indirect measurement approach (passive dosimetry). The total estimated dose using indirect measurements was 20.5 $\mu g/kg$ for the crawling infant. Using biomonitoring techniques and back calculating from the urinary TCP concentrations to the chlorpyrifos dose gave an estimated dose of 27 $\mu g/kg$. Plasma cholinesterase determinations before and after the four hour activity period did not indicate any exposure-related depressions. When these doses were compared to the single dose no observable effect level [NOEL] for chlorpyrifos in humans of 500 $\mu g/kg$, the margin of safety was eighteen fold or greater. It is very important that when studies involving broadcast treatments are conducted the protocol be carefully designed. Studies, to be meaningful, must follow labeled directions for ventilation and drying parameters.

Indoor Fogger Applications. A somewhat related approach to pest control is the use of foggers. Total release aerosols are sold over-the-counter and are also used by pest control professionals. There are a number of studies available addressing this type of application. Bohl *(16)* et al conducted a study using 1% chlorpyrifos-based foggers. Two portions of a duplex were treated for control of a number of insect species. At 2 hour post-release, airborne chlorpyrifos concentrations ranged from 40 $\mu g/m^3$ to 90 $\mu g/m^3$ in one portion of the duplex and 19 $\mu g/m^3$ to 20 $\mu g/m^3$ in the second duplex. At four hours post-release, the concentrations ranged from 3-16 $\mu g/m^3$ in the first duplex and 8-26 $\mu g/m^3$ in the second. After one day, the airborne chlorpyrifos ranged below 14 $\mu g/m^3$ in both duplexes and at 7 days below 1.5 $\mu g/m^3$. The highest deposition concentration from "fall-out" of the foggers was 11 $\mu g/cm^2$. This value agrees nicely with the labeled broadcast rate for carpets of 12.7 $\mu g/cm^2$ (Dursban LO Insecticide).

In a similar study *(17)*, a single total release fogger was released in a 1500 ft^2 dwelling. Thirty-six minutes later, the airborne concentration of chlorpyrifos was 4090 $\mu g/m^3$ in the living room and 2530 $\mu g/m^3$ in one of the bedrooms. At 2.9 hours post-release, airborne chlorpyrifos concentrations were 50 $\mu g/m^3$ and 80 $\mu g/m^3$ in the same areas. Eight and one-half (8.5) hours later, airborne chlorpyrifos concentrations were

20 μg/m^3 in both rooms. Twenty-five hours post-release, concentrations in both areas were 3-4 μg/m^3. The highest surface concentration was found on the floor near the release point and was 3.3 μg/cm^2.

Ross (18) et al at the California Department of Food and Agriculture (CDFA) conducted chlorpyrifos fogger experiments in a series of hotel rooms in Sacramento. Ross used a physicochemical and a biomonitoring approach to assess doses to leotard-adorned adult volunteers who conducted Jazzercise routines on the treated surface, and then he extrapolated the results to a 7.5 kg child. Airborne concentrations of chlorpyrifos in the first six hours averaged 14 μg/m^3, and 6 μg/m^3 from 6½ to 10½ hours post-release. Ross estimated, using physicochemical measurements, that the dose to a 7.5 kg child would be about 250 μg/kg; however, using urinary biomonitoring techniques he estimated a dose of less that 1 μg/kg.

Maddy (19) et al found that DDVP containing foggers produced airborne dichlorvos concentrations as high as 12.6 mg/m^3 in ventilated rooms following the use of a total release fogger. Twenty-four hour concentrations decline to 111 μg/m^3. It should be noted that the vapor pressure of dichlorvos is roughly 100 times that of chlorpyrifos. In an unventilated room, concentrations reached a high of 3075 μg/m^3 and were 186 μg/m^3 at 24 hours post-release.

These results leave little doubt in the mind of an investigator that fogging produces the highest airborne concentrations of any application. Also, foggers are indiscriminate as to where the active ingredient will finally reside.

Wood Treatment and Insecticidal Paints. A unique approach to pest control is the treatment of structural logs with chlorpyrifos for building log homes. One study (20) was conducted in a large log home built from pressure treated logs. The logs had been pressure-treated with a 1% chlorpyrifos-based organic solvent solution. Once the logs had been treated, they were air dried and transported to the building site in Wilmington, North Carolina. After construction of the home, two air sampling sessions were conducted, one in December and one in July. Airborne chlorpyrifos within the structure ranged below 1 μg/m^3 in December [ambient temperature about 40°F] before the heating system had been installed. In July, with air conditioning operational, airborne chlorpyrifos ranged from 3.3-5.3 μg/m^3. These low airborne concentrations in July were surprising, considering the large amount of chlorpyrifos potentially available for volatilization within the dwelling. Chlorpyrifos is strongly bound to organic matter, which would include porous wood fiber.

One rather unique approach to the control of indoor insect pests is the use of insecticidal paint. These paints may contain 0.75-1.0% active ingredient. Cockroach control may last for 9-12 months. The chlorpyrifos based paints work by diffusion to the surface where the insect makes physical contact and picks up a lethal dose on the legs. The obvious potential hazard would be similar to a broadcast application that being a large surface area for volatilization of the chlorpyrifos. If an entire house was treated with such a paint, airborne pesticide might be above established guidelines, but unlikely to be hazardous to mammalian health. The value of such a product is that it might be very beneficial in a kitchen or other food use/storage area. Ware and Cahill (21) conducted a study to compare airborne chlorpyrifos following the use of a chlorpyrifos-based paint and a typical 0.5% crack and crevice application for cockroach control. The paint contained 2% chlorpyrifos. The investigators found that airborne chlorpyrifos concentrations evolving from the paint application were 7.41 $\mu g/m^3$ one hour post-application, and 8.47 and 9.53 $\mu g/m^3$ [2 samples] 14 hours post-application. Airborne chlorpyrifos concentrations evolving from a 0.5% emulsion used in the crack and crevice application were 15.2 $\mu g/m^3$, post-application, and 18.0 and 16.6 $\mu g/m^3$ 15 hours post-application. In the first case the active insecticide bled slowly through the paint film precluding the development of high airborne concentration. On the other hand, the crack and crevice application produces aerosol particles that become airborne and diffuse throughout the room. In another study *(22)*, an apartment was treated with 0.85% chlorpyrifos-based paint. Only the kitchen and a small bathroom were treated. Airborne chlorpyrifos samples taken during a seven hour period following the completion of the painting ranged below 8 $\mu g/m^3$. The peak concentration [9 $\mu g/m^3$] was found about 6-8 hours post-application. Fifteen hours post-application the concentration was still about 9 $\mu g/m^3$ showing very little change. However, a poorly ventilated bathroom that was 7 $\mu g/m^3$ at 6 1/2 hours post-completion, was 16-17 $\mu g/m^3$ at 15 hours post-completion. One month later the average of two samples in the kitchen was 10 $\mu g/m^3$ (14 and 6 $\mu g/m^3$) and in the bathroom 9 $\mu g/m^3$ (10 and 8 $\mu g/m^3$). Four months later, 4 $\mu g/m^3$ of chlorpyrifos was measured in the kitchen and 2 $\mu g/m^3$ was measured in the bathroom. Volatilization was the main route of dissipation from the living environment.

CHLORPYRIFOS FORMULATION COMPONENTS: EXPOSURE

Solvents. Also of concern is the presence of airborne components in the home other than the active ingredient.   Chlorpyrifos formulations, especially emulsifiable concentrates, contain aromatic C8 and C9 hydrocarbons having an approximate molecular weight of 120. These compounds have vapor pressures of 2-10 mm of Hg at room temperature and therefore are 10,000 times more volatile than the active insecticide. The petroleum-based solvents consist of xylene (dimethylbenzene), mesitylene (trimethylbenzene), methyl ethyl benzene, cumene (isopropylbenzene) and a host of related compounds generally present at much lower concentrations. Volatilization of this solvent mixture can produce airborne concentrations of these aromatics above the odor threshold (1-5 ppm in air). The toxicity profile of the methylated benzenes and ethylated benzenes differs from that of benzene. These alkylated compounds have not been associated with aplastic anemia and other hematopoetic effects. They are common solvents producing typical narcotic effects at higher levels of exposure (> 200 ppm in air). The manufactures airborne guideline for control of these materials for a healthy working population is 50 ppm. However, xylene itself has a Threshold Limit Value [TLV] of 100 ppm (v/v). Odor following an indoor application is partially due to the rapid volatilization of these aromatic components. These airborne components rapidly dissipate. In a dwelling treated with 200 gallons of termiticide at the 1% chlorpyrifos rate, approximately 16.7 pounds of active is applied to the soil under the dwelling and about 10.2 pounds of solvent. Much of this solvent vaporizes in the first 24 hours and due to multiple air changes will leave the dwelling.

Studies conducted by The Dow Chemical Company to determine residual airborne solvent following termiticide applications indicated air concentrations of less than 5 ppm for the aromatic mixture. In addition to this, the air concentrations of the mixed aromatics are below the analytical limit of detection within 2 days. Although the solvent presents no known risk to the inhabitants of a dwelling, the air concentrations of the mixed aromatic solvent will sometimes exceed the odor threshold. The odor threshold for xylene has been reported to be about 5 ppm (v/v). Most dwelling inhabitants do not find the solvent odors particularly offensive, however a small portion of the population do find these odors irritating.

Volatile By-Products. In addition to solvent odors there are a number of by-products resulting from the synthesis of the chlorpyrifos. Although most by-products are removed in purification steps following isolation of the chlorpyrifos, some small quantities are present during application in the dwelling. Phosphorothioates will isomerize in the presence of traces of catalytic agents and heat *(23)*. The first step is a conversion of the parent compound to the S-ethyl derivative which results from the migration of the sulfur originally double-bonded to the phosphorous atom to a single ethoxy group, replacing the oxygen. The oxygen atom simply exchanges with the sulfur. The S-ethyl derivative formation is faster for some phosphorothiates than others, but in general is a minor conversion; that is only a small amount of the material is converted. An exception to this is parathion which will isomerize 90% in 24 hours when held at 150°C. Once the S-ethyl derivative forms it is converted to a series of alkyl polysulfides. This conversion is currently believed to be a free radical mechanism forming C_2H_5S. This free radical leads to disulfides, trisulfides, and tetrasulfides as well as ethyl mercaptan. Because of the low odor thresholds of these moderately volatile compounds, their presence following an application is obvious. These odor causing by-products are believed to be the source of odor associated with several other phosphorothioates. Alkyl polysulfides will have odor thresholds in the low ppb and even high ppt levels *(24)*. The odor is distasteful to most people, resembling garlic, rotten cabbage or pepper, and is often confused with the odor of the active ingredient. Pure chlorpyrifos has an odor threshold much higher than the polysulfides. The odor may have a detrimental effect on the senses; nausea and headache are common sensory responses to the odor-causing polysulfides. Despite these apparent "toxic signs", this is not true toxicity. It can be likened to ones response to smelling a skunk, smelling emesis or the contents of an infants dirty diaper.

SUMMARY

Chlorpyrifos is a widely used organophosphate insecticide. It finds utility in control of a wide variety of household pests and has an important use in the agricultural arena. Chlorpyrifos and Dursban Insecticide formulations have low to moderate acute toxicity in both laboratory animals *(25)* and human volunteers. Studies with laboratory animals indicate that chlorpyrifos is not a teratogen, not a mutagen, not a neurotoxin [OPIDN], does not cause reproductive effects and does not cause cancer in long term studies. Repeated studies in laboratory animals do not indicate any target organ effects. Chlorpyrifos does not accumulate in body depots and has a short physiological half-life of 24 hours. The material is poorly absorbed through human skin, precluding significant exposures by that route. The low vapor pressure also precludes significant exposure to vapor in the dwelling environment.

Chlorpyrifos is the most widely used termiticide in the United States today. Several studies have been conducted that indicate residual airborne concentrations of chlorpyrifos vapor are below the NAS guideline of 10 μg/m^3. These treatments can involve the use of 250 gallons of a 1% active, which means the use of nearly 21 pounds of chlorpyrifos. The chlorpyrifos has a strong attraction for organic matter resulting in low residual vapor in the living area of the treated dwelling. Some construction types will allow more chlorpyrifos to diffuse from the treatment zone than others. Crawlspace dwellings and plenum dwellings will yield slightly higher airborne chlorpyrifos concentrations than basements and slab type construction. Despite this fact residual air concentrations remain below the NAS guideline in all types of building construction.

Crack and crevice applications lead to low residual air concentrations due to the small amount of active ingredient applied. Often only a half gallon to one gallon will be used in a non-broadcast manner. Dissipation of these residual levels is quite rapid. Broadcast applications and the use of foggers appear to be of greatest concern to state and federal agencies. The concern is focused on crawling infants. Studies that follow labeled directions indicate estimated doses to crawling infants give a wide margin of safety when compared to NOEL's resulting from human studies. Studies involving human volunteers indicate that exposure-related cholinesterase depression is non-existent following childlike activities on a treated surface. The key to such applications is allowing enough time for the treated surface to dry completely. Although some insecticide may be dislodged onto skin, the amount is so small that the risk of injury is negligible. This is also true for pets such as dogs and cats. The key to total release fogger use is following the instructions on the label. Foggers initially produce relatively high air concentrations of chlorpyrifos because of aerosol particles, however air concentrations fall rapidly after release of the material. A rather unique method of controlling cockroaches is the use of insecticidal paint. Although a large surface area is generating chlorpyrifos vapor, airborne concentrations will fall below the NAS guideline at about one month post-painting.

Solvent concentrations in the air following applications have been historically low. Termiticide applications would be expected to produce the highest residual airborne solvent concentrations. Even with the relative abundance of liquid solvent, airborne solvent vapors remain at low levels and dissipate to below the analytical limit of detection within three days. Components of the xylene range aromatic solvent have not been shown to cause hematopoietic effects in mammals, such as those produced by benzene. A basic characteristic of phosphorothioates is the production of odorous by-products, sometimes confused with smelling the active ingredient. Although these sulfur compounds are unpleasant, low levels [1 ppb] are of no toxicological significance to the homeowner. With proper ventilation, these alkyl polysulfides dissipate within a few days.

Overall use of chlorpyrifos formulations produces an insect-free environment in residential homes. Some insects such as termites are capable of literally destroying a home. There is ample evidence from 30 years of use that chlorpyrifos-based formulations are effective and offer little or no risk to those who encounter them.

LITERATURE CITED

1. Coulston F. Instit. Exper. Toxicol., Albany Medical College [as sited by WHO, 1973].
2. Nolan R. J. *Toxicol. Appl. Pharmacol.* **1984**, *73*, 8-15.
3. Lewis R. *Pest Contr. Technol.* **1990**, May, 52.
4. Wright C. G., *Bull. Environ. Contam. Toxicol.*, **1991**, *46*, 686-689.
5. National Academy of Sciences. An assessment of the health risks of seven pesticides used for termite control. National Academy Press, Washington D.C., August 1992, 37-41.
6. Wright C. G. *Bull. Environ. Contam. Toxocol.* **1988**, *40*, 561-68.
7. Vaccaro J. R. et al, unpublished report of The Dow Chemical Co.; 1987, GHP-1310.
8. Wright C. G. and Leidy R. B. *Bull. Environ. Contam. Toxicol.*, **1978**, *19*, 340-344.
9. Wright C. G. *Bull. Environ. Contam. Toxicol.*, **1980**, *24*, 582-589.
10. Gold R. E. *J. Econ. Entomol.*, **1982**, *77(2)*.
11. Currie, K.L. *Am. Ind. Hyg. Assoc. J.*, **1990**, *51*, 23-27.
12. Nafzigger D. Down to Earth #41, Midland, Mich., The Dow Chemical Company, April 1985.
13. Vaccaro J. R. unpublished work, December 1991.
14. Fenske R. A. *Am. J. Public Health*, **1990**, *80*, 689-693.
15. Vaccaro J. R. Unpublished report, The Dow Chemical Company, 1990.
16. Bohl R. W. Unpublished report, The Dow Chemical Company, 1983.
17. Vaccaro J. R. and Nauer L. Unpublished report, The Dow Chemical Company.
18. Ross J. *Chemosphere*, **1990**, *20*, 349-360.
19. Maddy K. T. Unpublished report of The California Department of Food and Agriculture, HS-1259, 1984.
20. Vaccaro J. R. Wilmington, N.C., December and July 1983.
21. Ware G. W. and Cahill W. P. *Bull. Environ. Contam. Toxicol.* **1978**, *20*, 414-417.
22. Vaccaro J. R. Unpublished report, The Dow Chemical Company, 1981.
23. Eto M. Organophosphorous pesticides: organic and biological chemistry; CRC press, 1974, pp88-90.
24. Amoor J. E. *J. Appl. Toxicol.* **1983**, *3(6)*.
25. McCollister S. B. and Gehring P. J. *Food Cosmetic Toxicol.* **1974**, *12*, 45-61.

RECEIVED October 23, 1992

Chapter 26

Risk Analysis for Phenylmercuric Acetate in Indoor Latex House Paint

J. M. Blondell and S. M. Knott

Health Effects Division (H7509C), Office of Pesticide Programs, U.S. Environmental Protection Agency, 401 M Street, SW, Washington, DC 20460

Respiratory exposure to elemental mercury vapor, resulting from the use of interior latex paint preserved with mercurial biocides, can pose a potential health hazard to humans, especially children. The review of mercury house paint was initiated after a Michigan child developed acrodynia, a rare form of mercury poisoning. Use of paint containing 200 ppm mercury has been shown to lead to air levels of mercury as high as 200 $\mu g/m^3$ during application of the paint. Evidence for the risk of acrodynia was assessed from: case reports where liquid mercury had been spilled; studies involving mercury used in infant medicines and teething powder; and an incident where a mercury fungicide was used on diapers. Evidence from these studies suggested that infants displaying urinary levels above 50 μg mercury/g creatinine were at risk for acrodynia.

Mercury-containing biocides have previously been added to approximately 25 to 30% of interior latex paints *(1)*. The mercury biocide was added at low concentrations (200 ppm or less) to extend the shelf life of stored paints. It could also be added at higher concentrations to formulate a latex paint that would provide a mildew resistant coating. Recent evidence of mercury vaporization following application of indoor latex house paint raised questions about potential health effects. The recent occurrence of a childhood case of mercury-related disease brought to the attention of the U.S. Environmental Protection Agency the need to review potential exposure from previously unsuspected sources and estimate the dose and potential health effects. EPA's review resulted in voluntary cancellations of mercury containing biocides use in latex paints.

BRIEF HISTORY OF ACRODYNIA

Mercury-containing medicines and teething powders were often prescribed for young children during the first half of this century. During the same time period, hundreds of children developed a disease called acrodynia (meaning painful extremities) or pink disease (for the characteristic pink coloration of the hands and feet). Case series, with fatality rates of 3 to 17 percent, were reported in children in England, Australia, France, Switzerland, and the United States (2-7). Identification of causation was hampered by a delay of weeks or months from onset of exposure to onset of disease. One of the early clues that implicated mercury was the peak incidence in children under 2 years of age in England and Australia, where mercury was used most commonly in teething powder, and peak incidence in children more than 2 years old in France and Switzerland, where the most common source was from worm treatments often prescribed for children aged 3 to 10 (6).

The first signs of disease are usually changes in personality, including increased irritability, marked swings in mood, and restlessness (8). The skin of the hands and feet become red or pink starting at the tips of the fingers and toes. The tip of the nose, ears and cheeks may display a similar discoloration. As the disease progresses, the hands and feet become swollen, itchy, and painful. The skin on the palms and soles starts to flake and shed as if sunburned. These symptoms are usually accompanied by heavy sweating, loss of appetite, hypertension, pain in joints, and muscle weakness. As weakness progresses, the muscles loss their tone and the child may be unable to stand or walk. Photophobia is common, the child is less active, cries excessively, and is unable to sleep. In cases that go untreated, there may be loss of nails on fingers and toes and loss of teeth from severe gingivitis. Once the causative connection was made, starting in the late 1940s, use of mercury-containing medicines and teething powders was banned.

While appropriate treatment is now available for acrodynia, many of today's physicians would be unfamiliar with the symptomatology and might easily misdiagnose the disease. Modern pediatric texts often omit any discussion of acrodynia.

EXPOSURE TO MERCURY FROM THE USE OF LATEX PAINTS

The use of mercury-containing fungicides in latex house paints was not suspected of being a significant source of mercury exposure until Shalom Z. Hirschman, M.D., reported a case of acrodynia that coincided with the use of a paint containing phenylmercuric propionate (PMP) (9). Four months before the onset of symptoms, the five-year-old boy had helped his mother with the painting of two rooms in their home. The diagnosis of acrodynia was confirmed by the symptom complex and a measured urinary mercury concentration of 90 µg/l. The upper limit of the normal range of urinary mercury excretion is 25 µg/l (10). The concentration of mercury in the paint used was 0.02% or 0.036% phenylmercuric propionate (9). Ingestion of the paint and inhalation of its vapors were both considered as possible routes of exposure in this case.

To estimate exposure, Hirschman et al. (1963) placed a panel, painted with the paint containing mercury, in a sealed jar with an air flow of 1 liter per minute through the jar (9). The mercury concentration of the air exiting the jar at the end of 30 minutes was 170 µg/m^3 or a calculated average emission rate of 0.65 µg/min/ft^2. After 6 hours, the level fell to 100 µg/m^3 yielding an average emission rate of 0.38 µg/min/ft^2. The authors concluded that, since it was possible to exceed 100 µg/m^3 while using mercury-containing paints, inhalation exposure could have played a major role in the observed case of acrodynia.

These conclusions have been the subject of considerable criticism. The strongest argument against the emphasis on the inhalation exposure is the fact that the acrodynia patient's parents and siblings had no detectable urinary mercury excretions (9).

Additional studies of the emission of mercury from preserved latex paints evolved from the Hirschman et al. research and the resulting criticism. In the first of a series of experiments, Taylor formulated his own latex paints at low (0.02% Hg) and high (0.2% Hg) concentrations of phenylmercuric dodecenyl succinate (PMDS) that had been irradiated with neutrons to radiolabel the mercury *(11)*. These paints then were applied to aluminum panels resulting in 200 µg of mercury on panels with the low concentration paint and 1000 µg on the panels with the high. The total loss of mercury from each panel was measured at various time intervals using a Geiger counter. The data were corrected for background, decay of the ^{203}Hg, and variations in the reference standard. Panels were tested under low and high humidity conditions. Using the emission rate data, Taylor estimated the air level that could be achieved on day 100 after painting under static conditions in a 50.7m^3 room where the walls and ceiling (720 ft^2) had been painted. Air concentration levels for the low paint were 16 and 28 µg/m^3 in dry and wet air, respectively. The high mercury concentration paint resulted in levels of 140 and 250 µg/m^3 in dry and wet air, respectively.

Taylor concluded that the actual air concentrations that may be achieved during use of paints containing a mercury concentration of 0.02% would not pose a hazard to human health *(11)*. He reached this conclusion because he believed that the scenario he used (i.e., static conditions in a small room) was unrealistic. Also, he believed that the neutron labeling may have resulted in decomposition of the PMDS leading to an unusually high proportion of the more volatile elemental mercury in the experimental paint. However, it may not be appropriate to make such a conclusion using air concentrations achieved on day 100 when other investigations demonstrated that maximum concentrations occur during and right after paint application.

The information contained in the above described studies is not easily extrapolated to "real world" exposure situations. With this in mind, Jacobs and Goldwater (1965), collected mercury air concentration and human mercury excretion data under a "real world" exposure scenario *(12)*. In their study, latex paints containing 0.02% mercury (0.036% phenylmercuric acetate (PMA)) were applied by brush and roller to the walls and ceiling of a bedroom. A second room (control room) in the same house was painted concurrently with a mercury free latex paint. A Beckman ultraviolet mercury vapor meter and an impinger method were used to assess air concentrations of mercury periodically. During painting, the house was ventilated in the usual manner (i.e., doors and windows open). Immediately after the completion of painting, mercury air concentrations as high as 210 µg/m^3 were recorded. This corresponds to an average emission rate (assuming 1 air exchange per hour occurred in the bedroom) of 0.70 µg/min/ft^2, a value that compares well with the experimental value of 0.65 µg/min/ft^2 obtained by Hirschman et al. However, 6 hours after the completion of painting, the mercury air concentration had declined to 52 µg/m^3. Levels of mercury were found in the control room indicating either method interferences or dissipation of mercury from other rooms in the house. One painter and one occupant of the house experienced increases in urinary mercury excretion to just above the upper limit of normal(25 µg/l).

Due to the flaws in his 1965 study, Taylor conducted additional research in which the radiolabelled mercuric fungicide used (PMA) was manufactured using radioactive mercury (^{203}Hg) *(13)*. This deviation from the previous study avoided the decomposition observed during neutron labeling of the mercury containing biocide. The paints containing the PMA then were applied to glass panels, creating paint film thicknesses of 0.001 or 0.002 inches.

The painted panels then were subjected to a variety of environmental conditions including: zero humidity, darkness, indoor ambient conditions, sunlight, temperature of 50°C, and outdoor conditions.

Among the panels exposed to indoor conditions, those painted with a thin film (0.001 in.) of the low mercury paint (0.02% Hg) experienced an average loss of 61.4% after 236 days or an average emission rate of 0.0029 µg/min./ft.^{2} *(13)*. This same group exhibited a mercury loss of approximately 42% after 100 days or an average emission rate over the 100 day period of 0.0046 µg/min./ft.^{2}, a level approximately 3 times that determined in the earlier study using a paint with the same concentration of mercury but containing PMDS instead of PMA. Later study using both PMA and PMDS, under the same conditions, found only a 21% increase of emission from the PMA containing paint compared to the PMDS paint *(14)*.

Foote (1972) reported the results of a mercury air concentration survey conducted in homes and offices in the Dallas Texas area *(15)*. Mercury measurements were conducted by passing air through a device that collects elemental mercury vapor on a fine mesh gold screen. The accumulated mercury then was transferred to a second gold screen before proceeding into the beam of a spectrometer for detection. It is believed that the paints used in the homes contained diphenylmercuric dodecenyl succinate. Levels of 0.07 µg/m^3 mercury were detected in one home nearly 4 years after painting had occurred. Another home exhibited levels of around 0.15 µg/m^3 approximately 5 months after painting. In each case, these levels were above that found in the control home (0.01 µg/m^3).

Additional "real world" monitoring data were collected by Sibbett et al. *(16)*. In this study, mercury air concentrations were analyzed by passing air through a furnace containing a bed of hot (1200°F) cupric oxide to reduce any organic bound mercury to elemental vapor. The mercury vapor formed then was collected on a silver wire grid before being passed to an ultraviolet detector. A 57.8 m^3 room was painted with paint containing 0.0047% mercury (specific compound not identified). One week after painting, mercury air concentrations in the room without ventilation were about 1.5 µg/m^3. On day 10, an emission of 100 µg/day was calculated. The authors concluded that "sufficient mercury remains (in the painted surface) to sustain this rate for about 7.5 years" *(16)*.

The discussion of mercury exposure has, thus far, focused on emissions from painted surfaces and their contributions to mercury air concentrations. The exposure scenario would not be complete without considering, where possible, the fate of the airborne mercury vapor. Spedding and Hamilton (1982) reported their findings in a study designed to measure the capacity of certain household materials to adsorb elemental mercury vapor *(17)*. The study was conducted by placing various household materials in a chamber with approximately 300 µg/m^3 of mercury. After 20 days of exposure, the household materials were analyzed. Of the materials tested, water-based paint films and PVC flooring materials tended to adsorb elemental mercury vapor at a higher rate. These materials may cover a large surface area in a normal home, adsorbing a significant quantity of mercury that may be released into the air later. However, Spedding and Hamilton concluded that, overall, mercury vapor was relatively unreactive toward surfaces.

In the studies reviewed above, there is some disagreement about the form in which the airborne mercury is present. Hirschman et al. (1963) concluded that the mercury containing fungicide considered in his research (PMP) "decomposes to inorganic mercury, which is volatile" *(9)*. Taylor and Tickle (1969) discussed observations of mercury loss from test panels on the basis of the volatility of the parent organo-mercury compound used *(13)*.

There is considerable evidence that the airborne mercury is present as elemental vapor and not as an organic derivative *(18)*. In the paper industry in Sweden (where phenylmercuric compounds are used in the process as a fungicide), Lundgren and Swensson determined that the mercury in the atmosphere of the factory using phenyl-Hg or alkyl-Hg was metallic vapor resulting from decomposition of the organic compound *(19)*. In the exposure studies reviewed above, the mercury vapor detectors used by Hirschman et al., Jacobs and Goldwater, and Foote were designed to measure only elemental mercury vapor.

If it is accepted that the airborne mercury is elemental vapor resulting from decomposition of the parent compound in the paint, the next question is: what leads to the decomposition of the parent compound? Zepp et al. reported on the photo-decomposition of phenylmercuric compounds by sunlight *(20)*. They proposed that phenylmercuric salts, such as PMA, may dissociate, in the manner described in Figure 1, when dissolved in water. This dissociation could be expected to occur when these compounds are added to latex paints (many of which contain approximately 50% water). These studies indicated that phenylmercuric ion and phenylmercuric hydroxide photoreact to the same extent as the parent compound yielding elemental mercury.

Michigan Case Report. In 1989, a four-year-old boy in Michigan was diagnosed as having acrodynia *(21)*. The boy and the other four family members all had elevated mercury urine levels. The only significant source of mercury exposure identified by the Michigan Department of Public Health was from paint applied to the home's interior just 10 days before the onset of the child's illness *(22)*. Measurements conducted three months later of the air inside the home found a level of 1.0 µg/m³. Analysis of the paint that was used found it contained 930 ppm mercury in the form of phenylmercuric acetate (PMA).

The four-year-old developed most of the typical poisoning symptoms including marked personality change, excessive sweating, itching, hypertension, gingivitis, headaches, insomnia, weakness in the shoulders and hips, inability to walk, and red, swollen palms and soles and tip of nose. The child had stayed with grandparents during the day while the house was being painted. He and his family slept in the house at night with all the windows kept closed and the air conditioning on. The child was hospitalized for four months and received repeated treatment to increase mercury excretion from the body, after which nearly all the symptoms abated and the child could walk again.

CDC Investigation. The Centers for Disease Control (CDC) set up an investigation to determine whether persons in other homes using the same type of paint had exposure to mercury *(22)*. Nineteen exposed families were selected with 10 unexposed families. Data collected from each family included a questionnaire, first morning urine samples, indoor air mercury levels, and remaining paint samples. A total of 29 cans of paint were collected from the 19 exposed homes and found to contain a median level of 754 ppm mercury. Air samples taken from all the exposed homes had a median of 1.5 µg/m³ of mercury, with a range of undetectable to 10 µg/m³. No mercury was detected in the air of nine of 10 unexposed homes that were tested. Statistical analysis of the data from exposed homes

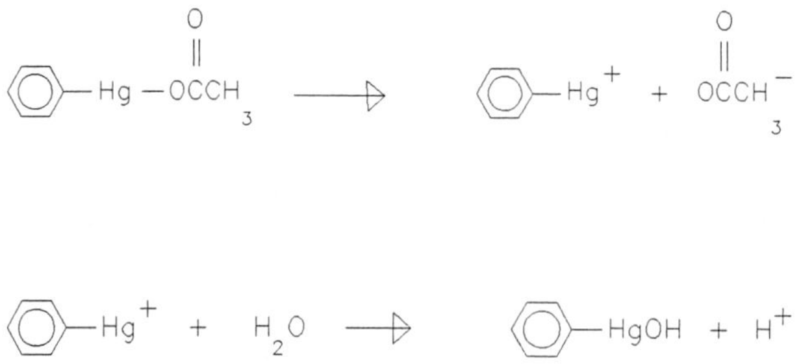

Figure 1. Dissociation of Phenylmercuric Acetate (Adapted from ref. 20.)

showed that air levels were significantly higher in homes that had more rooms painted or that were more recently painted. These two factors accounted for 51 percent of the variation among exposed homes.

In the exposed homes, 65 of the 74 persons provided first morning urine samples. In the unexposed homes, all 28 persons provided urine samples. The median urine level in exposed persons was 13.9 µg/l or 8.4 µg mercury per gram creatinine (gram creatinine was used to adjust for the variability in concentration from spot urine samples) and 3.4 µg/g or 1.8 µg mercury per gram creatinine (µg Hg/g Cr) in the unexposed. Stratification by age revealed that exposed children age 10 or under had the highest levels of mercury (a median of 17.4 µg/l in the 0-5 age group and a median of 17.3 µg/l in the 6-10 age group). Urine levels did not correlate with air levels among the exposed individuals.

MERCURY DOSE ASSOCIATED WITH ACRODYNIA

Levels Reported From Teething Powders and Medicines. Level of exposure in acrodynia cases before the 1950s are rarely available, except in the form of case reports. In a series of 28 case reports, only three cases reported the number of times mercury had been given to the child *(6)*. One child received teething powder on 14 occasions before the onset of acrodynia and another child received teething powders 24 times before the onset of symptoms. A third case developed the disease after exposure to 18 mercurial worm pills. The level of mercury in the teething powders or in the pills was not reported. Other reports put the level in teething powder at 42 mg each, in which case the child receiving 14 teething powders would have been exposed to 588 mg *(23)*. However, the level absorbed dermally in such cases is not known, nor is the amount ingested and absorbed by the gut.

Earlier data on urine values, however, have shown that acrodynia can develop in sensitive children with urinary concentrations as low as 50 µg/l *(24)*. One of the children in the CDC study had urine levels above 50 µg/l. Five of the 15 exposed children had unadjusted levels that were above 20 µg/l, the upper limit of normal. Unfortunately, individual urine levels are poor indicators of total body burden.

Acrodynia and Fungicidal Use of PMA on Diapers. Acrodynia from routine use of mercury in diaper rinses has been reported as far back as 1950 *(6)*. Cases continued to be reported from this use in the United States as recently as 1976 *(25)*. But the single largest epidemic of such exposure occurred in Buenos Aires, Argentina in 1980. The local diaper service there, serving 7,000 to 10,000 babies, used PMA in the diaper rinse *(26)*. Physicians that studied the exposure resulting from this episode reported three documented cases of acrodynia. However, examination of a large case series, 1,507 children selected from 4,230 requests for evaluation, determined that nearly half of them presented with symptoms attributable to their dermal exposure to mercury *(27)*. The most common symptoms reported in more than 20 percent of these children were excessive sweating, irritability, and gastrointestinal disturbances including diarrhea and constipation. Pink hands and feet were noted in 248 children or 16 percent of the case series and pink hands and feet with itching were noted in 44 cases (3%). Other symptoms suggestive of acrodynia included rash (12%), loss of appetite (10%), loss of muscle tone (6%), and photophobia (4%).

Acrodynia from Mercury Spilled in the Home. More useful data can be obtained from reports of acrodynia resulting when elemental mercury spilled in the home. In these cases the mercury vaporizes resulting in exposure by inhalation that is directly comparable to the current case in Michigan, because most of the mercury in air was probably in the form of elemental mercury. A listing of case reports of acrodynia from mercury in air is reported below with duration of exposure, levels of mercury in urine prior to treatment and level of mercury measured in air after the case was discovered (Table I). In some cases air levels may reflect lower levels of exposure than was initially present, immediately after the mercury was spilled.

Table I. Levels of Mercury in Air and Urine Associated with Cases of Acrodynia

Age of Case	Duration of Exposure	Urine Level	Air Level	Reference
8 yr.	not reported	250 µg/l	50 µg/m³	(28)
18 mo	1 month	70 µg/l	10-12 µg/m³ 300 µg/m³ at floor level	(29)[1]
14 mo	2 months	48 µg/24 hr. normal is < 20 µg/24 hr.	reported as unacceptably high	(30)
30 mo.	<1 month	214 µg/l	not reported	(31)
14 yr.	few days	522 µg/l	120 µg/m³	(32)[2]
41 yr.	<2 months	378 µg/l	120 µg/m³	
6 yr.	2 weeks	188 µg/l	not reported	(33)
3 yr.	2 weeks	88 µg/l	not reported	
23 mo.	4 months[3]	73 µg/l	5-54 µg/m³	(34)

[1]In this report, air levels at a height of 1.5 meters were 10-12 µg/m³ and levels near floor level where the mercury had been spilled were 300 µg/m³ *(29)*.

[2]In this report, two members of the household had acrodynia. The case in the father (41 year old) was relatively mild and time of onset of symptoms was not reported but was less than two months after mercury was spilled *(32)*.

[3]The case reported by Tunnessen et al. (1987) attributed the exposure to a box of fluorescent light bulbs that broke. The evidence presented in the article was inconsistent about the level of mercury likely to occur from these broken bulbs *(34)*.

RISK ASSESSMENT

Key populations at risk include painters, residents in homes painted in a given year, and, specifically, children living in those homes. An estimated 500,000 individuals are employed in housepainting in this country *(1)*. Assuming that the interior of homes are painted once every five years, that 78% of the interior paint used is latex rather than oil-based paint, and that one third of the interior latex paint contains mercury, about 13 million people each year may be exposed to mercury through painting *(1)*.

Painters are exposed to the highest levels of mercury. Even paint formulated at 200 ppm was shown to lead to exposures as high as 200 $\mu g/m^3$, 4 times the threshold limit value set by OSHA (Occupational and Safety Health Administration) and twice the acute ceiling level *(1)*.

Data from the CDC and other studies show that mercury levels in the home would be expected to be about 10 $\mu g/m^3$ 24 hours after painting and 6 $\mu g/m^3$ 1 month later. Because mercury has a half-life of 60 days, such exposures would likely lead to increased body burden for months following exposure *(35)*. Elevated urine levels of mercury in individuals living in homes in Michigan which had been painted months before support this hypothesis. In addition, the fetus and children may be at greater risk, both because of increased exposure and, possibly, increased sensitivity. Margins of exposure for acute and subchronic toxicity of mercury appear to be very small or nonexistent, based on the CDC Michigan data and other studies in the literature. It is difficult to estimate the number of individuals showing effects when margins of exposure are eliminated, but it is likely that some individuals will show some signs.

An estimated 3 million children were exposed to mercury-containing paint each year *(1)*. The percentage of these children who would have exposure sufficient to reach a urinary level of 50 $\mu g/l$ is not known. However, the CDC Michigan data found 10% of the children so affected with paint formulated at 3 times the normal level of mercury. For the purposes of estimating risk, two other percentages are assumed at 10 lower than this level (1% and 0.1%) to get a more representative range of potential exposures. Earlier literature from the 1940s suggests that only 1 in 500 children experiencing such exposure develop frank acrodynia *(7)*. If so, then the number of anticipated cases of acrodynia annually would be between 6 and 600. That only two such cases have been reported may be partly due to lack of recognition of cases by the treating physician who is unlikely to be familiar with the disease.

According to the World Health Organization (1976) review, continuous long-term exposure (24 hours/day, 7 days/week) to mercury vapor levels of 15 $\mu g/m^3$ would result in adverse effects in the most sensitive adults *(35)*. This level is supported by the NIOSH criteria document (1973) which relied principally on a high-quality study of workers exposed to mercury vapor *(36, 37)*. Other epidemiologic studies also supported this finding *(35, 36)*. The adverse effects cited by WHO and NIOSH were nonspecific symptoms such as weight loss, loss of appetite, and shyness. Overt poisoning signs (principally tremor with personality changes) would be expected at air levels above 30 $\mu g/m^3$. WHO notes that "this calculation does not take into account the sensitive groups in the general population" (e.g., infants, pregnant women). Dividing 15 $\mu g/m^3$ by an uncertainty factor of 10 to protect sensitive groups in the general population would result in a level of 1.5 $\mu g/m^3$ which was the median level observed in the exposed homes in Michigan one to five months after paint was applied. The dose is not directly comparable, however, because the initial exposure immediately after painting that was undoubtedly much higher is not known. How the cumulative dose of mercury, starting at relatively high levels and then dropping off, would affect the onset and incidence of poisoning symptoms is not known.

In July 1990, the U.S. Environmental Protection Agency took action in cooperation with paint manufacturers which resulted in voluntary cancellation of mercury biocides used in interior paints and labeling of exterior paints containing mercury to prohibit use indoors (1). In May 1991, the Agency announced voluntary cancellations of the remaining exterior paint uses, after the manufacturers decided not to submit additional studies required by EPA to better assess the risks of continued use in exterior paints (38).

LITERATURE CITED

1. U.S. Environmental Protection Agency Environmental Fact Sheet: Mercury Biocides in Paint, Voluntary Cancellation, Voluntary Deletion, and Amended Registration. Washington, DC, July 1990.
2. Chamberlain, J. L.; Quillian, W. W. *Clinical Pediatrics* **1963**, *2*, 439-443.
3. Clements, F. W. Med. *J. Australia* **1960**, *1*, 922-925.
4. Dathan, J. G.; Harvey, C. C. *British Medical Journal* **1965**, *1*, 1181-1182.
5. Holzel, A.; James, T. *Lancet* **1952**, *1*, 441-443.
6. Warkany, J.; Hubbard, D. M. *Journal of Pediatrics* **1953**, *42*, 365-386.
7. Warkany, J. *American Journal of Diseases in Children* **1966**, *112*, 147-156.
8. Cheek, D. B. In *Brennerman's Practice of Pediatrics*, vol. 1, Kelley, V. C., Ed.; , 1980), pp. 1-12. (Chapter 17)
9. Hirschman, S. Z.; Feingold, M.; Boylen, G. *NEJM* **1963**, *269*, 889-893.
10. Klaassen, C. C. In *The Pharmacological Basis for Therapeutics*, Goodman, L. S.; Gilman, A. G., Eds.; Macmillan Publishing Company: New York, **1985**).
11. Taylor, C. G. *J. Appl. Chem.* **1965**, *15*, 232-236.
12. Jacobs, M. B.; Goldwater, L. J. *Archives of Environmental Health* **1965**, *11*, 582-587.
13. Taylor, C. G.; Tickle, W. *J. Appl. Chem.* **1969**, *19*, 1-7.
14. Taylor, C. G.; Tickle, W. *J. Appl. Chem.* **1969**, *19*, 8-11.
15. Foote, R. S. *Science* **1972**, *177*, 513-514.
16. Sibbett, D. J.; Moyer, R.; Milly, G. Proceedings of the Division of Water, Air, and Waste Chemistry of the American Chemical Society, 20-27.
17. Spedding, D. J.; Hamilton, R. B. *Environmental Research* **1982**, *29*, 30-41.
18. Beusterien, K. M.; Etzel, R. A.; Agocs, M. M.; et al. *Arch. Environ. Contam. Toxicol.* **1991**, *21*, 62-64.
19. Lundgren, K. D.; Swenson, A. *Ind. Hyg. Assoc. J.* **1960**, 308-311.
20. Zepp, R. G.; Wolfe, N. L.; Gordon, J. A. *Chemosphere*, **1973**, *3*, 93-99.
21. Aronow, R.; Cubbage, C.; Wiener, R.; Johnson, B.; Hesse, J.; Bedford, J. *MMWR* **1990**, *39*, 125-126.
22. Agocs, M. M.; Etzel, R. A.; Parrish, G.; Paschal, D. C.; Campagna, P. R.; Cohen, D. S.; Kilborne, E. M.; Hesse, J. L. *NEJM* **1990**, *323*, 1096-1101.
23. Wilson, V. K.; Thomson, M. L.; Holzel, A. *British Medical Journal* **1952**, *1*, 358-360.

24. Warkany, J.; Hubbard, D. M. *Lancet* **1948**, *1*, 829-830.
25. Aronow, R.; Fleischmann. *Clinical Pediatrics* **1976**, *15*, 936-945.
26. Gotelli, C. A.; Astolfi, E.; Cox, C.; Cernichiari, E.; Clarkson, T. W. *Science* **1985**, *227*, 638-640.
27. Gimenez, E.; Vallejo, N. E.; Izurieta, E. M.; Albiano, N.; Plager, M. R.; Iarlori, R.; Guerra, B.; Fuscaldo, A.; Foppiano, M.; De Biase, P.; Barlotti, M. T. M. *Sociedad Argentina de Toxicologia* **1981**, *12*, 7-17.
28. Alexander, J. F.; Rosario, R. *Canadian Medical Association Journal* **1971**, 929-930.
29. Curtis, H. A.; Ferguson, S. D.; Kell, R. L.; Samuel, A. H. *Archives of Disease in Children* **1987**, *62*, 293-295.
30. Dinehart, S. M.; Dillard, R.; Raimer, S. S.; Diven, S.; Cobos, R.; Pupo, R. *Archives of Dermatology* **1988**, *124*, 107-109.
31. Foulds, D. M.; Copeland, K. C.; Franks, R. C. *American Journal of Diseases in Children* **1987**, *141*, 124-125.
32. McNeil, N. I.; Issler, H. C.; Olver, R. E.; Wrong, O. M. *Lancet* **1984**, *1*, 269-271.
33. Spiers, A. L. *British Medical Journal* **1959**, *2*, 142-143.
34. Tunnessen, W. W.; McMahon, K. J.; Baser, M. *Pediatrics* **1987**, *79*, 786-789.
35. World Health Organization. *Environmental Health Criteria* **1976**, *1*, 1-131.
36. NIOSH (National Institute of Occupational Safety and Health), *Criteria for a Recommended Standard -- Occupational Exposure to Inorganic Mercury* (U.S. Dept. of Health, Education, and Welfare, Washington, DC, **1973**).
37. Smith, R. G.; Vorwald, A. J.; Patil, L. S.; Mooney, T. F. *American Industrial Hygiene Association Journal* **1970**, *31*, 687-700.
38. U.S. Environmental Protection Agency Environmental Fact Sheet: Mercury. Notices of Receipt of Requests for Voluntary Cancellations. May 28, 1991.

RECEIVED November 9, 1992

URBAN PESTICIDES AND NONTARGET ANIMALS

Chapter 27

Avian Response to Organophosphorus Pesticides Applied to Turf

L. W. Brewer, R. A. Hummell, and R. J. Kendall

Department of Environmental Toxicology, and Institute of Wildlife and Environmental Toxicology, Clemson University, P.O. Box 709, Pendleton, SC 29670

The past decade has seen an increased demand, and improved methods for, evaluating non-target wildlife effects of pesticides used in turf management. Field studies have demonstrated the significance of urban lawns and other urban turf habitats to birds. Research designs for assessing the non-target wildlife effects of pesticide applications on turf have become more sophisticated. Studies have shown the susceptibility of certain birds to organophosphorus (OP) insecticides used on turf and have documented exposure to insecticides in some birds. Improved research techniques such as non-lethal exposure monitoring, radio telemetry and computer modeling hold promise for a better understanding of complex ecotoxicological relationships.

The use of agrochemicals in turf management is an expanding business and the environmental issues associated with the maintenance of home lawns, golf courses and other areas involving large areas of turf continue to increase in scope and complexity. Urban environments provide valuable bird habitat (1), and the significance of urban habitat will increase as human population and urbanization expand, reducing non-urban habitats. The National Wildlife Federation, recognizing this situation, encourages a "backyard program for wildlife" and issues certificates of recognition for those individuals that encourage wildlife habitat in urban environments. Bird watching and feeding have become important urban outdoor recreational activities in the United States (1). This suggests society is placing increasing value on urban bird habitat and the well being of birds in the urban environment. Concern for the hazards of pesticide applications on turf is not unique in that agricultural systems are receiving similar if not more scrutiny regarding potential ecological consequences of the use of these products (2). The currently evolving discipline of wildlife toxicology offers an opportunity to better understand the fate and effects relative to non-target wildlife species.

Wildlife toxicology has been defined as the science of effects of environmental contaminants on the reproduction, health and well-being of wildlife species (3). This was expanded by Hoffman et al. who primarily emphasized the integrated nature of the science involving both field and laboratory research *(4)*. Assessing the fate and effects of pesticides in wildlife species involves extensive use of wildlife ecology and biology, analytical chemistry and biochemistry in the study of both laboratory-and field-exposed wildlife.

BIRD KILLS RESULTING FROM ORGANOPHOSPHORUS INSECTICIDE USE ON TURF

Detailed accounts of bird kills resulting from OP and carbamate insecticide use on turf are not abundant in the literature. Grue et al. *(5)* provided one of the first assessments of the hazards of OP insecticides to wildlife. Stone and Gradoni *(6,7)* reported numerous wildlife kills resulting from the use of OP pesticides on turf in New York. Some of these incidents involved fairly large numbers of waterfowl, over 700 geese in one incident on a golf courses. The most abundant information involves incidents of waterfowl die offs. Zinkl et al. *(8)* reported a die-off of Canada geese (*Branta canadensis*) following a turf application of the OP insecticide, diazinon. Similarly, Kendall and Brewer *(9)* reported American wigeon (*Anas americana*) mortality following diazinon use on golf course turf. The grazing behavior of Canada geese and American wigeon make them susceptible to poisoning from OP insecticides applied to turf *(9)*. We believe the American robin (*Turdus migratorius*) may also be highly susceptible to turf-applied OP insecticides, particularly on urban lawns (S.L.Tank et al. and R.A.Hummell et al., unpublished data, The Institute of Wildlife and Environmental Toxicology, Clemson University) Their susceptibility to exposure appears to be related to their heavy foraging on earthworms.

The effects of OP insecticides on wildlife on turfgrass environments have precipitated an increased intensity of review of these chemical products by the Office of Pesticide Programs of the United States Environmental Protection Agency (Kendall, R.J. and Akerman J.M., *Environ. Toxicol. Chem.*, in press). In the past, large-scale die-offs of birds associated with agrochemicals (particularly organophosphate insecticides) received the most attention *(3)*; however, sublethal effects such as reproductive impairment are receiving increased scrutiny *(10)*. Herein we discuss some of these issues and the experimental designs used to assess the effects on wildlife of OP pesticides applied to turf.

Generally speaking, a homeowner, golf course superintendent, and other concerned person using an agrochemical might observe wildlife effects, including die-offs, after application. Such wildlife die-offs are often investigated by state agencies or the United States Fish and Wildlife Service. We now realize that many cases of wildlife mortality go undetected, but when reported they can provide valuable information about potential effects of specific chemical products on wildlife and the use conditions which led to non-target effects. Unfortunately, even when reported, wildlife mortalities are often not investigated with thorough chemical analyses and therefore, we cannot determine whether the effects are the result of appropriate use or misuse of the product.

FIELD RESEARCH AND WILDLIFE ECOTOXICOLOGY

Wildlife toxicology experienced a rapid increase in scientific development during the 1980s with the implementation of many field studies. This research was influenced by the EPA Guidance Document prepared by Fite et al.*(11)*, and many unique experimental designs have evolved to study the variety of geographic conditions, wildlife populations, and chemical products for ecological risk assessments *(11)*.

In the early 1980s, our research group did one of the first field studies ever requested for registration of an organophosphate product for turf environments. That product was Triumph, developed by CIBA GEIGY Corporation and the study was to address potential bird impacts associated with the use of Triumph on golf courses *(12)*. This work represented the early stages in development of field studies involving interdisciplinary approaches. It involved much environmental chemistry, avian censuses, monitoring of avian reproductive success, and mortality estimates. However, it did not involve the rigorous replication of study sites that is common in current study designs. This study was conducted on one golf course in contrast with a more recent and more complex study involving 48 individual urban turf sites treated with diazinon insecticide (R.A. Hummell, Institute of Wildlife and Environmental Toxicology, Clemson University, unpublished data).

If a pesticide kills wildlife, a less complex field study can reveal cause-effect relationships between the use of a pesticide and wildlife impacts. For instance, in studies in the Pacific Northwest, applying a relatively simple study design, we have determined that the American widgeon (*Anas americana*), owing to its grazing habits, is extremely vulnerable to exposure to turf applications of organophosphate insecticides *(9)*. If wigeon ingest relatively small amounts of organophosphates by grazing on treated turf, some may die within an hour. For this reason, we have recommended extreme caution in the use of such insecticides in areas that might be used by waterfowl which often feed, nest, or rest in turf environments such as golf courses.

The significance of urban environments to wildlife, particularly birds, has been demonstrated in field studies. A study in Florida identified fifty-eight species of birds inhabiting a single urban golf course *(13)*. Peak daily counts of just the six most frequently observed species accounting for an average 179 individual birds per day. During this study we noted 57 nest initiations and 20 nests producing eggs in habitats within 4 m above the ground. In the study of 48 urban lawn sites (discussed above) in South Carolina, we observed an average bird density of 14 birds per acre per day. This represented an average of 550 individual birds per day on all sites combined.

Relative frequency and relative abundance calculations from bird censuses in urban lawn environments can provide some information about the potential for bird exposure to lawn chemicals (Figure 1). However, a survey of activity and habitat use taken during censusing provides much more information about the relative potential for turf chemical exposure among various species (Figure 2). Clearly, turf dwelling birds such as the American robin, common grackle (*Quiscalus quiscula*), and the European starling (*Sturnus vulgaris*) that probe the thatch layer and upper centimeter of soil for invertebrates are at the greatest risk of exposure to turf chemicals from both direct contact and ingestion of contaminated foods.

Dietary studies of European starlings on urban lawns in South Carolina indicate a clear preference for the larvae of the family Noctuidae (Figure 3). Monitoring of chemical residues in Noctuidae larvae extracted from the soil of organophosphate-treated lawns by adult starlings indicated that these insect larvae do accumulate organophosphate residues and the residue levels are strongly correlated to the residue levels in the soil following application (Figure 4).

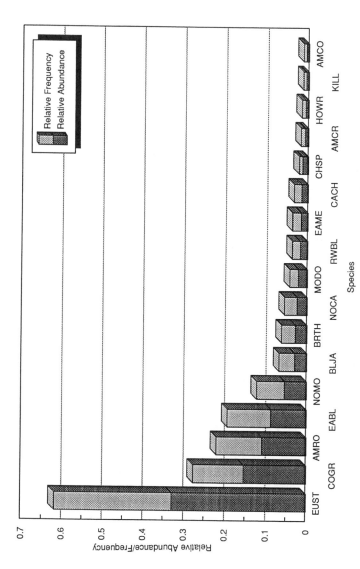

Figure 1. A figure representing the relative abundance and relative frequency of the top seventeen birds observed on turf sites.

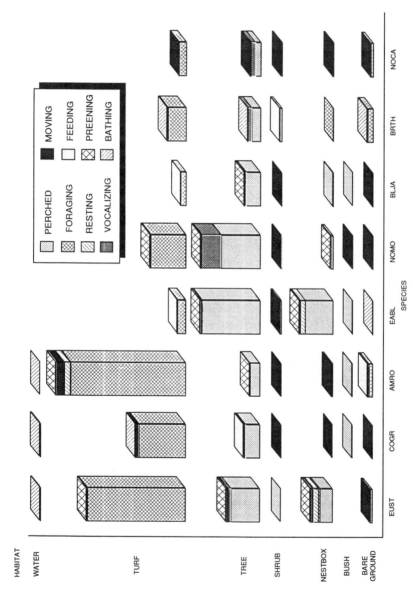

Figure 2. Activities of the eight most frequently recorded birds by habitat type.

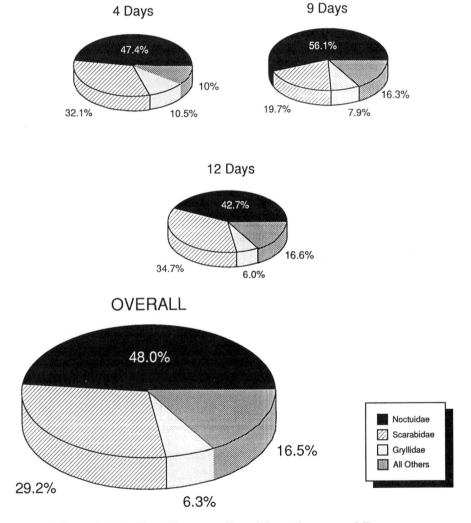

Figure 3. Families of insects collected from the crops of European starlings.

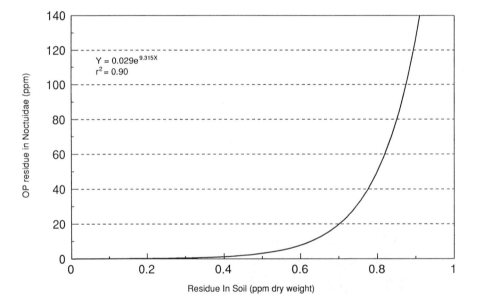

Figure 4. The correlation of OP found in the family Noctuidae to the OP residue found in the soil

We compiled the final evidence needed to verify food-chain transport of organophosphate insecticides by collecting fecal-urate samples from starling nestlings being reared in nestboxes on organophosphate treated study sites and correlating the diethylthiophosphate residues in the fecal-urates with parent compound residue levels in the soil (Figure 5). Considering that these nestlings are hatched and reared in nestboxes and never touch the treated turf, it is safe to conclude that the diethylthiophosphates in the fecal urates resulted from the organophosphate residues in their diet.

It is important to note that exposure of birds to pesticides does not necessarily have negative effects. Brewer et al. *(12)*, and Kendall et al. (J. Wildl. Diseases, in press) have observed low level exposure in passerine species and Canada geese to OP insecticides that did not cause obvious mortality or other adverse effects. During the Florida golf course study *(12)* we observed an increase in egg production on the treated study plots that was not observed on untreated reference plots. This increase may have been related to the abundance of dead or moribund insects on the turf for several days following chemical application. Conversely, in other studies we have also observed low level exposure to OP insecticides in starling nestlings to cause subtle reductions in nestling survival (R.S. Mellott, The Institute of Wildlife and Environmental Toxicology, Clemson University, unpublished data). Research results such as these point out the importance of performing well-designed field studies to accurately measure the extent and level of exposure and to identify and quantify effects prior to making regulatory or labeling decisions.

Fite et al. *(11)* described two levels of field studies to assess response of wildlife to pesticides. A Level 1 field study generally involves a study design to address the binomial question whether wildlife mortality does or does not occur after the use of a pesticide. A Level 1 study usually provides information which helps determine the need for more complex experimental designs, or a Level 2 study. A Level 2 study quantifies chemical effects on wildlife and usually involves more intensive environmental chemistry and biochemical evaluations to investigate cause-effect relationships. A Level 2 field study involving the use of pesticides in urban environments may involve 16 to 48 study sites on which to assess exposure and response of several bird and mammal species simultaneously.

The Future of Wildlife Toxicology in Assessing Response of Wildlife to Pesticides

Wildlife toxicology is an evolving discipline which in part deals with assessing the hazards of pesticides to wildlife. This current evolution involves the development of many new techniques, particularly sublethal methods, to assess response of wildlife to pesticide exposure *(13)*. Nonlethal assessment of pesticide exposure in wildlife can involve taking fecal-urate samples for residues and leaving groups, blood samples for cholinesterase measurements, and feather and foot washes for residues to assess dermal exposures or ingestion of pesticide products and the resultant biochemical response. With increasing concern for animal rights issues, the need to develop effective nonlethal assessment methods to evaluate exposure and response may become more pressing. The uses of radio-telemetry continue to evolve as effective methods to assess behavior, physiological functions, and survival of wildlife in ecotoxicology investigations *(13)*. The Avian Effects Dialogue Group of the Conservation Foundation will be holding an international meeting in 1993 on wildlife radio telemetry to evaluate the present and future potential of this technology in wildlife toxicology.

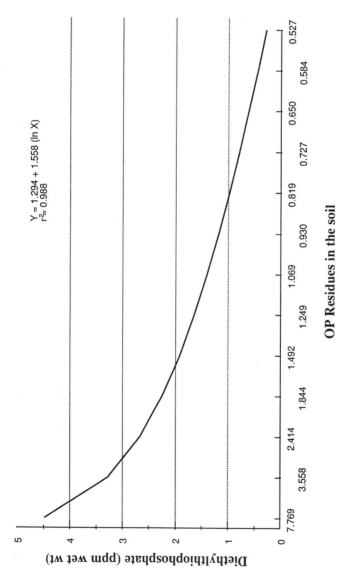

Figure 5. The significant correlation of diethylthiophosphate from fecal samples provides evidence of the exposure of the nestlings to the chemical in levels which are related to the concentration in the environment.

The effectiveness of nonlethal assessment techniques can be enhanced by utilizing biomarkers of exposure and effect that can be measured repeatedly during a study *(15)*. The use of appropriate biomarkers that do not require sacrificing wildlife allows the development of research designs that do not require removal of individuals from the study population. Non-removal studies help maintain strong sample size and allow the monitoring of the same individuals over time, enhancing our understanding of cause-effect relationships as well as recovery potential.

One particularly exciting area of development involves ecological modeling and the application of this technology towards ecological risk assessment. A symposium which occurred in July, 1990, brought together scientists from around the world to discuss the integration of population biology, wildlife toxicology and computer simulation modeling. This Symposium was intended to be a stimulus to further development of the use of computer modeling in assessing fate and biological effects of pesticides in wildlife populations *(16)*. Such disciplinary integration and further development of modeling applications are needed to advance our ability to conduct meaningful ecological risk assessments *(2)*. Ecotoxicological modeling will be instrumental in assessing the potential effects of, and regulating the use of the variety of pesticide products which might be utilized on turf in urban environments.

Reflecting on a decade of field and laboratory studies of the interaction between wildlife and pesticides, particularly regarding OP insecticides, we feel there are still many uncertainties about how local effects of pesticides relate to avian populations over all. The long term monitoring efforts needed to answer the question of population effects have not been conducted.

A great deal is yet to be understood about the physical and biological transport of pesticides and resultant effects on nontarget species in turf and other habitats. The rapid advance of the ecotoxicology discipline, and the application of multidisciplinary approaches to investigating ecotoxicological relationships are quickly bringing us to a better understanding of these relationships and should, in the near future, allow for more comprehensive environmental management of turf and other habitats that require chemical protection from pests. We believe this is not the time to relax in our pursuit of answers to these questions. Instead, we should aggressively apply sophisticated research designs to find the answers we need to guide us in the wisest use of chemicals in future turf and crop management.

LEGEND OF ABBREVIATIONS

AMCO	-	American cowbird
AMCR	-	American crow
AMRO	-	American robin
BLJA	-	bluejay
BRTH	-	brown thrasher
CACH	-	Carolina chickadee
CHSP	-	chipping sparrow
COGR	-	common grackle
EABL	-	eastern bluebird
EAME	-	eastern meadowlark
EUST	-	European starling

HOWR - house wren
KILL - killdeer
MODO - mourning dove
NOCA - northern cardinal
NOMO - northern mockingbird
RWBL - red-winged blackbird

LITERATURE CITED

1. Ehrlich, P.R.; Dobkin, D.S.; Wheye, D. *The Birder's Handbook. A Field Guide to the Natural History of North American Birds;* Simon and Schuster, Inc.: New York, 1988.
2. Kendall, R. J. *Environ. Sci. Technol.* **1992,** *26(2),* 239-244.
3. Kendall, R. J. *Environ. Sci. Technol.* **1982,** *16(8),* 448A-453A.
4. Hoffman, D. J.; Rattner, B. A.; Hall, R. J. *Environ. Sci. Technol.,* **1990,** *24,* 276-283.
5. Grue, C. E.; Fleming, W. S.; Busby, D. G.; Hill, E. F. *Trans. N. Amer. Wildl. Nat. Res. Conf.* **1983,** *48,* 200.
6. Stone, W.B. *NY Fish Game J.* **1979,** *26,* 37-47.
7. Stone, W. B.; Gradoni, P. B. *Northeast. Environ. Sci.* **1985,** *4,* 30-38.
8. Zinkl, J. G.; Rathert, J.; Hudson, P. R. *J. Wildl. Manage.* **1978,** *42,* 406-408.
9. Kendall, R. J.; Brewer, L. W.; Hitchcock, R. R.; Meyer, J. R. *J. Wildl. Diseases* **1992,** *28(2),* 263-267.
10. Avian Effects Dialogue Group *Pesticides and Birds: Improving Impact Assessment;* Report of the Avian Effects Dialogue Group; Conservation Foundation: Washington, DC, 1989; 68 pp.
11. Fite, E. C.; Turner, L. W.; Cook, N. J.; Stunkard, C.; Lee, R. M. *Guidance Document for Conducting Terrestrial Field Studies;* Ecological Effects Branch, Hazard Evaluation Division, Office of Pesticide Programs, United States Environ Protection Agency; 134 pp.
12. Brewer, L. W.; Driver, C. J.; Kendall, R.J.; Lacher, T. E. Jr.; J.C. Galindo *Environ. Toxicol. Chem.* **1988,** *7,* 391-401.
13. Hooper, M. J.; Brewer, L. W.; Cobb, G. P.; Kendall, R. J. In *Pesticide Effects on Terrestrial Wildlife* Somerville, L.; Walker, C. H., Eds.; Taylor & Francis: Basingstoke, Hampshire, 1990; pp 271-283.
14. Buerger, T. T., R. J. Kendall, B.S. Mueller, T. DeVos, and B.A. Williams *Environ. Toxicol. Chem.* **1991,** *10,* 527-532.
15. Huggett, A. R. (ed) **1991** *The Existing and Potential Value of Biomarkers in Evaluating Exposure and Environmental Effects of Toxic Chemicals;* Huggett, A. R., Ed.; Lewis Publishers, Chelsea, MI .
16. *The Population Ecology and Wildlife Toxicology of Agricultural Pesticide Use: A Modelling Initiative for Avian Species;* Kendall, R. J.; Lacher, T. E. Jr., Eds. Lewis Publishers: Chelsea, MI, 1993.

RECEIVED October 23, 1992

Chapter 28

Pesticide and Fertilizer Effects on Beneficial Invertebrates and Consequences for Thatch Degradation and Pest Outbreaks in Turfgrass

D. A. Potter

Department of Entomology, University of Kentucky, Lexington, KY 40546−0091

Effects of pesticides and fertilizers on beneficial invertebrates and processes such as degradation of thatch and natural regulation of pest populations were evaluated to understand their consequences for the long-term stability of the turfgrass ecosystem. Rates of thatch decomposition were greatly accelerated by earthworm activity. Certain pesticides applied to turfgrass at recommended rates caused severe and long-lasting reductions in earthworm populations, suggesting that their use could result in excessive thatch accumulation. Field experiments demonstrated high rates of predation on eggs and pupae of turfgrass pests. Insecticides kill arthropod predators as well as pests, and evidence of the increased survival or higher population densities of some pests following destruction of predators has been shown. Acquired resistance to insecticides, enhanced microbial degradation of pesticides, and other potential problems resulting from overuse of pesticides are discussed. Awareness of these adverse side-effects provides a compelling incentive for reducing non-essential pesticide use on turf.

Growing public concern about the potential hazards of urban pesticide use has created unprecedented pressure for the landscape maintenance industry to seek non-chemical solutions to turfgrass pest problems. The key controversies, especially regarding risks from acute or chronic exposure of humans or pets to pesticides and the potential for ground water contamination by pesticides (1), are likely to remain unresolved for many years. However, there are other compelling reasons why turfgrass managers may benefit from more selective and reduced use of pesticides. This Chapter summarizes recent studies on the effects of pesticides and fertilizers on beneficial invertebrates in turfgrass, and how these in turn can affect key processes such as thatch accumulation and outbreaks of pest insects. Awareness of these potential side-effects can be a tangible and powerful incentive for turfgrass managers to seek ways of reducing non-essential pesticide use.

0097−6156/93/0522−0331$06.00/0

REASONS FOR TRADITIONAL RELIANCE ON PESTICIDES

Turfgrasses are typically the most intensively-managed plantings in the urban landscape. The use of turfgrass in the United States has skyrocketed during the past 40 years as large tracts of land were developed to accommodate the growing urban population. Dense, dark green, uniform turf became valued increasingly as a symbol of social status and affluence, as an enhancement to property value, and for its aesthetic and recreational benefits. Use of pesticides and fertilizers on turfgrass also increased considerably *(2-4)*. The commercial lawn care industry grew at an average annual rate of 22% between 1977 and 1984; gross annual sales in 1983 were an estimated $2.2 billion *(5)*. The growing popularity of golf has encouraged higher standards for playing conditions *(6)*. Turfgrass culture, in its many forms, represents a $25 billion per year industry in the U.S. *(6)*, a significant portion of which involves the marketing and use of herbicides, insecticides, fungicides, growth regulators and fertilizers.

Preventative pesticide use on golf courses and home lawns is often motivated by the public's general intolerance of weeds, insects, or pest injury, and by the high replacement costs for damaged turf *(7)*. Furthermore, many of the currently available alternatives (e.g., entomogenous nematodes, microbial insecticides) are less effective and reliable, slower-acting, costlier, and more difficult to use than conventional pesticides. Indeed, the use of a chemical pesticide may sometimes be the only practical way to avoid extensive damage from an unexpected pest outbreak *(4)*.

Pesticides and fertilizers can have profound effects on the structure and stability of the turfgrass system. Because pesticides kill beneficial organisms as well as pests, their use can increase the risk of pest resurgences or secondary outbreaks. Pesticides and fertilizers can also affect energy flow, organic matter decomposition, and nutrient recycling in turfgrass by altering primary production or through their impact on soil organisms such as earthworms. Like many cultivated crops, turfgrass lacks the complexity of grassland and forest habitats and so may be relatively sensitive to pesticide-induced perturbations. Greater consideration of the ecotoxicological effects of pesticides, particularly with regard to preserving long-term stability of the turfgrass ecosystem will be important in the turf industry's transition toward integrated pest management.

THE TURFGRASS ECOSYSTEM

Turfgrass consists of the roots, stems, and leaves of grass plants together with the underlying thatch and soil. Together with the associated pest species *(8)*, this composite habitat supports a diverse community of non-pest invertebrates. For example, some 83 different taxa of invertebrates including insects, mites, nematodes, annelids, gastropods, and other groups were collected from a bluegrass-red fescue turf in New Jersey *(9)*. Similarly, dozens of species of Staphylinidae (rove beetles), Carabidae (ground beetles), Formicidae (ants), Araneae (spiders), and other groups of predominantly predaceous invertebrates were recovered from turfgrass sites in Kentucky *(10-13)*. Earthworms (Lumbricidae), oribatid mites (Cryptostigmata), Collembola, and other invertebrates important to plant litter decomposition and nutrient recycling in pastures and forests are also abundant in turfgrass soils *(9, 13-17)*.

These pest and non-pest invertebrates form a complex community that interacts with the living grass, thatch, and soil and contributes to the stability of the turfgrass system

(Fig. 1). It is noteworthy that excessive thatch accumulation and outbreaks of insects and diseases rarely occur in turfgrass under minimal maintenance. This implies that low-maintenance turf is a relatively stable habitat in which thatch accumulation is balanced by its decomposition and in which pests are held in check by predators, parasites, or natural plant resistance.

EFFECTS OF PESTICIDES ON THE NATURAL REGULATION OF PEST POPULATIONS

Broad-spectrum insecticides that are applied for the control of turfgrass insect pests are also toxic to predaceous and parasitic arthropods. For example, a single, surface application of chlorpyrifos reduced populations of spiders, staphylinid beetles and predatory mites in small (100 m²) plots of Kentucky bluegrass for at least 5 to 6 weeks (10). Similarly, application of isofenphos, a relatively persistent organophosphate, reduced populations of non-oribatid Acari, Collembola, Diplopoda, Diplura and Staphylinidae in home lawns for as long as 43 weeks (17). Not surprisingly, predatory arthropods were less abundant and diverse in turf receiving commercial lawn care than in lawns maintained without regular chemical treatments (12, 13, 18).

The fact that insect outbreaks are relatively uncommon in low-maintenance turfgrass suggests that some pests are normally held in check by indigenous natural enemies. Several authors (9 ,11, 19) have cautioned that repeated or heavy pesticide usage could reduce the stability of the turfgrass ecosystem and lead to pest resurgences or secondary pest outbreaks. Reinert (19) observed in Florida that southern chinch bug (*Blissus insularis* Barber) populations remained low in untreated St. Augustine grass lawns where natural enemies were abundant, but reached outbreak densities on lawns treated with insecticides. Resurgence of hairy chinch bug, *Blissus leucopterus hirtus* Montandon, populations following use of chlordane was attributed to reduced populations of predators (9, 20). In New Jersey, repeated carbaryl treatments to turfgrass were associated with outbreaks of winter grain mite, *Penthaleus major* (Duges), apparently due to suppression of acarine predators (21). Outbreaks of the greenbug, *Schizaphis graminum* (Rhondani) in Kentucky may be more common on high maintenance lawns than on untreated turf (22).

Relatively few studies have attempted to measure the impact of natural enemies on pest populations in turfgrass. Reinert (19) observed egg parasitism and predation on southern chinch bug in the laboratory and field, and suggested that the combined activity of predators and parasites contributed to collapse of the pest population in late summer. Cockfield and Potter (11) compared rates of natural predation on sod webworm (*Crambus* and *Pediasia* spp.) eggs in untreated Kentucky bluegrass and in turf that had received a single surface application of chlorpyrifos at the labeled rate. Groups of eggs were exposed in small dishes set level with the soil surface at 1, 3 and 5 weeks after treatment, and rates of predation were compared between treated and untreated plots. Predatory arthropods, especially ants, consumed or carried off as many as 75% of the eggs in the untreated plots within 48 hours. Predator populations and predation on eggs were significantly lower in the treated plots for at least 3 weeks after application (Table I). Predator populations had begun to recover after 5 weeks, at which time predation rates were similar in treated and untreated plots. Numerous species of predators collected from the study site consumed sod webworm eggs in the laboratory (11).

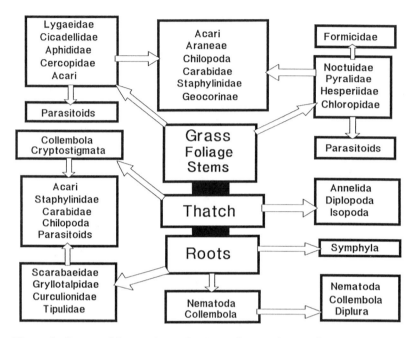

Figure 1. Proposed invertebrate food web in a typical turfgrass ecosystem.
Adapted from Streu (8).

Table I. Mean percentage of eggs eaten or carried off by predators in replicated
Kentucky bluegrass plots that were untreated or that received a single,
surface application of chlorpyrifos (Dursban 4 E) at the labelled rate.
Percentages are based upon cohorts of 500 total eggs placed in the turf for
48 hours at 1, 3, or 5 weeks after treatment

| | Percent Eggs Missing from | | |
Weeks Post-Treatment	Untreated Plots	Treated Plots	P Level[a]
1	37.7	0.9	P< 0.001
3	17.6	0.1	P< 0.05
5	75.4	61.3	P< 0.08

[a]Probability of a greater t statistic, one-sided paired t test. Reprinted with permission
from Cockfield and Potter.[11]

A more recent study documented high rates of predation on fall armyworm, *Spodoptera frugiperda* pupae and Japanese beetle, *Popillia japonica* eggs in Kentucky bluegrass turf, and possible interference by insecticides. Replicated plots (400 m²) were treated once with carbaryl, cyfluthrin, or isazophos in early June, and their impacts on invertebrate predators were measured with pitfall traps. Concurrently, groups of 20 newly-laid Japanese beetle eggs and 10 fall armyworm pupae were implanted beneath the turf in each plot at 1 and 3 weeks after treatment. Predation rates were determined by examining the eggs and pupae after 48 hours. Grub populations were measured by sampling the experimental plots in August.

Populations of ants, staphylinids, spiders, and certain other predators were reduced significantly by the insecticides, particularly isazophos and carbaryl. Predators killed up to 60% of the fall armyworm pupae, but the rate at which this occurred was not reduced significantly by the insecticides. In contrast, natural predation on Japanese beetle eggs was significantly lower in isazophos- and carbaryl-treated plots 3 weeks after treatment, presumably because of the destruction of predators. Most notably, naturally-occurring grub populations were significantly *higher* in plots previously treated with isazophos than in control plots (Fig. 2). These results demonstrate the potential for an improperly-timed insecticide treatment to induce higher scarabaeid grub populations by interfering with natural predation on the eggs or young larvae.

EARTHWORMS AND THATCH

Aristotle referred to earthworms as "the intestines of the earth". Earthworms and other soil invertebrates aid decomposition processes by fragmenting and conditioning plant debris in their guts before further breakdown by microorganisms *(23)*. Earthworms, in particular, enhance the chemical environment of soil by mixing organic matter into subsurface layers and by enriching the soil by their castings. Their burrowing activity increases aeration and water infiltration *(23, 24)*. These processes are especially important in lawns and golf fairways that are cultivated only through earthworm activity. This is sometimes most evident when earthworm populations are decreased by pesticides or through indirect effects of management *(25, 26)*, and soil compaction and thatch accumulation ensue.

Thatch is a tightly intermingled layer of roots, rhizomes, stolons, plant crowns, stems, and organic debris that accumulates between the soil surface and the green vegetation in turfgrass *(27)*. Thatch results from an imbalance between production and decomposition of organic matter at the soil surface *(28)*. Problems associated with excessive thatch include reduced water infiltration *(29)*, shallow root growth with increased vulnerability to heat and drought stress *(28)*, and restricted penetration of fertilizers *(30)* and adsorption of soil insecticides to the thatch *(31)*. Thatch accumulation is common in managed turfgrass, especially when high rates of nitrogen fertilizer are applied for several years *(14, 28)*.

Recent experiments *(15 ,16)* confirmed the importance of earthworms to thatch degradation in Kentucky bluegrass turf. Several hundred intact, pre-weighed pieces of thatch were buried in nylon bags having fine (53 microns), medium (1.2 mm) or coarse (5 mm) mesh to selectively admit or exclude certain components of the soil fauna. In a companion experiment, pieces of thatch were buried in identical, coarse mesh bags either in untreated plots with abundant earthworms, or in plots that had been treated with chlordane and carbofuran to eliminate earthworms. Samples were recovered periodically

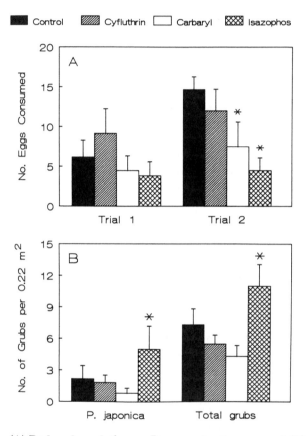

Figure 2. (A) Reduced predation on Japanese beetle eggs, and (B) higher densities of naturally-occurring white grubs in insecticide-treated turfgrass plots. The insecticides were applied in mid-June and eggs were implanted beneath the soil after 1 and 3 weeks. Grub populations were sampled in early August.

for 23 months and analyzed for mineral soil content and loss of organic matter by gravimetric methods. Subsamples of thatch were also tested for microbial respiration, indicative of rate of microbial decomposition.

Dramatic differences were apparent in both experiments after only three months. Without earthworms the thatch structure and composition remained nearly the same, but with earthworms the pieces were broken apart and dispersed. Worms, mainly *Apporectodea* spp. and *Lumbricus terrestris*, incorporated large amounts of mineral soil into the thatch matrix (Fig. 3). In both experiments, rates of net loss of organic matter and of relative microbial respiration were much greater when earthworms were present than when worms were excluded. There was only a small difference in degradation rates of thatch from medium and fine mesh bags, suggesting that the soil mesofauna (e.g., Cryptostigmata, Collembola) is less important than earthworms in the initial comminution of thatch.

Topdressing, i.e., the distribution of a thin layer of soil followed by physical incorporation of the soil into the thatch, is considered the best cultural method for reducing a thatch layer in turf *(28, 32)*. This process results in increased bulk density and moisture retention capacity, a higher cation exchange capacity, increased microbial decomposition, and better turfgrass growth *(32)*. However, topdressing may be too expensive for large turf areas. The aforementioned experiment *(15)* showed that earthworms perform a function similar to topdressing by rapidly incorporating soil into the thatch matrix. Preservation of earthworm populations is clearly important where thatch is a concern.

FERTILIZER AND PESTICIDE EFFECTS ON EARTHWORMS

Excessive fertilization may encourage thatch accumulation both by stimulating vegetative production and by inhibiting the decomposition processes. Nitrogen fertilization commonly results in soil acidification *(33)* which may in turn inhibit microbial activity *(34)*. Furthermore, the repellent nature of NH_4^+ can adversely affect soil invertebrates *(35)*. Earthworms, in particular, are generally sparse in acidic soils *(23)*. Heavy fertilization and thatch accumulation are often correlated *(36, 37)*, although this does not always occur *(38)*. High rates of ammonium nitrate fertilizer applied to Kentucky bluegrass for 7 years resulted in soil acidification, decreased populations of earthworms and some oribatid mites, and a significant increase in thatch *(14)*.

Use of pesticides can also contribute to thatch development. For example, certain fungicides may reduce soil pH, which can in turn inhibit activity of microorganisms important to thatch decomposition *(39)*. Alternatively, fungicides may increase rates of root and rhizome production, further contributing to thatch accumulation *(40)*.

Potter et al. *(16)* evaluated the comparative short-term and long-term toxicity to earthworms of 17 commonly used turfgrass pesticides in Kentucky bluegrass turf. A single application of the fungicide benomyl or of the insecticides ethoprop, carbaryl, or bendiocarb at recommended rates reduced earthworm populations by 60 to 99%, with significant effects lasting for at least 20 weeks. These compounds also reduced the rate at which earthworms incorporated mineral soil into buried pieces of thatch. Other insecticides, specifically diazinon, isofenphos, trichlorfon, chlorpyrifos and isazophos, caused less severe, but significant mortality in some tests (Table II). None of the

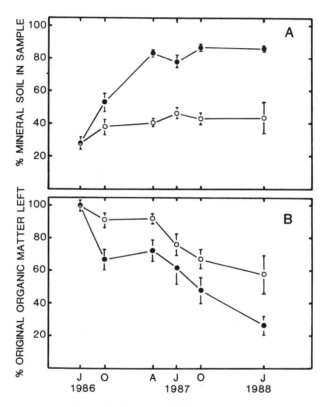

Figure 3. Incorporation of mineral soil (A) and net loss of organic matter (B) from thatch buried in coarse-mesh bags in untreated turf (•), or in plots treated with insecticides to eliminate earthworms and other soil invertebrates (o). Reprinted with permission from Potter et al. *(14)*

Table II. Relative toxicity of turfgrass pesticides to earthworms based upon the mean reduction in population density in two independent field tests. Treatments were applied to Kentucky bluegrass in April and watered in, and earthworms were sampled using formalin drenches after 7-9 days. Adapted from Potter et al.[16]

Treatment	Common Name	Rate kg (AI)/ha	Class[a]
Low toxicity (0-25% reduction)			
2,4-D	Dacamine 4D	2.24	H
Trichlopyr	Garlon 3 A	0.56	H
Dicamba	Banvel 4 E	0.56	H
Pendimethalin	Pre-M 60 WDG	3.36	H
Triodimefon	Bayleton 25 WDG	3.02	F
Fenarimol	Rubigan 50 WP	3.02	F
Propiconazole	Banner 1.1 EC	3.36	F
Chlorothalonil	Daconil 2787	12.66	F
Isofenphos	Oftanol 5 G	2.24	I-OP
Moderate toxicity (26-50% reduction)			
Trichlorfon	Proxol 80 WP	8.96	I-OP
Chlorpyrifos	Dursban 4 E	4.48	I-OP
Isazophos	Triumph 4 E	2.24	I-OP
Severe toxicity (51-75% reduction)			
Benomyl	Benlate 50 WP 1	2.21	F
Diazinon	Diazinon 14 G	4.48	I-OP
Very severe toxicity (76-99% reduction)			
Carbaryl	Sevin SL	8.96	I-C
Bendiocarb	Turcam 2.5 G	4.48	I-C
Ethoprop	Mocap 10 G	5.60	I-OP

[a]H= herbicide, F= fungicide, I-OP= organophosphate insecticide, I-C= carbamate insecticide

herbicides tested was toxic to earthworms in the field. The abundance of Cryptostigmata, Collembola, and ants may also be drastically reduced by some insecticides *(10, 16 ,17)*.

CUMULATIVE EFFECTS OF HIGH MAINTENANCE LAWN CARE

Although there is now ample evidence that use of certain turfgrass pesticides can affect beneficial invertebrates and processes such as thatch degradation and natural suppression of pest species adversely, another study *(13)* suggested that the cumulative side-effects of high maintenance lawn care programs may not necessarily be so severe. Replicated plots of Kentucky bluegrass were maintained for 4 years on a schedule of treatments similar to that used by many commercial lawn care companies, consisting of four fertilizer applications (225 kg [AI]/ha total nitrogen annually from urea), broadleaf weed control (2,4-D, MCPP, and dicamba) in spring and fall, early spring application of bensulide for preemergent crabgrass control, two applications of chlorpyrifos for surface-feeding insects, and granular diazinon applied for control of white grubs in late August. Control plots were unmanaged except for mowing. Changes in soil and thatch pH and thatch thickness were monitored, and the impact on earthworms and non-target arthropods was determined from pit-fall trap collections, soil and thatch extractions, and sweep-net and formalin-drench samples.

Even after 4 years on this relatively heavy treatment schedule, earthworm numbers were not reduced significantly in the treated plots, and numbers of oribatid mites actually increased. Moreover, there was only a slight decline in soil pH (6.2 to 5.9), possibly because the site was treated with agricultural limestone 2 years before the experiment began. Thatch accumulation was significantly greater in the high maintenance turf (10.7 mm vs. 3.3 mm in control plots), but was still not excessive. Predator populations, specifically Araneae, Staphylinidae, and Carabidae, were significantly reduced by the insecticides, particularly the late summer soil treatment with diazinon, but predators re-populated the treated plots by the following spring. Effects of the program on non-target herbivorous arthropods were variable; flea beetle (Chrysomelidae) populations were generally higher, and leafhopper (Cicadellidae) populations lower in the high maintenance plots.

The apparent recovery of turfgrass maintained on this relatively severe treatment schedule suggests that the impact of more moderate programs would be less severe and of shorter duration. However, thatch accumulation would probably have been greater had we used one or more of the pesticides that are especially toxic to earthworms, or had the insecticide applications been made in early spring or in the fall, when earthworms are more active at the soil surface. The rate at which predators, earthworms, and other beneficials would repopulate larger turf areas such as home lawns and golf courses is not currently known, but it would undoubtedly be slower than occurred in our study.

ACQUIRED RESISTANCE AND ENHANCED MICROBIAL DEGRADATION

Excessive or repeated use of certain pesticides on turfgrass may create problems such as acquired resistance of pests to insecticides or fungicides, or enhanced microbial degradation of pesticide residues.

Selection for resistant genotypes may occur when pest populations are exposed regularly to insecticides. Resistance of pests to cyclodiene insecticides had become widespread by the early 1970's, even before environmental concerns resulted in cancellation of their registrations for turf. Resistance to organophosphates or carbamates has been documented for chinch bugs and greenbugs *(41)* and in at least one instance for white grubs *(42)*. Metcalf *(43)* listed general resistance management tactics directed at reducing the single factor selection pressure on pest populations that occurs with conventional chemical control. These include 1) reducing the frequency and extent of pesticide treatments, 2) avoiding pesticides with long environmental persistence and slow release formulations, 3) reduced use of residual treatments, 4) avoidance of treatments that apply selection pressure on both immature and adult stages, and 5) increased use of cultural, biological, and other non-chemical methods in integrated pest management. All of these tactics are applicable to the turfgrass system.

Enhanced microbial degradation refers to a phenomenon in which pesticide residues are degraded more rapidly than usual by microorganisms in soils that have been conditioned by prior exposure to a pesticide. Enhanced degradation has been reported for isofenphos, diazinon, ethoprop, and other insecticides used on turf *(44)*, and it has been implicated in reduced residual effectiveness of isofenphos on golf courses previously treated with that chemical *(45)*. A more recent study *(46)* showed that residues of carbaryl and diazinon were degraded more rapidly in thatch from isofenphos-treated plots. Thatch from plots that had been treated previously with diazinon, chlorpyrifos, carbaryl, or isazophos degraded residues of these same chemicals rapidly. The risk of inducing a conditioned soil provides another compelling argument against the non-essential use of pesticides on lawns or golf courses.

CONCLUSION

The intent of this chapter is not to condemn all use of pesticides and fertilizers for turfgrass maintenance. Pesticides are powerful and indispensable tools of professional turf management, and they are likely to remain so until effective and reliable alternatives are developed. At present, use of a pesticide may be the only practical way to prevent severe damage from unexpected or heavy pest infestations. However, like human medicines, pesticide applications may have adverse side-effects which should be weighed against the overall benefit that the treatment will provide. Unnecessary or excessive use of pesticides can aggravate thatch and pest problems by interfering with the activities of beneficial organisms, or by encouraging development of acquired resistance or enhanced microbial degradation.

These potential problems should provide a strong incentive for turfgrass managers to select pesticides or alternative tactics that cause fewer known adverse side effects (e.g., earthworm toxicity), to apply them at the proper time and rate, and to use them only as needed to control specific problems. I suggest that most homeowners and professional turf managers are already concerned about the perceived and real hazards of pesticides, and that the added awareness of potential negative side-effects to beneficial invertebrates and processes further encourages more selective use of these tools on lawns and golf courses. The challenge now is for turfgrass scientists to provide safe, effective and reliable alternatives that are compatible with long-term stability of the turfgrass ecosystem.

ACKNOWLEDGMENTS

I am grateful to T.B. Arnold, M. Buxton, S. Cockfield, F.C. Gordon, C. Patterson, A. J. Powell, C. Redmond, M.S. Smith, P. Spicer, and L. Terry for their significant contributions to this research. This work was supported by USDA Grants SR89-57-E-KY, SR91-31-E-KY, and 91-34103-5836, and by grants from the U.S. Golf Association and the O.J. Noer Research Foundation, Inc.

LITERATURE CITED

1. U.S. General Accounting Office. *Lawn care pesticides. Risks remain uncertain while prohibited safety claims continue.* GAO/RCED-90-134, **1990**.
2. U.S. Environmental Protection Agency., *National Household Pesticide Usage Study, 1976-1977*, Rep. no. EPA/540/9-80-002, **1979**.
3. National Research Council, *Urban Pest Management*, National Academy Press, Washington, D.C., **1980**.
4. Potter, D. A.; Braman, S. K. *Annu. Rev. Entomol.* **1991**, *36*, 383-406.
5. Anonymous. *Lawn Care Ind.*, **1984**, *8*, 1.
6. Roberts, E. C.; Roberts, B. C., *Lawn and Sports Turf Benefits*, The Lawn Institute, Pleasant Hill, TN, **1987**.
7. Potter, D. A., *In Advances in Urban Pest Management*; Bennett, G. W.; Owens, J. M., Eds.; Van Nostrand Reinhold: New York, NY, **1986**; 219-251.
8. Tashiro, H. *Turfgrass Insects of the United States and Canada;* Cornell Univ. Press: Ithaca, NY, **1987**.
9. Streu, H. T. *Bull. Entomol. Soc. Am.* **1973**, *19*, 89-91.
10. Cockfield, S. D.; Potter, D. A. *Environ. Entomol.* **1983**, *12*, 1260-1264.
11. Cockfield, S. D.; Potter, D. A. *J. Econ. Entomol.* **1984**, *77*, 1542-1544.
12. Cockfield, S. D.; Potter, D. A. *Can. Entomol.* **1985**, *117*, 423-429.
13. Arnold, T. B.; Potter, D. A. *Environ. Entomol.* **1987**, *16*, 100-105.
14. Potter, D. A.; Bridges, B. L.; Gordon, F. C. *Agron. J.* **1985**, *77*, 367-372.
15. Potter, D. A.; Powell, A. J.; Smith, M. S. *J. Econ. Entomol.*, **1990**, *83*, 205-211.
16. Potter, D. A.; Buxton, M. C.; Redmond, C. T.; Patterson, C. G.; Powell, A. J. J. *Econ. Entomol.* **1990**, *83*, 2362-2369.
17. Vavrek, R. C.; Niemczyk, H. D. *Environ. Entomol.* **1990**, *19*, 1572-1577.
18. Short, D. E.; Reinert, J. A.; Atilano, R. A. In *Advances in Turfgrass Entomology;* Niemczyk, H. D.; Joyner, B. G., Eds.; Hammer Graphics: Piqua, OH, **1982**, 25-31.
19. Reinert, J. A. *Ann. Entomol. Soc. Am.* **1978**, *71*, 728-731.
20. Streu, H. T. Proc. Scotts *Turfgrass Res. Conf. I. Entomology*, O.M. Scott & Sons: Marysville, OH, **1969**, 53-59.
21. Streu, H. T.; Gingrich, J. B. *J. Econ. Entomol.* **1972**, *65*, 427-430.
22. Potter, D. A. *Amer. Lawn Applic.* **1982**, *3*, 20-25.
23. Lee, K. E. *Earthworms. Their Ecology and Relationships With Soil and Land Use, Academic Press:* New South Wales, Australia, **1985**.
24. Swift, M. J.; Heal, O. W.; Anderson, J. M. *Decomposition in terrestrial ecosystems. Studies in Ecology*, *5*, Blackwell Scientific: Oxford, England, **1979**.
25. Randell, R.; Butler, J. D.; Hughes, T. D. *HortScience 1972*, *7*, 64-65.

26. Turgeon, A. J.; Freeborg, R. P.; Bruce, W. N. *Agron. J.* **1975**, *67*, 563-565.
27. Ledeboer, F. B.; Skogley, C. R. *Agron. J.* **1967**, *59*, 320-323.
28. Beard, J. B. *Turfgrass: Science and Culture*, Prentice-Hall: Englewood Cliffs, NJ, **1973**.
29. Taylor, D. H.; Blake, G. R. *Soil Sci. Soc. Am.* **1982**, *46*, 616-619.
30. Nelson, K. E.; Turgeon, A. J.; Street, J. R. *Agron. J.* **1980**, *72*, 487-492.
31. Niemczyk, H. D.; Krueger, H. R. *J. Econ. Entomol.* **1987**, *80*, 950-952.
32. Danneberger, T. K.; Turgeon, A. J. *J. Amer. Sci. Hort. Sci.* **1984**, *111*, 184-186.
33. Pierre, W. H. *J. Amer. Soc. Agron.*, **1928**, *20*, 254-269.
34. Martin, D. P.; Beard, J. B. *Agron. J.*, **1975**, *67*, 835-836.
35. Marshall, V. G. *Commonwealth. Bur. Soils Spec. Pub.*, **1977**, 3.
36. Engle, R. E.; Aldefer, R. B. *N. J. Agric. Exp. Stn. Bull.* **1967**, *818*, 32-45.
37. Meinhold, J. H.; Duble, R. L.; Weaver, R. W.; Holt, E. C. *Agron. J.*, **1973**, *65*, 833-835.
38. Shearman, R. C.; Kinbacher, E. J.; Riordan, T. P.; Steinegger, D. H. *HortScience* **1980**, *15*, 312-313.
39. Smiley, R. W.; Craven Fowler, M. *Agron. J.*, **1986**, *78*, 633-636.
40. Smiley, R. W.; Craven Fowler, M.; Kane, R. T.; Petrovic, A. M.; White, R. A. *Agron. J.*, **1985**, *77*, 597-602.
41. Reinert, J. A. In *Advances in Turfgrass Entomology*; Niemczyk, H. D.; Joyner, B. G., Eds.; Hammer Graphics: Piqua, OH, **1982**, 71-76.
42. Ahmad, S.; Ng, Y. S. J. N.Y. *Entomol. Soc.*, **1981**, *89*, 34-39.
43. Metcalf, R. L. In *Integrated Pest Management for Turfgrass and Ornamentals;* Leslie, A.; Metcalf, R. L., Eds.; US-EPA: Washington, D.C., **1989**, 33-44.
44. Felsot, A. S. *Annu. Rev. Entomol.* **1989**, *34*, 453-476.
45. Niemczyk, H. D.; Chapman, R. A. *J. Econ. Entomol.*, **1987**, *80*, 880-882.
46. Niemczyk, H. D., Filary Z. *Proc. N.C.B. Meet. Entomol. Soc. Am.*, **1987**, (Abstr.).

RECEIVED November 12, 1992

Chapter 29

Pesticides and Pets

V. R. Beasley

Department of Veterinary Biosciences, College of Veterinary Medicine, University of Illinois, 2001 South Lincoln Avenue, Urbana, IL 61801

As compared to much older products containing "classical pesticides", such as the rodenticide warfarin and the insecticide carbaryl, many newer formulations are more hazardous to domestic animals in urban and suburban environments. Although progress has been marked in the area of insecticide baits for use in homes, at least one fly bait which is particularly lethal to dogs is still widely available. In the case of rodenticides, recent experience has reflected generally negative progress with regard to small animal safety. Indeed, some products relatively new to the marketplace routinely cause prolonged suffering, necessitate expensive and often ineffective therapies, and can induce permanent organ damage despite vigorous treatment of the inadvertently exposed pet animal.

Selectivity, which pertains to the effectiveness of a product as an agent to control a pest relative to the risk it poses to nontarget species is a key concept in pesticide development. Over the past fifteen years, pesticides new to the marketplace and to the environments of pet animals have included products with both highly desirable and those with highly undesirable degrees of selectivity. There are a number of straightforward reasons why certain formulations of pesticides currently in wide use in urban and suburban environments pose unacceptable hazards to pet animals (1). These include: that the products have replaced considerably less hazardous products in the marketplace; that there are no effective and/or reasonably economical antidotal therapies; that nontarget animals are likely to suffer irreparable damage to vital organs despite vigorous therapeutic intervention; or that the agents act so rapidly that therapeutic intervention is often impossible or unlikely to be administered in time to preserve the life of the animal.

Another problem with some products currently on the market is that simple label warnings would be most unlikely to protect against common animal poisonings, yet such labels have been the sole means of implementing control of the attendant hazards. Practices which fail to allow for a reasonable degree of human frailty are inconsistent with reality, and dismissal of any responsibility for product use beyond the label when such use

0097–6156/93/0522–0344$06.00/0

could logically be predicted, or even after it has been documented repeatedly, is equivalent to dismissing both the humanity of the responsible parties and the suffering on the part of the animal.

Companion animals play important roles in the lives of human beings. Recent evidence has repeatedly demonstrated that development of a human-animal bond can help relieve stress and promote physical wellbeing, enable children having difficulty relating to adults or other children to have an accepting "friend" to help ease them back toward the ability to interact with their fellowman, alleviate feelings of isolation, detachment, and inability to communicate in elderly people, contribute to the accelerated rehabilitation of persons convicted of criminal behaviors, and substantially assist in a range of other forms of psychotherapeutic treatment. Organisms which can contribute to all these benefits for mankind must surely have inherent value.

Control of certain rodent and insect pests in urban environments is essential to human health. In addition, insects that parasitize domestic animals may not only cause suffering on the part of the host, such as that related to pruritis, flea-allergy or anemia, but they may also transmit diseases among pets, or bite the human co-inhabitants of the home. Clearly, judicious treatment of homes and yards to control rodent and insect pests is often of significant benefit to animal owners and/or their pets.

A number of highly desirable, from a safety point of view, pesticidal products have been introduced to the marketplace in recent times. Such products allow for variation in human traits whether intellectual, emotional, or situational. It is in this direction that pesticides for use in urban environments must progress; and progress in this direction should be achieved without the retrogression toward hazardous products that we have often witnessed over the past fifteen years.

In the use of any product involving costs and benefits, one must have a frame of reference. In the case of pesticides, certain widely used formulations of a given class (i.e. rodenticide, or insecticide) can serve as a standard to gauge progress or lack thereof in terms of safety toward nontarget pet animal species. Using this approach, in the following discussion, the clinical experiences of the author are drawn upon in consideration of the emergence of new pesticide products.

RODENTICIDES

Anticoagulant Rodenticides. Of all rodenticidal compounds, one of the most widely used has been the anticoagulant warfarin. Thus, for the purposes of this discussion of hazards posed to pet animals, the toxicologic attributes of once common formulations using warfarin are compared with those of more recently developed products based on other active ingredients. Warfarin-based rodenticidal products often contained 0.025% or 0.05% active ingredient. Generally, because of the low toxicity of the compound following a one-time ingestion, a single exposure to warfarin was unlikely to result in clinical toxicosis in small domestic animals. To the author's knowledge, the lowest LD_{50} reported for warfarin would be equivalent to 81 grams of bait per kg of body weight, based on bait containing warfarin at a concentration of 250 ppm *(2)*.

Although acute onset of hemorrhage (i.e. within a day or so of ingestion) is theoretically possible with such warfarin products, the common three-day delay before the onset of clinical signs often allows time for the owner to discover evidence of exposure and to present the animal for veterinary care *(3)*. When begun prior to the onset of illness, vitamin-K_1 is a highly effective antidote. Vitamin K tablets are readily given by the owner with the animal at home, it is needed for no longer than ten days, it is a highly effective and reliable therapy, and it is generally given without any notable side effects (3). When animals are presented after the onset of hemorrhage, a blood transfusion sufficient to restore adequate perfusion of vital organs and provide clotting factors in conjunction with vitamin K_1 therapy is sometimes highly effective. Of course, some animals, especially those repeatedly exposed and not closely monitored by their owners, die as a result of a lethal degree of hemorrhage. However, animals that survive clinical toxicosis as a result of either a sublethal degree of hemorrhage or therapeutic intervention generally make a complete recovery with no permanent sequelae. The anticoagulants tend to be more toxic on a repeated dosing basis as compared to a single exposure (3). Resistance on the part of rodents is one reason to abandon warfarin in favor of newer compounds, but as indicated below, the change to newer active ingredients and the formulations selected have also resulted in increased hazards for pet animals.

Rodenticide formulations containing either brodifacoum or diphacinone are examples of products that are much more acutely toxic, and which exert much more persistent effects on the nontarget animal as compared to those containing warfarin (3,4). LD_{50}s found in the literature for brodifacoum-containing products range from 0.25-3.56 mg/kg (5,6). Brodifacoum baits are commonly sold in 20g wax bars, 50 g placepacks, and single or grouped boxes containing 42.5, 85, 171, 342, or 1,362 grams of bait. If one uses the lowest LD_{50} value of 0.25 mg/kg, and the common bait concentration of .005%, then, to consume a LD_{50}, a dog must consume bait in an amount as low as 5 g/kg (7). In view of the range of LD_{50} values, there appears to be considerable variability among dogs with regard to sensitivity to brodifacoum, but the author has repeatedly encountered complaints regarding clinically hemorrhaging dogs which had been exposed to the bait in the range of 5 g/kg. Similarly, the lowest LD_{50} found for diphacinone-containing products (concentration in bait of .005 %) was 18.7 grams of bait per kg of body weight (2). As a consequence of the much lower total amount of bait necessary to cause poisoning, the occurrence of toxicosis following a single exposure is substantially increased with these products as compared to warfarin. Due to the exceedingly long persistence of the active ingredients in the exposed individual, treatment of the pet animal with vitamin K must generally take place for approximately one month; and consequently it is much more expensive. Moreover, when therapy is not sufficiently prolonged, reoccurrence of hemorrhage and associated clinical manifestations, including hemorrhagic crisis, readily occur (8,9).

When compared with the acute toxicity of the other second generation anticoagulants just mentioned, bromadiolone (also formulated at (0.005%) is an example of a step forward. The lowest LD_{50} found for bromadiolone in dogs was 8.1 mg/kg (average of 10.7 for males and 6.3 for females) (10). The 8.1 mg/kg dose translates to approximately 162 grams of bait per kg of body weight. Although bromadiolone exposure may mandate treatment for a period of three to four weeks, because of its lower toxicity, clinical toxicoses as a result of single dose exposures when 50 g place packs are used are less likely. Unfortunately, this generic is also marketted to pest control operators in bulk drums of loose pellets, as well as wax blocks, and seed bait.

Zinc Phosphide. Zinc phosphide is a less commonly encountered rodenticide. It has been on the market since World War II, but it seems to reemerge in popularity from time to time *(11)*. A typical product contains 2% active ingredient although more concentrated forms may be encountered. It is sometimes sold in quantities of one to 50 pounds *(12)*. A single dose of zinc phosphide bait at 40 mg/kg can be lethal to dogs *(12)*. Thus, two grams of bait per kilogram of body weight may be a lethal dose. Zinc phosphide bait has the potential, following a single exposure, to cause vomiting, lung damage, hemorrhagic gastroenteritis, signs suggestive of intense abdominal pain, seizures similar to those induced by strychnine, and often death. In addition, there is no effective antidote for zinc phosphide toxicosis. Survivors of acute poisoning may later experience liver failure *(11,12,13)*. The hazard of zinc phosphide containing baits, relative to that of warfarin, is extremely high.

Bromethalin. Bromethalin-containing rodent baits, which typically contain 0.01% active ingredient, have both advantages and notable disadvantages. The theory behind the use of these products is that the high metabolic rate of rodents and their small size relative to that of most domestic animals are such that the former are likely to ingest a much larger dose than the latter. Although dogs are relatively resistant to the material (minimum lethal dose of 25 grams of bait per kg of body weight), cats are much more sensitive (minimum lethal dose of 4.5 grams of bait/kg) *(2)*. Because of the smaller size of cats relative to most dogs and their greater susceptibility, they are the species most at risk when small quantities are available, such as those in single place packs which contain 21 to 42 grams of bait. Unfortunately, however, the material is also available in bulk such that pest control operators sometimes put out amounts hazardous to dogs.

Another disadvantage of bromethalin toxicosis is that it can masquerade as a myriad of other central nervous system maladies. The compound causes brain damage in the form of intramyelinic edema and secondary axonal damage, which is only partially reversible. Clinical manifestations are dose-dependent, but may include severe muscle tremors, hyperthermia, excitement and seizures, depression, coma, and hind limb paralysis. Undoubtedly, because of the nonspecificity of certain of these clinical signs and the overlap with such common diseases as cerebral trauma, canine distemper, other convulsive disorders, and spinal cord trauma including thoracolumbar disc herniation *(14)*, the syndrome is likely to be underdiagnosed as well as misdiagnosed in veterinary practice.

Initial suggestions by the manufacturers, based on early studies with rats, suggested that therapy for bromethalin toxicosis, such as the use of osmotic diuretics, would be highly effective and that treated animals would be left with no permanent sequelae. Unfortunately, such predictions have proven entirely incorrect. In fact, a major disadvantage of bromethalin is that there is currently no effective therapy for the toxicosis apart from initial evacuation of the gastrointestinal tract and administration of activated charcoal. Quite often animals are not presented in time for this to be a feasible alternative. More recently, an extract of *Gingko biloba* (EGB, Tebonin[R], Dr. Wilmar Schwabe, Arzneimittel, Karlsruhe, FRG) experimentally provided some alleviation in the severity of sublethal toxicoses in rats *(14)*. This substance alters cerebral blood flow, is an antioxidant, reduces oxygen demand, and reduces cerebral edema. However, the extract is not available to veterinary practitioners in the USA, its efficacy in supralethally-exposed animals of any species has not been explored, and its safety and efficacy in bromethalin-poisoned small domestic animals have not been studied.

Cholecalciferol. Cholecalciferol-containing rodenticides are a worst case example of apparently good intentions gone awry. It appears that the idea behind the development of cholecalciferol as a rodenticide was that, as in the case of the bromethalin, it was expected that the product would be consumed in much greater proportional amounts by rodents than by domestic animals. Based on initial toxicity trials with oral dosing of the technical material in the canine, it was predicted that dogs would not be significantly at risk. In fact, the compound was initially promoted as essentially a hazard-free rodenticide. The oral LD$_{50}$ of the 100 percent technical material was 88 mg/kg body weight *(2)*. By contrast, a rodenticide bait containing cholecalciferol, was lethal to dogs experimentally at an oral dose of 10 mg of active ingredient per kg body weight *(15)*. Of even greater concern is the fact that there have been field reports of toxicoses in dogs exposed to as little bait as 1 gram/kg body weight (2 to 3 mg of cholecalciferol/kg) *(2,16)*. The active ingredient, is bioactivated in a two-step process in the liver and kidneys to the most active form, 1,25-dihydroxy-cholecalciferol. Elevated serum calcium is compatible with a cholecalciferol toxicosis. In conjunction with elevated serum 25-hydroxy-cholecalciferol (assays not routinely available) and exposure history, a diagnosis is readily confirmed. Elevation of both serum calcium and phosphorus are common and when these are sufficiently marked, mineralization of a number of tissues begins. Mineralization of vessels in the brain may lead to central nervous system dysfunction. Mineralization of vessels in the lungs or stomach may result in clinical evidence of hemorrhage, and mineralization in the heart may lead to cardiac problems. Of greatest importance is mineralization of the kidneys, and cholecalciferol toxicosis not only destroys the tubular epithelial cells, but also damages the basement membranes which are essential for regeneration of the tissue.

Animals are often presented to veterinarians after the onset of the toxicosis such that it is too late to evacuate the digestive tract, and hypercalcemia is already present. The goal in such instances is to lower the serum calcium, minimize the effects of renal failure and promote renal blood flow. Therapeutic agents used to lower serum calcium include normal saline solution, the diuretic furosemide, corticosteroids, and a rather expensive hormonal drug, salmon calcitonin. Multiple assays of serum for calcium, as well as for indicators of renal function such as urea nitrogen, and creatinine are essential in order to tailor therapy to the individual inpatient, and to know when therapy can subside. Animals must often be treated for three weeks. Survivors may be left with seriously compromised renal function.

The much higher frequency of toxicosis as compared to predictions, the suffering on the part of the animal associated with the dystrophic mineralization of organs especially including the kidneys, heart, etc., the prolonged nature of the toxicosis, the necessary clinical and biochemical monitoring, and the vigorous and expensive multicomponent therapy which are often essential to give the patient a chance of reasonable health after exposure, combine to make this a highly inappropriate domestic rodenticide formulation.

INSECTICIDES

For the purposes of the discussion with regard to the progress in insecticides, the experience with carbaryl as an insecticide will be referred to as many people are familiar with the product. This generic compound is commonly employed as a 5% dust in such products as flea powder for use on dogs and in tomato dust. LD$_{50}$ values for carbaryl in mammals range from 200 to 759 mg/kg body weight, with dogs being at the high end of this scale. Concern with regard to reports of teratogenesis in dogs *(17)* are probably unwarranted as such effects are not often, if ever, recognized in veterinary practice. In acute toxicosis situations, as may occur with relatively massive exposures, carbaryl can act quite rapidly such that there is not always sufficient time to implement appropriate therapies. However, when animals are treated successfully (i.e. with adsorbents such as activated charcoal, and possibly atropine, or in a worst case situation, artificial respiration with oxygen), they typically recover to near normal function within a period of less than one day. In addition, unless the animal has become severely hypoxic during the toxicosis, which is rare, a rapid and uneventful recovery is the rule.

Methomyl. In contrast to formulations of carbaryl, each unit of the less widely sold generic methomyl (when formulated into sugar-based baits containing 1 % of the active ingredient) poses a much greater hazard for acutely lethal toxicosis. The LD_{50} of methomyl (rat) is only 17 mg/kg body weight, and large containers of baits are often both available and lethal to dogs (i.e. within minutes) before treatment can be attempted *(4)*. Clinical manifestations are typical of most cholinesterase inhibiting insecticides.

Chlorpyrifos. Chlorpyrifos is an example of an insecticide that is much more widely used than most others, and which has an acceptable safety record in some formulations, but not in others. In the author's experience, chlorpyrifos has often been the insecticidal compound most often associated with lethal toxicoses in domestic cats *(4,18)*. Chlorpyrifos dip solutions may contain a concentration of approximately 600 mg/l after dilution. A complicating factor is that the clinical effects of chlorpyrifos in exposed cats are atypical as compared to most other insecticides of the organophosphorus group. The compound has the capability to cause prolonged behavioral changes (weeks), inappetance (days to weeks) and, at massive intramuscular doses (300 mg/kg) in cats surviving as a result of antidotal therapy, delayed neuropathy (19, Fikes, J. D., Zachary, J. F., Parker, A. J., and Beasley, V. R. *Neurotoxicology*, in press).

Although cats are apparently poisoned by a range of types of chlorpyrifos-containing products, the formulations which are most prone to cause life-threatening toxicoses are those intended for use as dips to kill fleas and ticks on dogs *(4)*. In hindsight, it should have been predicted that persons who have recently dipped their dogs are also highly likely to dip their cats without always rereading the label or recalling precautions against other uses of such products. A simple solution to this problem would be to abandon such formulations either voluntarily or through regulation.

Intermediate Success in Developing Selective Insecticidal Formulations. The trend toward increased use of pyrethrins has been slowed as the material has become harder to obtain and as pyrethroid products have entered the marketplace. Generally, few life-threatening toxicoses are attributable to the pyrethrin-containing products, but toxicoses do occur with animals typically displaying clinical signs such as hypersalivation, tremors, and hyperexcitability or depression *(4,20,21)*. Among the pyrethroid containing products most implicated in clinically significant toxicoses in small domestic animals is an aerosol combining the alpha-cyano pyrethroid, fenvalerate (0.09%), and the insect repellent, n,n-diethyltoluamide (DEET) and related isomers at 9% *(21)*. Alpha cyano pyrethroids tend to act both at sodium channels (as do non-alpha cyano pyrethroids and natural pyrethrins) and at gamma amino butyric acid (GABA) mediated chloride channels. The action at the latter sites probably contributes to their greater neurotoxicity *(20,21,22)*. Typical treatment regimens for pyrethrin- or pyrethroid-exposed cats and dogs include bathing in detergent, diazepam if seizures are present and supportive care, which usually is not required for more than 24-48 hours.

Positive Developments in Insecticide Formulations. Many new products have emerged in the pesticide marketplace which reflect progress in the direction of selectivity against the offending pests and in behalf of safety for pet animals. Among such products are ant traps which contain propoxur, and roach baits containing either n-ethyl perfluoro-octanesulfonamide, or hydramethylnon. These products have generally been formulated so as to contain amounts of active ingredient which, when a single bait is ingested, are insufficient to cause clinical evidence of toxic effects in domestic dogs or cats *(4)*.

The insect hormone mimic methoprene is another compound without notable toxicity and for which toxicoses are not a significant problem *(4)*. Since this product is of considerable value in the control of fleas, it is often particularly appropriate for use around animals.

Microencapsulation of insecticides is a technology which often confers the advantage of decreased acute toxicity as compared to other forms of a compound, and thereby the risk of exposure is typically reduced. Combining increased use of microencapsulation with selection of generics of low toxicity, and formulation into products which deposit relatively low total amounts of pesticide would undoubtedly result in safer pesticides for use on and around domestic animals.

SUMMARY

Pesticide poisoning of pets is a common problem for which ethical behavior demands control. Control can be achieved by means of increased consideration of likely patterns of exposure prior to product formulation and marketing, thorough testing of final formulations in species likely to be accidentally overexposed in urban and suburban environments, and reevaluations of the safety of such products in pets through implementation of routine monitoring of illness in exposed or overexposed pets. Products causing rapid onset of lethal toxicoses thereby precluding early intervention, those for which intervention is often ineffective or highly expensive, and those which commonly induce significant permanent damage in the overexposed nontarget animal should be candidates for reformulation or withdrawal from the marketplace.

LITERATURE CITED

1. Beasley, V. R. *Veterinary Clinics of North America*, **1990**, 20, xv-xvii.
2. Dorman, D. C. *Veterinary Clinics of North America*, **1990a**, 20, 339-352.
3. Beasley, V. R., and Buck, W. B. in *Current Veterinary Therapy VIII*, Kirk, R. W., Ed.; Saunders: Philadelphia, PA, **1983**; 101-106.
4. Beasley, V. R., and Trammel, H. L. in *Current Veterinary Therapy X*, Kirk, R. W., Ed.; Saunders: Philadelphia, PA, **1989**; 97-113.

5. Rammell, C. G., and Fleming, P. A. *Compound 1080, propertie and use of sodium monofluoroacetate in New Zealand*; Animal Health Division, Ministry of Agriculture and Fisheries: Wellington, NZ, **1978**; pp 76-112.

6. Godfrey, M. E. R., Reid, T. C., and McAllum, H. J. F. *N. Z J. of Exp. Agric.*, **1981**, 9, 147-149.

7. Dubock, A. C., and Kaukeinen, D. E. Paper presented at 8th Vertebrate Pest Conference. **1978**, 1-25.

8. Mount, M. E., and Feldman, B. F. *Am. J. Vet. Res.*, **1983**, 44, 2009.

9. Mount, M. E., Feldman, B. F., and Buffington, T. *J. Am Vet. Med. Assoc.*, **1982**, 180, 1354.

10. Poche, R. M. *Bull. OEPP/EPPO Bull.*, **1988**, 18, 323-330.

11. Stowe, C. M., Nelson, R., Werdin, R., Fangmann, G., Fredrick, P. Weaver, G., and Arendt, T. D. *J. Am. Vet. Med Assoc.*, **1978**, 173, 270.

12. Osweiler, G. D., Carson, T. L., Buck, W. B., and Van Gelder, G. A. *Clinical and Diagnostic Veterinary Toxicology*; Kendall Hunt: Dubuque, IA, **1976**; 353-354.

13. Casteel, S. W., and Bailey, E. M. *Vet. Hum. Toxicol.*, **1986**, 28, 151-153.

14. Dorman, D. C. Ph.D. Thesis, **1990b**, University of Illinois.

15. Gunther, R. Felice. L. J., Nelson, R. K. et al. *J. Am. Vet. Med. Assoc.*, **1988**, 193, 211-214.

16. Dorman, D. C., and Beasley, V. R. in *Current Veterinar Therapy X*, Kirk, R. W., Ed.; Saunders: Philadelphia, PA, **1989**; 148-150.

17. Smalley, H. E., Curtis, J. M., and Earl, F. L. *Tox. Appl Pharmacol.*, **1968**, 13, 392-403.

18. Beasley, V. R. in *Current Veterinary Therapy IX*; Kirk, R. W., Ed.; Saunders: Philadelphia, PA, **1986**; 120-129.

19. Fikes, J. D. MS Thesis, **1989**, University of Illinois.

20. Valentine, W. M., and Beasley, V. R. in *Current Veterinary Therapy X*; Kirk, R. W., Ed.; Saunders: Philadelphia, PA, **1989**; 137-140.

21. Dorman, D. C., and Beasley, V. R. *Vet. Hum. Toxicol.*, **1991**, 33, 238-243.

22. Valentine, W. M. *Veterinary Clinics of North America*, **1990**, 20, 375-382.

RECEIVED December 3, 1992

Chapter 30

Nontarget Organism Evaluations for Rodenticides

D. E. Kaukeinen

Professional Products Group, ICI Americas, Inc., Delaware Corporate Center II, Wilmington, DE 19897

Rodenticides have the potential to cause toxicity to nontarget animals that might become accidently exposed to such materials, and various experimental techniques have been developed to determine whether rodenticides cause nontarget hazard under various use conditions. Distinctions between toxicity and hazard are important. Determinations need to be made as to what nontarget animals are present near rodenticide applications and how potential exposure can occur. Various formulation and application parameters may be experimentally modified to reduce hazard, and to determine resultant effects upon both target and nontarget species. Aversive agents have been evaluated that may increase rodenticide selectivity to the target species. Wildlife hazard evaluations require basic toxicity testing, and primary hazard may be reduced through formulation and application modifications. Secondary hazard requires a knowledge of a nontarget species foraging behavior versus rodenticide application in terms of habitat used or affected, and prey preference versus pest species controlled. Simulated field studies or large scale field studies utilizing radiotelemetry techniques (concurrent with rodenticide applications) may provide the most realistic data on hazard.

Commensal rodent pests are those living in association with man, and are most commonly represented by the Norway rat, Rattus norvegicus and the House mouse, Mus musculus, throughout the USA. In warmer west coast and gulf coast areas, an additional species, the roof rat Rattus rattus, is a problem. These species cause tremendous damage by gnawing of structures and wiring, consumption and contamination of foodstuffs, damage to paper and wood products, and disease transmission. Commensal rodents are frequent vectors of leptospirosis, salmonellosis, and other human maladies, and rats bite countless children yearly; particularly in inner-city areas. Pest rodents are incriminated in transmission of various livestock diseases such as trichinosis, toxoplasmosis and other ailments.

0097–6156/93/0522–0352$06.00/0

In addition to these common commensal pests infesting structures throughout most of the U.S., other species such as deer mice (Peromyscus spp.) and voles (Microtus spp.) damage turf by their tunnels and trees and ornamental plantings by their gnawing damage, particularly in colder winter months.

Rodent control is practiced by homeowners and farmers, by professional pest control operators, by municipal vector control or sanitation workers, and others. Control of these rodent pests involves integrated pest management including, where possible, elements of sanitation, rodent proofing or exclusion, and rodent killing. Rodent killing principally relies upon chemical toxicants, namely rodenticidal baits, and to a much lesser extend upon trapping. Most currently registered rodenticides are equally available to homeowners, farmers, and professional applicators.

RODENTICIDES

Rodenticides have many factors offering value in pest rodent management. They have a long use history, they provide a practical means of control, they are economical to use, they offer specificity to the pest species by various means, they can be controlled through application and removal, and they are currently registered and available. A variety of physical forms of rodenticides are sold, including meals, pellets, and paraffin blocks.

Rodenticides are, by definition, mammalian toxicants. The more hazardous materials of the past are no longer registered, such as arsenic and sodium fluoroacetate (Compound 1080). However, most of the remaining rodenticidal products can be shown in the laboratory to be toxic at some dose to non-target animals. This chapter will review some research methodologies and approaches to reduce and define hazard in the process of formulation development and product registration. For rodenticides, as with most pesticides, a tiered testing system is followed beginning with LD50 and LC50 studies, and progressing, if warranted, through pen or simulated field studies, and then potentially to full scale field studies involving radiotelemetry or other techniques to evaluate nontarget effects *(1)*.

Toxicity Versus Hazard: It is important to distinguish between toxicity and hazard, the latter involving the determination of the probability of injurious effects based on both toxicology and real world (exposure) data. Examples of study techniques will primarily focus on ICI's anticoagulant rodenticide brodifacoum, which is a single-feeding, second-generation product. Although anticoagulants have been used in rodent control for some 50 years, brodifacoum possesses some novel properties that stimulated considerable research concerning potential non-target hazard *(2)* (Figure 1).

Types of Hazard: From the point that rodenticidal bait is applied, usually in a sheltered or protected location, animal species potentially at risk must be considered. Generally, for rodenticides, the possible nontarget categories are humans, pets such as dogs and cats, domestic animals such as poultry and livestock, and wildlife. Wildlife hazard from a rodenticide may involve direct or primary hazard, such as to seed-eating birds, or involve secondary hazard to predatory or scavenging animals that consume poisoned prey.

PRIMARY (DIRECT) TOXICITY AND HAZARD

Evaluations of Hazard Reduction. There must be a clear picture of the proposed rodenticide use pattern when determining the need for and nature of hazard evaluations. There must also be adequate information on the biology, behavior, and ecology of nontarget animals which may be at risk. There are certain things that researchers and registrants can do to reduce potential hazards of rodenticidal products, and the potential for primary poisoning is perhaps the easier to reduce. The EPA specifies for most rodenticides that baiting be conducted in a tamper-proof bait station, or in an area inaccessible to children, pets, domestic animals and wildlife.

An approach involving a toxic rodent wick in a protective container has been described which offers increased selectivity for house mouse control, while reducing nontarget hazard by eliminating the need for a toxic bait; rodents press against the wick in entering the container and ingest the toxicant when grooming their fur *(3)*. For rodent pests of turf and ornamental plantings, finely broadcast small bait particles may prevent pets or livestock from obtaining sufficient contact with the bait for toxic effects to occur *(4)*.

User education is also a key component that must be provided along with the rodenticide product to further reduce hazard concerns. Consumer users of rodenticides are generally less well-informed of nontarget hazards as compared to professional users. However, such consumers generally apply far less quantities of rodenticidal bait and are more likely to restrict bait placement to limited, indoor areas rather than the more extensive indoor and outdoor locations often treated by professional applicators.

Use of Aversive Agents. Aversive colors, textures, tastes, emetics or stenches may reduce the likelihood of exposure for some nontarget species. All such additives must be thoroughly tested to ensure that rodenticidal efficacy to the target species is maintained. Denatonium benzoate, an intensely bitter substance known commercially as Bitrex, has recently been added to several rodenticide products with the discovery that rodents will readily accept Bitrex levels that are highly aversive to children. This has been documented with ICI's brodifacoum rodenticidal formulations in human taste tests (samples without anticoagulant), showing that palatability of pellets/blocks had shifted significantly toward sample rejection with the inclusion of 10 ppm denatonium benzoate *(5)*. Unfortunately, levels that might be effective in discouraging nontargets such as dogs, cats, or seed-eating birds are too high to also allow rodent acceptability as a general bait additive. The larger body size of dogs and cats provides considerable differential effect with accidental intake of anticoagulant rodenticides via primary or secondary routes.

WILDLIFE HAZARD

Wildlife are the most difficult animal group to protect and constitute the primary concern of most governmental regulatory authorities. The remaining sections of this chapter are limited to discussions of study techniques to determine potential wildlife hazard.

Basic Toxicity Testing. Extensive LD50 and LC50 toxicity studies may be needed, such as on various bird and mammal species, to better indicate what non-target species may require further consideration. However, pharmacological sensitivity may be a poor predictor of ecological vulnerability. Additionally, the toxicity of a rodenticide to one avian species, such as a mallard duck or pheasant, may differ dramatically from that observed with another avian such as a passerine bird.

Toxicant Considerations. Use of a particular rodenticide, must be considered in conjunction with its toxic properties and characteristics of the formulation or carrier involved; the persistence of the chemical and its mobility; the frequency, method and timing of its application; its use pattern; and, especially for predatory wildlife, how it affects the target rodent species.

Nontarget Animal Considerations. Ecological considerations must include what species are present in the use area, their sensitivity to the chemical, and how the chemical application relates to the nontarget species habitat, behavior, breeding and feeding habits, and life stage.

Evaluations of Broadcast Rodenticides. For rodent pests of turf, ornamental plantings, and grassy areas of orchards, the mechanical broadcast of small rodenticidal pellets is a cost-effective method to treat large acreages *(4)*. However, broadcast applications potentially provide wide exposure to nontarget animals. Initial laboratory research with captive nontargets such as pheasants and quail can be used to evaluate formulation changes that may selectively reduce acceptability to such species. Rodents are color-blind, yet color is an important cue for feeding behavior of many animals, such as birds. For example, red and black pellets were equally mixed and offered to pheasants for 24 hours in the laboratory. At the end of this period, red pellets had been selectively taken to a greater extent than the black *(6)*, (Figure 2). Such initial research suggested a number of hazard-reduction approaches to further explore.

For example, two potential distasteful additives and two colorants were tested for effects on acceptance by target rodents (voles) and rock doves. Preliminary bird research verified all additives provided significant rejection. However, some of these additives also caused rodent rejection *(7)*. Figure 3 gives the average of 2 replicates of 4-way choice tests of aversive agents vs. untreated pellets with voles and rock doves. Additives that continued to show promise were subsequently evaluated in large-scale pen tests utilizing ring-necked pheasants. Studies in such pens in Virginia evaluated the effects of various rodenticide particle shapes, colors and ingredients on bird acceptance or rejection. The tests involved 4 replicated trials of 3 rates plus controls, using 12 adjacent pens of over 46.4 sq m (500 sq ft) each, housing groups of 6 female pheasants per pen. Birds also had access to whole grain. This work resulted in significantly reduced bird mortality through formulation and application rate changes *(8)* (Figure 4).

SECONDARY TOXICITY AND HAZARD

Secondary poisoning hazard occurs when a toxicant enters the food chain and affects an organism other than the target species. With rodenticides, the most likely scenario is a predator or scavenger ingesting poisoned rodent prey. Secondary poisoning of wildlife with anticoagulant rodenticides has not been reported as a significant problem in the

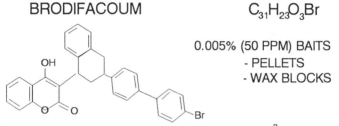

BRODIFACOUM $C_{31}H_{23}O_3Br$

0.005% (50 PPM) BAITS
- PELLETS
- WAX BLOCKS

PCO PRODUCT NAME: TALON RODENTICIDE [R] ICI AMERICAS
              TALON WEATHERBLOK [R]   "

RAT LD_{50} 100% TECHNICAL - 0.26 MG/KG (1.3 G BAIT)
MOUSE LD_{50} 100% TECHNICAL - 0.4 MG/KG (0.2 G BAIT)

ACTION: INTERFERES WITH PRODUCTION OF CLOTTING FACTORS,
CAUSING INTERNAL AND EXTERNAL BLEEDING AND DEATH IN 4-10 DAYS

Figure 1. Brodifacoum Rodenticide

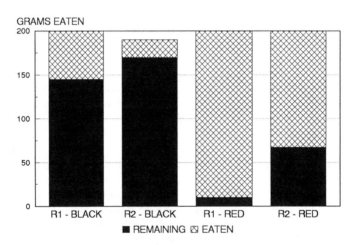

**Figure 2. Comparative Acceptance over 24 Hrs of Red and Black Pellets
Mixed Equally (100 g each) in the Same Food Container with 2 Groups of
5 Female Ring-Necked Pheasants (No Alternate Food Available)**

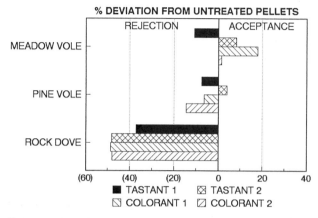

Figure 3. Comparative Acceptance of Various Colors and Taste Additives in Tests with Voles and Rock Doves

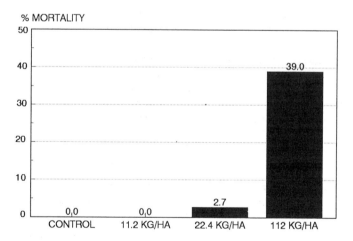

Figure 4. Results of Different Application Rates of Broadcast Brodifacoum Rodenticide with Aversive Agents Using Penned Pheasants

United States (9), but second-generation anticoagulants such as brodifacoum required further evaluations to verify this impression. Research on formulation changes will not readily affect secondary poisoning, but rodenticide concentration and application rate reductions, application timing, and use restrictions can reduce hazard in some situations. Birds of prey, with their smaller body size and more common rodent diet, may be more appropriate for secondary hazard investigation than are many mammalian predators or scavengers.

Some raptorial species such as vultures will readily take dead animals, and thus research to document or enhance the tendency for target rodents to die from rodenticides in below-ground or inaccessible areas is desirable. In urban situations, removal of poisoned rodent carcasses should be encouraged where possible, not only to reduce potential risk to scavenging animals, but to also eliminate potential disease and odor problems. For many wildlife predator species which normally take only living prey, investigations may involve determining the extent and duration that poisoned, possibly moribund but active rodent prey are available following rodenticide treatment.

Residue Studies. Studies of residues of toxicant remaining in target rodent carcasses have been conducted with brodifacoum, comparing two application techniques. Pulsed baiting produced more carcasses containing lower residues than typical, sustained baiting (10). Figure 5 gives a plot comparing residue values from samples of 50 rats (limit of detection was 0.002 ppm) for the two baiting approaches. Pulsed baiting is a technique of placing limited amounts of rodenticide at timed intervals, rather than maintaining a surplus. This may extend the time to control and increase labor (which may be unacceptable for some use patterns), but the method can reduce the quantity of toxicant placed in the environment at any given time. Knowledge of chemical residues in target species allows calculations to be made for toxic quantities for predators; in this case the information indicated that the secondary hazard potential to most mammalian predators from anticoagulant-killed rodents was slight. Minimal rates and careful equipment calibration can reduce toxicant exposures, such as in the broadcast application of rodenticides for rodent pests of grassland areas. Analysis of voles fed in the lab on 10 ppm and 50 ppm brodifacoum baits (Table I) indicated that body burdens of toxicants were reduced greater than 5-fold by the lower concentration.

Table I. Vole Residues from No-Choice Laboratory Feeding

Brodifacoum Concentration	Sex	Mean Vole Tissue Residue (ppm)
10 ppm	M	0.53 (+/- 0.24)
	F	0.40 (+/- 0.20)
50 ppm	M	5.21 (+/- 2.06)
	F	2.17 (+/- 1.17)

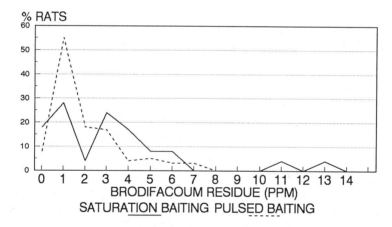

Figure 5. Brodifacoum Residues in Norway Rats from UK Farms after Baiting with 0.005% Brodifacoum by Two Methods

Potential Effects on Nontarget Animals. Secondary hazard is difficult to assess, as the likelihood of poisoned prey and predator interaction needs to be known. Effects can occur to individuals, and individual impacts may potentially effect local populations, depending upon the extent of toxicant use. Such effects can be temporary or sustained if rodenticide application and exposure is frequent. Initial laboratory findings can determine additional research needed. For example, with brodifacoum, toxicity studies with captive barn owls indicated poisoning could occur, and gave some guidance on what exposure to poisoned prey would be necessary *(11)*. However, lab studies cannot assess the probability in the field of predator/poisoned prey interaction and resultant predator risk.

Large-Scale Telemetry Field Study. A telemetry field study for the EPA was designed to address the question of potential secondary hazard to a raptor species for one intended brodifacoum rodenticide use pattern. This use pattern involved application of 50 ppm brodifacoum baits in and around farm structures for commensal rodent control. The study was conducted in cooperation with the U. S. Fish and Wildlife Service under the conditions of an experimental use permit secured from the EPA *(12)*. In this study, the barn owl was chosen as the indicator species. The barn owl is considered as a threatened or endangered species in much of its eastern or midwestern range in the U.S. and it is also the raptor species most closely associated with structures where rodent baiting might occur.

An extensive literature review of barn owls was undertaken, and site selection was begun. Part of this selection was based on potential study impacts, how many owls would need to be monitored, the best means of monitoring and of applying the brodifacoum rodenticide in the study area, and how to measure and evaluate the predator/prey interactions and effects.

After evaluations of several potential sites around the U.S., an area of some 400 sq mi (1036 km sq) in southwest New Jersey was chosen *(12)*. This area consisted of a mosaic of different land use patterns; with towns and residences, farms and agricultural lands, and woods and marshes along Delaware Bay. The selection was made because there was an abundance of old structures such as barns and silos favored by the owls for nesting. The barn owl population in the area was healthy and therefore the study impact, even if significant locally, would not further endanger this species on a regional or national basis. Finally, the area and the farm structures had infestations of commensal rats and mice *(13)*.

Teams of researchers systematically searched the area by road and by foot, investigating and marking potential nesting and roosting sites on maps. Such potential sites included old water tanks, silos and barns, and large trees with nesting cavities. Farmers and homeowners were cooperative and often led researchers to locations of nesting owls on their properties. Other nest sites were located at night by listening for begging owl chicks. Additional study sites were augmented by installation of owl nest boxes, many of which were subsequently utilized.

Owls like most raptors regurgitate the bones, hair and other indigestible portions of their prey in balls called pellets. Because these pellets provide a convenient means of determining prey species, an effort was made to collect recent pellets from the nesting areas under observation. Eventually, over one hundred nest sites were located. Particular attention was given to finding nest sites on farmsteads with rodent problems. Rodent census techniques of food consumption and tracking patches *(13, 14)* revealed 25 farms suitable for rodenticide treatment. Ten of these farms had owls present.

Owls were captured by several techniques. Some birds were netted at roost or nest sites during daytime, whereas others were captured at night with mist nets. Radiotelemetry transmitters were attached to 26 adult nesting owls and 8 fledged young of the year. Selected farms were treated with brodifacoum rodenticide according to standard techniques, and populations of rodents were mesured by indirect census methods before and after treatment *(13, 14)*. In addition, a bait additive, demethylchlorotetracycline (DMCT) was used. This material chelates with calcium and fluoresces under UV light. By examination of bones from regurgitated owl pellets collected on study sites, a determination could also be made of whether rodent prey had ingested the rodenticide.

Transmitters were fastened to the base of the owl's central tail feathers. Since brodifacoum is an anticoagulant, it was believed that other attachment methods might cause some irritation or hemorrhage and possibly influence results of the study. Twenty of the 34 transmitters had a mortality circuit that changed pulse rate if it remained still for about 45 minutes. From the ground, by foot or vehicle, range was 2-4 km (1-3 mi). Tracking by aircraft extended this range for 20-45 km (10-30 mi) *(12)*. Triangulation of bird location was taken several times daily by simultaneous bearings plotted on Geological Survey maps utilizing 2-way radio communication. Telemetry helped in determining of whether owls actually used the rodenticide-treated farmsteads for roosting or feeding, and enabled the recovery of any owl that died in the study.

Analysis of regurgitated pellets revealed that meadow voles were the most common prey at all sites *(12, 15)*. Although some Norway rats and house mice were recovered, they made up only a small percentage of prey taken. Examination of bones from regurgitated pellets under UV light did not indicate that rodents had fed on rodenticidal bait. However, a number of causes of owl mortality were documented: two electrocutions, 2 highway kills, 2 predator kills, and another reportedly shot *(12)*.

Owls typically hunted away from treated farmsteads, and some owls regularly hunted more than 3 km (2 mi) from the nest site. Individual owl home range was as much as 3278 ha, but averaged about 750 ha. Owls preferred vole prey. Voles were inhabiting grass fields and marsh areas, which were not treated with brodifacoum rodenticide. Thus, although lab toxicity studies indicated a potential for owl mortality from secondary feeding of poisoned prey, this field study demonstrated that barn owls seldom fed on the commensal rodent species and in the habitat being exposed to rodenticide. The researchers concluded that the chance for owl mortality from this use pattern of brodifacoum rodenticide appeared low *(12, 15)*. In consideration of these and other data and considerations, the U.S. EPA granted approval for the use of brodifacoum formulations for exterior baiting around farm structures. This is a clearance yet to be achieved with other second-generation anticoagulants, such as bromadiolone.

Similarly, a pilot study in Virginia evaluated rodent and raptor residues following experimental rodenticide application to grasslands involving a different brodifacoum formulation for vole control *(16)*. Results of that study suggested a large-scale telemetry study was necessary to evaluate possible effects to screech owls. The subsequent large-scale study and computer modelling indicated that some raptors, such as screech owls that feed on voles, were at potential risk from this use pattern *(17, 18)*. Methods developed during these evaluations *(19)* should prove useful in further research utilizing other active ingredients and formulations.

CONCLUSIONS

This chapter has illustrated a range of approaches to evaluate hazards to nontarget animals from application of rodenticides in non-crop situations such as around residential or farm structures, and in grassland areas. Examples have been given of methodologies to evaluate different formulations and application techniques for potential hazards to nontarget species, particularly wildlife, in both the laboratory and the field. Secondary hazard studies are probably the most complex of rodenticide hazard evaluations, and the steps in making these assessments have been summarized.

Only with the best and most well-informed opinion of all involved (manufacturer, outside scientists, USEPA), can real-world risks be estimated and potential hazards determined. Continued monitoring and product stewardship after registration is necessary to ensure that research findings parallel hazard observations under actual use. In some cases, it may be necessary to "go back to the drawing board" to further evaluate or improve particular products and application techniques. Regular research involving hazard reduction techniques must be ongoing, and discoveries applied to existing and future products to further protect both individual nontarget animals, as well as the health and stability of their population and the desirable diversity of the environment.

LITERATURE CITED

1. Kaukeinen, D.E. Potential non-target effects from the use of vertebrate toxicants. Proc Conf. Organization & Practice of Pest Control, Elvetham Hall, Hampshire, England, **1984**, pp. 589-618.
2. Kaukeinen, D.E. and Rampaud, M. A review of brodifacoum efficacy in the U.S. and worldwide. Proc. 12th. Vertebrate Pest Conf., Davis CA, **1986**, pp. 16-50.
3. Kaukeinen, D.E., Morris, K.D. and Proctor, R.D. Design and evaluation criteria for development of toxic wicks for rodent control. Vertebrate Pest Control and Management Materials, American Society for Testing and Materials, Philadelphia, PA, ASTM STP 817, **1983**, pp. 165-182.
4. Kaukeinen, D.E. *Microtus* problems and control in North America and the development of VOLID rodenticide. Proc. Conf. Organization and Practice of Vertebrate Pest Control, Hampshire, England, **1984**, pp. 589-618.
5. Kaukeinen, D.E. and Buckle, S.P. Evaluation of Denatonium Benzoate (Bitrex) Bittering Agent as a commensal Rodenticide Additive, Proc. 15th. Vertebrate Pest Conf., Newport Beach CA, 3-5 Mar. **1992**, in press.
6. Morris, K.D. and Kaukeinen, D.E. ICI Americas, unpublished report TMUD3625/B, **1981**.
7. Morris, K.D. and Kaukeinen, D.E. Stepwise approach to selection and addition of agents to lessen avian primary toxicity to broad cast applied rodenticides for field rodents. Proc. 6th Biodeterioration Symposium, CAB International, Farnham House UK, **1986**, pp. 54-60.
8. Kaukeinen, D.E. A test protocol for assessment of primary poisoning hazard to ground-feeding birds from broadcast pelletized rodenticides. Vertebrate Pest Control and Management Materials, American Society for Testing and Materials, Philadelphia PA, ASTM STP 817, **1984**, pp. 110-117.

9. Kaukeinen, D.E. A review of the secondary poisoning hazard to wildlife from the use of anticoagulant rodenticides. *Pest Manage.* **1982**, 1(11): *10*, 12-14; 1(12): *16*, 18-19.

10. Dubock, A.C. Pulsed baiting - a new technique for high potency, slow acting rodenticides. Proc. 10th. Vertebrate Pest Conf., Monterey CA, **1982**, pp. 123-136.

11. Mendenhall, V.M. and Pank, L.F. Secondary poisoning of owls by anticoagulant rodenticides. *Wildl. Soc. Bull.*, **1980**, *8*: 311-315.

12. Hegdal, P.L. and Blaskiewicz, R.W. Evaluation of the potential hazard to barn owls of Talon (Brodifacoum bait) used to control rats and house mice. *Env. Toxicol. Chem.*, **1984**, *3*:167-179.

13. Morris, K.D. and Kaukeinen, D.E. ICI Americas, unpublished report TMUD3335/B, **1980**.

14. Kaukeinen, D.E. Field methods for census taking of commensal rodents in rodenticide evaluations. Vertebrate Pest Control and Management Materials, American Society for Testing and Materials, Philadelphia PA, ASTM STP 680, **1979**, pp. 68-83.

15. Kaukeinen, D.E. and Tysowsky, M. Portrait of the Barn Owl. A Closer Look. ICI Americas, Inc. Science Series, No. 1, **1985**, 8 pp.

16. Merson, M.H. , Byers, R.E. and Kaukeinen, D.E. Residues of the rodenticide brodifacoum in voles and raptors after orchard treatment. J. Wildlife Manage., **1984**, *48*(1): 212-216.

17. Hegdal, P.L. and Colvin, B.A. Potential hazard to eastern Screech-owls and other raptors of brodifacoum bait used for vole control in orchards. Env. Toxicol. Chem., **1988**, *7*: 245-260.

18. North, P.M. A computer modelling study of the population dynamics of the screech owl *(Otus asio)*. *Ecol. Model.*, **1985**, *30*: 105-143.

19. Colvin, B.A. and Hegdal, P.L. Procedures for assessing secondary poisoning hazards of rodenticides to owls. Vertebrate Pest Control and Management Materials, American Society for Testing and Materials, Philadelphia PA, ASTM STP 974, **1988**, pp. 64-71.

RECEIVED October 23, 1992

INDEXES

Author Index

Affiliation Index

Subject Index

Production: Paula M. Bérard
Indexing: Deborah H. Steiner
Acquisition: Barbara C. Tansill

Printed and bound by Maple Press, York, PA

Bestsellers from ACS Books

The ACS Style Guide: A Manual for Authors and Editors
Edited by Janet S. Dodd
264 pp; clothbound ISBN 0–8412–0917–0; paperback ISBN 0–8412–0943–X

The Basics of Technical Communicating
By B. Edward Cain
ACS Professional Reference Book; 198 pp;
clothbound ISBN 0–8412–1451–4; paperback ISBN 0–8412–1452–2

Chemical Activities (student and teacher editions)
By Christie L. Borgford and Lee R. Summerlin
330 pp; spiralbound ISBN 0–8412–1417–4; teacher ed. ISBN 0–8412–1416–6

Chemical Demonstrations: A Sourcebook for Teachers,
Volumes 1 and 2, Second Edition
Volume 1 by Lee R. Summerlin and James L. Ealy, Jr.;
Vol. 1, 198 pp; spiralbound ISBN 0–8412–1481–6;
Volume 2 by Lee R. Summerlin, Christie L. Borgford, and Julie B. Ealy
Vol. 2, 234 pp; spiralbound ISBN 0–8412–1535–9

Chemistry and Crime: From Sherlock Holmes to Today's Courtroom
Edited by Samuel M. Gerber
135 pp; clothbound ISBN 0–8412–0784–4; paperback ISBN 0–8412–0785–2

Writing the Laboratory Notebook
By Howard M. Kanare
145 pp; clothbound ISBN 0–8412–0906–5; paperback ISBN 0–8412–0933–2

Developing a Chemical Hygiene Plan
By Jay A. Young, Warren K. Kingsley, and George H. Wahl, Jr.
paperback ISBN 0–8412–1876–5

Introduction to Microwave Sample Preparation: Theory and Practice
Edited by H. M. Kingston and Lois B. Jassie
263 pp; clothbound ISBN 0–8412–1450–6

Principles of Environmental Sampling
Edited by Lawrence H. Keith
ACS Professional Reference Book; 458 pp;
clothbound ISBN 0–8412–1173–6; paperback ISBN 0–8412–1437–9

Biotechnology and Materials Science: Chemistry for the Future
Edited by Mary L. Good (Jacqueline K. Barton, Associate Editor)
135 pp; clothbound ISBN 0–8412–1472–7; paperback ISBN 0–8412–1473–5

For further information and a free catalog of ACS books, contact:
American Chemical Society
Distribution Office, Department 225
1155 16th Street, NW, Washington, DC 20036
Telephone 800–227–5558